Art and Worship in the Insular World

Elizabeth (Betty) Coatsworth at the launch of her 2008 book *Corpus of Anglo-Saxon Stone Sculpture*. VIII. *Western Yorkshire* at Leeds University. Photo: Gale R. Owen-Crocker

Art and Worship in the Insular World

Papers in Honour of Elizabeth Coatsworth

Edited by

Gale R. Owen-Crocker
Maren Clegg Hyer

BRILL

LEIDEN | BOSTON

Cover illustration: The late eighth-/early ninth-century Hereford Gospels in their seventeenth-century chained binding, open at the St Mark *Incipit* page, fols 35v–36r. Courtesy of the Dean and Chapter, Hereford Cathedral.

The Library of Congress Cataloging-in-Publication Data is available online at http://catalog.loc.gov
LC record available at http://lccn.loc.gov/2021019711

Typeface for the Latin, Greek, and Cyrillic scripts: "Brill". See and download: brill.com/brill-typeface.

ISBN 978-90-04-46699-9 (hardback)
ISBN 978-90-04-46751-4 (e-book)

Foreword

Professor Dame Rosemary Cramp

Betty's work on textiles, for which she is a major source of reference, has been mentioned by other contributors. I know her however not only from this, but as a very efficient organiser on the excavations of the Anglo-Saxon site at Jarrow. Here she ran the 'finds' reception, and was a stern monitor of whether the excavators had filled in their background data adequately!

For anyone working in the field of Anglo-Saxon studies her publications, especially on 'The Crucifixion', are essential points of reference, and she is also the recognised consultant for any new discoveries in this field. I am personally indebted to her expertise in my own work on Anglo-Saxon sculpture, and would like to record my gratitude for her informed support.

Elizabeth (Betty) Coatsworth: Her Life and Times

Gale R. Owen-Crocker

Coatsworth is an English surname, and in England is most commonly found in County Durham in the north-east of the country. Elizabeth (Betty) Coatsworth was born on 21 October 1941, the eldest child of Ernest Wilfrid Coatsworth, a tenant farmer of Shildon, County Durham, and his wife Doris, a teacher. Betty's sister Joan was born two and a half years later; Ann and Mary followed. Betty's vivid childhood memories depict a by-gone era in rural England. Doris having declined to live in the farm house, since, although picturesque, it lacked the basic amenities of running water, gas, and electricity, the family lived in an old-fashioned terraced house. It was gradually updated, part of the general catching up after the recession of the 1930s and the war, which had delayed a lot of modernisation. The straggle of outbuildings at the back, which included an outside toilet and a small laundry with a huge gas-fired "copper" for heating water (the house had been built before electricity became available) was replaced by a ground-floor bathroom and the old black kitchen range gave way to modern cooking facilities. The terrace had fields of the farm both back and front, and what would have been its back garden served only as a "drying green" for the family laundry, as it was sometimes required as an entry into the fields for large farm machinery.

A very early memory of Betty's is of a plane crashing into one of the farm's fields nearby: this was at the end of April 1944, during the Second World War. It was not caused by enemy action but was a training flight for a British bomber which went sadly wrong, killing all on board. Betty remembers it not for the crash, but because she accompanied her father to the field to meet the civil and military authorities who came to explain how the situation was to be dealt with – it was the tight group of important men, many in uniform, plus the spokesman who was a civilian in what she saw as his "Sunday Best" (and her father's mysterious explanation of him as the "man from the ministry"), which stuck in her memory.

Betty recalls her hardworking parents with great affection and respect. Principled, Christian, politically-aware people, they were as generous to others in the hard times during and after the war as they could be, though money was never plentiful in their own home. One way in which for many years her father supported his community was by allowing one of his fields to be used for a communal bonfire on Bonfire Night – 5 November. The local boys made the guy and collected the wood for the fire, and people brought potatoes and chestnuts to roast in the blaze, and fireworks to share. These events gradually stopped as people got better off, and held their own parties, or went to bigger, more organised events.

Doris had continued in her teaching profession after marriage and motherhood, which was rather unusual at the time, and so Betty early became responsible for shepherding the little group of sisters to Sunday School and cinema, as well as helping on the farm – as did her mother, and her sisters as they grew older. She remembers hoeing the fields after school (in areas where whatever weed-killing sprays were used then had missed), and helping to carry food and drink to seasonal workers – when the potatoes were picked and at hay time. At harvest time some workers, probably mainly the men who came with the threshing machine, had a cooked dinner at the end of the day. On these occasions tables were pushed together, unmatching chairs brought from all over the house, and a padded bench (upholstered by Doris) brought from the outbuilding where it was stored for such occasions. Providing food and drink was part of the work of the farm and took considerable effort to provision and organise – it was always much appreciated! There was no room for the family to eat at the same time – Betty's memory is of herself and sisters carefully carrying from the kitchen one filled plate at a time – a literally heavy responsibility.

In the earlier years of Betty's childhood, the heavy work on the farm was powered by horses. Ernest loved his horses, and it was a great grief to him when they "had to go" to be replaced by machinery. Although each farm owned some of the necessary machinery, including a tractor, other heavy machinery was lent/borrowed between farms or hired, and Ernest had no option but to go along with the move to mechanisation. Betty feels he would have been delighted to know that his own great bond with horses has been passed down to his descendants, some of whom both ride and work with horses.

Potato planting was a semi-mechanised process: Betty remembers sitting on a machine attached to the back of the tractor, facing either her mother or a sister, and feeding seed potatoes by hand, down a chute – when a bell rang – more or less frequently depending on the speed of the tractor, leading to some family arguments if it got too fast! She also remembers riding on the back of the tractor in order for her father to take her to school during a bus strike, which would offend Health and Safety regulations these days. She also recalls walking home from school on occasion, a distance of over three miles.

Betty was an academic child and she attended Bishop Auckland Girls' Grammar School, followed by Durham University. "Betty" had been her father's pet name for her, otherwise she had been known as "Elizabeth" up to this point, but it was at University that an old school friend introduced her to people saying, "They call her Betty at home," and "Betty" stuck, though she still uses Elizabeth in formal situations and for her publications.

She graduated in 1963 with an Honours Degree in English Language and Literature, and immediately proceeded to a Post Graduate Certificate in Education at London University Institute of Education, which she completed in 1964. The same year she returned to north-east England to a teaching post at Jarrow Grammar School, County Durham, followed by another at Rutherford Comprehensive School, Newcastle upon Tyne. They were happy and successful years. Betty learned to drive and bought a car, becoming quite adventurous, including taking her car on a holiday to Greece, with friends to share the driving. This was in 1967 – which the more politically aware may remember was the year there was a military coup in Greece. Betty remembers the alarm of some local people, when, on a bus trip in Athens, a line of tanks rumbled past. Oddly, not one of the many people who had helped her plan the journey had mentioned that this might be a problem – and there were plenty of other equally clueless (or unconcerned) tourists around.

In 1970 she returned to Durham University to take up the post (initially part-time, full-time from 1972) of Research Assistant to Professor Rosemary Cramp at the inception of the British Academy-funded Corpus of Anglo-Saxon Sculpture Project. In 1971 she also became a part-time Tutor in the Department of Archaeology and, from 1971, College (now called Personal) Tutor at Durham University's St Mary's College. Simultaneously her own doctoral research on Anglo-Saxon sculpture progressed and she was awarded her PhD in 1979 for her two-volume thesis, "The Iconography of the Crucifixion in Pre-Conquest Sculpture in England."

At this time she began the steady stream of publications on Anglo-Saxon sculpture which would continue throughout her career, peaking in the 2008 volume *Corpus of Anglo-Saxon Sculpture. VIII. Western Yorkshire* and her forthcoming book provisionally entitled *The Crucifixion Imagined in Anglo-Saxon England*. She was also inspired by other treasures of Durham, and contributed a study of its crucifixion illumination and other decoration to a collaborative facsimile edition of the Durham Gospels manuscript A. II. 17 (with Christopher Verey and Julian Brown) which was published in 1980, and an acclaimed chapter on metal items associated with the relics of St Cuthbert in Durham Cathedral, "The Pectoral Cross and Portable Altar from the Tomb of St Cuthbert," in *St Cuthbert: his Cult and Community to AD 1200*, a highly regarded collection of essays edited by Gerald Bonner, David Rollason, and Clare Stancliffe, published in 1989.

In December 1969 she moved to Manchester, taking up the post of Warden of Loxford Tower Hall, and a half-time Senior Lectureship in the Department of

History of Art and Design, in the then Manchester Polytechnic, now Manchester Metropolitan University (MMU). She was Secretary of the National Association of Principals and Wardens of Halls of Residence from 1982 to 1987. She left her Wardenship in 1987, when her Senior Lectureship became full time, and she added the duties of Tutor/Slide Librarian in 1993, continuing in both capacities until her retirement in 2004. She was energetic and successful in applications for grants towards the development of the Manchester Metropolitan University Slide Library, raising well over £100,000 in awards for the cataloguing, conservation, and digitization of the collection, particularly the slide collection of the Design Council, which was deposited at MMU, chosen from a number of candidates, in 1995 on the closure of the Design Centre. This online resource for the visual arts (researched and implemented by John Davis) is available at https://vads.ac.uk/learning/dcsc/slide.html (accessed 22 May 2020).

As part of her work for the Department of History of Art and Design Betty was able to use her knowledge of Anglo-Saxon and wider medieval material culture for Design History students and also for students of Art and Design (future designers). This drew once again on her experience at Durham, since the embroidered vestments among the relics of St Cuthbert in Durham Cathedral are an outstanding early example of the art in medieval England, and she became interested in the famous *Opus anglicanum* embroidery of the later medieval period and the influence of all this early work on later nineteenth- and early twentieth-century art and design designers and movements. This made her aware of how difficult access to this early material was for people without her background in medieval art and archaeology. She thought that the best way to document the numerous textiles surviving from the British Isles might be through a database, and so took a Master of Science degree in Computing at the (then) University of Manchester Institute of Science and Technology in 1992. This experience fed into the database for the slide collections noted above.

In these years at Manchester Betty developed two major collaborations, the first with Michael Pinder, then Senior Lecturer in Metalwork, in the Department of Architecture, Landscape, and Three-Dimensional Design, Manchester Metropolitan University, and a practising goldsmith. Together they wrote *The Art of the Anglo-Saxon Goldsmith: Fine Metalwork in Anglo-Saxon England: its Practice and Practitioners*, which is described in its publishers' advertising as "the first [book] to look at the goldsmiths' products through the eyes of both a specialist in the period and a practical craftsman." The second was with Gale R. Owen-Crocker, then Lecturer in English at the nearby Victoria University of Manchester (now The University of Manchester), who shared Betty's interest in textiles, her special knowledge of the Anglo-Saxon period, and incidentally, her north-east origins and university education. Together

they established the Manchester Medieval Textiles Project, successfully applying for a number of grants which funded two successive Research Assistants,
Maria FitzGerald and Christina Lee (both of whom went on to distinguished
careers), some very useful research travel, and the publication of *An Annotated
Bibliography of the Medieval Textiles of the British Isles* (2007). They brought
the existence of textiles to the notice of Anglo-Saxon specialists in more traditional fields by means of a presentation at the Stanford, California, conference of the International Society for Anglo-Saxonists in 1995 and became
regular attenders at the annual Medieval Congresses in Kalamazoo, Michigan,
sometimes taking the opportunity to visit American collections of medieval
European textiles *en route*.

At Kalamazoo Betty was a founding member of the group known as DISTAFF
(Discussion, Interpretation, and Study of Textile Arts, Fabrics, and Fashion)
and has written a number of papers for its associated, peer-reviewed journal,
Medieval Clothing and Textiles, joining the journal's Editorial Board in 2018.
DISTAFF is always represented at the Leeds, UK, Medieval Congresses, also,
where Betty has been, and still is, a regular presence. In 2012, after over five
years of research and writing, Betty and Gale, together with Maria Hayward,
produced the *Encyclopedia of Medieval Dress and Textiles of the British Isles
c. 450–1450*, with Betty acting as editor for entries on textiles. Many of these
she commissioned from experts in the field. Others she wrote herself, and the
range of her knowledge and command of the subject is well demonstrated
by the entries for 2012 in the bibliography of her works in this volume (pp.
XV–XXI). Impressed by the number of surviving near-complete garments
from the medieval period in galleries and museums (a pleasant contrast to
Anglo-Saxon fragments which are mostly brown, brittle, and tiny), Betty and
Gale jointly wrote *Clothing the Past: Surviving Garments from Early Medieval to
Early Modern Western Europe*, published in 2018.

Although she was the only "Anglo-Saxonist," in her Department at MMU,
Betty worked only 10 minutes' walk away from The University of Manchester,
where medieval studies were well established, and where lecturers in English,
History, Art History, and most modern languages were teaching and carrying
out research on the medieval period. Salford University, not far away, also
supported some medieval studies. The Manchester Medieval Society, long
established at The University of Manchester, was opened to non-academics
under the presidency of Professor C.R. Dodwell, and greatly benefitted from
that augmentation. Betty served as Secretary (2004–2008), President (1993–
1995), and committee member (until 2016). The University of Manchester's
Extra-Mural Department ran a successful Certificate in Anglo-Saxon Studies
for many years. Betty was a tutor on that course. The Manchester Centre for

Anglo-Saxon Studies (MANCASS), founded in 1984, brought international scholars to Manchester for its annual conferences and published a series of volumes. Betty was an Assistant Director of MANCASS from its inception, and frequently contributed to conferences and publications. The Centre organized a part-time MA in Anglo-Saxon Studies, taught over three years, with remarkable success. A number of students went on to doctorates and publications. Betty was a tutor on that degree and a member of the MA Examining Board. In recent years a cluster of MA and research students at The University of Manchester took an interest in medieval textiles and a successful series of seminars was instituted, attracting considerable numbers of interested staff and students. Betty was again a stalwart attender.

Betty's career has coincided with what, in many ways, has been a golden era for Anglo-Saxon studies. University Archaeology Departments, which had long been dominated by interest in Classical and Near Eastern excavations, began to open up to medieval European topics in the mid-twentieth century. Many scholars who originated in English Departments turned to Anglo-Saxon Art and Archaeology, initially to augment their knowledge and teaching of Old English texts, but rapidly recognising the wealth of information there for its own sake. Cemetery archaeology flourished, and long-term excavations of urban sites including York and London provided hitherto undreamed-of evidence, including organic remains such as textile and leather. The annual *Anglo-Saxon England*, established in 1970, published interdisciplinary collections of papers by both leading scholars and beginners, and pioneered an interdisciplinary annual bibliography of Anglo-Saxon studies. The *Old English Newsletter*, established in 1977, continued the interdisciplinary approach and became a valuable resource for its annotated bibliographies, reports on current research, and other immediate issues. Betty co-ordinated the bibliographic entries on Archaeology, Numismatics, and Sculpture for *Old English Newsletter* from 2001 to 2008. The biennial conferences of the International Society of Anglo-Saxonists (ISAS) were important meeting places for scholars of various nationalities where ideas were exchanged, new collaborations arranged, and some memorable excursions organized.[1]

---

1 Sadly ISAS imploded in 2019, and later changed its name, since the term "Anglo-Saxon" which, to specialist academics, meant the culture of a particular era (*c.* 449–1066) in a particular place (England), has been misappropriated, causing many scholars, in particular American ones, now to shun it, generally choosing to refer to "early medieval English" topics instead. The organization has been re-established as the International Society for the Study of Early Medieval England (ISSEME) with new officers and firm statements against prejudice of any kind in its constitution.

Betty retired from the Department of History of Art and Design and from the Slide Library at MMU in 2004, transferring as a part-time Research Fellow to MIRIAD (Manchester Institute for Research and Innovation in Art and Design) from 2004 to 2008 and thereafter as an Honorary Fellow until 2015. In retirement she served for four years as Chair of MEDATS (the Medieval Dress and Textiles Society) and continues her academic work as an independent scholar.

When she ceased to be Warden of Loxford Tower Hall, which was situated in one of the most traffic-polluted parts of the city of Manchester, Betty moved full time to the leafier suburbs, where she had already bought the first of several houses, initially in Heaton Mersey, next in Heaton Norris, finally Heaton Mersey again, near her church. In all her houses, she displayed a talent for interior design, and was also daring in altering and extending her properties. Such changes rarely took place trouble-free: none of Betty's friends will forget her months of anguish, effectively living on a building site, when an unmapped drain was discovered running through the foundation trench of her proposed new living room at Heaton Mersey, to the horror of the builder, Betty, and the local council. All was resolved in the end, and many convivial evenings and productive working lunches were enjoyed in the extended house.

St John's Church, Heaton Mersey, played a major role in Betty's life for many years. A regular worshipper, she served as a Lay Assistant, an elected member of the Parochial Church Council, and at various times Deanery Synod Representative and Gift Aid Secretary. She also founded and for a long time ran a much-needed monthly "Wednesday Club," for, mainly, retired people, with varied activities including invited speakers on various topics; worked hard for a regular play-meeting for young Mums/Carers and Tots; and attended a Bible Study Discussion Group.

In 2019 she made the life-changing decision to return to Durham to be near her family, selling her loved home in Heaton Mersey and buying a new-build house in the city of Durham, within walking distance of the University library. There, despite difficulties, not least those caused by the Corona Virus pandemic, she has been working to finish her latest book, on the representation of the Crucifixion in Anglo-Saxon England, and to create a garden. Her friends and relatives confidently expected that in time she would extend or otherwise develop the house. Instead, she has announced a move to a traditional stone-built terraced property rather like the house where she was brought up, which coincidentally has the same street name, a rather satisfying return to origins. Meanwhile she is greatly missed by her Manchester friends. There is another textiles book just waiting to be written when she has time …

The Published Work of Elizabeth Coatsworth

2018 (With G.R. Owen-Crocker) *Clothing the Past: Surviving Garments from Early Medieval to Early Modern Western Europe* (Leiden & Boston: Brill).

2017 "Depiction of Martyrdom in Anglo-Saxon Art and Literature: Contexts and Contrasts," in *Crossing Boundaries: Interdisciplinary Approaches to the Art, Material Culture, Language and Literature of the Early Medieval World*, ed. E. Cambridge and J. Hawkes (Oxford), pp. 23–35.

2017 (With G.R. Owen-Crocker) "Textiles," in *A Cultural History of Dress and Fashion in the Medieval Age* (The Cultural History of Dress and Fashion 2), ed. S.-G. Heller (London and New York), pp. 11–28.

2017 Exhibition Review: "Opus Anglicanum: Masterpieces of English Medieval Embroidery: London," *Burlington Magazine*, 159, January, pp. 56–57.

2016 "Opus What? The Textual History of Medieval Embroidery Terms and Their Relationship to the Surviving Embroideries c. 800–1400," in *Textiles, Text, Intertext: Essays in Honour of Gale R. Owen-Crocker*, ed. M.C. Hyer and J. Frederick (Woodbridge), pp. 43–68.

2015 "Landmarks of Faith: Crosses and Other Freestanding Stones," in *The Material Culture of the Built Environment in the Anglo-Saxon World* (Daily Living in the Anglo-Saxon World 2), ed. M.C. Hyer and G.R. Owen-Crocker (Liverpool), pp. 117–36.

2015 Book Review: "Shirley Ann Brown, *The Bayeux Tapestry (Bayeux, Mediathèque municipale: MS. 1): A Sourcebook* (Publications of the Journal of Medieval Latin 9) (Turnhout, 2013)," *Speculum* 90.1, 216–18.

2014 "'A formidable undertaking': Mrs A.G.I. Christie and *English Medieval Embroidery*," *Medieval Clothing and Textiles* 10, 165–93.

2014 Book Review: "*Envisioning Christ on the Cross: Ireland and the Early Medieval West*, ed. Janet Mullins, Jenifer Ní Ghradáigh, and Richard Hawtree," *Medieval Archaeology* 58 (2014), pp. 422–23.

2014 Book Review: "Jan Keupp, *Die Wahl des Gewandes. Mode, Macht und Möglichkeitssinn in Gesellschaft und Politik des Mittelalters* (Mittelalter-Forschungen 33) (Ostfildern, 2010)," online at https://perspectivia.net//receive/ploneimport2_mods _00005031.

2012 *Encyclopedia of Dress and Textiles in the British Isles c. 450–1450*, ed. with G.R. Owen-Crocker and M. Hayward (Leiden and Boston).

2012 (With G.R. Owen-Crocker) "Alb," in *Encyclopedia*, p. 31, and "Amice," pp. 36–37.

2012 "Apparel," in *Encyclopedia*, p. 37.

2012 (With G.R. Owen-Crocker), "Appliqué," in *Encyclopedia*, pp. 37–38.

2012 (With M. Chambers) "Baudekin," in *Encyclopedia*, pp. 56–57.

2012 "Becket, St Thomas: Life and Textile Relics," in *Encyclopedia*, pp. 64–68.

2012 "Embroidery," in *Encyclopedia*, p. 196.

2012 "Felbrigge Psalter: Embroidered Book Cover," in *Encyclopedia*, pp. 205–06.

2012 "Felt," in *Encyclopedia*, pp. 206–07.

2012 "Finger Loop Braiding," in *Encyclopedia*, pp. 207–08.

2012 "Finishing," in *Encyclopedia*, pp. 208–09.

2012 "Fraternity," in *Encyclopedia*, p. 210.

2012 (With M. Chambers) "Frieze," in *Encyclopedia*, p. 211.

2012 "Fringes and Tassels," in *Encyclopedia*, pp. 211–12.

2012 "Fuller's Earth," in *Encyclopedia*, pp. 213–14.

2012 "Fustian," in *Encyclopedia*, pp. 222–23.

2012 (With M. Hayward) "Gold and Silver Wire and Wire Drawing," in *Encyclopedia*, pp. 239–41.

2012 "Goscelin," in *Encyclopedia*, pp. 242–43.

2012 (With M. Chambers) "Haberget," in *Encyclopedia*, p. 260.

2012 "Heckle," in *Encyclopedia*, p. 264.

2012 "Hemming (1)," in *Encyclopedia*, p. 266.

2012 "Horse trapper, Musée Cluny, Paris," in *Encyclopedia*, p. 277.

2012 "Iconography and Symbolism on Textiles," in *Encyclopedia*, pp. 285–89.

2012 "Inscriptions on Textiles," in *Encyclopedia*, pp. 289–91.

2012 "Johanna Beverlai Altar Frontlet," in *Encyclopedia*, p. 298.

2012 "John of Thanet," in *Encyclopedia*, pp. 298–99.

2012 "Kendal," in *Encyclopedia*, p. 301.

2012 "Kersey," in *Encyclopedia*, p. 302.

2012 "Lampas," in *Encyclopedia*, p. 311.

2012 "Last," in *Encyclopedia*, p. 313.

2012 "Lawn," in *Encyclopedia*, p. 316.

2012 "Leathersellers," in *Encyclopedia*, p. 323.

2012 "Lebuin, St, Relic of," in *Encyclopedia*, pp. 323–24.

2012 "Liber Pontificalis," in *Encyclopedia*, pp. 324–25.

2012 "Liturgical Textiles: ante-1100," in *Encyclopedia*, pp. 330–33.

2012 "Maaseik Textiles," in *Encyclopedia*, pp. 354–57.

2012 "Mercers," in *Encyclopedia*, p. 366.

2012 "Merchant Taylors," in *Encyclopedia*, p. 367.

2012 "Mitre," in *Encyclopedia*, p. 370.

2012 "Narrow Wares," in *Encyclopedia*, p. 380.

2012 "Needle," in *Encyclopedia*, p. 381.

2012 "Opus anglicanum," in *Encyclopedia*, pp. 392–97.

2012 "Patrons and Patronage," in *Encyclopedia*, pp. 407–09.

2012 "Piece," in *Encyclopedia*, p. 417.

2012 "Pienza Cope," in *Encyclopedia*, pp. 417–18.

2012 "Pinners," in *Encyclopedia*, p. 419.

2012 (With M. Chambers) "Plunket," in *Encyclopedia*, p. 421.

2012 "Pouches and Purses: ante-1100," in *Encyclopedia*, pp. 428–29.

2012 "Pouchmakers," in *Encyclopedia*, p. 432.

2012 "Purser," in *Encyclopedia*, p. 438.

2012 "Ray," in *Encyclopedia*, p. 441.

2012 "Relics of St Cuthbert," in *Encyclopedia*, pp. 451–55.

2012 (With M. Chambers) "Russet," in *Encyclopedia*, p. 469.

2012 "Sack," in *Encyclopedia*, p. 470.

2012 "Samite," in *Encyclopedia*, p. 475.

2012 "Sarpler," in *Encyclopedia*, p. 475.

2012 "Sarsenet," in *Encyclopedia*, p. 476.

2012 "Satin," in *Encyclopedia*, p. 476.

2012 (With M. Chambers) "Say," in *Encyclopedia*, pp. 476–77.

2012 "Sculpture: ante-1100, Evidence for Dress," in *Encyclopedia*, pp. 481–84.

2012 "Sculpture: ante-1100, Skeuomorphs of Textile Techniques," in *Encyclopedia*, pp. 485–86.

2012 "Sendal," in *Encyclopedia*, p. 500.

2012 "Shearman's Hook," in *Encyclopedia*, p. 508.

2012 "Shearmen," in *Encyclopedia*, p. 508.

2012 "Shopping," in *Encyclopedia*, pp. 511–14.

2012 "Skinners," in *Encyclopedia*, p. 523.

2012 "Soft Furnishings and Textiles: ante-1100," in *Encyclopedia*, pp. 526–30.

2012 "Soft Furnishings and Textiles: post-1100," in *Encyclopedia*, pp. 530–34.

2012 "Stone," in *Encyclopedia*, pp. 565–66.

2012 "Straits," in *Encyclopedia*, p. 566.

2012 "Surviving Medieval Textiles of the British Isles," in *Encyclopedia*, pp. 568–69.

2012 "Syon Cope," in *Encyclopedia*, pp. 569–70.

2012 "Taffeta," in *Encyclopedia*, p. 577.

2012 "Tapestry," in *Encyclopedia*, pp. 577–78.

2012 "Tartarin," in *Encyclopedia*, p. 579.

2012 "Tinsel," in *Encyclopedia*, p. 585.

2012 "Tiretaine," in *Encyclopedia*, p. 587.

2012 "Tissue," in *Encyclopedia*, pp. 587–88.

2012 "Tod," in *Encyclopedia*, p. 588.

2012 "Tucker," in *Encyclopedia*, p. 606.

2012 "Vegetable Fibre," in *Encyclopedia*, pp. 610–11.

2012 (With G.R. Owen-Crocker) "Velvet," in *Encyclopedia*, p. 613.

2012 "Verge," in *Encyclopedia*, p. 613.

2012 "Wadmal," in *Encyclopedia*, p. 615.

2012 "Waterford," in *Encyclopedia*, pp. 617–18.

2012 "Weaving (weaves)," in *Encyclopedia*, pp. 620–24.

2012 "Wey," in *Encyclopedia*, p. 626.

2012 "Whitawyer," in *Encyclopedia*, p. 626.

2012 "Wills and Inventories: ante-1100," in *Encyclopedia*, pp. 626–28.

2012 "Winder," in *Encyclopedia*, pp. 630–31.

2012 "Wiredrawers," in *Encyclopedia*, p. 631.

2012 "Woolbrogger," in *Encyclopedia*, pp. 650–51.

2012 "Wrappings," in *Encyclopedia*, pp. 654–55.

2012 "Yard," in *Encyclopedia*, p. 656.

2012 Book Review: "*Europäische Stickereien 1250–1650 [European Embroideries 1250–1650]*, ed. Uta-Christiane Bergemann (Regensberg)," *Medieval Clothing and Textiles* 8, 156–57.

2011 "The Material Culture of the Anglo-Saxon Church," *The Oxford Handbook of Anglo-Saxon Archaeology*, ed. H. Hamerow, S. Crawford, and D.A. Hinton (Oxford), pp. 779–96.

2011 (With Michael Pinder) "Sight, Insight and Hand: Some Reflections on the Design of the Fuller Brooch," in *The Material Culture of Daily Living in the Anglo-Saxon World*, ed. M.C. Hyer and G.R. Owen-Crocker (Exeter), pp. 258–74.

2010 "Anglo-Saxon Liturgical Textiles," in *The English Parish Church through the Centuries: Daily Life and Spirituality, Art and Architecture, Literature and Music*, ed. Dee Dyas, Interactive DVD-ROM.

2010 Book Review: "*The Medieval Broadcloth: Changing Trends in Fashion, Manufacturing and Consumption* (Ancient Textiles Series 6), ed. Kathrine Vestergård Pederson and Marie-Louise Nosche (Oxford, 2009)," *Medieval Clothing and Textiles* 6, 210–11.

2009 Book Review: "Seiichi Suzuki, *Anglo-Saxon Button Brooches: Typology, Genealogy, Chronology* (Woodbridge, 2008)," *Medieval Clothing and Textiles* 5, 189.

2008 *Corpus of Anglo-Saxon Stone Sculpture. VIII. Western Yorkshire* (Oxford).

2008 "Design in the Past: Metalwork and Textile Influences on Pre-Conquest Sculpture in England," in *Aedificia Nova: Studies in Honour of Rosemary Cramp*, ed. C. Karkov and H. Damico (Kalamazoo, MI), pp. 139–61.

2008 (With C. Lee and F. Altvater) "Archaeology, Numismatics, Sculpture," *Old English Newsletter* 41.2, 216–49.

2007 (With G.R. Owen-Crocker) *An Annotated Bibliography of the Medieval Textiles of the British Isles, 450–1100* (BAR British Series 445) (Oxford).

2007 "Cushioning Medieval Life: Domestic Textiles in Early Medieval England," *Medieval Clothing and Textiles* 3, 1–12.

2007 "Text and Textile," in *Text, Image, Interpretation: Studies in Anglo-Saxon Literature and its Insular Context in Honour of Eamonn Ó'Carragáin*, ed. A. Minnis and J. Roberts (Turnhout: Brepols), pp. 187–207.

2007 (With C. Lee and F. Altvater) "Archaeology, Sculpture, Inscriptions, Numismatics," *Old English Newsletter* 40.2, 205–21.

2006 "Inscriptions on Textiles Associated with Anglo-Saxon England," in *Writing and Texts in Anglo-Saxon England* (Publications of the Manchester Centre for Anglo-Saxon Studies 5), ed. A.R. Rumble (Woodbridge), pp. 71–95.

2006 "The Cross in the West Riding of Yorkshire," in *The Place of the Cross in Anglo-Saxon England* (Sancta Crux/Halig Rod Series 2, Publications of the Manchester Centre for Anglo-Saxon Studies 4), ed. C. Karkov, S.L. Keefer, and K.L. Jolly (Woodbridge), pp. 14–28.

2006 (With F. Altvater and C. Karkov) "Archaeology, Numismatics, Sculpture," *Old English Newsletter* 39.2, 188–225.

2005 (With R. Wood and L. Butler) *Early Sculptures in Burnsall Church* (Burnsall).

2005 "Stitches in Time: Establishing a History of Anglo-Saxon Embroidery," *Medieval Clothing and Textiles* 1, 1–27.

2004 (With F. Altvater and G. Fisher) "Archaeology, Numismatics, Sculpture," *Old English Newsletter* 37.2, 178–95.

2003 "The Book of Enoch and Anglo-Saxon Art," in *Apocryphal Texts and Traditions in Anglo-Saxon England* (Publications of the Manchester Centre for Anglo-Saxon Studies 2), ed. K. Powell and D. Scragg (Woodbridge), pp. 135–50.

2003 "Archaeology, Numismatics, Sculpture for 2000," *Old English Newsletter* 36.2, 153–54.

2002 (With M. Pinder) *The Art of the Anglo-Saxon Goldsmith* (Woodbridge).

2001 (With M. Fitzgerald) "Anglo-Saxon Textiles in the Mayer/Faussett Collection," *Medieval Archaeology* 45, 1–14.

2001 "The Embroideries from the Tomb of St Cuthbert," in *Edward the Elder 899–924*, ed. N.J. Higham and D. Hill (London and New York), pp. 292–306.

2001 (With A. Gannon) "Archaeology and Numismatics," *Old English Newsletter* 34.2, 114–27.

2000 "The 'Robed Christ' in Pre-Conquest Sculptures of the Crucifixion," *Anglo-Saxon England* 29, 153–76.

1999 "East Riddlesden Hall," *Durham University Journal* 14–15, pp. 107–10.

1998 "Clothmaking and the Virgin Mary in Anglo-Saxon Literature and Art," in *Medieval Art: Recent Perspectives: A Memorial Tribute to C.R. Dodwell*, ed. G.R. Owen-Crocker and T. Graham (Manchester), pp. 8–25.

1998 "Embroidery," in *The Blackwell Encyclopaedia of Anglo-Saxon England*, ed. M. Lapidge, J. Blair, S. Keynes, and D. Scragg (Oxford), pp. 167–69.

1998 "Textiles," in *The Blackwell Encyclopaedia*, pp. 442–43.

1996 (With M. Fitzgerald, K. Leahy and G.R. Owen Crocker) "Anglo-Saxon Textiles from Cleatham, Humberside," *Textile History* 27.1, 1–37.

1991 "Byrhtnoth's Tomb," in *The Battle of Maldon AD 991*, ed. D. Scragg (Oxford), pp. 279–88.

1989 "The Pectoral Cross and Portable Altar from the Tomb of St Cuthbert," in *St Cuthbert: His Cult and Community to 1200 AD*, ed. G. Bonner *et al.* (Woodbridge), pp. 287–301.

1988 "Late Pre-Conquest Sculptures with the Crucifixion South of the Humber," in *Bishop Aethelwold: His Career and Influence*, ed. B. Yorke (Woodbridge (revised ed. 1997)), pp. 161–93.

1987 "Pre-Conquest Cross Head with Crucifixion," in *St Mary Bishophill Junior and St Mary Castlegate, The Archaeology of York* (8.12), ed. L.P. Wenham, R.A. Hall, C.M. Biden, and D.A. Stocker (London), pp. 161–63.

1983 "The Angel Stone in Manchester Cathedral," in *Medieval Manchester: A Regional Study* (The Archaeology of Greater Manchester 1), ed. M. Morris (Manchester), pp. 9–12.

1981 *The Carved Stones of Woodhorn Church* (Ashington, Northumberland: Wansbeck District Council).

1980 (With C. Verey and T.J. Brown) *The Durham Gospels* (Early English Manuscripts in Facsimile 20) (Copenhagen).

1978 "The Crucifixion Scenes on a Cross at Aycliffe, Co Durham," in *Anglo-Saxon and Viking Age Sculpture: Papers from the Collingwood Symposium on Insular Sculpture from 800 to 1066* (BAR British Series 49), ed. J.T. Lang (Oxford), pp. 114–16.

1978 "The Four Crossheads from the Chapter House, Durham," in *Anglo-Saxon and Viking Age Sculpture*, pp. 85–92.

1977 "The Crucifixion on the Alnmouth Cross," *Archaeologia Aeliana* 55, 198–201.

1974 "An Unnoticed Sculpture Fragment in Durham Cathedral Library," *Transactions of the Architectural and Archaeological Society of Durham and Northumberland* NS 3, 109–10.

1974 "Two Examples of the Crucifixion at Hexham," in *St Wilfrid at Hexham*, ed. D.P. Kirby (Newcastle upon Tyne), pp. 180–84.

1973 "Two Representations of the Crucifixion on Late Pre-Conquest Carved Stones from Bothal, Northumberland," *Archaeologia Aeliana*, 15, 234–36.

Illustrations

Tables

Contributors

Richard N. Bailey
is Emeritus Professor of Anglo-Saxon Civilisation at Newcastle University, where he was Deputy Vice-Chancellor. He has written widely on Anglo-Saxon metalwork, manuscripts, and the relics of Northumbrian saints. His main research interest, however, has been in pre-Norman sculpture on which he has written two overview books – *Viking Age Sculpture* (Collins, 1980) and *England's Earliest Sculptors* (Pontifical Institute for Medieval Studies, 1996) – as well as being the author of two volumes in the British Academy's *Corpus of Anglo-Saxon Stone Sculpture* series.

Michelle P. Brown
FSA is Professor Emeritus of Medieval Manuscript Studies at the School of Advanced Study, University of London, and Visiting Professor at University College London. She was formerly the Curator of Illuminated Manuscripts at the British Library, a Visiting Professor at Leeds and Baylor Universities and a Senior Research Fellow of Oslo University. A specialist in History, Art History, and Archaeology, she brings these skills to bear upon the art, buildings, and artefacts of an age to give insight into the lives of those who made and used them. She has lectured, published, and broadcast widely. Her books include: *The British Library Guide to Historical Scripts*, *How Christianity Came to Britain and Ireland*, *Understanding Illuminated Manuscripts*, *The Historical Source-Book for Scribes*, *The Lindisfarne Gospels: Society, Spirituality and the Scribe*, *The Book and the Transformation of Britain*, and *Art of the Islands: Celtic, Pictish, Anglo-Saxon and Viking Visual Culture c. 450–1050*.

Peter Furniss
spent his professional career in Marine, Mechanical, and Electrical Engineering, becoming a Chartered Engineer in 1990 and spending the last 20 years of his career as University Engineer for Wolverhampton. His hobby of rock climbing was cut short by a serious road accident, and he took up calligraphy as a new hobby in the mid-1990s, becoming Chairman of Shropshire Scribes in 2004. His interest in calligraphy has mainly centred around pre-gothic scripts and has led to research of Insular scripts and associated manuscript production, together with the history of the Anglo-Saxon period. Since retirement from engineering in 2008, he has worked as a guide at Shrewsbury Abbey, writes calligraphy-related articles, and teaches calligraphy courses for various

community groups. In 2018 he wrote and co-edited the book, *20 Scripts over 20 Centuries* to celebrate the 20th anniversary of Shropshire Scribes.

Jane Hawkes

is Professor of Art History at the University of York. She has published widely in the field of Anglo-Saxon art with a specialist interest in the art and architecture of late antiquity and early medieval Europe with reference to the roles of sculpture as public art in the Insular world, the cultural cross-currents between Ireland, Britain, and Europe, and relationships between text and image.

David A. Hinton

is an Emeritus Professor Archaeology, University of Southampton. He was editor of the journal *Medieval Archaeology* from 1979 to 1989, and is a past President of the Royal Archaeological Institute. His publications include *Archaeology, Economy and Society: England from the Fifth to the Fifteenth Century* (Routledge, 1990) and *Gold and Gilt, Pots and Pins: Possessions and People in Medieval Britain* (Oxford University Press, 2005).

Maren Clegg Hyer

is Professor of English at Valdosta State University (Georgia, USA). She specializes in researching textiles and other elements of material culture in the literary imagery of early medieval England. Her projects include *The Material Culture of Daily Living in Anglo-Saxon England* and its subsequent four volumes, most recently *Sense and Feeling in Daily Living in the Early Medieval English World* (Daily Living in the Anglo-Saxon World 4) (with Gale R. Owen-Crocker, Liverpool, 2020); *Textiles, Text, Intertext: Essays in Honour of Gale R. Owen-Crocker* (with Jill Frederick, Boydell, 2016); and *Studies in Medieval Literature and Lexicology in Honor of Antonette di Paolo Healey* (with Haruko Momma and Samantha Zacher, Boydell, 2020).

Catherine E. Karkov

is Chair of Art History in the School of Fine Art, History of Art, and Cultural Studies at the University of Leeds. She has written and edited numerous books and articles on early medieval English Art, including *The Art of Anglo-Saxon England* (Boydell, 2004) and, most recently, *Imagining Anglo-Saxon: Utopia, Heterotopia, Dystopia* (Boydell 2020). She is currently completing a book on *Form and Image in Early Medieval England*.

Alexandra Lester-Makin

is a professional embroiderer, trained at the Royal School of Needlework, and a textile archaeologist. She holds a PhD from Manchester University, specializing in early medieval embroidery and is the University of Glasgow's textiles and leather Post-doctoral Research Associate on the AHRC funded "Unwrapping the Galloway Hoard" Project, led by the National Museum of Scotland. Her book, *The Lost Art of the Anglo-Saxon World: The Sacred and Secular Power of Embroidery*, was published in 2019. She is currently recreating part of the St Cuthbert Maniple, funded by a Janet Arnold Grant (Society of Antiquaries, London). She is co-editing a volume exploring collaborative work methods between researchers, conservators, curators, and makers for studying early medieval textiles. She founded and runs the *Early Medieval (mostly) Textiles* blog and the Early Medieval Textiles YouTube channel.

Christina Lee

is an Associate Professor in Viking Studies at the University of Nottingham. Her research interests have been in the definitions of illness, health, and impairment in Anglo-Saxon England. She has published on leprosy, trauma, and disability, as well as medical textiles. Her work considers the cultural implications of illness and the experiences of those who were affected and she is currently completing a book on *Health and Healing in Early Medieval England*. In 2013 she began a project with a group of scientists (the 'AncientBiotics') to query if there was any efficacy in the medicine in early medieval England which resulted in an ongoing collaboration between the Arts and Sciences and a Royal Society APEX award.

Donncha MacGabhann

is an independent researcher. His professional career in teaching Art History and Art (MA, Fine Art, NCAD, Dublin, 1998), and his work as an artist have significantly informed his study of Insular manuscripts over the past fifteen years. He completed his PhD under the supervision of Prof Michelle Brown (SAS, Univ. of London, 2016). His research, with a particular focus on the Book of Kells, is ongoing, as is his commitment to communicating this work through publication, lecturing, and presenting papers at major conferences. Publications to date include articles in the proceedings of the most recent International Insular Art Conferences (2017 and 2020).

Éamonn Ó Carragáin

is Professor Emeritus of Old and Middle English at University College Cork, and a Member of the Royal Irish Academy. He has published on *Beowulf,* the

Vercelli Book and Old English poetry; artistic, ecclesiastical, and liturgical contacts between the Atlantic Islands and Rome in the early Middle Ages; Botticelli in the Sistine Chapel; the Renaissance church of San Giovanni Crisostomo in Venice. He is committed to Adult and Continuing Education, and for years ran the UCC Seminar on Medieval Rome based on the British School at Rome; more recent courses have included Paris, Constantinople and Venice.

Gale R. Owen-Crocker

FSA (Editor) is Professor Emerita of The University of Manchester; she was formerly Professor of Anglo-Saxon Culture and Director of the Manchester Centre for Anglo-Saxon Studies. She co-founded and for 15 years co-edited the journal *Medieval Clothing and Textiles*; and directed the Manchester Lexis of Cloth and Clothing Project, producing the database http://lexisproject.arts.manchester. ac.uk/. Her recent books include *Clothing the Past: Surviving Garments from Early Medieval to Early Modern Western Europe* (with Elizabeth Coatsworth, Brill, 2018); and *Sense and Feeling in Daily Living in the Early Medieval English World* (Daily Living in the Anglo-Saxon World 4) (with Maren Clegg Hyer, Liverpool, 2020).

Frances Pritchard

is an Honorary Research Fellow of The University of Manchester. As a museum professional her career encompassed sixteen years in the Department of Urban Archaeology, Museum of London, and twenty-three years as Curator (Textiles) at the Whitworth Art Gallery. She has also acted as a consultant on textiles to the British Museum, National Museum of Ireland and English Heritage. Most of her many publications have focused on textiles from excavations in London, Dublin and Egypt.

Penelope Walton Rogers

is proprietor of The Anglo-Saxon Laboratory, Visiting Fellow at the University of York, and currently serves as Chair of the Early Textiles Study Group. As an archaeological project manager she has brought to completion a series of excavation reports and as an academic collaborator she participates in funded European research projects. Her particular research interests lie in the reconstruction of women's lives from the archaeological record; regional, cultural, and political borders; migration patterns; costume and textiles; and the many facets of ritual practice and religion.

Introduction

Gale R. Owen-Crocker and Maren Clegg Hyer

Our honoree graduated with a degree in English, subsequently taught English, then worked and taught in an Archaeology department and later in a Department of The History of Art and Design. She has published on archaeology, sculpture, metalwork, illuminated manuscripts, text, dress, and textiles, mostly from the Anglo-Saxon period,[1] and has always had a particular interest in the North East of England, both because of her own birth there and because of the historical importance of the so-called 'Golden Age of Northumbria.' Our authors, invited to contribute chapters on any, or multiple, topics featured in her career, have produced a stimulating and wide-ranging collection of papers, many of them multidisciplinary. Readers will find archaeology in Chapters 5, 7, and 12, sculpture in 8–11, metalwork in 5, 9, 11, and 12, manuscript art in 1–2 and 13, text in 2, 4, 9, 11, and 12, liturgy in 11, dress and appearance in 1–7, textiles in 4–7, specifically embroidery, a particular interest of the honoree, at 4 and 6–7. The 'Golden Age of Northumbria' features in Chapters 5, 9, 11, and 12 and Anglo-Norman Durham in 7.

The first seven papers have been grouped as Representation: Art and Worship through Text, Textile, and Tool. The first two chapters demonstrate how figural art, whether realistic or imaginative, was used to enhance the learning and contemplation of the most holy of Christian scriptures. Donncha MacGabhann's "Figurative Art in the Book of Kells: Absurd Anatomies, See-through Tunics and Diverse Hairstyles" (1) focuses on one of the most accomplished and famous of Insular illuminated manuscripts, the late eighth- to early ninth-century gospels known as the Book of Kells, which teems with figural decoration, both anthropomorphic and zoomorphic. Identifying two artists, MacGabhann provides a detailed analysis, concentrating particularly on hair.

---

1 In past controversies, white nationalists have attempted to appropriate the term 'Anglo-Saxon' for use as a term of identity. That is not how the term is used in this edited volume. The ethnic groups scholars label 'Anglo-Saxon' (largely out of convenience and overlapping ancestry and interests) lived in England from the early 400s, dominating the regional landscape until the 1100s and blending with other groups in the region then and thereafter. As scholars, we consider these peoples as biologically and culturally 'other' to all groups now living and accord them the respect due to an 'other' entitled to their own identity. In this text, wherever the term 'Anglo-Saxon' is used by any of our authors, it should be considered equivalent to 'early medieval English'.

© KONINKLIJKE BRILL NV, LEIDEN, 2021 | DOI:10.1163/9789004467514_002

Christina Lee, in "The Art of Looking Good: Hair and Beauty Remedies in Early Medieval Texts and Contexts" (2) also considers the subject of hair and head, discussing hair as a marker of social identity in both religious and secular life and the performative importance of cutting or covering the hair in literary contexts. Pointing out the relationship of clean hair and healthy hair, the paper discusses personal grooming tools, headdress, maladies and parasites of the head and hair, and remedies against them.

Gale R. Owen-Crocker's "Dress and Undress, Real and Unreal, in the Drawings of Harley Psalter Artist F" (3) also considers matters of appearance, in this case in the work of an artist working *c.* 1020, who illustrated most of two quires of a manuscript already in progress, acknowledging the tradition of his predecessors, but, unlike them, not copying his images from the Utrecht Psalter. The artist depicts unusual and unique details of dress that were perhaps in vogue in his day, as well as creating imagined details through decorative flourishes in the style of his models. Alone among English artists of his era, he shows great awareness of the anatomy of his subjects, particularly using male nudity in semiotic ways.

Dress and textiles again feature in Maren Clegg Hyer's "Adorning Medieval Life: Domestic and Dress Textiles as Expressions of Worship in Early Medieval England" (4), which examines the documentary evidence for donation of garments and textiles to ecclesiastical establishments, showing how gifts of prestigious items of this kind were expressions of both art and worship, and also how gifts of more utilitarian domestic textiles might enhance worship. Contrasting attitudes to fine dress are also examined, showing how ostentatious dress might be condemned as worldly, but might also play a welcome role in worship.

Personal tools, both for grooming and for cloth making, together with material remains of textile and dress accessories, are among the archaeological finds from the site of Whitby. In "In Search of Hild: A Review of the Context of Abbess Hild's Life, her Religious Establishment, and the Relevance of Recent Archaeological Finds from Whitby Abbey" (5) Penelope Walton Rogers explores the known biographical details of this influential seventh-century female saint. In a life spent at a crucial point in the establishment of Christianity in Northumbria, and spanning periods of political turmoil, Hild presided over a community that was not only famous for its spirituality and scholarship, but also an economic and trading unit.

While the Whitby community is likely to have produced textiles of good, but not *de luxe* standard, the linen cloth discussed in Frances Pritchard's "Embroidery on Spin-patterned Linen in the 6th to 9th centuries" (6) was one that required special materials and skilled weaving and finishing. The uses of such cloth include linings of prestige garments and ground fabric for embroideries sometimes associated with the elite, notably, though not exclusively, in religious contexts, and not just coloured embroidery, but also as an early manifestation of whitework.

Continuing the topic of elite embroidery, Alexandra Lester-Makin's "The Embroidered Fragments from the Tomb of Bishop William of St Calais, Durham: an Analysis and Biography" (7) examines in detail two neglected eleventh-century fragments from Durham. Placing the embroideries in their contexts, and applying object biography methods, the author concludes that one fragment was a recycled piece; and the other, probably commissioned by Bishop William himself, in England, was part of a specific episcopal vestment, a particularly unusual survival.

Similarly meaningful devotional objects and expressions of worship are explored in the second half of the volume. The last seven papers have been grouped as PART 2: In their Contexts: Art and Worship through Sculpture, Carving, and Manuscript. "Framing Fragmentation: (Re)Constructing Anglo-Saxon Sculpture" by Jane Hawkes (8) explains how iconoclasm resulted in most surviving Anglo-Saxon stone sculptures being in a fragmentary state and argues that, with a few notable exceptions, they are displayed in ways that misinterpret them and minimize their impact, both in visual terms and in comparison to the accepted appreciation of classical art. Hawkes presents a striking reimagining of Anglo-Saxon stone sculpture, coloured and glittering with glass inserts and metal attachments which enhanced their three-dimensional nature, making them a particularly effective vehicle for divine imagery.

Catherine E. Karkov, in "The Thread of Ornament (aka the Bewcastle Cross)" (9) examines the meaningful nature of ornament on Anglo-Saxon artefacts, focusing on one of the few stone sculptures still in its original place. She considers the significance of that place, and of the static nature of the stone monument which demands that the viewer walk around it, experiencing different lights on different sides and being drawn in to contemplation of and meditation on the multiple meanings of its ornament.

In "A Newly Identified Anglo-Saxon Sculpture in Great Chalfield Church, Wiltshire" (10), David A. Hinton continues the themes of stone sculpture, fragmentation, and context. Two fragments now identified as parts of an Anglo-Saxon carving survive in the environment of a church of which there is no evidence before the fourteenth century, apart from a possibly thirteenth-century font. Considering the material and the ornament, Hinton identifies the fragments as belonging to an arch framing a figure in a panel of an ecclesiastical sculpture, suggesting that a tradition of stone sculpture as an aid to Christian worship existed in the area considerably earlier than other survivals would imply.

Éamonn Ó Carragháin's "The Company they Keep: Scholarly Discussion, 2005–2020 of the Original Settings for the Poems in the 'Dream of the Rood' Tradition" (11) concerns the related poems on the Ruthwell and Brussels crosses, and in the Vercelli Book, but chiefly focuses on developments in scholarship about the runic poem on the Ruthwell Cross since the publication of the author's major monograph in 2005. The author's own work explores the biblical, liturgical, and doctrinal associations of the cross and its internal patterning, while other scholars have variously questioned and asserted these relationships as well as the integrity of the monument and the relevance of the runic poem to the iconography. The article is enriched by photographs of the upper stone at Ruthwell generously provided by Catherine Karkov.

Continuing consideration of the Golden Age of Northumbria, in "Bishop Acca's Portable Altar: Authentic Relic or Twelfth-century Hexham Fiction?" (12), Richard N. Bailey examines the career, burial, and cult of a major ecclesiastical figure who has received remarkably little attention from modern scholars. Noting that a single twelfth-century source describes in detail a portable altar said to have been buried with Bishop Acca of Hexham, Bailey considers whether this was an elaborate invention to compete with the portable altar already found with the remains of St Cuthbert at Durham, or whether, in the light of its intriguing, highly intellectual inscription, it was documenting a genuine eighth- or early ninth-century object.

The final chapter, Michelle P. Brown and Peter Furniss' "The Hereford Gospels Reappraised" (13), provides a detailed analysis of a small, lesser-known, late eighth-, or more probably, early ninth-century gospel book, showing its affinities with earlier Hiberno-Saxon and contemporary Mercian manuscript art. The authors suggest plausibly that it might have been made at Hereford, under the influence of Lichfield, itself a daughter-house of Lindisfarne, for the shrine of King Ethelbert the King or for the bishop of Hereford.

The papers deliver important insights into the lived experience of worship in early medieval England and Ireland, from the public experience of church and free-standing stone sculptures, through non-liturgical aspects of the religious life including the cult of relics, to personal identity and imagination. Long-term contemplation of illuminations in manuscripts and on carved monuments would gradually awaken monastic scholars to wider significance of their faith. Public worship took place in a colourful environment, including painted sculptures studded with gems or glass, augmented by shining metal attachments. The Gospels and Psalter discussed here, books that would have been available and open in church for readings, were brightly illuminated. Mass was celebrated by ecclesiastics in colourful vestments. The finest silks and linens, decorated with rich embroidery, sometimes including gold, were employed for liturgical textiles. The acquisition and veneration of relics was another important feature of medieval Christianity. They were gathered from graves, sometimes stolen, wrapped in precious textiles, enclosed in decorated shrines, and recorded in histories and inventories. All of these devotional objects enhanced and informed the lived experience of art and worship in early medieval England.

Religious life did not take place entirely within church. Worship included study and contemplation as well as physical labour. Archaeological finds explored in this volume demonstrate the simple dress, intimate tools for grooming, and implements for daily work employed by the women of the Whitby community. For other monastics, learning and transmitting medical remedies were daily work, revealing a surprising interest in personal appearance and grooming, which included maintaining an attractive appearance as well as curing maladies.

The monastic life also included study, rote learning, contemplation, and *compunctio*. That artists illuminated and illustrated manuscripts of the most important texts in the imaginative way they did, to aid memorisation and deep understanding of the holy word, is apparent from the manuscripts discussed here. The use of inherited traditions of iconography and decoration added the authority of spiritual ancestry to new works, but the use of them in new combinations, along with novel, inventive devices, such as scenes from contemporary ceremonial or fantasy creatures, made them living aids to worship. It is clear that the decorative arts were not there merely to delight the eye of medieval man and woman. They existed to aid profound understanding, to stimulate the personal imagination that enabled the audience, in the long hours of book learning or standing in contemplation of carved stone, to engage personally with the Scriptures. Art promoted worship, and worship generated some outstanding art. It is to these explorations that we will now turn.

Acknowledgements

The editors would like to thank all of the authors for completing their work in the *annus horribilis* of 2020–21, when university departments and libraries were closed because of the COVID-19 pandemic, and to express their gratitude to all those authors and non-authors for their kind cooperation by providing page numbers from their bookshelves and from American libraries when British ones were closed, photographs from their folders, and memories of events when the authors did not have the means to check things themselves. They also thank Professor Dame Rosemary Cramp for her Foreword in appreciation of Betty.

PART 1

Representation: Art and Worship through Text, Textile, and Tool

∵

Figurative Art in the Book of Kells: Absurd Anatomies, See-through Tunics, and Diverse Hairstyles

Donncha MacGabhann

In view of Elizabeth Coatsworth's studies of the Durham Gospels (which were of particular importance in my own research on Insular art) and on medieval dress and textiles, I trust this article is an appropriate offering in celebration of her work.

∵

Introduction

Insular illuminators (working in the islands of Ireland and Britain *c.* 550–900) are not renowned for their proficiency as figurative artists. They are more famous for their repertoire of curvilinear and geometrically-based motifs, while figurative work, zoomorphic or anthropomorphic, tends to be stylised rather than being concerned with accurately rendering literal and visual details. Their backgrounds and training are rooted in ancient and enduring traditions which, as Jonathan Alexander states, have "survived to us mainly in metalwork."[1]

With the conversion of these islands to Christianity, and the consequent demand for the ceremonial objects and accessories required for worship, native artists frequently struggled in their efforts to interpret and reproduce the classically-derived figurative motifs associated with the new religion. In their treatment of the body Insular artists often display an imperfect understanding of the compositional types, conventional poses, and draperies present in their models and exemplars; typically these were ultimately derived from Mediterranean and Byzantine archetypes.[2] This is particularly evident in

---

1 J.J.G. Alexander, *A Survey of Manuscripts Illuminated in the British Isles Vol. 1 Insular Manuscripts: 6th to the 9th Century* (London, 1978), p. 10.
2 Alexander, *Insular Manuscripts*, pp. 9–16. See also Nancy Netzer, "Style: a History of Uses and Abuses in the Study of Insular Art," in *Pattern and Purpose in Insular Art: Proceedings of*

© KONINKLIJKE BRILL NV, LEIDEN, 2021 | DOI:10.1163/9789004467514_003

the tradition of Insular book production, a wholly novel medium in cultures which up to then were almost totally non-literate. In some instances artists appear to favour the invention of fantastic draperies which seem unrelated to any classical conventions, as, for example, the Matthew symbol in the Echternach Gospels (fol. 18v).[3] Werckmeister, however, convincingly identifies the non-classical models from which this figure, and others, are ultimately derived.[4] The draperies and figures of the crucified Christ in the St Gall Gospels (p. 266) and the Durham Gospels (fol. 38³v) are also unusual.[5] Our honorand, in discussing the latter, observes that "this method of designing the human figure, very different though it is from the classical method, was able to cope in its own terms with the depiction of iconographical detail."[6] It would appear that other artists strive to replicate the classical models more faithfully and their efforts are realised with varying degrees of success. Compare, for example, the 'portrait' of Luke in the Trier Gospels (fol. 125v)[7] with those in the Lindisfarne (fol. 137v)[8] and Barberini Gospels (fol. 79v).[9] Of these the image

the Fourth International Conference on Insular Art held at the National Museum and Gallery Cardiff 3–6 September 1998, ed. Mark Redknap, Nancy Edwards, Susan Youngs, Alan Lane, and Jeremy Knight (Oxford, 2001), pp. 169–77; and Douglas Mac Lean, "The Book of Kells and the Northumbrian Type of Classical Drapery," in The Book of Kells: Proceedings of a Conference at Trinity College Dublin, 6–9 September 1992, ed. Felicity O'Mahony (Aldershot, 1994), pp. 301–10. While Mac Lean does not address issues of attribution and authorship, his observations on the series of variations of the Northumbrian model which are found in Kells speak to the thesis proposed in the present paper (pp. 303–06).

3 Paris, Bibliothèque nationale de France, lat. 9389: https://gallica.bnf.fr/ark:/12148/btv1b 530193948/f42.item.r=lat (accessed 10 January 2020).

4 Otto Karl Werckmeister, "Three Problems of Tradition in Pre-Carolingian Figure-Style: From Visigothic to Insular Illumination," Proceedings of the Royal Irish Academy 63 (1962–4), pp. 167–89. Werckmeister also discusses related figures from the Book of Dimma (Dublin, Trinity College, A. 4. 23 [59]), the Book of Deer (Cambridge, Cambridge University Library, Ii. 6. 32), and St Gallen, Stiftsbibliothek, Cod. Sang. 60. See also, e.g. figures of Mark (p. 142) and Luke (p. 218) in the Lichfield/Chad Gospels (Lichfield Cathedral Library, 1).

5 St Gallen, Stiftsbibliothek, Cod. Sang. 51, http://www.e-codices.unifr.ch/en/csg/0051/266 and Durham Cathedral Library, A. II. 17, https://iiif.durham.ac.uk/index.html?manifest=t2mmp 48sc76z&canvas=t2t9z902z95m (both accessed 10 January 2020).

6 Elizabeth Coatsworth, "The Decoration of the Durham Gospels," in The Durham Gospels, together with Fragments of a Gospel Book in Uncial: Durham, Cathedral Library, MS A. II. 17, ed. Christopher D. Verey, T. Julian Brown, and Elizabeth Coatsworth (Early English Manuscripts in Facsimile 20) (Copenhagen, 1980), pp. 53–63 at 60. Werckmeister, "Three Problems of Tradition," pp. 185–89, also discusses this image.

7 Trier Domschatz, Cod. 61: see Alexander, Insular Manuscripts, fig. 176.

8 London, British Library, Cotton Nero D. iv: http://www.bl.uk/manuscripts/Viewer.aspx? ref=cotton_ms_nero_d_iv_f002r (accessed 10 January 2020).

9 Biblioteca Apostolica Vaticana, Barb. lat. 570, https://digi.vatlib.it/view/MSS_Barb.lat.570 (accessed 10 January 2020).

in Trier is the poorest, that in Barberini the most sophisticated, while somewhere in between lies Lindisfarne, in which at least, as our honorand observes,
"an attempt was made to use the rules of perspective in the depiction of the
human figure."[10] Among this group of artists we can include the Scribe-Artist
of the late eighth- to early ninth-century Gospel Book known as the Book of
Kells (*Codex Cenannensis*, Dublin, Trinity College Library, A. I. [58]), who, as
will be demonstrated, struggles more than most in his efforts to deal with classical anatomy and drapery.

Over the past seventy years or so there has been much debate regarding the
number of scribes and artists involved in making the Book of Kells. The present
author's research concludes that it was entirely the work of a two-man team,
identified by the present author as the Master-Artist and the Scribe-Artist.[11] As
their names indicate, only the latter was responsible for script while both were
artists. In their illumination of the manuscript it is proposed that they worked
on some pages individually while collaborating on others.[12] It is suggested that
the Master-Artist was the senior illuminator and in this capacity also acted as
mentor to his colleague. It is further proposed that, following some significant
hiatus in the course of its creation, only the Scribe-Artist survived to complete
both script and illumination in a second campaign.[13] This work is characterized by a decline in the Scribe-Artist's faculties. A further deterioration is
identifiable in the later phase of this campaign; there are indications that as
it progressed this may have included cognitive as well as physical failings. The
working and mentoring relationships between the two artists and the separate campaigns inevitably led to much variation in Kells' art. This is further
complicated by the incorporation of variation in the work of both individuals;

---

10   Coatsworth, "The Decoration of the Durham Gospels," pp. 59–60.

11   Donncha MacGabhann, "The Making of the Book of Kells: Two Masters and Two
      Campaigns," PhD thesis (University of London, School of Advanced Study, 2016), available
      online: https://sas-space.sas.ac.uk/6920/ (accessed 23 July 2020). See also MacGabhann,
      "The *et*–ligature in the Book of Kells: Revealing the 'Calligraphic Imagination' of its
      Great Scribe," in *Islands in a Global Context: Proceedings of the Seventh International
      Conference on Insular Art*, ed. Conor Newman, Mags Mannion, and Fiona Gavin (Dublin,
      2017), pp. 138–48 and MacGabhann, "Turning the Tables: An Alternative Approach to
      Understanding the Canon Tables in the Book of Kells," in *Peopling Insular Art: Practice,
      Performance, Perception: Proceedings of the Eighth International Conference on Insular Art,
      Glasgow 2017*, ed. Cynthia Thickpenny, Katherine Forsyth, Jane Geddes, and Kate Mathis
      (Oxford and Philadelphia, 2020), pp. 13–22.

12   MacGabhann, "The Making of the Book of Kells," p. 12.

13   This challenges other theories including Meehan's recent opinion that the manuscript
      seems to have been "produced without overall coordination or collaboration by scribes
      and artists who worked at different times and may not necessarily have known each
      other" in Bernard Meehan, *The Book of Kells, Official Guide* (London, 2018), p. 11.

while long-recognized as a typical feature of Insular art, this is taken to unprecedented levels by the Scribe-Artist in both his artistic and scribal work.[14] To date this variation in Kells has typically been understood as indicating it is the work, as Françoise Henry suggested, of "a whole scriptorium" involving many artists and apprentices.[15] However, Alexander, one of the most eminent commentators on Kells' art, states that "a more extensive and detailed examination of the question of the division of hands is undoubtedly needed to produce better founded conclusions."[16] Such remarks have inspired the present author's attempt to provide a comprehensive and detailed reading of the evidence.

Having earlier established the personae of Kells' two artists (above), this essay teases out the peculiarities of their figurative work. The identification of distinctive traits and recurring patterns in work attributed to both individuals strengthens the argument for this two-man team. This also deepens our understanding of their particular talents (and limitations) and the extent of their respective contributions in creating the Book of Kells. It begins with a brief examination of the role of the Master-Artist in the creation of the manuscript and outlines the graphic style evident in his handling of animals and figures. The much larger body of this work attributed to the Scribe-Artist requires more extensive analysis; his figures, for example, are examined by separately addressing their bodies (and clothing), facial features, and hairstyles. This leads to analysis of the hairstyles and head-related decorative motifs in Kells' profusion of anthropomorphic and zoomorphic initials.[17]

---

14   MacGabhann, "The Making of the Book of Kells," pp. 13–14 *passim*. This summarizes the defining characteristics of the Scribe-Artist's work as evident in his treatment of a whole range of letterforms, motifs, and other features. All of these are subject to his constant predilection for variation (including the creation of unique variants), random distribution, and occasional clustering. Throughout there is consistency both in the imagination which informs their design and in the graphic/calligraphic qualities of their execution. See also MacGabhann, "The *et*–ligature in the Book of Kells."

15   Françoise Henry, *The Book of Kells* (London, 1974), p. 212 and *Irish Art During the Viking Invasions 800–1020 AD* (New York, 1967), pp. 68–95 at 73.

16   J.J.G. Alexander, "The Illumination," in *The Book of Kells, MS 58, Trinity College Library Dublin*, 2 vols, facsimile and commentary, ed. Peter Fox (Lucerne, 1990), 2, pp. 265–89, at 287. To date Alexander and Henry have been the most prominent commentators on Kells' illuminators. However, neither of their schemes for the division of hands comprehensively addresses all of its illumination (see also note 39 below). See also Roger Stalley, "The Book of Kells: Unfinished Business," in Newman *et al.*, *Islands in a Global Context*, pp. 189–97 at 192. Regarding scholarship on the art and artists in the Book of Kells, Prof. Stalley states that "a fresh examination is long overdue."

17   The reader will find the complete facsimile of the Book of Kells useful: available online at https://digitalcollections.tcd.ie/concern/works/hm50tr726?locale=en; or at https://

The Figurative Work of the Master-Artist

The *Chi-rho* page and the Eight-Circle Cross carpet-page (fols 34r and 33r), which share similarly fine and precise decoration, are both attributed by Henry to an artist she calls "the Goldsmith."[18] In the present author's research this individual's role in the creation of the manuscript is much developed; he is credited with more of the illumination and is also identified as the lead artist in the two-man team. Renaming him the 'Master-Artist' reflects this expanded role. He is something of a perfectionist and his distinctive work is easily recognisable on the pages noted above and on the *incipits* (opening pages) to each of the Gospels (fols 29r, 130r, 188r and 292r).[19] His work is characterized by a fine linear precision, complemented by a refined elegance and restraint in his use of decorative elements, the most prominent of which in his figurative work is a scroll-motif.[20] In the unfinished border on fol. 30v we find perhaps the clearest example of his work in a pair of aggressively engaged creatures, where their meticulous appearance has not been obscured by the later addition of paint (Fig. 1.59).[21] This is also largely the case with a pair of opposed lions at the top of fol. 29r (Fig. 1.60). Such painting, or later graphic additions, tend to complicate the identification of his work in some instances, as, for example, on fols 4v, 187v, and 292r (Figs 1.61–63). Separate from his more typical work in the illumination of borders and decorative panels, the Master-Artist is also responsible for a limited number of more 'free-standing' animals and figures. These share the same traits as his other work and our discussion begins with a look at an image of Christ.

---

www.tcd.ie/library/digitalcollections/home/#folder_id=14&pidtopage=MS58_291r&
entry_point=1 (both accessed 19 September 2020).

18   Henry, *Irish Art*, p. 74 and also *The Book of Kells*, p. 212.

19   Significant contributions attributed here to the Master-Artist are also identified in the Canon Tables (fols 1v–5r), fols 7v, 8r, 13r, 16v, 19v, 27v, 28v, 29v–30r, 32v, 129v, 187v, 203r, 285r, and 290v. He may also be considered as the primary artist responsible for the design/layout of most of these pages. Less significant contributions by the Master-Artist are found on fols 114r, 114v, 124r, and 291v, while minor contributions attributed to him also occur, among the clearest examples of which are the finely interlaced zoomorphs added to a pair of *et*-ligature initials on fol. 156v, lines 9 and 12 and to another on fol. 157r, line 11.

20   This curved motif with a spiral-knob terminal is similar to those derived from a French-Curve template as might be used by a modern draughtsman. One needs only to recall the splendid lion on fol. 75v in the Echternach Gospels to appreciate that this motif is not unique to Kells.

21   The decoration and painting of the Matthean genealogy (fols 29v–31v) is unfinished; see Stalley, "The Book of Kells: Unfinished Business," pp. 189–97.

On fol. 34r the Greek letter *rho* terminates in a human head; as part of Christ's monogram it can reasonably be read as representing Him (Fig. 1.9). Although surrounded by broader motifs in red (also added to his hair),[22] we can identify a finely executed drawing with well-proportioned facial details, including the ear which is correctly aligned with the nose. In terms of the classical tradition this head is probably the most accomplished human representation in the manuscript and its graphic quality is consistent with the Master-Artist's other work on the page. Also attributable to him here are the three angels to the left of the great *x*-shaped *Chi* (Figs 1.10–11). While the legs of the two full-length angels have been adapted to the restricted space, the arms and gripping hands of all three are reasonably well-proportioned and correctly portrayed. However, the high positioning of the ears in each case might suggest some involvement by the Scribe-Artist (see discussion of his work below). Other heads attributable to the Master-Artist include that of the Christ Child on fol. 7v, that at the bottom of fol. 16v (inverted), those of the man wrestling a beast at the upper right on fol. 130r, and another similarly engaged (in a panel of display-lettering) at the lower right on fol. 292r (Figs 1.13–16). The fine graphic quality of the head at the top of the framing-border on fol. 8r and that commencing the *qui fuit* column on fol. 200r suggest that these might also be primarily his work.

At the top of fol. 29r, a three-quarter length, book-holding figure is also well-proportioned. Its presence on a page dominated by the Master-Artist's typical repertoire of exquisite and precise decoration may support its attribution to him.[23] On fol. 7v the graphic quality of the main figures of the Virgin and Child suggest these may be attributed to the Master-Artist. Both figures are reasonably well-proportioned while their arms and hands constitute a touching essay in maternal affection. Some anatomical problems may be

---

22   The red in the hair and the simple interlace and stepped motifs in the small adjacent panels are here understood as second campaign additions by the Scribe-Artist (see notes 26, 41, and 42). For further discussion of these red additions (and related features) as they occur throughout the manuscript see MacGabhann, "The Making of the Book of Kells," pp. 337–67 and figs 6.1–90. These include Kells' remarkably varied line-filling motifs, many of which are also in orange-red (see pp. 230–38 and figs 4.93–146). These marks are variously attributed to the "clumsy ... Master of the Felt Marker" (Mark Van Stone, "Ornamental Techniques in Kells and its Kin," in O'Mahoney, *The Book of Kells*, pp. 234–42 at 239), or "the lesser breed of young painters and muddlers" (Henry, *Irish Art*, pp. 76–77). However, the graphic sensibility which informs these marks and motifs, and their remarkable variation, are characteristic of the Scribe-Artist's work, as is their random distribution.

23   The head, hair, and facial details have more in common with those of the large full-length figure on the same page (lower left), both of which are attributed to the Scribe-Artist (Figs 1.31–32). See discussion below in the context of his work.

FIGURES 1.1–2   The Book of Kells, Evangelist symbols on fol. 1v (above) and fol. 2r (below).
All images are reproduced from the "Faksimile Verlag" facsimile of the Book
of Kells by permission of inmediaONE GmbH (a 100% subsidiary company of
Bertelsmann SE & Co. KGaA)

observed in the relationship of the Virgin's legs to her torso, while both she and
the Christ-child also show pairs of the same foot, and only the fingers of the
Virgin's left hand are accurately 'stepped.'[24] Rather than any misunderstanding
of classical conventions these may reflect the stylisations present in contemporary (or earlier) icons; the Virgin's facial features and mesmeric eyes may
also owe their inspiration to such models (Fig. 1.12).[25] The possibility of some
collaboration in the creation of these figures cannot be ruled out and some
later additions including over-drawing and painting are certainly compatible
with the Scribe-Artist's work.[26]

---

24   Rendering the Christ-child as a miniature bearded adult may be understood as a contemporary convention (Fig. 1.13).

25   Many scholars suggest that Coptic icons may have ultimately provided the inspiration for
these figures, in what is considered to be the earliest surviving image of the Virgin and
Child in a Western manuscript (see, e.g. Henry, *The Book of Kells*, p. 186).

26   These include the red strokes in the Virgin's golden headdress and the child's hair, while
the sets of red triple dots added to his brown tunic and the various sets of white triple dots

FIGURES 1.3–8 Figures with 'see-through' legs and variously
               compromised arms and hands attributed to the
               Scribe-Artist.
               Fig. 1.3, fol. 1v; Fig. 1.4, fol. 2v; Fig. 1.5, fol. 183r; Fig. 1.6,
               fol. 187v; Figs 1.7–8, fol. 114r

This brings us to the Master-Artist's figurative work on Kells' Canon Tables, in particular the compositions of the evangelist symbols at the top of both fols 1v and 5r. In finely rendered detail on fol. 1v, the confronted heads of the central creatures (lion and calf) are linked by the delicate kiss of the lion's tongue, while their extremities elegantly respond to the edges of the frame (Fig. 1.1). A noble-headed eagle is also exquisitely drafted, and his wings are hinged on a

---

also seem compatible with this work (see notes 22, 41, and 42). The rudimentary drawing
of breasts outlined on the Virgin's cloak might suggest these are also attributable to the
Scribe-Artist.

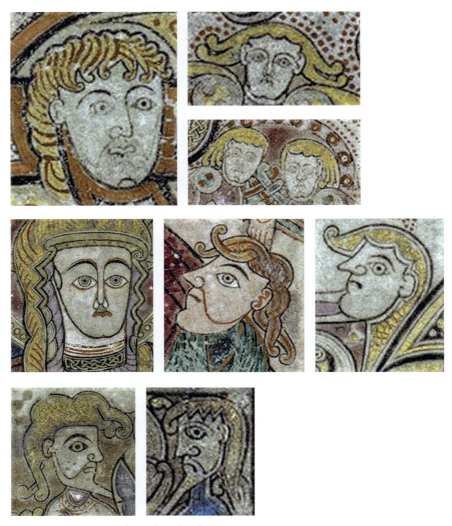

FIGURES 1.9–16   Heads attributed to the Master-Artist.
Figs 1.9–11, fol. 34r; Figs 1.12–13, fol. 7v; Fig. 1.14, fol. 16v; Fig. 1.15, fol. 130r;
Fig. 1.16, fol. 292r

fine double-spiralled breastplate. Although closely grouped, the composition is not overcrowded, and the creatures are set off against a balanced pattern of negative spaces.

This graceful drawing style is also evident in the Master-Artist's rendering of the half-length figure of Matthew's symbol, the winged man. His long-fingered hand correctly grips the evangelist's Gospel book (now barely visible), while his cloak is draped convincingly over his extended forearm. However, as with the figure at the top of fol. 29r, the facial features are less satisfactorily rendered and, as will be discussed below, may have been added by the Scribe-Artist.[27]

The quality of the illumination at the top of fol. 5r has been much lauded, including Henry's appraisal that it "is by far one of the most impressive compositions in the whole book."[28] Complementing the arrangement of those on fol. 1v, the elegant lion and calf are here addorsed, while the eagle and the man are outside the tympanum frame. The eagle presents a book with an elegant long-fingered hand which mirrors that of the man on fol. 1v. Although not anatomically perfect, the rendering of the winged man on fol. 5r is generally convincing in the accuracy of its visual detail, including the facial features.

In attempting a three-quarter view (where the figure is turned slightly sideways) the arm is not perfectly aligned with the shoulder; however, it is well-proportioned and the gripping hand is correctly drawn. Consideration of the remaining figures and creatures in Kells' Canon Tables leads to the examination of work here attributed to the Scribe-Artist.

The Figurative Work of the Scribe-Artist[29]

The Matthew symbol on fol. 2r stands in marked contrast to the winged men on fols 1v and 5r which have just been discussed; differences are particularly obvious when comparing the facing pages of the first opening (Figs 1.1–2). On fol. 2r the head is too large for the body and is impossibly angled above the shoulders. There is little sense of the torso beneath the tunic and a rudimentary white arm seems merely appended to it. This is also the case with the relatively short legs which are depicted in a somewhat stylised version of a

---

27 The unusual presence of a double lower-jaw line might indicate the entire head was the Scribe-Artist's work (see also notes 23 and 38).

28 Henry credits this composition to her "Goldsmith" (here the Master-Artist); Henry, *The Book of Kells*, p. 171.

29 While it is proposed that contributions by the Scribe-Artist occur on all the illuminated pages, he is identified as the primary artist on fols 2r, 2v, 4r 12r, 15v, 18r, 124r, and 291v, and the sole creator of fols 183r and 202v.

classical *contrapposto*. This rendering of legs and feet, and their 'see-through' appearance as if beneath a diaphanous tunic (another classical convention), frequently occurs in the Scribe-Artist's work; unfortunately these are often most distinguished by the inadequacies of his efforts to connect the legs to the body. While appearing to lack skill and confidence in handling human forms his artistic achievements are considerable in other respects, as will be discussed below.

The graphic quality of the animal symbols on fol. 2r is also less sophisticated than those across the opening, both in their overall form and in their detail. The lion's thick tongue and his tail, plopped on the eagle's head, for example, lack the subtlety and elegance of those on the page opposite, as does the more densely packed composition of the whole panel.[30] This is also true of the creature's abundant mane, more extravagant variations of which are prominently worn by his companions on fols 2v, 3v, 27v, and 129v (Figs 1.64–67). While the lion on fol. 3r sports a similarly ample mane, its poorer graphic quality suggests it may belong to the later phase of the second campaign (Fig. 1.69). In contrast to the work of the Master-Artist, the Scribe-Artist's handling of the various decorative elements (including the scroll-motif) is subject to much greater variation, while his grouping of these and other elements is looser and more flamboyant.[31] Further variation is prominent in some of his unique lion manes as found on fol. 4r (below the centre arch), fol. 28v (Fig. 1.68), fol. 188r (at the top), and fol. 188v, lines 11–17 (initial-*f*).[32]

Returning to the figures, we encounter more of the Scribe-Artist's compromised classical models in most of the other instances in the manuscript. Revisiting fol. 1v, we come across a little man seated at the top of the first column of numerals (Fig. 1.3). He is shown in profile, with oversized facial features, while an exaggerated thumb occurs at the end of an oversized arm.[33] His legs are juxtaposed beside this arm (the figure seems to lack any torso) and are revealed beneath another instance of the see-through tunic; these legs end in the Scribe-Artist's much-repeated version of *contrapposto* feet. Turning the page to fol. 2v we find similar legs and feet in another version of the Matthew symbol, where again there is little sense of any upper body (Fig. 1.4). These

---

30   MacGabhann, "The Making of the Book of Kells," pp. 37–108, provides a detailed analysis of the artists' collaboration in the Canon Tables. See also MacGabhann, "Turning the Tables."

31   His use of a curved and pointed motif on the calf symbols on fols 28v and 290v may be intended to represent their coats, while its appearance on the calf at the bottom right on fol. 129v is very mane-like.

32   The creation of unique variants is a characteristic of the Scribe-Artist's work (see note 14).

33   Compare with the 'cock-a-snoot' figure at the lower-right on fol. 8r.

recurring features can begin to be seen as 'trademarks' of the Scribe-Artist's figurative work. Yet another trademark feature occurs in the book-holding arm of this Matthew symbol on fol. 2v. From its bent elbow, the lower part of the limb seems to be elongated with the addition of a second forearm, and to compound the blunder this right arm ends with a left hand. More examples of these muddled limbs occur on the page opposite (fol. 3r), while another is found on the man presenting a book at the lower left on the *Liber* page (fol. 29r). Similar inconsistencies in the rendering of arms and hands occur throughout the manuscript, including those of the seated figure on fol. 183r, the winged figure on fol. 187v, and the men flanking Christ on fol. 114r (Figs 1.5–8).[34]

The full-page illuminations on fols 7v, 202v, and 285r each include four attendant figures, all of whom have variously jumbled limbs and generally impossible bodies. Anomalies are especially evident when we try to link the legs and torsos of the four angels in the upper section of the Temptation scene on fol. 202v. Turning to the seated angels at the tomb on fol. 285r, the Scribe-Artist's muddled anatomy is particularly apparent when trying to make sense of their legs. On fol. 7v the legs of the four upright, winged figures are more reasonably proportioned, however, their arms and hands are much confused, while the heads of the lower angels are simply appended at an angle, looking upwards to draw our attention to the Virgin and Child (Fig. 1.39).

It is concluded here that many of these features are indicative of a working process where elements seem to be somewhat 'copied-and-pasted,' an approach which seems evident in most of the figures discussed above.[35] Appearing to lack any coherent sense of anatomy, the Scribe-Artist compensates by adopting such a system. Figures appear to be assembled from disparate elements,

---

34   In his *Fac-similes of the Miniatures and Ornaments of Anglo-Saxon & Irish Manuscripts* (London, 1868, repr. New York, 2007), fig. 51, illustrations Plate 1, J.O. Westwood (or perhaps his lithographer) obligingly 'corrects' the left hand of the figure on the left-side to show both hands gripping Christ's forearm. This is available online: https://archive.org/stream/facsimilesofminioowest#page/n385 (accessed 3 September 2020).

35   Other prominent 'impossible bodies' include the Christ on fol. 32v and the figure at the top of fol. 292r; in both cases it is difficult to make sense of their draped-hands (presenting books) and the arms to which these should be connected. Another problematic limb occurs in the 'portrait' of John on fol. 291v where the arm, again presenting a book, is not linked to the saint's shoulder but seems rather to emanate from the middle of his chest. This is also the case with the left arm of the central figure of Christ on fol. 202v. Both arms of the central Christ figure on fol. 114r are again similarly depicted, as the Scribe-Artist distorts all four limbs to form a symbolic *Chi*. On fol. 3v the book-holding man (under the first arch) initially seems posed on a long cushion typical of those in many evangelist portraits (a classical convention). However, this cushion is cleverly repurposed to represent the legs of the Matthew symbol, lending him something of a gnome-like appearance.

often with little sense of how these should be combined and proportioned. In light of the Master-Artist's apparently superior knowledge of anatomy, it may seem odd that he has not more successfully imparted this to his colleague. However, this may indicate that much of the Scribe-Artist's figurative work was executed during the second campaign; in addition to working without the supervision of his erstwhile mentor, it was noted earlier (p. 11) that his faculties were deteriorating at this time.

Facial Features and Hairstyles

Analysis of Kells' figurative work undertaken in the present study included a collective examination of all the heads in the manuscript.[36] Among its most interesting outcomes was the revelation of a formulaic pattern in the eyes-nose-mouth grouping of facial features in work attributed to the Scribe-Artist. In those facing frontally, the oversized eyes are framed by the emphatic curve of brows which then sweep down to outline both sides of the nose (e.g. Figs 1.24–29). When the head is slightly turned (in three-quarter view), the nose is usually drawn as a single line (e.g. Figs 1.30–32).[37] Most likely the Scribe-Artist was initially inspired by the Master-Artist's heads – the single line on fol. 34r and the double line on fol. 7v (Figs 1.9 and 1.12). Typically, the Scribe-Artist's versions of these facial features are poorly centred and over-sized (again somewhat copied-and-pasted). They are frequently accompanied by ears rendered as part of the hairline and almost always incorrectly set in line with the forehead (such features are apparent in all of the Scribe-Artist's figures discussed earlier). It would appear that he also added the facial features (if not the entire heads) to figures otherwise attributed to the Master-Artist, as noted above in relation to the Matthew symbol on fol. 1v and the book-holding figure at the top of fol. 29r (Figs 1.1 and 1.32).[38]

---

36   A comprehensive and detailed analysis of all features, both scribal and artistic, has under-pinned the present author's research on the Book of Kells. In this process, features with shared elements are grouped into arbitrary categories to facilitate analysis and discussion. However, such categorization of the Scribe-Artist's work is never entirely satisfactory as different motifs (and letterforms etc.) randomly merge with each other in unpredictable combinations creating further sub-categories or mutating into unique variants (see notes 45 and 58 below).

37   Heads in profile avoid the more complicated challenge of rendering the nose frontally.

38   It is impossible to determine whether these were added as part of the two artists' ongoing collaboration in the first campaign or were completions of unfinished work in the second campaign (see also notes 23 and 27).

It is useful to examine the facial features on some of Kells' larger figures on fols 28v, 32v, 114r, and 291v (Figs 1.24–27).[39] All four heads are remarkably similar, each with the same oversized eyes and, as noted earlier, with lines extending from both eyebrows to form the nose. They also share the same mouth and chin surrounded by a beard, the upper edge of which is exactly repeated in each case (also in Figs 1.28–29). In the detailing of this facial hair we can begin to see the Scribe-Artist's fondness for variation, with subtle differences apparent throughout. This tendency, however, is given much greater scope in their hairstyles, as will be demonstrated in the following discussion.

While the recurrence of compromised anatomy and poor facial details to some extent provide the 'Morellian' evidence identifying most of Kells' figures and heads as the work of a single individual, the treatment of hair, in particular its remarkable variation, seems to confirm this individual is the Scribe-Artist (see note 14).[40] The comprehensive analysis of Kells' heads revealed a veritable 'salon catalogue' of hairstyles. At their most basic these present relatively simple outline shapes, while the internal articulation of locks and curls in some appears to have been added in the red much-associated with the second campaign (Figs 1.17–23).[41] Decorative elaborations are almost totally absent from the relatively plain instances in this first group; however, those in the next category are composed almost exclusively of the scroll-motif (Figs 1.24–32). We have seen these in much of the work discussed earlier, from their restrained presence in the Master-Artist's border-lion on fol. 30v or in his heads (Fig. 1.59 and Figs 1.9–16), to the Scribe-Artist's more excessive mane-variants (Figs 1.64–69). The Scribe-Artist's typical variations are again most prominent when we return to examine the hairstyles of the four large figures discussed above (Figs 1.24–27). In their broader outlines these display little difference, but a closer inspection is more revealing. Longer or shorter versions of the scroll-motifs are composed and layered in combinations that constitute a

---

39   In commenting on these pages Henry attributes fol. 114r to her "Illustrator" and the others to her "Portrait Painter" (Henry, *The Book of Kells*, p. 212), while Alexander attributes fol. 32v to his Artist A and the others to his Artist B (Alexander, "The Illumination," pp. 286–87).

40   The nineteenth-century art critic Giovanni Morelli developed a technique of distinguishing the work of different painters through the identification of diagnostic features especially in minor details. In the absence of a general study on Morelli, see Edgar Wind, *Art and Anarchy*, 3rd ed. ([Evanston, Ill.,] 1985), pp. 32–46 and Carlo Ginzburg, "Morelli, Freud and Sherlock Holmes: Clues and Scientific Method," [*Oxford Academic*] *History Workshop Journal*, 9.1 (Spring 1980), 5–36, available online: https://academic.oup.com/hwj/article/9/1/5/609389 (accessed 11 June 2020).

41   Such marks are also sometimes added, e.g. to manes and wings as in Fig. 1.2, Figs 1.4–6, Figs 1.64–65, and Fig. 1.69. See also Figs 1.93 and 1.106 and see notes 22, 26, and 42.

FIGURES 1.17–23   Simple hairstyles – these heads and those in the following Figs 1.24–
58 are attributed to the Scribe-Artist.
Fig. 1.17, fol. 4r; Fig. 1.18, fol. 201v; Fig. 1.19, fol. 89r; Fig. 1.20, fol. 2r;
Fig. 1.21, fol. 3r; Fig. 1.22, fol. 3r; Fig. 1.23, fol. 129v

FIGURES 1.24–32   Hairstyles variously formed of 'french-curve' elements.
Fig. 1.24, fol. 32v; Fig. 1.25, fol. 114r; Fig. 1.26, fol. 291v; Fig. 1.27, fol. 28v; Fig. 1.28, fol. 292r;
Fig. 1.29, fol. 12r; Fig. 1.30, fol. 202v; Figs 1.31–32, fol. 29r

delightful series of 'variations on a theme.' In those illustrated we see two other frontally facing heads display further, if simpler, variations on the same theme (Figs 1.28–29), as do the three heads rendered in three-quarter view (Figs 1.30–32 and see also the Matthew symbol on fol. 3v and the 'merman' on fol. 213r, line 8).

The last two of these hairstyles (Figs 1.31–32), both on fol. 29r, and both quite different, could be described to some extent as 'bouffant,' which seems an adequate descriptor for the next grouping (Figs 1.33–39). These again show the Scribe-Artist's predilection for variation and it is interesting to note the subtle differences between those worn by the pairs of heads on both fols 114r and 202v (Figs 1.35–37). Differences are also evident in the groups of attendant figures on fols 7v, 32v, and 285r: fringe details are varied significantly, as are the overall styles, including some which are rounded and puffed out. Others with more bouffant styles include the Matthew symbols on fols 1r and 187v (Fig. 1.6), the unfinished head of the small angel at the upper left on fol. 29r, and the Christ figure at the upper right on fol. 183r.

The individuality of some of the Scribe-Artist's hairstyles is such that they do not fit easily within any of the arbitrary categories (Figs 1.40–45). While they may include scroll-motifs or be somewhat bouffant, the extent of their differences suggest they should be considered more as unique variants (see notes 14 and 32). Among those illustrated, the 'mop-top' with angular fringe details worn by the warrior on fol. 200r looks decidedly contemporary (Fig. 1.43). Other distinctive styles are found on the head of the book-holding figure above the architectural-frame on fol. 4r sporting 'pig-tails,' the winged figure on fol. 183r with a saw-toothed fringe (Fig. 1.5), and the tonsured head of the horseman on fol. 255v, line 4 (also with a zig-zag fringe).

As mentioned earlier in relation to the heads on fols 7v and 34r, most of these have added red lines, usually curved, augmenting the articulation of the hair and which are attributable to the second campaign. These additions indicating tresses, tufts, curls, or quiffs are themselves subject to the Scribe-Artist's patterns of constant variation and support their attribution to him. Consider, for example, the spiral-curls added to the pair of angels directly above Christ on fol. 202v, their rudimentary execution suggesting they were added in the later phase of the second campaign (Fig. 1.37). Their subtle variation, however, shows that even in these relatively impoverished graphic additions (as his faculties decline) his commitment to variation is unfailing. Staying with fol. 202v, we can see many related second campaign additions to the hair of those in the figure-groups below and beside the temple; the greater variation in the hairstyles of the latter group was no doubt intentional, probably reflecting some

FIGURES 1.33–39 Varied bouffant hairstyles (note the similarities between the heads in Figs 1.38–39 on fols 202v and 7v).

Fig. 1.33, fol. 3r; Fig. 1.34, fol. 27v; Figs 1.35–36, fol. 114r; Figs 1.37–38, fol. 202v; Fig. 1.39, fol. 7v

FIGURES 1.40–45   Unique variations in hairstyles.
Fig. 1.40, fol. 7v; Fig. 1.41, fol. 290v; Fig. 1.42, fol. 202r; Fig. 1.43,
fol. 200r; Fig. 1.44, fol. 202v; Fig. 1.45, fol. 201r

iconographic distinction between those closer to the Christ figure and those lower down.[42]

Anthropomorphic and Zoomorphic Initials/Larger Letters

Among Kells' multitude of initials/larger letters, just over fifty incorporate human figures and heads. Fourteen of these show a head within the bowl of the letter, usually *h* and *m*, with eight occurring in two clusters in John's Gospel (between fols 294r–311v and fols 327v–335v), while a further cluster of three is found in Mark (between fols 179v and 182r – seven of the fourteen are shown in Figs 1.46–52).[43] These heads continue to display the Scribe-Artist's fondness for variation, which again is most apparent in the treatment of hair. Subtle variations are found on the four heads incorporated into the column of *b*-initials on fol. 40v, lines 1–6. In some instances the hairstyles are relatively simple (Figs 1.46–49), while others are elaborated with interlace (Figs 1.50–52). More complex hair-interlace occurs, for example, in those on fols 80v, line 7, 96r, line 12, 245r, line 4, and 253v, line 6, while some also include spiral terminals similar to that on fol. 309r, line 6 (Fig. 1.52). Further variations include some bouffant hairdos on fols 53v, line 6 and 58v, line 3, while the figures on fols 97v, line 10 and 253v, line 6, are shown pulling their beards, as is the figure squatting beside the *IN*-monogram on fol. 329v, line 9. Finally, a number of these hairstyles highlight the Scribe-Artist's tendency for occasionally creating unique instances; while incorporating familiar elements and motifs these are sufficiently different to warrant separate consideration (Figs 1.53–58). Like the modern 'mop-top' mentioned above (Fig. 1.43), we might ask if we are looking at an early medieval 'mullet' haircut[44] in the figure attached to the *et*-ligature on fol. 95r, line 6 (Fig. 1.53)? Is the head inside the initial-*m* on fol. 182r, line 7

---

42   Like those at the bottom of this page, the hairstyles of the smaller figure groups on fols 7v and 124r are simple in outline, although all are variously articulated with short red (or black) strokes (see notes 22, 26, and 41).

43   Clustering of features is identified as one of several signature traits prominent in the Scribe-Artist's work throughout the manuscript – randomly distributed, these may occur on a single page or over several neighbouring pages (see note 14). See MacGabhann, "The *et*–Ligature in the Book of Kells," pp. 145–46 and see also Peter Meyer, "Notes on the Art and Ornament of the Book of Kells," in *The Book of Kells: evangeliorum quattuor codex Cenannensis*, 3 vols, ed. Ernest H. Alton, Peter Meyer, and George O. Simms (Berne, 1950–51), 3, pp. 25–52 at 28, and Erika Eisenlohr, "The Puzzle of the Scribes: Some Palaeographical Observations," in O'Mahoney, *The Book of Kells*, pp. 196–208 at 207.

44   A style where hair is cut short at the front and sides, but worn long at the back, popular in the 1980s and 1990s.

FIGURES 1.46–52   Heads added to initials. Figs 1.46–49 show relatively simple hairstyles, while Figs 1.50–52 show instances with variously interlaced terminals (note the differences between Figs 1.47 and 1.52 which occur on the same page).
Fig. 1.46, fol. 103v; Fig. 1.47, fol. 309r; Fig. 1.48, fol. 161v; Fig. 1.49, fol. 327v; Fig. 1.50, fol. 125r; Fig. 1.51, fol. 179v; Fig. 1.52, fol. 309r

FIGURES 1.53–58   Initials showing heads with unique hairstyles (note the differences between Figs 1.55–56 which occur on the same page).
Fig. 1.53, fol. 95r; Fig. 1.54, fol. 100v; Figs 1.55–56, fol. 182r; Fig. 1.57, fol. 255v; Fig. 1.58, fol. 286r

FIGURES 1.59–63
Lion-heads with manes attributed to the
Master-Artist. Paint and some other additions
are attributable to the Scribe-Artist (e.g. the
longer scroll-motifs in Fig. 1.62).
Fig. 1.59, fol. 30v; Fig. 1.60, fol. 29r; Fig. 1.61,
fol. 4v; Fig. 1.62, fol. 187v; Fig. 1.63, fol. 292r

FIGURES 1.64–69   Lion-heads – these and the following Figs 1.70–112
are attributed to the Scribe-Artist.
Fig. 1.64, fol. 27v; Fig. 1.65, fol. 2v; Fig. 1.66, fol. 3v;
Fig. 1.67, fol. 129v; Fig. 1.68, fol. 28v; Fig. 1.69, fol. 3r

tonsured or is he wearing some kind of headgear (Fig. 1.56)? In any case he stands in sharp contrast to his companion a few lines above, whose long locks would suit a rock star, as indeed might his acrobatic performance (Fig. 1.55). Our examination of heads and hairstyles continues, shifting slightly to look at some closely related aspects of Kells' zoomorphic initials/larger letters.

We have already met some of the book's remarkable menagerie of playful pets and prowling predators, those who variously stand guard on elaborate borders, report for symbolic duty, or shepherd stray phrases and wandering words. Our attention now turns to an examination of the hordes who more stealthily infiltrate the chorus of shapeshifting initials relentlessly punctuating the Gospel texts. The behaviour of these contorted creatures may often puzzle or surprise but rarely fails to delight. Although among its most celebrated features, to date Kells' remarkable initials/larger letters have not been the subject of much scholarly analysis.[45] These are occasionally humorous, often enigmatic, always unpredictable, and constantly subject to the Scribe-Artist's seemingly endless capacity for variation.

Over two hundred and sixty of these letterforms may be described as fully zoomorphic (i.e. complete with bodies and limbs), while over four hundred and seventy only incorporate animal heads. In some cases a letter may be formed of more than one creature or have more than one head.[46] In total there are over eight hundred and fifty such heads.[47] As with the human heads discussed

---

45   Heather Pulliam has made a significant contribution to this work in her *Word and Image in the Book of Kells* (Dublin, 2006) and "'Therefore do I speak to them in parables': Meaning in the Margins of the Book of Kells," in *Making and Meaning in Insular Art: Proceedings of the Fifth International Conference on Insular Art Held at Trinity College Dublin, 25–28 August 2005*, ed. Rachel Moss (Dublin, 2007), pp. 257–67. See also MacGabhann, "The Making of the Book of Kells," pp. 281–319 and figs 5.1–391. There are around four thousand initials/larger letters in the manuscript; this total separately counts those letters which are combined in monograms or otherwise grouped together. Of the total, about eighteen hundred may be described as large. The form of the letters themselves is subject to much variation and most are further elaborated with elements drawn from the usual Insular types. The extent to which individual motifs from this repertoire are varied in Kells is without precedent in Insular art. They are combined in ever-changing permutations, and those traditionally used as discrete motifs may be merged as mutant forms are conjured up (see notes 36 and 58). A freer, more fluid approach pervades this work which has parallels in the more flamboyant phases of other art-historical styles.

46   Almost one hundred initials/larger letters show pairs of heads, while thirteen have three. These are randomly distributed throughout very different sections of the manuscript, as are the unique instances, one with four heads on fol. 72r, line 16 and another with five on fol. 264v, line 9.

47   Tightly fitted inside the bowls of certain letterforms we find another two hundred creatures. On the outsides, variously attached to some letter terminals are a further thirty small birds and animals. Similar to the multiples mentioned in the previous note, these

above, the basic shape of these animal heads is largely formulaic and graphically consistent and again it is in their elaboration that we find the Scribe-Artist enjoying freer rein as he pursues ever more imaginative variations. The commonest of these features might be described as a 'neck-trail,' a simple linear extension emanating from the back of the head; prominent examples include those on the initial-*i* felines on fols 24r, line 1 and 34v, line 5.[48] The following analysis focuses on features that might best be described as crests, 'eye-trails,' manes, and cockscombs, and these can be understood as paralleling (and continuing) the earlier analyses of animal manes and human hair.

Examining the initials/larger letters with animal heads we find about thirty lacking any elaborations, representing the lower end of the Scribe-Artist's spectrum of variations. Just above these on the scale are about another one hundred showing only ears or ear-like additions.[49] These, and the occasional assortment of protruding 'tongues' are largely excluded from the following discussion.[50] It is only possible to show a small selection of variants, and again it is important to note that these are consistently drawn from very different sections of the manuscript.

The most basic head elaborations may be described as 'crests.' Many of these are relatively simple (Figs 1.70–73), while others may be terminated with spiral-knobs (Figs 1.74–76) or spirals (Figs 1.77–79). On some letters crested creatures may occur in pairs, with those illustrated sharing numerous features (Figs 1.80–82 and see also Fig. 1.102). Some crests may be quite intricate and in the examples shown are developed into complex interlacings (Figs 1.83–85); note that in two of these, on fols 333r, line 6 and 46r, line 7, the convoluted crests are combined with separate 'tongue' interlace (Figs 1.83–84). Among the multitude of crests are some rare variants and again these are found in very different sections of the book. Included here are some unusual conical instances, as if each creature was wearing a dunce's cap (Figs 1.86–89). On a few occasions the crest is bifurcated and ends in two scrolled terminals (Figs 1.90–91),

---

varied creatures randomly occur in pairs on about thirty occasions, in threes on seven (e.g. fols 64r, line 2, 133r, line 1, and 304v, line 7) and in fours only on fols 152v, line 7 and 309r, line 1.

48   The 'neck-trail' does not require much additional space and can be streamlined with the body. It is often the starting point for the fine secondary interlace threaded through the complex zoomorphic borders on the illuminated pages.

49   For variants with one ear see, e.g. fols 294r, line 18, 107r, line 13, and 200r, line 3 and with two, e.g. fols 316r, line 18, 146r, line 13, and 259v, line 11.

50   'Tongues' often extended and elaborated, are also subject to much variation. Several of these and other mouth-related features are evident in the illustrations (also occurring in some anthropomorphic letters). See also the various animal 'tongues' in several of the Figs 1.59–69.

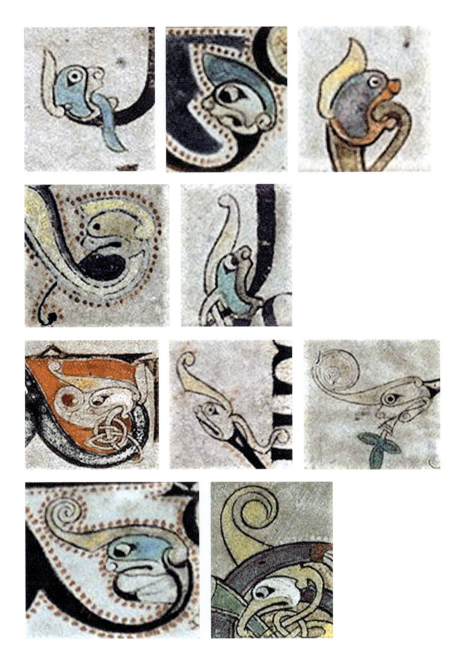

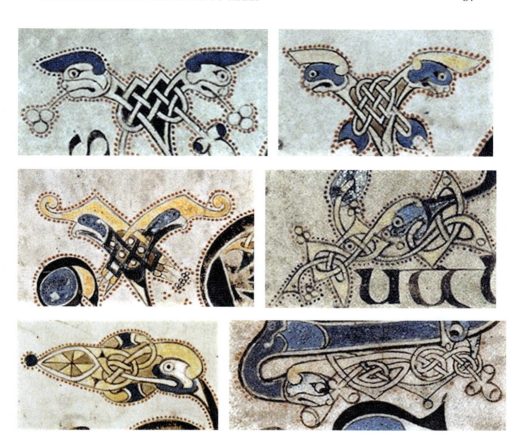

FIGURES 1.70–85   Initial-zoomorphs showing crest variations (note the differences between Figs 1.70, 1.74 and 1.77 found on the opening at fols 298v–299r).
Fig. 1.70, fol. 298v; Fig. 1.71, fol. 153v; Fig. 1.72, fol. 249v; Fig. 1.73, fol. 127v; Fig. 1.74, fol. 298v; Fig. 1.75, fol. 70r; Fig. 1.76, fol. 93r; Fig. 1.77, fol. 299r; Fig. 1.78, fol. 141v; Fig. 1.79, fol. 115v; Fig. 1.80, fol. 310r; Fig. 1.81, fol. 279r; Fig. 1.82, fol. 82v; Fig. 1.83, fol. 333r; Fig. 1.84, fol. 46r; Fig. 1.85, fol. 93v

or it culminates in a type of 'fruit' that is common throughout Kells, perhaps an Insular interpretation of olives (Figs 1.92–93 and see also Fig. 1.89). While the trumpet-spiral motif is widespread throughout the manuscript, it makes an unlikely appearance on four crests; these are quite small and include tiny versions of the lentoid element which defines the trumpet-mouth (Figs 1.94–97).

FIGURES 1.86–97   Rare crest-elaborations.
Fig. 1.86, fol. 296v; Fig. 1.87, fol. 254r; Fig. 1.88, fol. 174v; Fig. 1.89, fol. 73r; Fig. 1.90, fol. 332v; Fig. 1.91, fol. 278v; Fig. 1.92, fol. 328v; Fig. 1.93, fol. 39v; Fig. 1.94, fol. 315v; Fig. 1.95, fol. 244v; Fig. 1.96, fol. 211r; Fig. 1.97, fol. 61r

Linear extensions emanating from some creatures' eyes are another type of head elaboration and may be described as 'eye-trails' (not unlike the 'neck-trails' mentioned earlier). These range from relatively simple versions (Figs 1.98–99) to more complex instances where they are developed as interlace (Figs 1.100–102). Among the most unusual head elaborations are the spectacular pair of eye-trails on fol. 171v, lines 6 and 14 (this small cluster is closely paralleled in a related pair on fol. 177r, lines 3 and 7). As mentioned above, these clusters are typical of the Scribe-Artist's work-process and patterns of distribution (see notes 14 and 43) and, while displaying differences, the zoomorphic additions to these pairs of initials share many common features, as do the four parent-letters (all rectilinear variants of the *et*-ligature).

Manes were addressed earlier and from time to time appear on the heads associated with the initials/larger letters. These include some relatively simple instances (Figs 1.103–106), while more unusual variants occur, for example, on fols 120r, line 11 and 283v, line 2; the latter instances recalling the longer flowing manes worn, for example, by the lions on fols 2v and 3v (Figs 1.65–66). Another rare head elaboration may be identified as a cockscomb. While some are accurate in their literal and visual detail, others seem to be products of the Scribe-Artist's imaginative virtuosity (Figs 1.106–11). More extravagant cockscomb variants occur, for example, on fols 57r, line 10, 170r, line 7, and 259r, line 16. Another rare head elaboration may be described as 'lobed,' often combining elements of both crests and cockscombs.[51] These range from relatively simple instances with a single lobe, as found, for example, on fols 316v, line 8 and 234v, line 15, to quite complex versions with shared features as on fols 70v, line 4 and 255r, line 3, or those on fols 50v, line 12 and 281r, line 11. Between these extremes are versions with two or three lobes which seem directly to overlap with the cockscomb (Figs 1.106 and 1.109). Although not connected with any letterform, the bird marking a turn-in-path on fol. 309r, line 3, wears an unusual head elaboration (Fig. 1.111). This may be understood as a hastily executed version of the lobed crest/cockscomb (with added dots as in Figs 1.109–10). Sketchily painted in green, this is consistent with similar additions here attributed to the Scribe-Artist in the later phase of the second campaign. However, despite the apparently casual nature of its execution, it is nonetheless rendered with the confidence of a seasoned draughtsman. Other rare and exotic crest elaborations include those with 'foliate' ends, as, for example, on fols 56v, line 8, 125r, line 2, and 271r, line 8.

---

51   A lobed elaboration is added to an extended-*m* on fol. 177r, line 6. The presence of this feature on the four zoomorphic finials attached to the outside of the framing-border on fol. 33r is also interesting.

FIGURES 1.98–112   Variations of simpler and more complex 'eye-trails' (Figs 1.98–102), manes
(Figs 1.103–106), 'cockscombs' (Figs 1.106–111), and unique (Fig. 1.112).
Fig. 1.98, fol. 25r; Fig. 1.99, fol. 177r; Fig. 1.100, fol. 331r; Fig. 1.101, fol. 125r;
Fig. 1.102, fol. 127v; Fig. 1.103, fol. 111r; Fig. 1.104, fol. 324v; Fig. 1.105, fol. 26r;
Fig. 1.106, fol. 45r; Fig. 1.107, fol. 176v; Fig. 1.108, fol. 198r; Fig. 1.109, fol. 257v;
Fig. 1.110, fol. 277r; Fig. 1.111, fol. 309r; Fig. 1.112, fol. 130v

Perhaps the most unusual of all the head elaborations is that terminating the *et*-ligature on fol. 130v, line 14 (Fig. 1.112). Instead of a crest or one of the other features just discussed, uniquely this small head has a shock of long human hair.[52] In addition, the wide profile, typical of these creatures' heads, seems to have been compressed to give it more human proportions. Is this a merely decorative appendage or might it have some deeper relevance? It seems to present something of a puzzle that might engage a curious reader. It could perhaps be understood in the context of its Gospel text, giving a visual description of John the Baptist – *et erat iohannis vestitus pellis camelli et zona pellicia circa lumbos suos* (Mark 1:6).[53] This strange hybrid creature with flowing blonde tresses seems to subtly evoke a sense of this man of the desert who "ate locusts and wild honey." It is but one of many such interventions throughout Kells and seems indicative of this extraordinary manuscript and the extent to which the Scribe-Artist has reimagined how the Gospel texts might be presented.

Conclusion

Variation in the treatment of human hair or in the elaboration of animal heads is not unique to Kells. Consider, for example, the Lindisfarne Gospels showing different hairstyles on each of the three figures in the Matthew 'portrait' page (fol. 25v) or the spiral extensions to the animal heads of the wonderful *ma*-monogram on fol. 18v. Variation is an integral element in all Insular art; however, the Scribe-Artist's idiosyncratic approach is unique among the corpus of surviving Insular books. It is consistently identifiable through the two proposed campaigns of work, persisting even in the more impoverished red additions associated with the later phase of the second campaign. As the present author has demonstrated elsewhere, the Scribe-Artist's distinctive approach is easily recognized, when, for example, *et*-ligatures, marginal arabesques, line-fillers, or uncial-*a* at line-ends are subject to collective analysis.[54] It is also readily observable in the 'family' of extended letterforms, over seven

---

52 This also neatly confirms the link between the various head elaborations and the hairstyles.

53 "And John was clothed with camel's hair, and a leathern girdle about his loins."

54 These are all comprehensively addressed in MacGabhann, "The Making of the Book of Kells," pp. 126–27 and figs 3.149–212 (*et*-ligature, script), pp. 284–85, 291–94, and 315–16, and figs 5.17–30, 5.123–246, and 5.345–53 (*et*-ligature, initials/larger letters), pp. 220–25 and figs 4.40–68 (marginal arabesques), pp. 230–38 and figs 4.93–146 (line fillers), and pp. 171–75 and figs 3.357–92 (uncial-a at line-ends).

hundred of which are randomly distributed throughout the manuscript.[55] Yet further 'families' or categories of features are identified in the hairstyles and head elaborations presented here.[56]

There are no surviving books with which to compare Kells' thousands of initials, each one of which, as Nicolette Gray suggests "is different and seems to have its own personality."[57] However, it is partly in the very manner of their variation that their overall 'familial' homogeneity can be recognized as they are continuously informed by a distinctive and idiosyncratic quality of imagination. In addition, underlying their variation is a singular graphic consistency, which we have also seen in the Scribe-Artist's figure drawing. Such graphic and imaginative coherence cannot easily be explained as the work of a "whole scriptorium" or by scribes and artists who may not have been acquainted (see notes 13 and 15). Art Historian and Kells' scholar Peter Meyer, who also attributes all of Kells' script to a single scribe, states that:

> It is impossible to say which of the two is the more admirable – the incredible perseverance which maintains a supreme standard of formal beauty for more than six-hundred pages, or the vigilance and skill which find a variation for every form of every letter or fresh mutations of a basic form.[58]

This elegantly encapsulates the Scribe-Artist's sublime calligraphic performance and, with some minor adjustments, could equally describe his variation of the initials/larger letters.

Had the Book of Kells been the work of a large team of artists, it would be possible to tease out individual contributions; however, until now Kells has not been subjected to a sufficiently detailed (and painstaking) analysis.[59] Having

---

55   MacGabhann, "The Making of the Book of Kells," pp. 151–65 and figs 3.259–317.

56   The analysis of hairstyles and head elaborations presented here could be replicated by any one of several others, e.g. looking at the details of the letterforms themselves or a whole range of other elements added within and around them as decoration (see MacGabhann, "The Making of the Book of Kells," pp. 282–322 (chapter five) and related illustrations). A good example is found in the horizontal stroke of the *et*-ligature (see MacGabhann, "The Making of the Book of Kells," figs 5.123–246 and see also, MacGabhann, "The *et*–ligature," pp. 142–45 and figs 6–12).

57   Nicolette Gray, *Lettering as Drawing: Contour and Silhouette* (Oxford, 1970), p. 26.

58   Meyer, "Notes on the Art and Ornament," p. 27. Palaeographer Julian Brown also attributes all of Kells' script to "one great scribe"; T.J. Brown and C.D. Verey, "Northumbria and the Book of Kells," *Anglo-Saxon England* 1 (1972), 219–46, at p. 236.

59   The work of Walter Oakeshott in his book *The Artists of the Winchester Bible* (London, 1945) provides an interesting parallel to the present analysis. See also, Claire Donovan,

identified the Master-Artist's relatively competent figurative art, the vast majority of this work is attributed to the Scribe-Artist, making him the main subject of this paper. If the present reading of the evidence is close to the truth, he was quite a remarkable and complex character. He was certainly a knowledgeable scriptural scholar and he was a great scribe. He appears to have been an assiduous student of the Master-Artist and also his dedicated collaborator, faithful to the end in his efforts to complete their shared *magnum opus*. His attempts at figure drawing fail to match the high standards of his other work (the present author's career as an Art-Teacher would readily confirm that he is not alone in appearing to have something of a 'mental block' in this regard). In contrast to these inadequacies (and free of any classical conventions) he seems to have embraced the freedom of transforming creatures into letterforms and discovering how the word (or at least the initial letters) might be 'made flesh' in the bodies of his willing accomplices.

Pulliam's work has pioneered the investigation of the initials and other minor artwork in Kells, often revealing the depth of their connections with the text, which supersedes that of mere ornament and decoration.[60] However, these letters and additions never appear in its Gospel episodes with any formulaic or predictable regularity, are absent when we might most expect them, and frequently lack any simple or straightforward connection with the narrative (at least to modern readers). This is another aspect of the Scribe-Artist's random distribution, adding yet a further layer to the variation permeating every aspect of Kells' art and script. Ultimately it begs the question as to why such trouble is taken to make these texts, already complex and challenging, even more puzzling. Pulliam concludes that in Kells "meaning emerges not in a sequential orderly fashion, but rather as something that must be sought out, chewed over and, even then, provides only a partial and imperfect glimpse of the unknowable perfection of God."[61] Evidence for this is consistent throughout all four Gospel texts in Kells, and its idiosyncratic nature further supports their attribution to a single individual. No mere copyist, this is the work of a sophisticated 'scribe-exegete,'[62] perhaps the greatest of those whose work has survived from this period. These aspects of the Scribe-Artist's unique vision of how such sacred texts might be celebrated and transmitted merits further investigation.

The Winchester Bible (Winchester Cathedral, 1993); I am grateful to Claire (RIP 2019) for generously sharing her great knowledge of this manuscript.

60 Pulliam, *Word and Image.*

61 Pulliam, *Word and Image*, p. 210.

62 Laura Kendrick, *Animating the Letter* (Columbus, OH, 1999), pp. 36–64.

Acknowledgements

Thank you to Anita MacGabhann, Gale R. Owen-Crocker, and Maren Clegg Hyer for comments during various drafts of this paper. Thanks also to Michelle Brown. Thank you to the Libraries of Durham Cathedral and Lichfield Cathedral, British Library (London), Bibliothèque nationale de France (Paris), Biblioteca Apostolica Vaticana (Rome), Bodleian (Oxford), and Corpus Christi College (Cambridge) for generous access to original manuscripts.

CHAPTER 2

The Art of Looking Good: Hair and Beauty Remedies in Early Medieval Texts and Contexts

Christina Lee

I worked as the research assistant for the "Manchester Medieval Textiles Project," run by Betty and Gale Owen-Crocker between 1998 and 2001. My job was to add examples from archaeological remains to a database set up by Betty. This experience was transformative: I learned an enormous amount during these years and it was the making of me as an academic. Betty and I shared a minute office and I will always remember her generosity and patience. During the textiles project, I also had the advantage of being the first to hear about Betty's research. It was here where I first encountered Aldhelm's disdain of people in religious orders wearing clothes with colourful borders, which were presumably tablet-woven silk borders.[1] Aldhelm, as well as his compatriot Boniface, regarded splendid dress as a slippery slope which could lead to all kinds of sin and deprivations. In a letter dated to AD 747 to Archbishop Cuthbert of Canterbury, Boniface responds to a previous letter of advice written to him by pointing out a number of failings in the behaviour of Cuthbert's clergy, among which seems to be the wearing of bright purple strips which: *significantia signa ... arrogantiae et superbiae et luxuriae et vanitatis* ("signify the signs of ... insolence, and pride, and extravagance, and vanity"). Colourful garments, according to Boniface, endanger the souls of their young wearers since they pave the way for the Antichrist. Indeed, he concludes, they are sent by the Devil and will lead religious people to neglect their prayers and the reading of scripture. Instead they will engage in sinful acts in their cell.[2] Such rare glimpses into the domestic lives of early nuns and monks show, among other things, that monastic populations valued their personal possessions. Betty's work on embroidery has given us an idea of what such borders may have looked like.[3] Clothing, however, was not the only means with which nuns and monks tried to make themselves more attractive.

---

1 Gale R. Owen-Crocker, *Dress in Anglo-Saxon England: Revised and Enlarged Edition* (Woodbridge, 2004), p. 134; for Aldhelm's Prose *De Virginitate* see: *Aldhelm: The Prose Works*, ed. Michael Lapidge and Michael Herren (Ipswich: Brewer, 1979), p. 128.

2 *Die Briefe des Bonifatius, Willibalds Leben des Bonifatius Nebst einingen zeitgenössischen Dokumenten*, ed. and trans. Reinhold Rau (Darmstadt, 1968), pp. 238–55 at 252–54.

3 For example, "Stitches in Time: Establishing a History of Anglo-Saxon Embroidery," *Medieval Clothing and Textiles* 1 (2005), 1–28.

© KONINKLIJKE BRILL NV, LEIDEN, 2021 | DOI:10.1163/9789004467514_004

Aldhelm talks about curling irons used on forelocks and the hair showing at their temples.[4] Such passages give us a rare window into the fashions and concepts of beauty in early medieval England. Religious dress was not yet formalised and a variety of dress styles seems to have been possible for people in orders. These garments allowed for the necessary covering of the head and body, but they also were an act of underlining the beauty, status and gender of the wearer.

•.•

While it may come as a bit of a surprise that religious people cared about something as frivolous as their hairdos, it is worth remembering that hair was an important marker of religious allegiance, at least by men, who shaved part of their head for the tonsure. Hair, of course, plays an important role in all cultures. Hair can cover and reveal, and cuts and styles are linked to all kinds of signifiers: from sexuality, to status to devotion.[5] It is the "exceptional" hair (*capillorum quoque forme egregia*) of the slaves from England which attracts the attention of Pope Gregory, according to Bede.[6] Hair is a marker of distinction, and despite much archaeological evidence for combs and pins we seem to pay little attention to the way people kept their tresses in check. My essay will look at some of the evidence for the importance of hair and beauty from a range of sources from early medieval England and the Continent: historical and literary texts, material culture, as well as remedies from early medieval sources which tell us about hair care. I would like to see this essay as an extension to important work that Carl Phelpstead has published on the tonsure and hair loss in medieval Scandinavian sources.[7] Phelpstead's essay shows that the involuntary cutting of hair for men can be an act of emasculation. Hair is connected to virility, and baldness a sign of old age and loss of power.[8] He shows that even the voluntary loss of hair through tonsure is seen as an act of effeminisation in Old Norse sources.

---

4   Lapidge and Herren, *Aldhelm: Prose Virginitate*, p. 128.

5   For an interesting wider take, see Ian Wood, "Hair and Beards in the Early Medieval West," *Al-Masāq* 30.1 (2018), 107–16.

6   *Bede's Ecclesiastical History of the English People*, ed. and trans. Bertram Colgrave and R.A.B. Mynors (Oxford, 1969), 2.1, p. 132.

7   Carl Phelpstead, "Hair Today, Gone Tomorrow: Hair Loss, the Tonsure, and Masculinity in Medieval Iceland," *Scandinavian Studies* 85.1 (2013), 1–19.

8   Phelpstead, "Hair Today," esp. pp. 5–8.

The tonsure signifies that the wearer has agreed to become part of a religious order with all rights and privileges, but also the acceptance of rules and obedience to the Church. On one level this constitutes a loss of individual independence and self-determination, and this loss may have put them closer to the ways in which women gained influence, i.e. by connecting with other families. Women could gain agency and status through marriage, similarly those joining religious orders could enhance their influence by becoming part of a new, monastic 'family'. There had been a connection between long hair and status in some parts of classical antiquity and among the Merovingian elites which equated such styles with being a free man of a certain rank.[9] However, illustrations of men in pre-Conquest manuscripts such as the *Junius Psalter* (Oxford, Bodleian Library, Junius 27), or the *Old English Illustrated Hexateuch* (London, British Library, Cotton Claudius B. iv) show that they favoured shorter hair and beards for those not in orders. Generally religious men are depicted with short hair and shaven. In some places, such as the tenth-century *Harley Psalter* (London, British Library, Harley 603), it is the demons who have longer (and unkempt) hair (Fig. 2.1)

Shorter hair does not necessarily mean less 'power.' Hair remains a symbol of individual dignity and status. It is not, in early medieval contexts, the length which seems to matter, but the presence of hair, since a loss of it can be a sign of decline, as for example in *Vercelli Homily IX* where one of the terrors of hell is old age and includes the loss of hair.[10] Such negative ideas about old age appear in contrast to other instances where grey hair is associated with wisdom, as for example in the combination *har hilderinc* ("hoary/grey-haired warrior") which is used for Byrhtnoth in *The Battle of Maldon*, or King Hrothgar in *Beowulf*.[11] The difference in these two examples is that a loss of hair appears to be a marker of decrepitude, whereas the presence of hair is connected to leadership. Thijs Porck's recent examination of old age in early medieval England shows that the final stage of life was presented as a bit of a mixed bag.[12] In many cases old age is seen a period of decline, but there are the occasional figures who possess the wisdom of age. Porck quotes the popular example of the Three Magi in which Melchior is depicted with white hair.[13] The Magi who

---

9   Wood, "Hair and Beards," pp. 108–09.

10   *The Vercelli Homilies and Related Texts* (Early English Text Society (EETS) os 300), ed. Donald Scragg (Oxford, 1992), p. 168.

11   *The Anglo-Saxon Minor Poems* (Anglo-Saxon Poetic Records 6), ed. Elliot von Kirk Dobbie (London: Routledge, 1942), p. 11, line 169a; *Klaeber's Beowulf and the Fight at Finnsburg*, 4th ed., ed. R.D. Fulk, Robert E. Bjork, and John D. Niles (Toronto, 2008), p. 46, line 1308a.

12   Thijs Porck, *Old Age in Early Medieval England: a Cultural History* (Woodbridge, 2019).

13   Porck, *Old Age*, p. 25.

FIGURE 2.1   London, BL, Harley 603, fol. 3v detail. Devils with long, unkempt hair.
                © The British Library Board

have come to worship the infant Christ are clearly positive and significant figures. They are the first princes to recognise and worship Christ as a king. The
image of the Magi worshipping the infant Christ appears in various sources,
from art, as on the front panel of the eighth-century Franks Casket, to Ælfric's
Homily on Epiphany.[14] While Ælfric does not give a description of the *tungel-
witegan* ("Magi"), the panel on the Casket shows a bearded man with a full
head of hair. While the presence or absence of hair seems to be an indicator
of ability, for the few grey-haired women of Old English literature it is mainly
a marker of age, for example, Exeter Book Riddle 74 contrasts a *fæmne geong*

---

14   *Ælfric's Catholic Homilies: The First Series* (EETS ss 17), ed. Malcolm Godden (Oxford,
        1997), pp. 232–240, esp. 233–34.

("young virgin") with a *feaxhar cwen* ("grey-haired woman").[15] We may, however, note that the monk Zosimus, when he finds aged and grey-haired Mary of Egypt in the desert, considers her to be holy.[16]

Further evidence for the significance associated with hair comes from laws, such as §33 of the code of the late sixth-century King Æthelberht of Kent, in which the "seizing of hair" (*feaxfang*) carries a compensation of 50 *sceattas*, indicating that the forceful pulling of hair is seen as a violation.[17] The passage does not stipulate if this is male or female hair, but follows the misdeeds of a free man (*friman*). The amount of penalty is higher in this case than the killing of a freedman of third rank and suggests that such acts are demeaning, rather than deforming.

However, abundance of hair is not in all cases necessarily seen as a sign of strength. Unkempt or unruly hair, as seen above, is used to symbolise deviance. In the homily on the "Twelfth Sunday after Pentecost," Ælfric uses the example of Nebuchadnezzar from the Book of Daniel to illustrate pride and its consequences. He adapts the biblical version from which the hair of the king had grown like feathers of eagles and his nails like talons of birds (Daniel 4:33) to "so that his hair that grew like that of women and nails like eagle's claws" (*þæt his feax weox swa swa wimmanna and his næglas swa swa earnes clawa*).[18] Ælfric thus chooses to illustrate Nebuchadnezzar's loss of power and sanity by changing his appearance to be more like that of women and beasts. The length of hair is clearly linked to gender since by cutting their hair women can move into male spheres, and sometimes even operate as men. For example, St Eugenia is able to join a male monastery after cutting her hair,[19] and St Thecla cuts her hair and puts on men's clothing to accompany the Apostle Paul.[20] Writers

---

15   *The Exeter Book* (Anglo-Saxon Poetic Records 3), ed. George Krapp and Elliot van Kirk Dobbie (London, 1936), p. 234. For a translation and possible solutions of the riddle see James Paz's contribution to the *Riddle Age* https://theriddleages.wordpress.com/2018/02/12/riddle-74-or-72/ (accessed 20 May 2020).

16   *The Old English Life of Saint Mary of Egypt*, ed. and trans. Hugh Magennis (Exeter, 2002), p. 72.

17   The laws are recorded in the twelfth-century *Textus Roffensis* (Rochester Cathedral Library, A. 3.5). The standard edition for Anglo-Saxon laws is still Felix Liebermann, *Die Gesetze der Angelsachsen*, 3 vols (Halle, 1903–1916), but for this code we are lucky to have a new edition from the late Lisi Oliver, *The Beginnings of English Law* (Toronto, 2012), pp. 60–81. The hair-seizing passage is on p. 71.

18   *Ælfric's Catholic Homilies: The Second Series* (EETS ss 5), ed. Malcolm Godden (London, 1979), p. 253; see also Godden, *Ælfric's Catholic Homilies: Introduction, Commentary and Glossary* (EETS ss 18) (Oxford, 2000), p. 587.

19   *The Old English Martyrology*, ed. and trans. Christine Rauer (Cambridge, 2013), p. 36.

20   Rauer, *The Old English Martyrology*, p. 188.

in early medieval England will have been familiar with Isidore's definition of 'hair' in the *Etymologies*, in which he explains that a head of hair is in need of being shorn, but only for men.[21] Ælfric's emendation to *wimmanna feax* thus has two purposes: one to show Nebuchadnezzar's loss of agency over his own life, but also to show a change in the king's life. (In fulfilment of Daniel's prophesy, on account of his sins Nebuchadnezzar is driven out and lives like an animal for seven "times" – seasons or years.)

Depictions of women with uncovered hair in illustrations as well as textual sources occur in exceptional situations, and are connected to change. We may think of the Geatish woman of *Beowulf* line 3151b who, with her hair *bundenheord* ("bound up"), bewails the hero's death and the doom to come. The manuscript is damaged in this place and the *hapax legomenon bundenheord* is a reconstruction; so it is not quite clear how we should imagine the lady's hairdo. Megan Cavell has pointed out the singularity of using *bunden* in connection with hair. She refers to Carol Clover's suggestion that this should really read *wundenheorde* ("wound" (wavy) hair), which is the opposite to a formal hairdo: it refers to hair flowing freely down.[22] Nevertheless, if we accept that this word refers to a particular type of hair style it may suggest that this is a special way to dress her hair for the funeral which perhaps even indicates a relation to the dead hero.[23] In this case hair becomes part of a ritual of mourning the dead. Mourning is a transitory state – it alters someone's relationship with the now-dead person, but also indicates a change of the living in their wider community; it is a place in which present and future coexist. The uncovered hair is thus part of a grief performance: Beowulf's life is undone, and the future of his people is not yet done. It is always debatable whether literary texts are representative of real life ceremony, especially in a work as complex as *Beowulf* which 'remembers' a fictional past. The (un)bound hair of the Geatish woman seems to be more metaphor than memory of an act that has taken place. While the dating of the poem is still a matter of furious debate, illustrations which are contemporaneous with the manuscript (*c.* 975–1050)

---

21   *The Etymologies of Isidore of Seville*, ed. and trans. Stephen Barney, W.L. Lewis, J.A. Beach, and Oliver Berghof (Cambridge, 2006), p. 232. Short(er) hair for women is clearly noteworthy; one may think of Mary of Egypt who has *loccas … swa hwit swa wull and þa na siddran þonne oþ þonne swuran* ("hair … as white as wool and no longer than down to her neck"), *The Old English Mary of Egypt*, pp. 72–73.

22   Megan Cavell, "Old English 'Wundenlocc' Hair in Context," *Medium Ævum* 82.1 (2013), 119–25, at p. 122. Carol Clover, "Hildigunnr's Lament," in *Structure and Meaning in Old Norse Literature*, ed. John Lindow, Lars Lönnroth, and Gerd Wolfgang Weber (Odense, 1986), pp. 141–83, at 167.

23   *Klaeber's Beowulf*, p. 107, line 3151. I would like to express my thanks to Paul Cavill for a thoughtful exchange on this passage.

show women wearing extensive veils in funerary contexts. Grief, however, may lead women to expose their hair. In Ælfric's "Second Homily for the Feast of St Stephen," a widow is so grief-struck over the death of her husband that she is deluded by a devil to curse her children (who become sick as a consequence).[24] Ælfric explains that she was experiencing *maran wodnysse* ("great insanity") which made her unbind her hair (*tolysde hire feax*) and dip it in the font while she utters her curse. Unusual hair is not just a sign of sinfulness or effeminisation as in the case of Nebuchadnezzar, it may also signify otherness; we may think of those Homodubii in the *Marvels of the East* who have beards reaching to their knees.[25]

Hair, whether covered or uncovered, needs to be kept tidy and for the implements of grooming we need to turn to material culture. While actual hair seldom survives, combs and hair tools are ubiquitous and recently hair care has come into focus of archaeological research.[26] Studies of combs and hair accessories have been recently published by Steve Ashby, who has examined evidence for hair care from archaeological sources.[27] He observes that the 'grooming kit,' found among grave-goods, is typically gendered: men get iron razors, a pair of shears, and sometimes an iron knife, whereas women are buried with a 'toilet set': an ear scoop and one or two long picks or pins. These, he suggests, may be used for nail and skin maintenance and they were most likely to be personal ornaments which might have been worn from a belt. Ashby underlines that the male kit is concerned with facial or head hair whereas the female set is dedicated to beauty more generally.[28] Combs are more often buried with women than men and he suggests that women may have been buried with ornaments in their hair.[29]

---

24   *Ælfric's Catholic Homilies* 2, p. 11.

25   Andy Orchard, *Pride and Prodigies: Studies in the Monsters of the "Beowulf"-Manuscript* (Toronto: 2003). The idea that hair reaches the knees may be one of those "strange appearances." In *The Old English Martyrology* the false god of the Indians is described as having hair down to his knees (Rauer, p. 166).

26   Steve Ashby has explained the past neglect: "The fact that hair does not play a more central role in the archaeological study of identity is no doubt a result of its chemistry, which renders it an infrequent survivor in archaeological deposits …"; "Archaeologies of Hair: an introduction," *Internet Archaeology* 42 http://dx.doi.org/10.11141/ia.42.6.1 (accessed 17 February 2021). His monograph *A Viking way of life: combs and communities in early Medieval Britain* (Stroud: 2014) shows the importance of combs as grave goods, their technique and manufacture.

27   Steve Ashby, "Technologies of Appearance: Hair Behaviour in Early Medieval Europe," *Archaeological Journal* 171.1 (2014), 151–84.

28   Ashby, "Hair Behaviour," p. 166.

29   Ashby, "Hair Behaviour," p. 170.

Combs were made from antler and animal bone and they were produced for different functions: thus there are combs to tame the head hair, to look after beards but to also potentially comb nits out.[30] Just as today, combing hair with a fine-toothed comb will have helped to get rid of nits. However, combing was not just a way of keeping the hair tidy and perhaps louse-free, in at least one example it is also connected to some more esoteric uses. In the main manuscript versions of the *Medicina de Quadrupedibus*, a woman who suffers from severe menses is recommended to only use only her own comb and to comb her hair under a mulberry tree. A similar treatment is also prescribed for those who want their periods to come.[31] Thus combs and hairs were not just objects of grooming but associated with the individual person and their problems. This kind of individual possession may also be indicated in cases and coverings for combs, which have been found from the Viking world. Aside from practical reasons, such as keeping the teeth intact, decorated cases mean that combs can be easily transported in bags or even suspended from belts.

It is not just ordinary men and women who had to look good: an example of a two-sided comb from the tomb of St Cuthbert,[32] and a gift to Alcuin of York from Archbishop Riculf of Mainz show that combs were not just personal objects, but they also served as important gifts in exchanges.[33] Hair, as Ashby reminds us, is bound up with identity, and this could be group, status and religious identity.[34] It is therefore not surprising to find grooming implements, such as 'ear scoops,' tweezers, and tooth picks, as well as combs, are ubiquitous in cremation and to a lesser extent in pre-Conversion inhumation burial.[35] They have been associated with the status of the deceased, and as personal utilitarian objects, and, less so, as having amuletic function. Instead

---

30   For an overview see Steven Ashby, *A Viking way of Life* (Stroud, 2014). For production in Early Medieval England see Ian Riddler and Nicola Trzaska-Nartowski, 'Chanting upon a Dunghill: working skeletal remains', in *The Material Culture of Daily Living in the Anglo-Saxon World*, ed. Maren Clegg Hyer and Gale R. Owen-Crocker (Exeter, 2011), pp. 116–141.

31   *The Old English Herbarium and Medicina de quadrupedibus* (EETS, os 286), ed. Hubert J. De Vriend (London, 1984), pp. 238–9. De Vriend points out that this passage is out of place since it is not connected to animals, p. lxiv.

32   Ashby, *A Viking Way of Life*, pp. 102–03.

33   Steve Ashby and C.E. Batey, "Evidence of Exchange Networks: the Combs and Other Worked Skeletal Material," in *Being an Islander*, ed. James Barrett (Cambridge, 2012), pp. 229–43.

34   Ashby, *A Viking Way of Life*, 72 and *passim*. While most of the book deals with Viking and Anglo-Scandinavian evidence Ashby offers a very useful historical and anthropological survey in his book.

35   Howard Williams, "Tressed for Death in Early Anglo-Saxon England," *Internet Archaeology* 42 (2016), http://dx.doi.org/10.11141/ia.42.6.7 (accessed 13 May 2020).

of considering them entirely as something that the deceased may have used in their lives, Howard Williams suggests that such items may have been part of rituals which prepared the dead for the grave: "Combs, tweezers, shears, razors, and sometimes ear scoops too, can be profitably interpreted as key elements of 'technologies of remembrance': chains of operations enacted during the mortuary process and serving in the selective remembering and forgetting the dead."[36] The idea that the dead, and particularly the princely dead, were groomed for their final appearance is appealing. It may suggest that not just the mourners, but also the mourned, were dressed in a specific way. Williams points out that there is evidence for female grooming in high status conversion graves at Harford Farm in Norfolk.

It is often assumed that high-ranking women wore veils in the early Anglo-Saxon period, but the surviving evidence is limited.[37] In the archaeological contexts of the pre-Conversion phase this consists mostly of fine, often metal-replaced scraps of textile from brooches worn on the shoulders of women and from gold fillets at some Kentish cemeteries (Mill Hill and Sarre). Female skeletons in conversion period cemeteries, as pointed out by Gale R. Owen-Crocker, are occasionally buried with pins that are interpreted as fastening a thin veil. Penelope Walton Rogers shows that such pins were found throughout England, but with an easterly bias.[38] Her research demonstrates that while head coverings may not have been uniform across the various religious houses, nuns had adopted the habit of covering their hair with veils.

More evidence for the wearing of veils comes from later illustrations, and, perhaps unsurprisingly, many of the illustrated are religious figures, such as the St Æthelthryth in the *Benedictional of St Æthelwold* (London, British Library, Additional 49598, fol. 90v) or the Virgin Mary on the frontispiece of the *New Minster Charter* (London, British Library, Cotton Vespasian A. viii, fol. 2v). Manuscript images from the end of the period, such as the Old English illustrated Hexateuch (London, British Library, Cotton Claudius B. iv), habitually show women with their hair covered. This covering also included the neck, as for example the illustration of Queen Emma/Ælfgifu on the frontispiece of the

36   Williams, "Tressed."

37   Desirée Koslin and Gale R. Owen-Crocker, "Veil," *Encyclopedia of Medieval Dress and Textile of the British Isles c. 450–1450*, ed. Gale R. Owen-Crocker, Elizabeth Coatsworth, and Maria Hayward (Leiden, 2012), pp. 611–13, https://referenceworks-brillonline-com.ezproxy.not tingham.ac.uk/entries/encyclopedia-of-medieval-dress-and-textiles/veil-SIM_000878? s.num=3 (accessed 30 April 2020).

38   See Penelope Walton Rogers, "In Search of Hild: A Review of the Context of Abbess Hild's Life, her Religious Establishment, and the Relevance of Recent Archaeological Finds from Whitby Abbey," Chapter 5 in this volume.

New Minster *Liber Vitae* (London, British Library, Stowe 944, fol. 6r). Exceptions of women with their hair uncovered are Eve in the Junius 11 manuscript (Oxford, Bodleian Library) and some of the figures in the illustrations of Prudentius's *Psychomachia*, such as *Ira* (Anger) in the manuscript London, British Library, Cotton Cleopatra C. viii, fol. 12r. This manuscript of the *Psychmachia* is one of three surviving from the period, which although produced in England were based on continental examples.[39] In a recent essay Stephenie McGucken has observed that while the vices and virtues in the manuscripts from early medieval England are mostly depicted as women, these also exhibit behaviour traditionally associated with men, such as war.[40]

There have been some suggestions that the covering of women's hair may be connected to their marital status.[41] As we have seen above, religious women, who will have included the virgin daughters of high ranking families, chose to cover their heads. Covering the hair may be linked to being bound to a family, either by marriage or by being a member of a religious 'family'. It may be that the uncovering of hair also signifies that this character is not tied by any promises or bonds. A good example for a woman who is defying a new attachment is the famous *wundenlocc* hair of Judith in the Old English poem of that name which is usually translated as "curly-haired," although Megan Cavell has pointed out that this may also refer to braided hair (in analogy to the *wundenfeax* of a horse's mane in *Beowulf*, line 1400).[42] Unlike her biblical namesake, the Old English Judith is not a widow or married, but described as a *mægð* (maid), so anything between a virgin and a young woman.[43] Her uncovered locks may thus underline her status as an unmarried, and possibly virginal, woman. The audience of Old English poetry often remains speculative but other versions of the story of Judith seems to be particularly cognisant of a

---

39   Gernot Wieland, "The origin and development of the Anglo-Saxon *Psychomachia* illustrations," *Anglo-Saxon England* 26 (1997), pp. 169–86.

40   "Vice & Virtue As Woman?: The Iconography of Gender Identity in the Late Anglo-Saxon *Psychomachia* Illustrations," *Medieval feminist forum* 55: 1 (2019–10), pp. 42–63, at 47.

41   See Oliver, *Beginnings of English Law*, p. 110. Oliver points out comparisons with Lombard law which distinguish *in capillo/capillis* to mark between married and unmarried women. See also Gabriela Signori, "Veil, Hat or Hair? Reflections on an Asymmetrical Relationship," *The Medieval History Journal* 8.1 (2005), 25–47, at p. 31.

42   Cavell, "Old English 'Wundenlocc' Hair", p. 121. Cavell is using Hugh Magennis's interpretation of this word here. She also provides a useful overview of the long-standing discussion of Judith's hair and sexuality.

43   Mary Dockray Miller, "Female Community in the Old English *Judith*," *Studia Neophilologica* 70 (1998), 165–72, at p. 171.

female monastic audience, and this kind of association of Judith with virginity
may have appealed to a monastic audience.[44]

Getting It Covered

The covering of women's hair has its roots in biblical pronouncements such as
Paul's instruction for women to cover their heads in 1 Corinthians 11:6. However,
as with many other religious conventions, it also met with practices that served
more pragmatic purposes; long hair is protected from dirt and potentially
all kinds of pests. Veils for consecrated women had been around since the
fourth century AD after they had been advocated by influential writers, such
as Tertullian, and by the twelfth century the wimple became a status marker
for married women.[45] Head coverings may have indicated a specific rank and
status and luscious locks indicated youth and beauty, but we should not forget
that hair and health are connected and that perhaps such coverings served a
useful purpose. Sometimes the rules set up by the Church in handbooks, such
as those given to confessors (penitentials) demonstrate a good portion of common sense. For example, the eating of carrion is forbidden in several penitentials. This injunction has no tangible benefit for the soul, but makes good sense
in terms of hygiene.[46] This kind of enforcement of sensible behaviour through
religious practice is an indicator that there was some understanding of basic
ideas of why people get sick. The washing of the head, and with it the hair, is
explicitly allowed on Sundays in the *Penitential of Theodore*.[47] Despite the fact
that most other activities are disallowed on Sundays, keeping clean is seen as

---

44   See, for example, Mary Clayton, "Ælfric's *Judith*: Manipulative or Manipulated," *Anglo-
       Saxon England* 23 (1994), 215–27 and Rebecca Stephenson, "Judith as Spiritual Warrior:
       Female Models of Monastic Masculinity in Ælfric's *Judith* and Byrhtferth's *Enchiridion*,"
       English Studies 101 (2020), 79–95.
45   Signori, "Veil, Hat or Hair," pp. 27, 31.
46   See for example, *Scriftboc* chapter vi, cited from Allen Frantzen, *Anglo-Saxon Peniten-
       tials: a Cultural Database*, http://www.anglo-saxon.net/penance/index.php?p=JUNIUS
       _88b&anchor=X04.02.01 (accessed 20 May 2020); see also *Das altenglische Bussbuch* (*sog.
       Confessionale pseudo-Egberti): ein Beitrag zu den kirchlichen Gesetzen der Angelsachen*, ed.
       Robert Spindler (Leipzig, 1893), p. 177. The *Canons of Theodore* state that stags or red deer
       should not be eaten if found dead; *The Old English Canons of Theodore* (EETS ss 25), ed.
       Robert Fulk and Stefan Jurasinski (Oxford, 2012), p. 4. The Penitential and the canons of
       Theodore come from the same source, but the various manuscript versions have slightly
       different renderings.
47   In *Die Bussordnungen der abendländischen Kirche*, ed. Friedrich Wasserschleben (Halle,
       1851), p. 178.

important. Not only does clean hair indicate a good standard of hygiene, but looking after one's hair may also have been seen as an important aspect of hygiene and health.

Ectoparasites such as lice and fleas are vectors for the transmission of dangerous diseases, such as plague and malaria. Head lice (*Pediculus humanus capitis*) belong to the same species as body lice (*Pediculus humanus humanus*), and these are not just unpleasant creatures but can also be health hazards, by transmitting bacteria which cause diseases such as typhus or trench fever.[48] Body lice are not normally transmitted in hair, but they attach themselves to clothes and thus get close to the skin. More significantly, human fleas (*Pulex irritans*) have recently been identified as a vector for the high morbidity of the second plague pandemic in Europe (1348–1353).[49] Evidence that the first, Justinianic pandemic affected England is now firmly established, which makes caring for hair and body no longer just a question of beauty, but also health.[50] While it was impossible for medieval people to know about bacterial transmission, they could have well seen a connection between having lice and fleas and becoming sick, particularly if lice had been identified as a source of sickness in their influential medical sources from Antiquity.

Lice remedies thus appear in a range of medical collections. One of our early remedies against 'lice' from the so-called *Lorscher Arzneibuch* (Bamberg, Staatsbibliothek, med. 1) is the oldest medical compilation in Europe.[51] Written in Latin in the first quarter of the ninth century at the abbey at Lorsch (Hesse, Germany), it is a compendium of medical texts, as well as an unusual defence for the necessity of medical treatments (fols 1r–4v).[52] The writer evidently had access to medical knowledge from classical traditions, but also to plants and

---

48   Didier Raoult and Véronique Roux, "The Body Louse as a Vector of Re-emerging Human Diseases," *Clinical Infectious Diseases* 29.4 (1999), 888–911.

49   Karen Dean *et al.*, "Human Ectoparasites and the Spread of Plague in Europe during the Second Pandemic," *Proceedings of the National Academy of the United States of America* 115 (2018), 1304–09.

50   Marcel Keller *et al.*, "Ancient Yersinia Pestis Genomes from across Western Europe Reveal Early Diversification during the First Pandemic (541–750)," *Proceedings of the National Academy of the United States of America* 116 (2019), 12363–72. Positive genomic evidence was recovered from four burials at the seventh-century cemetery at Barrington, Edix Hill, Cambridgeshire.

51   *Das "Lorscher Arzneibuch": Ein medizinhistorisches Kompendium des 8. Jahrhunderts (Codex Bambergensis medicinalis 1): Text, Übersetzung und Fachglossar*, trans. Ulrich Stoll (Stuttgart, 1992).

52   The digitized manuscript and facing German translation of the first part, based on Stoll's translation, is available at https://www.bayerische-landesbibliothek-online.de/arznei buch (accessed 20 May 2020). Quoted by folio number.

and Ayurvedic healing, continues to seek solutions from historical remedies by applying modern methods of chemical analysis which, if efficacious, are then subjected to the same clinical trials as conventional Western drug development. Medieval remedies may inform modern research where to look for efficacious new chemical combinations which can inform novel cures.[97]

In some cases medieval remedies treat the same diseases with mixtures of plant-based remedies which are similar to those used in Chinese Traditional Medicine. For example, Bald's Leechbook lists *lencten adl* in the section of remedies against fever. The other plants listed for the cure are *wermod, eoforprote, elehtre, wegbræde, ribbe, cerfille, attorlaðe, feferfuge, alexandre, bisceopwyrt, lufestice, saluie, cassuc* ("wormwood, carline thistle, lupin, plantago major, ribwort, chervil, betony or nightshade, feverfew, a type of alexander (*Smyrnium olusatrum*), marsh mallow, lovage, common sage, sedge (grass)"). The physician is instructed to *wyrc to drence on welscum ealað, do halig wæter to springwyrt* ("work them into a drink with Welsh ale, add Holy Water and caper spurge").[98] As usual there is no information on the quantity of ingredients and several of them (wormwood/absinth, lupine, and nightshade) are actually poisonous. Notable here is that the artemisinin in wormwood/*Artemisia absinthium* has recently been shown to have powerful antimalarial qualities. The Chinese scientist Tu You-You discovered the use of artemisinin in traditional Chinese medical texts from the fourth century AD and developed an antimalarial drug by essentially following the instruction in the text to the letter.[99]

Much of medieval medicine will not have 'worked,' in the same way as much of modern pharmacology is not working for everyone.[100] While single ingredients or 'superfoods' often do not fulfil the promises of the laboratory in clinical trials, combinations of ingredients seem to indicate more stable results. The fact that remedies use combinations of plants which activate the

---

97   Erin Connelly, Charo del Genio and Freya Harrison, "Data Mining a Medieval Medical Text Reveals Patterns in Ingredient Choice That Reflect Biological Activity against Infectious Agents," *mBio* 11: 1 (2020) doi: 10.1128/mBio.03136-19 (accessed 28 February 2021).

98   *Leechdoms* II, p. 334.

99   Tu You-You, "New Antimalarial Drug – Qinghaosu and Dihydro-Qinghaosu," *Chinese Journal of Integrated Traditional and Western Medicine* 3 (1997), p. 312. For this work she was awarded the Nobel Prize in Medicine and Physiology in 2016.

100   An important essay on the possibilities of research has been recently published by Erin Connelly and Freya Harrison of the AncientBiotics project: "Could Medieval Medicine Help the Fight Against Antimicrobial Resistance?" in *Making the Medieval Relevant: How Medieval Studies Contribute to Improving our Understanding of the Present*, ed. Chris Jones, Conor Kostik, and Klaus Oschema (Berlin, 2019), pp. 113–34. See https://doi .org/10.1515/9783110546316-005 (accessed 13 May 2020). Their work shows the possibilities for modern research, but also the necessity for true interdisciplinary collaboration.

potential of other plant chemicals, or inhibit the harmful effects of more toxic species in medieval remedies, suggests a certain amount of observation. Even if species have changed with cultivation and we may not be completely sure that we can positively identify all ingredients in a physician's repertoire we may appreciate that there is some understanding of chemical processes. Such observation matters because it represents an overlooked aspect of the history of science, which tends to cut out medieval medicine as an 'irrelevant' aberration in human progress. Medieval observation is not the same as present day research, but it demonstrates human ingenuity and curiosity. It also matters for research today since plant-based treatments have not disappeared. Even a cursory search of a patent database shows a range of nettle tonics which are designed to strengthen hair roots and help with hair loss,[101] but our work has shown that medieval physicians knew that combinations of plants unlock, and often enhance the efficacy of single ingredients. In terms of understanding the efficacy of such remedies, the multiple ingredients make testing and research more complex.

There is a tendency in popular culture to depict medieval people as shaggy-haired barbarians who did not care about cleanliness or hygiene.[102] Such views stand in contrast to the evidence from archaeology and manuscripts which indicate that people in early medieval England did not just like to look after their appearances but also understood that there is a connection between health and keeping oneself clean. The various remedies against parasites indicate that keeping themselves free from insects was an important part of self-care. Continental manuscripts give us a glimpse that not all of this care was utilitarian: aging skin and wrinkled lips were clearly seen as undesirable. While religious men may have been highly critical about such vanity, as well as the wearing of colourful dress, or any other frivolity which may have distracted them from worship and contemplation, there is a fair bit of evidence that beauty mattered to people in early medieval Europe, and perhaps even to those who lived behind the walls of the cloister.

---

101   Nettles may increase bactericide properties of other ingredients. They may also encourage plants to strengthen certain chemical processes. Our analysis was interrupted by the outbreak of Covid-19 but continues in 2021.

102   For a good survey, albeit with a later medieval focus, of this idea see Carol Rawcliffe, *Urban Bodies: Communal Health in Late Medieval English Towns and Cities* (Woodbridge, 2013), pp. 12–53.

Acknowledgements

Research for this paper is partly based on work undertaken for the Royal Society/Leverhulme APEX Grant "Nettles and Networks" (APX\R1\180053) and my sincere thanks go to the funders and my colleagues on the project: Freya Harrison, Erin Connelly, and Charo Del Genio. I would like to thank Paul Cavill and Erin Connelly for reading an earlier draft of this paper as well as the anonymous reviewer and editors for helpful comments. All mistakes are mine.

CHAPTER 3

Dress and Undress, Real and Unreal, in the Drawings of Harley Psalter Artist F

Gale R. Owen-Crocker

Having worked on medieval dress and textiles in collaboration with Betty Coatsworth for many years, there was no question about my choice of topic. As a personal friend I was well aware of the importance of her Christian faith to her and of the contributions she made to worship and community at her local church in Manchester. She loves books and has published on medieval manuscripts. I therefore hope this contribution, on dress (and undress) as illustrated in a manuscript, a holy book used in personal and communal worship, forms a fitting tribute to her.

∴

The Psalter and Worship

The Psalter, or book of the psalms, was central to Christian worship. Medieval monks were expected to learn the entire collection of 150 psalms by heart, and, ideally at least, all the psalms were chanted or recited in the course of each week in monasteries.[1] Psalms were at the heart of the liturgy, and were also used for private prayer, for example by monks after waking and before attending to their personal needs.[2] Every monastery and church needed at least one copy of the Psalter, and devout, literate seculars also read the psalms, sometimes with the aid of translations or glosses. More Psalters survive from

---

1 This was required by the Benedictine Rule, Chapter 18; the Latin text may be found at http://www.intratext.com/IXT/LAT0011/_PJ.HTM and a translation, *St. Benedict's Rule for Monasteries*, translated from the Latin by Leonard J. Doyle (Collegeville, MI, 2015), e-book http://www.gutenberg.org/ebooks/50040 (both accessed 1 February 2021). Evidently some failed to live up to this standard: "For those monks show themselves too lazy in the service to which they are vowed, who chant less than the Psalter with the customary canticles in the course of a week, whereas we read that our holy Fathers strenuously fulfilled that task in a single day" (XVIII, pp. 24–25 in the Latin, 18, [40] in the translation). I am grateful to Sarah Anderson for this reference.

2 M.J. Toswell, *The Anglo-Saxon Psalter* (Turnhout, Belgium, 2014), pp. 3–5, 7–9, 23–24.

© KONINKLIJKE BRILL NV, LEIDEN, 2021 | DOI:10.1163/9789004467514_005

Anglo-Saxon England than any other text, and the Psalter was evidently the commonest book in the country at that time.[3]

The Harley Psalter and the Utrecht Psalter

The Psalter now British Library Manuscript Harley 603 has been called "one of the most important of all pre-Conquest English illuminated manuscripts."[4] Making this book was an ambitious project, ultimately employing, according to William Noel's estimation, twelve hands: two scribes, two artist-scribes, and eight artists.[5] It was begun about AD 1000, and work continued, or was resumed, for over 100 years, probably in Canterbury.[6] Initially scribes and artists copied the layout and *mises-en-scène* of a ninth-century Carolingian manuscript now called the Utrecht Psalter,[7] which has three columns of text, accompanied by drawings at the head of every psalm, canticle, and prayer, running across all three columns of text. The English scribes, however, used a different, more compact script,[8] ultimately causing problems for the layout of the new

---

3   Toswell, *The Anglo-Saxon Psalter*, p. 20. Over fifty Psalters, or parts of Psalters, survive.

4   J.M.B[ackhouse], "The Harley Psalter," in *The Golden Age of Anglo-Saxon Art*, ed. Janet Backhouse, D.H. Turner, and Leslie Webster (London, 1984), pp. 74–75 at 74. The colour facsimile, which can be enlarged, may be found on http://www.bl.uk/manuscripts/Viewer .aspx?ref=harley_ms_603_fs001r (accessed 18 May 2021). The commentary on the website gives guidance as to which psalm and verse is referenced in the illustrations. The commentary to Ohlgren's black and white facsimile also provides useful shortcuts to relevant verses: Thomas H. Ohlgren, *Anglo-Saxon Textual Illustration: Photographs of Sixteen Manuscripts with Descriptions and Index* (Kalamazoo, MI, 1992), pp. 18–41.

5   William Noel, *The Harley Psalter* (Cambridge, 1995), p. 2.

6   Noel, *The Harley Psalter*, pp. 3–6 discusses opinions about the origins and date of the manuscript, including voices for St Augustine's, Canterbury, and opinions that some drawings may have been done at Glastonbury, others by visiting Winchester artists. At pp. 140–45 Noel argues firmly for Christ Church, Canterbury, accepted as a probability by Francis Wormald, *English Drawings of the Tenth and Eleventh Centuries* (London, 1952), no. 34, p. 69; a Christ Church origin is also accepted by Janet Backhouse, "The Making of the Harley Psalter," *Electronic British Library Journal*, 1984 articles, Chapter 8, pp. 97–113, at 98, https://www.bl.uk/ eblj/1984articles/articles.html (accessed 25 January 2021); and Ohlgren, *Anglo-Saxon Textual Illustration*, p. 2.

7   Now Utrecht, Universiteitsbibliotheek, Utrecht Hs. 32; https://www.uu.nl/en/utrecht-univer sity-library-special-collections/the-treasury/manuscripts-from-the-treasury/the-utrecht -psalter and https://psalter.library.uu.nl/ (accessed 18 May 2021). The Library description states, "Most experts agree that the Utrecht Psalter was made in 820–830, in Reims or in the nearby abbey of Hautvilliers, and was perhaps commissioned by arch bishop [*sic*] Ebbo."

8   The Utrecht University Library Special Collections website describes Utrecht as Carolingian *capitalis rustica*, headings in uncial and *capitalis quadrata* (fols 1–92); insular uncial, headings in *capitalis rustica* (fols 94–105). Harley is Caroline minuscule; Noel, *The Harley Psalter*, p. 9.

manuscript and the placing of the illustrations. They also used a different Latin text: since the Harley text is mostly the Roman version of the Psalter,[9] Utrecht the Gallican,[10] the text being copied must have come from elsewhere. A significant difference between the illustrations of the Utrecht and Harley Psalters is that the former is monochrome – executed in light brown ink with darker brown touches added – while Harley is executed in colour, though different artists use the colours in different ways (discussed further below, pp. 77–78, 91).

Very probably the Utrecht Psalter was revolutionary in its time. While the ninth-century artists are likely to have copied individual images from earlier manuscripts,[11] the way they were combined into lively and detailed illustrations of (parts of) the psalms was entirely new:

> A comparison between the drawings in the Utrecht Psalter with those in other manuscripts from the same or previous periods shows clearly their originality, innovation and modernity. It is as if art has made a big leap forward, as if a revolution has taken place in the almost sketch-like depiction of the scenes illustrating the psalm verses. We see buildings, landscapes and heavens, full of kings, soldiers, angels, saints, sinners, craftsmen, musicians, children or a selection from the animal kingdom. Christ, the psalmist or David often play central parts. But also Atlas, the mouth of the Hell or demons with tridents appear on the scene.[12]

---

9   Preamble to the British Library online facsimile: "The illustration of the manuscript is copied from the Utrecht Psalter (Utrecht, Universiteitsbibliotheek, MS 32), however the text is mostly the Roman version, except Psalms 100–105 which are Gallican." This Gallican intrusion is in Quire 9, on fols 50r–54r column a, line 23, which coincides exactly with the writing of a single artist/scribe (D2) who worked only on this quire; Noel, *The Harley Psalter*, pp. 23, 212.

10   The Roman version of the Psalter is the oldest version (now usually dated to AD 84, though once thought to be St Jerome's earliest version), and was popular in Anglo-Saxon England. The Gallican version (once thought to be Jerome's second version, but probably his first, dating to 388–392) was popular throughout Gaul; Toswell, *The Anglo-Saxon Psalter*, pp. 11–12.

11   Koert van der Horst thinks it probable that the ninth-century Utrecht artists were using much older models, including late Antique drawings of the fourth to fifth centuries as well as a sixth- to seventh-century evangeliary or gospel book; K. van der Horst, William Noel, and Wilhelmina C.M. Wüsterfeld, *The Utrecht Psalter in Medieval Art* (Amsterdam, 1996), pp. 73–81.

12   Website of Utrecht University Library Special Collections page on the Utrecht Psalter, https://www.uu.nl/en/utrecht-university-library-special-collections/the-treasury/manuscripts-from-the-treasury/the-utrecht-psalter (accessed 6 March 2021).

The Utrecht Psalter was highly influential. Arriving in Canterbury at some unknown time in the late tenth century, certainly there by the year 1000, its illustrations were directly copied both as a set[13] and individually, appearing for example in both the bilingual, Anglo-Saxon *Paris Psalter*[14] and the Anglo-Norman Bayeux Tapestry.[15] Features of its "Reims Style," particularly its active, often hunched, figures with fluttering drapery, were transmitted into Anglo-Saxon art, though swirling textiles are to be found earlier in the tenth-century Winchester Style, reflecting Carolingian influence even before the arrival of the Utrecht Psalter in England.

Patronage, Purpose and Use in Worship

Utrecht's method of illustrating the Psalter by literal visualisation of the psalms texts was probably a tool in monastic worship and study. With its large size, approximately 370 × 310 mm (14.56 × 12.2 in),[16] and lavish use of illustration, the book was probably displayed as one of the treasures of its monastery; nevertheless its order, with the psalms arranged numerically, suggests it was designed for study, rather than for liturgical use.[17] Medieval methods of learning by heart involved creating mental pictures. Van der Horst suggested the "possible mnemonic function of drawings" in relation to the Utrecht Psalter[18] citing the work of Mary Carruthers on medieval memorisation[19] and relating the technique to that described by Hugh of St Victor in his version of the anonymous classical treatise *Ad Herrenium*.[20] Carruthers suggests that Utrecht's images belong to a long tradition of *imagines rerum* associated with the psalm

---

13   In addition to Harley 603, the drawings were copied in the twelfth-century Eadwine Psalter (Cambridge, Trinity College, R. 17. 1) and from there into the later twelfth-century Paris Psalter, now Paris, Bibliothèque nationale, Lat. 8846.

14   Paris, Bibliothèque nationale, fonds lat. 8824, mid-eleventh century, perhaps from St Augustine's Canterbury.

15   Probably dating from the 1070s to 1080s, but certainly post 1066, probably designed at St Augustine's, Canterbury, and made in southern England.

16   Kooert van der Horst, "Chapter 2 The Utrecht Psalter: Picturing the Psalms of David," in Van der Horst *et al.*, *The Utrecht Psalter in Medieval Art*, pp. 22–84 at 82.

17   Van der Horst dismisses the possibility that the Utrecht Psalter was made for liturgical use if only because the numerical arrangement would be inconvenient for monks in the choir as they would have to leaf back and forth through the book; ibid, p. 81.

18   Ibid.

19   Mary Carruthers, *The Book of Memory: A Study of Memory in Medieval Culture* (Cambridge, [first edition 1990] second edition 2008), pp. 282–85.

20   Translated as Appendix A in Carruthers, *The Book of Memory*, 2nd ed., pp. 339–44.

texts. She argues strongly that the images were not used only as *imagines verborum* as clues to specific syllables and therefore to remembering the psalms by heart, but that they signalled the chief topics and key ideas of each psalm. Therefore they were not only for novices beginning to memorise the psalms but also for advanced study by persons who already knew them by heart.[21]

Arguably the illustrations also evoked empathy, compunction, in the student, whatever that person's level of theological education. The delightful variety of images, their liveliness, and the way in which human figures are situated in landscapes and buildings, interacting with each other and with objects, must have triggered responses in viewers who were unused to the concept of textual illustration, realising the psalms for them and assisting memory of them, which could be employed not just for the recitation of the texts but in other situations from private prayer to public preaching to teaching and commentating.

The Harley Psalter, at 380 × 310 mm (14.96 × 12.2 in) is even larger than Utrecht, and, with its programme of coloured illustrations, was intended to be even more impressive, had it been completed. Its purpose and use remain mysterious. Like its model, the Utrecht Psalter, its psalms appear in numerical order. This, together with the lack of other liturgical matter, suggests it was probably not made primarily for liturgical use. Nor does it contain extra material which would identify it as a study manuscript or one for private devotional use.[22] Its first initial, the B of *Beatus* on fol. 2r, shows a tonsured

---

21   Carruthers, *The Book of Memory*, 2nd ed., pp. 282–83.

22   See note 17 above. If it was intended to contain only the Psalms the manuscript would be what Peter Kidd calls "very uncommon." He continues "Much more common are manuscripts arranged primarily for the purposes of study, usually containing extra apparatus intended to make the theological meaning of the text clearer. This extra material often takes the form of marginal and interlinear glosses, which explain the meaning of individual words and expound the general meaning of longer passages; these volumes are more accurately called Glossed psalters. Manuscripts that arrange the psalms not in numerical order, but in the order in which they are recited liturgically, usually with other liturgical material interspersed, are called by various names such as 'Choir psalter' and 'Ferial psalter', because they represent the order in which the psalms are chanted in the choir of a church, arranged according to the feria (days of the week). Alternatively, a psalter may be designed primarily for private devotional use ... The ultimate liturgical origin of such psalters is manifest in two ways. First, the presence of divisions of the text reflect liturgical practice; and second, the presence of certain kinds of supplementary matter: psalters are usually preceded by a calendar, and followed by canticles, a litany of saints, petitions, collects, and often other prayers. In addition to these common texts, a wide diversity of other material can be found in manuscript psalters; for these one has to devise hybrid names such as 'Psalter-Hours', 'Psalter-Hymnary', 'Psalter-Collectar', and 'Psalter-Antiphoner'"; Peter Kidd, "Contents and Codicology," in *Dombibliothek Hildesheim: The Albani Psalter*,

figure in an archbishop's pallium, prostrate before Christ, which led Kathleen Doyle, in the book accompanying a major British Library exhibition of 2018 to suggest the manuscript was, originally at least, intended for an ecclesiastical audience;[23] there are cowled and tonsured figures elsewhere among the illustrations (including Artist F's folio 66v with its depiction of the monastic Maundy ceremony, Fig. 3.1, left), and the text is entirely in Latin, not the vernacular; but even without this evidence of ecclesiastical focus, there is little doubt that the manuscript was written and illustrated in a monastery, since this is where eleventh-century scriptoria were mostly situated.[24] The opening initial may suggest a specific archiepiscopal patron or moving spirit for the manuscript. Suggested candidates are Archbishop Ælfric (who died in 1005) or Æthelnoth (archbishop 1020–38);[25] both were monks and abbots, as indeed were the archbishops between them Ælfheah and Lyfing (who do not appear to have been suggested). The manuscript was so long in the making that plans for its eventual gifting may have changed over time. It has been suggested that it was started for King Æthelred II (reigned 978–1016) and intended to be completed for King Cnut (reigned 1016–1035).[26] Queen Ælfgifu/Emma (died 1052), who was married sequentially to both of them, had a keen awareness of books, was a generous benefactor of monasteries, and took a personal interest in Christ Church, Canterbury (being present, with her son King Harthacnut,

---

Commentary by Jochen Bepler, Peter Kidd, and Jane Geddes (Simbach am Inn: Verlag Muller and Schindler, 2008), pp. 10–156, Section 1.2.5 "What is a Manuscript Psalter?", p. 50, on line at http://www.manuscripts.org.uk/albani/Kidd%20essay%20in%20St%20 Albans%20Psalter%20commentary%20volume.pdf (accessed 14 February 2021). I am grateful to Margaret Jane Toswell for this reference.

23   K. D[oyle], "The Harley Psalter," in *Anglo-Saxon Kingdoms: Art, Word, War*, ed. Claire Breay and Joanna Story (London, 2018), p. 345. Doyle assumes the Beatus initial belongs to the earliest phase of illustration. Cf note 25. Janet Backhouse suggests that it would be plausible for "a dignitary of Canterbury to aspire to ownership of a copy of the Utrecht Psalter"; "The Making," p. 110.

24   There was secular record keeping, especially associated with the royal court, but this concerned law, land and tax issues rather than biblical copying; see Alexander R. Rumble, "Anglo-Saxon Royal Archives: Their Nature, Extent, Survival and Loss," in *Kingship, Legislation and Power in Anglo-Saxon England*, ed. Gale R. Owen-Crocker and Brian W. Schneider (Publications of the Manchester Centre for Anglo-Saxon Studies 13) (Woodbridge, 2013), pp. 185–99.

25   Noel, *The Harley Psalter*, pp. 1, 3, 6. Backhouse, who believed the Beatus initial was added by Hand E in the 1020s, suggested that Æthelnoth was the ecclesiastic represented in the initial and favoured him as the prospective owner, and his death in 1038 as bringing an end to the project. (She suggested the later sections were to replace lost parts.) She compared the initial to owner-donor miniatures in contemporary manuscripts; "The Making," pp. 108–10.

26   Noel, *The Harley Psalter*, p. 6.

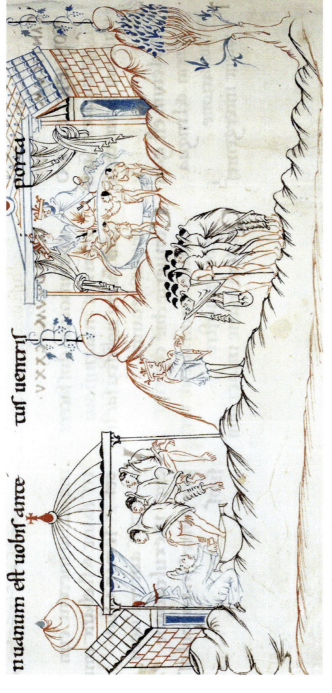

FIGURE 3.1   London, BL, Harley 603, fol. 66v, lower, Psalm 127 (128). A crowned king and queen at table. Below, left, a Maundy ceremony. Right, a crowned king gives alms to the foremost of a group of beggars.
© The British Library Board

at the translation of St Ælfheah's bones in 1023),[27] should be included among potential royal recipients.[28]

The Making of the Harley Psalter

The Utrecht Psalter was probably unbound for the making of Harley, so that parts could be distributed to different artists, and in the case of one short section, an additional scribe.[29] William Noel asserts that the work of Quires 1–4 and 9 "was executed within a few months," perhaps in the second decade of the eleventh century.[30] The fact that the manuscript was never finished did not preclude it circulating, being studied and imitated. Scribes and artists would certainly not have been working on a bound volume as Evangelists are shown doing in medieval illuminated manuscripts, since work proceeded simultaneously on different quires.[31] Completed sections are likely to have been available as individual quires or booklets for reading, memorisation, and meditation.

The ambitious plan for Harley included illustrations in colour. Each colour comes in darker and lighter shades, the former for lines and the ink more diluted for colour wash. Richard Gameson has made the important point that using coloured inks complicated the illustration process considerably: instead of working systematically through the composition, drawing complete images, the artists necessarily drew only part or parts of a figure, building, tree, or other item in one stint, returning to draw another part in a different coloured ink.[32] Such a method would appear to be contrary to spontaneity; however the likelihood of under-drawing reconciles the conflict between spontaneity and piecemeal ink drawing. Images were first drawn, some possibly traced, in lead point

---

27   Judith E. Duffey, "The Inventive Group of Illustrations in the Harley Psalter," PhD dissertation, University of California at Berkeley, 1997, pp. 168–69. Emma and Cnut received books as gifts, and Emma gave a psalter containing pictures to her brother Robert, Archbishop of Rouen; T.A. Heslop, "The Production of *de luxe* Manuscripts and the Patronage of King Cnut and Queen Emma," *Anglo-Saxon England* 19 (1990), 151–95 at pp. 159–60, 158, respectively. She also commissioned a book, the so-called *Encomium Emmae Reginae*.

28   Duffy, "The Inventive Group," pp. 160–67, suggests that certain scenes drawn by Artist F may relate directly to the reign of Cnut and Queen Emma; see also Mary Olsen, "'He has given birth to iniquity': Gender and the Reading Subject in MS Harley 603," *Browsing Enarratio: Publications of the Medieval Association of the Midwest* 8 (2001), 85–119, esp. 98–99, 108.

29   Noel, *The Harley Psalter*, pp. 134–35, 137.

30   Noel, *The Harley Psalter*, pp. 136–37, quotation from 137.

31   It is unlikely that scribes and artists ever did so, except when annotating or adding to existing, bound books.

32   Richard Gameson, *The Role of Art in the Late Anglo-Saxon Church* (Oxford, 1995), p. 13.

(a precursor of the modern pencil) or some other hard point stylus, which left grooves in the vellum that could be drawn over in different coloured inks then enhanced with colour wash.[33] Scriptoria were accustomed to teamwork, sometimes with one person revisiting a section of the project, but often with different individuals contributing to what was eventually a finished page or quire, from pricking and ruling, to writing the text, to adding decorated initials, rubrication,[34] and corrections, and illustrating it.

The Harley Psalter made subtle modifications to Utrecht's drawings. All the Harley artists used ruled lines for buildings, whereas Utrecht's were drawn freehand.[35] As Martin Carver has shown, alongside "image fossils," representations of things in Utrecht that were already archaic, Roman in origin, the Harley artists made changes to both buildings and objects as they appeared in Utrecht, in some cases perhaps drawing on eleventh-century life, in others on more recent manuscript models.[36] Some artists were more inclined to alter Utrecht than others. Artist A (fols 1v–11v, 16r, 16v) in particular "demonstrates a dynamic involvement with the text," developing not only inanimate objects but also living creatures and spatial relationships.[37]

Two early eleventh-century artists, now known as Hands E and F, diverged from the drawings in the Utrecht Psalter, perhaps because that manuscript was unavailable when they were working or perhaps because a decision was made to be independent of it. Artist E, who added *tituli* to most of the text written so far (Quires 1–4 and 9),[38] inserted his rather crude, spikey drawings into spaces and made additions to existing illustrations, as well as illustrating folios

---

33   Judith Duffey stated that all the Harley drawings were first completely laid out in lead point, and subsequently inked by drawing over the lines, colour by colour, with a fine pen, not always following the layout lines precisely. They were completed using a broader pen and possibly a small brush for wider sweeps of colour; Duffey, "The Inventive Group," p. 20. Her generalisation about all drawings has since been modified; Noel, *The Harley Psalter*, pp. 33–36 states that there is clear evidence only for artist B that under-drawing in lead point was used consistently. Artist D2 used hard point for buildings and landscape. "There is, however, no indication that he used lead point or hard point to articulate his figures," ibid., p. 60. I have adopted Noel's alphabetical designations of the artists, which are slight modifications of those presented in Wormald, *English Drawings*, No. 34, pp. 69–70.

34   Insertion of headings and important letters in red.

35   Noel writes of Utrecht's "agitated impressionism that allowed wooden and stone structures to appear to be battling against a gale in the same way as the figures that crowd the landscape. In Harley by contrast, every architectural structure was executed using a straight edge." Noel, *The Harley Psalter*, p. 11.

36   M.O.H. Carver, "Contemporary Artefacts Illustrated in Late Saxon Manuscripts," *Archaeologia* 108 (1986), 117–145, quotation from p. 117.

37   Noel, *The Harley Psalter*, pp. 49–59.

38   Duffey, "The Inventive Group," pp. 209–10.

15v, 23v, 25v, 52v, and 61r–62v.[39] William Noel explains that Scribe 1, who wrote quires 10 and 11 (fols 58r–73v), did not follow the Utrecht Psalter in the placing of his text and that he wrote the text before the artist added the drawings.[40] Artist F, the main illustrator of quires 10 and 11 (Psalms 112 (113)–143 (144)),[41] following the layout set by Scribe 1, was therefore working with different spaces from the Utrecht artist. Some of his illustrations draw on models from elsewhere in Harley, and are thus in the Utrecht tradition; others appear to be original, and it is this work which is the focus of the second part of this chapter. His work has been tentatively dated to *c.* 1020.[42]

The central quires, 5–8 (fols 28r–49v), were added later. The scribe has been identified as Eadui Basan, a very experienced scribe identified by name from other manuscripts, probably working in his old age as his handwriting appears to have deteriorated, in the third or fourth quarter of the 11th century.[43] The artists who followed him in illustrating Quire 5 and three pages of Quire 6 were more faithful to the Utrecht Psalter than E and F had been, the former (G) illustrating only fols 28r and v, but also making many additions to the work of earlier artists. The later of the two (H; illustrating fols 29r–35r, after which there are no more drawings), probably working in the first half of the 12th century, develops the Utrecht drawings in a noticeably later style.[44]

Artist F and Dress

Freed from slavish copying of Utrecht, Artist F composed what are believed to be new images. The following discussion will consider these drawings and the manner and extent to which the artist used this freedom in depiction of the dress – and undress – of human figures, an aspect of F's work not previously considered.

---

39   His drawing has been identified on fols 10v, 15v, 25v, 53r, 58v, 61r, 61v, 62v, and, adding to the work of Artist F, on fols 67r, 70r, 70v, and 72v; Noel, *The Harley Psalter*, pp. 208–09, 212–13.

40   Noel, *The Harley Psalter*, pp. 76–77.

41   The psalms in medieval Psalters are conventionally numbered today with two sets of numerals. The first are the medieval numbers which correspond to the Vulgate and ultimately the Greek Psalter; the second are the ones used in most modern Protestant bibles, which follow the older Hebrew tradition. The Douai (Catholic) bible follows the Vulgate, Latin tradition. The differences are due to different ways of dividing certain psalms. Quotations from the psalms given here are from the King James Version.

42   Noel, *The Harley Psalter*, p. 138; Wormald had considered Artists E and F slightly later (1025–50); Wormald, *English Drawings*, pp. 69–70; Carver follows Wormald's dating, "Contemporary Artefacts," p. 121.

43   Noel, *The Harley Psalter*, pp. 137–39, 210–11.

44   Noel, *The Harley Psalter*, p. 140.

Artist F's drawings are among the more colourful in the manuscript.[45] While the earliest artists had generally used brown or black for human faces and hands, Artist F follows Artist D2, who had illustrated the previous quire, in depicting human skin – faces, hands, bare feet, and legs – in red, though applying this much more systematically than Artist D2 had done,[46] and sometimes drawing devils (59r, 72r) and 'wicked' figures (65v) in black, the colour-contrast directing the viewer to the morality of the image.

Like the other Harley artists, Artist F inherited certain conventions about clothing from Utrecht. God, Christ, and angels wear classical (Roman) clothing, an ankle-length, long-sleeved robe, the *tunica*, sometimes topped with a cloak, the *pallium*, which is worn asymmetrically, over the left shoulder and under the right arm. The Psalmist is depicted in a long *tunica* suggesting a status somewhere between the spiritual figures and the human. Other human garments are gendered, some male costumes probably monastic. Artist F had also inherited a semiotic use of nudity from the Utrecht Psalter and earlier Harley artists.

Nudity

Nudity is often used for children, indicating their vulnerability, though prosperous children, such as those on Harley fol. 14r (Artist C, following Utrecht fol. 14r) are clothed. In this case the Psalm 24 (25):13 says "His soul shall dwell at ease and his seed shall inherit the earth." The mother is making a donation into a large vessel from which items are being distributed to the poor. In contrast a bare-headed and -breasted woman on Harley fol. 56r (Artist D2, Utrecht 64r, Psalm 108 (109)) is a mourning widow. Her orphaned children are naked. In this case the lack of clothing is a convention indicating the misery of destitution.

Artist F develops the depiction of partial nudity to emphasise extreme poverty. At the bottom right of fol. 66v (Fig. 3.1) is a scene of charity, where a crowned king gives alms to the foremost of a group of men. The recipients are barefoot and barelegged, and appear to be huddled into the same kind of sleeveless garments as the men undergoing foot-washing to the left of the same illustration (see further below pp. 83–84). The foremost recipient is naked under this garment: he has bare buttocks, and a bare penis is faintly

---

45   Artists B and E are noticeably un-colourful, confining themselves to reddish-brown and
      black. Artist F works initially (fol. 58r) in red, blue, brown, and black-brown, then adding
      green (from fols 59r, 59v, 60r, 60v, 64r, 64v), after which the use of green is reduced to rare
      touches of colourwash (65v, 68v, 69r, 69v). From 71r green becomes more prominent and
      the use of blue is reduced. There is no blue at all on 72v–73v. These variations probably
      reflect the supply of inks available at particular times.

46   There are a few exceptions about faces, which occasionally appear in black, such as the
      foremost recipient on fol. 66v, Fig. 3.1.

populi   iniquitate manui fuaf.   hel

FIGURE 3.2   Harley 603, fol. 66r, Psalm 125 (126). Workers plough, sow and carry home the
                    harvest.
                    © The British Library Board

drawn, partly covered by the garment. He is supported by a crutch and bears
a large collecting bag, fastened by, when the image is enlarged, what appear
to be three knots with dangling threads.[47] The figures may have been inspired
by earlier Harley images. One possibility is a group of four figures of poor and
crippled men at fol. 8r (Artist A, copying Utrecht fol. 8r), who wear similar
upper garments and carry staffs, though they do not display nudity: they wear
tunics below the short garment, and shoes. Another possible source is a group
of three men facing the opposite way at fol. 57v (Artist D2, copying Utrecht fol.
65v), where the front figure is bare beneath the garment, but genitalia are not
indicated. These, and the collecting bag, hanging round the neck of Harley's
foremost beggar, are Artist F's innovations.[48]

47   At actual size they resemble animal tails or the tassels that today decorate Scottish spor-
      rans, which can be made of fur or horsehair.
48   The adaptation of the image by Artist F, and that of foot washing to the left, was proba-
      bly inspired by one of the ceremonies described in the *Regularis Concordia*, which took
      place on Maundy Thursday of Holy Week, in which the feet of an unspecified number of
      poor men were washed, they were offered water for their hands and fed, and money was
      distributed to them. The text specifies that the abbot should provide for the men. The
      depiction of a king is not consistent with the text, but might reflect actual practice. Duffey
      ("The Inventive Group," pp. 130–35) notes King Cnut's documented acts of charity and
      surmises that the ceremony, which is practiced in Great Britain today, of the monarch giv-
      ing money on Maundy Thursday, already existed in the eleventh century. The attendance
      of the monarch has certainly not been continuous, however, and the role was delegated
      from the seventeenth to early twentieth centuries.

In other cases Artist F's attention to anatomy makes it very clear that working men are bare beneath tunics: workmen bringing home the harvest (fol. 66r, Fig. 3.2) have garments which cling into the cleft between their buttocks, the result of sweaty work on a summer day;[49] a man ploughing with oxen wears a short tunic tucked up at the back. He is bare-legged and bare-bottomed, genitals visible. The ploughman is obviously very poor. The image relates to Psalm 125 (126):5 "They that sow in tears shall reap in joy."

This partial nudity sometimes gives other messages, however. At fol. 66v the upper illustration shows the building of what Psalm 126 (127):1 initially called a "house" and later a "city": "Except the Lord build the house, they labour in vain that build it: except the Lord keep the city, the watchman waketh but in vain" (Fig. 3.3).[50] The workmen are barefoot; some have tucked-up tunics and their buttocks are revealed, and the genitals of the right-hand workman dangle beneath the V of his tunic skirt, again demonstrating a lack of underwear. No doubt such labourers would not be rich, but the message of the partial nudity is not, here, poverty, rather it shows the vigour of their exertions by the minimalisation of their clothing. Tucked-up tunics are common for men doing physical work in other late Anglo-Saxon manuscript art, and in the Bayeux Tapestry, though sometimes the back of the tunic is shown covering the buttocks as in Harley fol. 2v (Artist A).[51] Artist F's emphasis on muscular buttocks and bare genitals is individual. At fol. 67r upper, Psalm 128 (129), it is wicked men torturing another who wear tucked-up tunics and show bare buttocks. They are engaged in vigorous activity, but the nudity here is perhaps not social observation so much as moral comment.

Apart from this last example, Harley's use of nudity is unlike that usually found in Anglo-Saxon art and literature, where it generally indicates sin, sexuality, or shame.[52] Though Harley's recipients of charity might conceivably feel shame at their poverty, they are not indicating embarrassment at their nudity by any gesture. The workmen of folio 66v evidently do not "labour in vain" since the Lord, his right hand raised in blessing, takes an eager interest in their

---

49   I am grateful to Christopher Monk for this observation.

50   The commentary in the British Library manuscript viewer is misleading in claiming the illustration is "Building the city of Jerusalem." The psalm refers to a generic building.

51   Gale R. Owen-Crocker, *Dress in Anglo-Saxon England: Revised and Enlarged Edition* (Woodbridge, 2004), p. 254. This partial nudity is very different from the sexualised nudity of monsters in late Anglo-Saxon art, see Christopher Monk, "A Context for the Sexualisation of Monsters in *The Wonders of the East*," *Anglo-Saxon England* 41 (2013), 79–99, esp. pp. 80–89.

52   See Catherine E. Karkov, "Exiles from the Kingdom: the Naked and the Damned in Anglo-Saxon Art," and Jonathan Wilcox, "Naked in Old English: the Embarrassed and the Shamed," both in *Naked Before God: Uncovering the Body in Anglo-Saxon England*, ed. Benjamin C. Withers and Jonathan Wilcox (Morgantown, 2003), pp. 181–220 and 275–309, respectively.

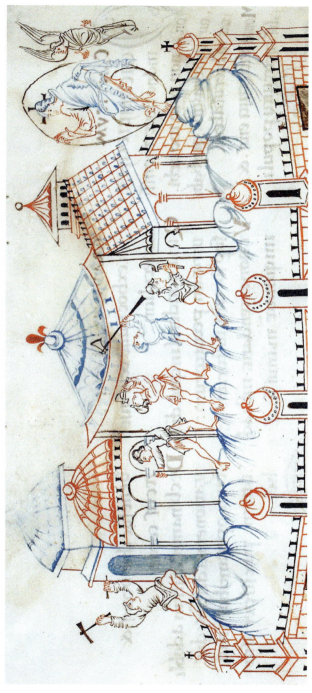

FIGURE 3.3   Harley 603, fol. 66v, upper, Psalm 126 (127). Building of a city.
© The British Library Board

work from a mandorla at the upper right of the image. Like the ploughman on fol. 66r, they demonstrate virtuous labour.

It is entirely possible that underwear was not common until later in the Middle Ages and that glimpses of private parts of the anatomy were not unusual in everyday life when men undertook vigorous physical activity. If so, however, the Utrecht Psalter artists and the other Harley artists preferred not to depict them. Artist F may have chosen to do so for subtle effect. I have suggested the nudity of Artist F's workman and ploughman emphasise the vigour of their masculine labour. Christopher Monk has previously taken a similar view of exposed male genitalia in the borders of the Bayeux Tapestry arguing that they convey "overt masculinity" and as such are "a metonymic commentary on the main register" of the Tapestry.[53]

As Christopher Monk has pointed out to me[54] the assumption that an artist-monk was unwaveringly spiritual is to ignore the evidence of monks composing penis riddles (for example Exeter Book Riddle 25, "Onion") and enjoying *double entendre* over a horn in Ælfric Bata's *Colloquies*. It is possible that the inclusion of sowing in the text of Psalm 125 (126) invited Artist F to draw a slightly salacious image. As Jonathan Wilcox has mentioned to me,[55] Exeter Book Riddle 2, "Plough" creates a sexualised image of ploughing and this may have been an accepted association. Indeed, quite apart from the phallic possibilities of the ploughshare pushing its way into the soil, the goad of the Harley scene is also angled suggestively,[56] though the hard-working ploughman himself is not particularly sexualised, despite his visible genitals.

---

53 Christopher Monk, "Figuring out Nakedness in the Borders of the Bayeux Tapestry," in *Making Sense of the Bayeux Tapestry: Readings and Reworkings*, ed. Anna C. Henderson with Gale R. Owen-Crocker (Manchester, 2016), pp. 54–74, quotations from pp. 56 and 69, respectively. There are always ambiguities, potential plural meanings, in the Bayeux Tapestry: the little figure in the lower border beneath Scenes 6–7, part of a hunting scene, whose genitals dangle below his tunic rather like those of the Harley workman, is directly underneath the capture of Harold by Guy of Pontieu. It is quite possible that the exposure reflects Harold's embarrassment at his situation, as well as a clash of machismos. The naked woodworker, in the lower border of Scene 15, has often been given a sexual interpretation by commentators, in relation to the enigmatic Ælfgiva, the unknown woman pictured above him to the right, as well as Monk's association of him with the forceful discussion going on between William and Harold above him to the left. The images are best seen in David Wilson, *The Bayeux Tapestry* (London, 1985), pp. 7, 17.

54 Personal communication 8 May 2020; also Christopher Monk, "Bedship and Sex-play: Sex and Sensuality in Early Medieval England," in *Sense and Feeling in Daily Living in the Early Medieval English World*, ed. Maren Clegg Hyer and Gale R. Owen-Crocker (Liverpool, 2020).

55 Personal communication 8 May 2020.

56 The goad is quite different from those in the ploughing scenes in the Anglo-Saxon Calendars in London, British Library, Cotton Julius A. vi and Tiberius B. v, where they are wielded by the ploughman's boy from in front of the oxen, at shoulder height.

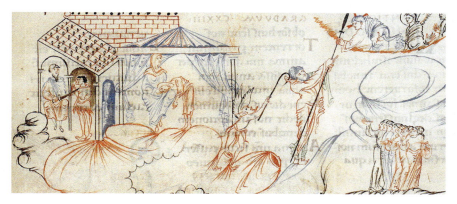

FIGURE 3.4   Harley 603, fol. 65r Psalm 122 (123). Left, a master touches his servant with a
sword, centre left a maid lays her head in her mistress's lap, centre right a devil
hooks the Psalmist who (right) receives a spear from God.
© The British Library Board

It is interesting that, although Artist F illustrated 25 folios, the three occur-
rences of bare genitals cluster entirely on two sides of a single leaf (fols 66r–v,
with the bare buttocks of the torturers on the following page, fol. 67r), giving
insight into the mind of the artist at a particular point in his working life. The
genitalia in all three cases are partially covered, and those of the workman
and the recipient of charity are drawn in a very pale shade of the red ink. If it
were not for the excellent digital photographs now available and the capacity
to enlarge them, these two examples might not be noticed at all, and that dis-
cretion cannot be accidental.[57] Yet these exposed private parts appear to be
very deliberately drawn, and the artist's attention to muscular bare buttocks is
noticeable. Artist F's mind was evidently running on masculine loins though
he used them semiotically to represent poverty and vigorous labour in his
interpretation of the psalms.

Male Underwear
Loin cloths were certainly familiar to the Anglo-Saxons: the Old English
words *gyrdels*, *underwrædel*, and *wædbrec* were all used for this concept.[58]
Artist F depicts a man with bare chest and loin cloth, carrying a basket at fol.
64v, Psalm 120 (121) upper, illustrating v. 8: "The Lord shall preserve thy going
out and thy coming in." Devils wear similar loin cloths, for example at fol. 65r
(Fig. 3.4, centre).

Artist F, uniquely in Anglo-Saxon art, also depicts long undergarments.
They can be found in both the ceremonies illustrated at the bottom of fol. 66v

---

57   They are not discernible in Ohlgren's black and white facsimile.
58   Owen-Crocker, *Dress*, p. 253 and note 75.

(Fig. 3.1). On the left is a Maundy scene, taking place in a building surmounted by a cross, indicating a church. One man in a cowled, sleeved robe, kneeling, washes the feet of another, while two more await the ceremony. The kneeling man probably represents an abbot, though as his portrait is unfinished there is no tonsure to confirm that he is a monk.[59] The middle, seated figure awaiting the washing of his feet wears a garment or garments which cover his legs but not his feet. The seated men are probably tonsured,[60] and they wear garments with cowls or hoods, so they are probably meant to be monks (though the front two are peculiar garments, without sleeves, poncho-like; in the case of the figure having his feet washed, his hand appears from beneath the garment). Duffey suggests the scene directly refers to a daily practice described in the *Regularis Concordia*, the rule book dated to *c*.973, issued for English monasteries at the Benedictine Reform.[61] The rear figure in the crowd of men receiving alms from the king at bottom right of the folio also wears the long-legged undergarment(s) (again under the poncho-like, cowled garment).

The Old English version of the Benedictine Rule indicates that monks' dress in the tenth century included *hosan* as well as socks (*meon* or *soccas*), and the *Indicia Monasterialia*, a manual of sign language for silent monks indicates that the *hosan* covered the lower legs;[62] the same text includes a mime for *brec*, "breeches" which involved making a gesture up the thighs with both hands.[63] On balance it seems more likely that the Harley figures wear breeches (joined like trousers) rather than individual stockings, since trousers had a long tradition in north-west Europe, from the Roman period to the Migration Age, at least.[64] Separate-leg hose are only known, according to present evidence, from later medieval times.[65]

---

59   Duffey, "The Inventive Group of Illustrations," pp. 132–34, suggests that the artist has adapted an image of Christ washing the disciples' feet, which would account for the unfinished head of the kneeling man (omitting Christ's halo) and the awkward right hand of the foremost figure (omitting Peter's gesture of raising his right hand to his head).

60   A flatness at the front of the head often suggests tonsure in the work of F, but the artist never paints the top of the head in red, always in the same colour as the hair.

61   This specifies a Maundy (service and footwashing) ceremony should take place in a specified place where three poor men from among those supported by the monastery should be washed and provided with food. The text implies that the beneficiaries would be secular men, but Artist F, in depicting cowled garments and tonsures, seems to have chosen to depict monks.

62   Owen-Crocker, *Dress*, pp. 256–57 and n. 83. Though "hose" came to mean a garment like a stocking, later still tights, we cannot be sure what the term meant to the Anglo-Saxons.

63   Owen-Crocker, *Dress*, p. 256 and n. 82.

64   Owen-Crocker, *Dress*, pp. 18, 115–17.

65   Later medieval hose consisted of single-leg stockings which sometimes had a strap under the foot and sometimes covered the foot; they were suspended from a belt worn under the tunic. See, for example Elizabeth Coatsworth and Gale R. Owen-Crocker, *Clothing the*

FIGURE 3.5   Harley 603, fol. 59v, lower, Psalm 116 (117). A group of seculars and possibly monks praise the Lord, depicted above right with angels.
© The British Library Board

Male Figures in Long Dress

In other cases, male figures in long garments depicted by Artist F may be monastic. For example on fol. 59v (lower), a group of men in long garments stand in front of a larger group which includes men in short secular dress and women (Fig. 3.5). Since one of the front figures has a garment with a collared effect which is perhaps a cowl, worn down, this group may, as Duffey suggest, represent monks.[66] This same collar is to be seen on the seated figures at fol. 68v (Fig. 3.6). Although the drawing is unlike the equivalent illustration of Psalm 132 (133) in Utrecht, both have the anointing of Aaron as central, and it may be relevant to the interpretation of Harley that Utrecht has groups of tonsured figures standing on either side of the anointing illustrating the "brethren [who] dwell together in unity" of verse 1. In Utrecht the "brethren" are conceived as monks so it is possible that the Harley figures are also ecclesiastics, though this is not clear except in one case. In Harley the "brethren" are depicted in the form of six men and a woman seated beneath a triangular roof.[67] They wear floor-length robes and shoes. The men may wear one

Past: Surviving Medieval Garments from Early Medieval to Early Modern Western Europe (Leiden, 2018), Bocksten Hose, pp. 281–82, Greenland Stocking, p. 185. Footed hose were sometimes supplied with leather soles, attached by shoemakers, a separate transaction from the purchase of the hose; Christine Meek, "*Calciamentum*: Footwear in Late Medieval Lucca," *Medieval Clothing and Textiles* 13 (2017), 83–105, at pp. 86, 88, 102. Joined hose came into fashion in the second half of the fourteenth century, in conjunction with the very short tunics condemned by moralists, Coatsworth and Owen-Crocker, *Clothing the Past*, p. 274.

66   Duffey, "The Inventive Group of Illustrations," p. 43.

67   This appears to be an original drawing, though there are plenty of examples in Harley and Utrecht of figures beneath triangular roofs – usually the gable ends of buildings rather

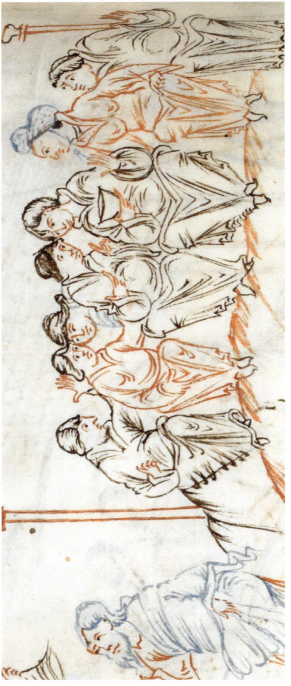

FIGURE 3.6   Harley 603, fol. 68v Psalm 132 (133). Left, partly shown, the anointing of Aaron, right, seated figures ("brethren") in a building, one of them female.

© The British Library Board

FIGURE 3.7   Harley 603, fol. 6or Psalm 117 (118). The "righteous".
© The British Library Board

garment over another – there are stylised rolls of cloth at the thighs which could be rucking up of one garment or the hem of an upper garment. The men's garments have V necks and a collared effect, and the sleeves fit loosely round the wrists. The central man, with a vessel in his right hand, holds his left arm up and there is a suggestion of a tighter inner sleeve. The necklines and collared effect suggest cowls, but only the figure at the right-hand side is clearly tonsured. (The woman is discussed below, pp. 96–98).

At fol. 6or the artist appears to use long robes for "the righteous,"[68] including two figures who have the roll collar (Fig. 3.7); in this case short tunics are worn by the enemies surrounding the Psalmist in the lower register. Long garments distinguish Moses, who with his rod, is about to lead the Israelites across the Red Sea, and his companion (perhaps his brother Aaron) from the other Israelites in medieval secular dress (Fig. 3.8). While early medieval artists do not strive for continuity in the modern sense,[69] and Artist F uses both long and short costumes for male Israelites at different times, he does in this case appear to use the contrast between short garments of ordinary men and the

---

than freestanding structures like this. The closest parallel is probably on fol. 53v (by Artist D2), a close copy of Utrecht fol. 62r, where four men are seated beneath the gable end of a building described on the Utrecht Psalter website as "a tabernacle."

68   Identified as such by Ohlgren, *Anglo-Saxon Textual Illustration*, p. 35, in reference to verse 15.

69   The composers of the narrative sequences in the Anglo-Saxon manuscript London, British Library, Cotton Claudius B. iv (the illustrated Hexateuch) and the Anglo-Norman Bayeux Tapestry do not colour the clothing of the same character the same way, even in consecutive scenes.

FIGURE 3.8   Harley 603, fol. 58r, lower, Psalm 113 (114–115). Moses and Aaron (?) lead the
               Israelites to the Red Sea.
               © The British Library Board

classical garments of the two prophets (dictated by convention) to show their
superior status.

The issue of who wore long garments and when, is complicated by the artistic convention of depicting seated figures in long clothing. Three crowned
"Princes" depicted in Fig. 3.9 wear shin-length garments, the one who is perhaps of highest rank, since he wears an arched, 'imperial' crown, distinguished
by a front panel to his gown; but a fourth seated man, to the right, who wears
a Phrygian hat and who perhaps represents the poor and needy made by the
Lord to sit with princes (v. 8) is also given a long garment.[70] The seated figures contrast with the group of men in tunics to the left of the composition,
whose skirts all stop well above the knee. King David, enthroned with his
harp at Fig. 3.10, also wears long garments in the conventional way of seated
kings in Anglo-Saxon art. In this case his cloak is looped through his shoulder
brooch, which is unusual but not unique in late Anglo-Saxon art[71] and is perhaps depicted here to indicate rank; and he wears unusual round segmented
headgear, which Ohlgren assumes to be a crown.[72] Men seated on the ground
at fol. 67v lower (Psalm 130 (131):1 "my heart is not haughty, nor mine eyes lofty",
Fig. 3.11) are depicted in longish tunics, though they are not obviously of high
rank. This seems to be attributable to the convention of depicting a seated

---

70   The 'imperial' crown is worn by the second man from the left, to whom all the others turn,
      and the only one not holding a sword. He is slightly taller than the others, his feet are
      daintily crossed, and his clothing is coloured differently. See Duffey, "The Inventive Group
      of Illustrations," pp. 109–10, where it is suggested that some kind of hierarchical ceremony
      is represented, the other figures demonstrating subjection to the superior king.

71   Owen-Crocker, *Dress*, p. 236 and p. 235, Fig. 195. This feature is not always a sign of rank.

72   Ohlgren, *Anglo-Saxon Textual Illustration*, p. 38.

FIGURE 3.9   Harley 603, fol. 58r, upper, Psalm 112 (113). Above, "Princes" and the poor made
to sit with them. Below, the barren woman given a home and made a joyful
mother of children.
© The British Library Board

FIGURE 3.10   Harley 603, fol. 68r Psalm 131 (132). King David, enthroned, flanked by a
woman and two armed men.
© The British Library Board

FIGURE 3.11   Harley 603, fol. 67v lower, Psalm 130 (131). Left, humble men seated on the
               ground. Right, a woman gives a ring to her departing son.
               © The British Library Board

figure decently clad, even though, in their humility, they do not sit on chairs
or thrones.

Male Figures in the Short Tunic and Its Accessories

Other male figures, workers, soldiers, by-standers, and the crowned king who
stands distributing alms (Fig. 3.1), are generally depicted in what is assumed
to be authentic medieval dress: a short tunic, often topped with a short cloak,
fastened on one shoulder, leaving the other arm free. Tunics appear to be worn
pouched over a belt or girdle at the waist. This is similar to tunics in other
late Anglo-Saxon manuscripts, but different from those in the Bayeux Tapestry,
which have belts or girdles in contrasting colours worn entirely over the tunics.

There are variations in the depictions of tunics. At Fig. 3.4, left, a seated
"master," in long garments, touches his "servant" with a sword. The servant's
tunic has a jagged edge which perhaps denotes a court entertainer.[73] The tunic
is sometimes tucked up at the sides for physical exertion, where the wearer is
usually barefoot, as at Fig. 3.3, which is common in late Anglo-Saxon manuscript art.[74] Unusually, a man waiting at table (Fig. 3.1) has a tunic tucked up at
one side only. He is not barefoot.

Men dressed in tunics normally wear shoes, but Artist F sometimes makes
footwear more prominent than other Harley artists. On fol. 70v the artist
includes flared upper edges on the ankle shoes; there and at fol. 67v (Fig. 3.11)

---

73   There is a similar tunic in the Bayeux Tapestry. There was a long tradition of entertainers
      wearing jagged-edged clothing; Gale R. Owen-Crocker, "Fools in the Bayeux Tapestry," *Text*
      42 (2014–15), 4–11.

74   Owen-Crocker, *Dress*, p. 254 and Figs 203–04.

a line or double line is drawn down the centre of the foot. This medial line, often found in other Anglo-Saxon art, may represent a seam, though surviving Anglo-Saxon shoes are not constructed this way.[75] More likely it represents ornament, since an embroidered vamp stripe has been found on some late Anglo-Saxon shoes.[76]

The leg clothing of male figures in short tunics is more problematic. The Utrecht Psalter, rather intermittently, adds sketchy parallel lines to the lower legs of some shod men, which could be interpreted as socks, gartering, or even the upper parts of boots.[77] The Harley artists, using colour, depict the legs of men mostly in brown-black or red, with the occasional blue, and follow Utrecht's use of the parallel lines, colouring them in the same shade as the outline of the legs, until Artist D2, at fols 55v and 57v, colours the lines in a different ink from the legs, making them appear like garter bands wound round the shins. On the same folio the artist draws some of the lines diagonally instead of horizontally. In support of the possibility that these parallel lines indicate garters, is a barefoot female figure on horseback, representing the vice *Superbia*, in the London, British Library, Additional 24199 version of Prudentius's *Psychomachia*, fol. 12r. The figure clearly wears garters wrapped round the leg and tied in a knot at the ankle.[78] Artist F, beginning at fol. 58r, continues to draw the lines diagonally, but, in contrast to D2, colours them the same as the legs, variously brown, red, blue, and green. In accordance with the principle that all the artists generally observe of using different colours for different garments, this would suggest that Artist F was not drawing separate garters but rather loose hose, which were bound to the leg with (unseen) garters at intervals that accordingly formed folds round the shins.[79]

---

75 Marquita Volken, *Archaeological Footwear: Development of Shoe Patterns and Styles from Prehistory till the 1600's* (Zwolle, 2014), p. 131 shows only one shoe type with front seam from this period: Oslo Style (1025–50).

76 Alexandra Lester-Makin, *The Lost Art of the Anglo-Saxon World: the Sacred and Secular Power of Embroidery* (Oxford, 2019), pp. 165–66, identifies two examples from London (both 1070s–1080s).

77 There are folios where no lines are drawn on the legs (for instance they do not appear until fol. 13v, and disappear again from 29r to 40r), images in which some men have them but others do not, and of course folios in which no men in this costume are depicted.

78 http://www.bl.uk/catalogues/illuminatedmanuscripts/ILLUMIN.ASP?Size=mid &IllID=60663 (accessed 17 December 2019). Male figures in the same picture wear similar leg coverings, but the lower extremities are concealed by their shoes.

79 Until the arrival of knitting in Western Europe in the later Middle Ages, wool and linen garments were woven and did not have the elasticity we take for granted today.

FIGURE 3.12   Harley 603, fol. 68v lower Psalm 133 (134). "… servants of the Lord … in the
                house of the Lord".
                © The British Library Board

Male Garments with Rolled Collar

A recurrent feature of dress in the hand of Artist F is a V-neckline with what looks like a rolled collar, indicated by pairs of lines at either side. Where a figure is seen from the side, this extends into a cowl or small hood at the back. Possibly Artist F took as his model a figure on fol. 51r (the work of Artist D2), in classical dress representing a father who "pitieth his children," Psalm 102 (103):13, where the folds of the pallium at the left neck are matched by an extra line on the tunic to the right of the neck. The effect of a collar was perhaps unintentional: Artist D2's image copies the original at fol. 59r of the Utrecht Psalter, where the extra line is clearly the edge of the beard meeting the neck, not a collar on the garment.

The majority of figures wearing this neckline in the work of Artist F wear long garments and may represent monks. The most sustained use of this detail is on the group[80] of seated figures at Fig. 3.6, who illustrate Psalm 132 (133):1 "Behold how good and how pleasant for brethren to dwell together in unity!" In the lower miniature on the same folio, depicting Psalm 133 (134), eight figures are seen against an arcaded building (Fig. 3.12). They illustrate v. 1: "… servants of the Lord, which by night stand in the house of the Lord," so are probably monks. One of them (third from the right) wears the collared costume. Possibly the second from the left does so also but his arm, in a wide sleeve, conceals part of his body. The other figures wear long garments, and two may have symmetrical cloaks, unfastened, over their shoulders.

---

80   There are seven heads but only six seated bodies.

The roll collar effect is also visible on the foremost of a group of bearded men, in long garments, standing in front of a larger group which includes men in short secular dress carrying spears and, in the background, women's heads, at Fig. 3.5. Since the collared effect on the garment of the front figure is perhaps a cowl, this group in long garments may, as Duffey suggest, represent monks.[81] The artist is perhaps choosing to represent variety by the dress of the combined group (male, female, soldier, cleric): the first verse of the short Psalm reads, "O praise the Lord all ye nations: praise him all ye people."[82] At Fig. 3.7, where Artist F appears to use long robes to indicate "the righteous," one figure in red at the front and another in green at the centre of the group have the roll collar. Again they could be monks, though they lack the characteristic tonsure. It is interesting that in several cases the figures in this dress are in the minority in their groups. Perhaps the artist is distinguishing rank in some way. The seated "brethren" of Fig. 3.6 are perhaps high-ranking monastics. On the other hand, the same roll collar/cowl effect can be seen on the men experiencing the washing of feet and receiving alms from the king at Fig. 3.1, one of the most original and interesting miniatures of Artist F (discussed above, pp. 83–84). The costumes suggest that the recipients of charity are wearing monastic clothing, different from the usual secular male costume, but in this context of receiving charity they are unlikely to be high ranking. Possibly these costumes might have been donned as part of a charitable ceremony,[83] but if so, I know of no written evidence of it.

Artist F occasionally used the collared/hood effect on the dress of what are clearly secular men in short tunics. Fig. 3.2, right, shows agricultural workers carrying sheaves and ploughing with oxen. They wear tunics with a slight cowled effect at the back. At Fig. 3.10, too, a tunic-clad man with spear to the right has a V neckline with double lines either side giving the effect of a roll collar. There is no independent evidence of a hooded tunic in Anglo-Saxon England, so possibly in these cases the extra lines and curls are simply decorative features of Artist F's style.

The artist also uses this hood or cowl effect in a way that is amusing, to the modern observer at least. In the centre right of Fig. 3.4 a bearded man in long garments (representing the Psalmist) looks and reaches up to God above, "our eyes wait upon the Lord our God, until that he have mercy on us" (Psalm 122 (123): 2), and God hands down a spear, presumably as a weapon of spiritual warfare to protect the man against evil and temptation, which the Psalm expresses

---

81   Duffey, "The Inventive Group of Illustrations," p. 43.

82   The Utrecht Psalter, fol. 67v, depicts the psalm quite differently, with four separate groups of secular men and the psalmist, centre, elevated on a rock, all looking up.

83   I thank Sarah M. Anderson for this suggestion.

as "for we are filled with contempt ... with the contempt of the proud" (vv. 3–4). The man's potential regression is presented graphically by a devil hooking the hood of the man's garment to pull him back.

Artistic Flourishes

Figures drawn by Artist F frequently have what appear to be strips of textile dangling from their garments, often executed in distinctive zig-zag pen strokes. They appear on different garments; for example, the pallium of Moses in Fig. 3.8, as extensions to cloaks worn by a seated king (Fig. 3.1) and an agricultural worker sowing seed (Fig. 3.2), and dangling from the poncho-like garment of a recipient of alms (Fig. 3.1). Similar flourishes appear in the work of other Harley 603 artists and ultimately derive from the Utrecht Psalter. When attached to women's sleeves (Figs 3.10, 13) they bear some resemblance to the streamers worn in the 14th century, commonly called "tippets" by costume historians, but they cannot logically belong to such a range of different garments. If they were real, fashionable dress, they would indicate conspicuous consumption of material; but as similar features appear on the costume of poor men receiving alms on fol. 66r, this is unlikely. Nor do they look like ragged edges of aged garments. They are probably decorative flourishes characteristic of the inherited style.

Women's Outer Garments

Women in Anglo-Saxon art are generally identifiable by their headdress, which covers all the hair, the sides of the face, and the neck and conceals the neckline of any garment worn underneath.[84] This is worn indoors and out, even (in art at least) in bed. Throughout the Harley Psalter most of the (infrequent) female figures wear the gendered costume of long garments and this headdress. Elsewhere in Anglo-Saxon art this is sometimes worn over a poncho- or chasuble-shaped cloak, itself worn over a longer gown[85] but, although it appears elsewhere in Harley (fol. 8r, Artist A), Artist F never depicts this cloak, always showing the headdress over a sleeved gown. Sometimes headdress and gown are depicted in different colours, showing clearly that they are different garments, for example at the right of Fig. 3.11 where a woman, seated underneath a building, gives a ring to her departing son. Sometimes, because the headdress and gown are shown in the same colours, it is possible that they belong to the same garment, for example at the costume of the foremost Israelite woman approaching the Red Sea, Fig. 3.8, though the strongly drawn

---

84   The only exception known to this author is the small figure fleeing a burning building in Scene 47 of the Bayeux Tapestry, whose headdress is tucked into the round neckline of her gown.

85   In some cases the head covering appears to be integral to the cloak.

FIGURE 3.13   Harley 603, fol. 71r Psalm 138 (139). The Three Marys at the Sepulchre.
© The British Library Board

lines suggest separate garments. It may be that the artist chose not to distinguish garments by colour when dealing with minor or subservient female figures: the illustration to Psalm 122 (123) v. 2 "... as the eyes of a maid to the hand of her mistress ..." depicts a seated woman (the mistress) in a blue gown with red headdress to the shoulders. Her maid, who bends over to lay her head at the hand of her mistress, in the mistress's lap, is dressed entirely in red (Fig. 3.4, centre left).

In what are probably the earliest examples from surviving Anglo-Saxon manuscript art, Artist F shows women's gowns with elongated sleeves. The Israelite woman at Fig. 3.8 wears a long gown with a long pointed sleeve, over a tighter inner sleeve. A queen seated at table on Fig. 3.1, identified as such by the crown worn over her headdress, wears a gown with an extended, narrow sleeve. A woman standing before King David (Fig. 3.10) appears to have a tippet dangling down from her arm, though this may be simply an artistic flourish as described above. At Fig. 3.6 a woman in unique costume – 'The woman in the blue hairnet' discussed in detail below – has long, pointed sleeves to her roll-collared gown. Fig. 3.13, which depicts the three Marys at the sepulchre, shows each woman with different, but elaborate sleeves, left to right, with a wide sleeve possibly decorated with a 'tippet,' in the centre long and narrow with 'tippet'-like ends and, on the right, narrow and pointed. Obviously wishing to distinguish the women from one another, the artist uses the sleeves to make his point.

Artist F does not show the woman's gown as belted, but, in accordance with the awareness of human anatomy he demonstrates in male figures (above, p. 80), he uses curved lines to indicate women's breasts beneath their garments. Other artists of Harley 603, like Anglo-Saxon artists elsewhere, show women's upper bodies in shapeless clothing which gives no indication of the shape

underneath. While Artist F may simply have been less inhibited about drawing female bodies than other artists, it is also possible that he was responding
to an increased sophistication in tailoring which led to better-fitting clothes.
Surviving garments from the 12th century have gores, which were inserted to
widen a garment to fit the contours of the body. They may have been known in
the 11th century.[86]

The Woman in the Blue Hairnet

The woman at Fig. 3.6 sits among the "brethren" in a gabled building, her feminine shape clearly indicated by curved lines, though there is nothing in the
accompanying psalm (132 (133)) to warrant the inclusion of a woman.

Like the "brethren" with whom she is pictured, the woman wears a garment with a V neck and collar, but there is a double line drawn round her neck
which may be the edging of another garment beneath, or a necklace. Her left
sleeve – the only one visible – is somewhat extended, and pointed. In drawing
the woman's head the artist appears to have first drawn her face, neck and part
of her head in red. Her headgear evidently came after, the blue line crossing
the red at her temple and at her chin where the garment is tied under her chin
with 2 strings and a looped knot. Her hair, eye, and the neck of an undergar-
ment (or necklace) were probably added later, in black. The blue headdress
is unique in Anglo-Saxon art. Although this artist does sometime use blue for
hair (as for Aaron to the left of the same Fig.) the woman has some dark hair
showing in the area of her left ear, so the blue area is clearly a head covering,
not hair. Duffey describes it as "an elongated blue double-ended hat."[87] Faint
lines, and other marks in blue upon it, could represent embroidery, but it looks
more like a hairnet. Her face is drawn in profile and the headdress bulges high
on the top of her head and also slightly at the back of her head, but perhaps
the artist is rather awkwardly depicting a hairnet over hair which is flat in the
middle and bunched either side. (This artist favours for men a hairstyle parted
and flat in the middle and rather wide at the sides.)

Hairnets of knotted silk mesh have been found in Viking archaeological contexts from eleventh- and twelfth-century Ireland, and it is very likely that this
fashion was known in Anglo-Viking England, though the earliest finds from

---

86   Olivier Renaudeau has suggested gores are depicted in men's skirts in the Bayeux Tapestry,
      which is probably late eleventh-century; "The Bayeux Tapestry and Its Depiction of
      Costume: the Problems of Interpretation," in *The Bayeux Tapestry: Embroidering the Facts
      of History: Proceedings of the Cerisy Colloquium* (1999), ed. Pierre Bouet, Brian Levy, and
      François Neveux (Caen, 2004), pp. 237–59, at 238–39.
87   Duffey, "The Inventive Group of Illustrations," p. 72.

London are thirteenth-century.[88] Possibly the hair was first plaited, bunched, or knotted close to the head, then a hairnet was tied over it.[89] The mesh covering may have been worn underneath the formal swathed headdress, and pins used to secure that headdress were probably buried into the mound of netted hair.[90] Perhaps, despite artistic conventions, in reality the voluminous headdress was removed indoors, and Artist F is giving us a rare glimpse of how a woman really appeared in such a context.

The woman is prominently positioned next to the man with a chalice, and is the tallest figure in the group. The man to her left is slightly behind her, but her arm is behind that of the man with the chalice. The implication of the position is that she is a prominent member of the group but not the most senior. She leans towards the central figures and faces them, appearing to be eager to engage with them, though they lean towards one another, heads together, and do not look at her. She is with them but not quite of them. She does not wear a crown, therefore is not being signalled as a queen.[91] The lack of crown makes it unlikely that the visit of Ælfgifu-Emma and Harthacnut to Christ Church, Canterbury in 1023 (see above, pp. 73–75) is being represented here. Duffey suggests that the woman might be an abbess or a prominent secular person, who in view of the proposed interpretation of other scenes by Artist F as referring to contemporary royalty, may be a member of the royal house.[92] It would be strange if an abbess were not depicted in a veil, since this was the characteristic dress of nuns.[93] There may have been visits to the male monastic establishments by prominent women which were important to the community and

88   Cynthia Myers, "Hairnet," in Gale R. Owen-Crocker, Elizabeth Coatsworth, and Maria Hayward, *Encyclopedia of Medieval Dress and Textiles of the British Isles c. 450–1450* (Leiden and Boston, 2012), pp. 261–62.

89   This hairstyle could be found in Denmark and among ex-patriate Danish women up to the middle of the twentieth century; personal communication from Maren Clegg Hyer.

90   Seamus Ross notes that (earlier) pins from Barking Abbey are gilded only for about 2 mm of their length, suggesting that the lower part of the shaft was not intended to be seen, perhaps embedded in the headdress [or hair]. Simple pins increase considerably from the late Anglo-Saxon period and were evidently mass-produced; Seamus Ross, "Dress Pins from Anglo-Saxon England: Their Production and Typo-chronological Development," D.Phil thesis, University of Oxford, 1991, respectively, pp. 124, 149.

91   Though Ælfgifu-Emma does not wear a crown in the illustration of her in London, British Library, Stowe 944, fol. 6r, despite being identified there as "Regina," http://www.bl.uk/manuscripts/Viewer.aspx?ref=stowe_ms_944_f006r (accessed 27 July 2019).

92   Duffey, "The Inventive Group of Illustrations," p. 151, though making a case for Emma at pp. 168–9, which is taken up by Olsen, "'He has given birth'," p. 99.

93   Though again there is precedent in the seal of Godgitha, described as "a nun dedicated to God" but depicted bare-headed; Backhouse *et al.*, *Golden Age*, pp. 113–14, No. 112; Owen-Crocker, *Dress*, pp. 219–20, 225.

to Artist F, but record of which do not survive. The woman's identity remains a mystery.

An Enveloping Veil

The lower image on Fig. 3.9 is of a seated woman hugging children, within a building. The reference is to Psalm 112 (113):9 "He [the Lord] maketh the barren woman to keep house, and to be making her a joyful mother of children." Her headdress and lower garment are blue, but over her shoulders and upper body she wears a brown garment, which wraps round her arms and dangles down in the characteristic extensions, like wings helping to enclose the naked children on either side of her. The brown item is implausible as a garment, and seems to be a hybrid of a wrap round her shoulders, and a wrap extended across the front of her body. The artist perhaps took inspiration from the veils sometimes used in the medieval Church to cover the hands as ecclesiastics handled sacred objects. In the Roman Catholic Church today the humeral veil is worn round the shoulders and hanging down over the arms.[94] Though no doubt women did use rectangles of cloth to wrap babies and children, this illustration, which shows a woman enclosing six small children in her embrace, is unrealistic and so is the veil she employs.

Conclusion

Artist F draws in a style that harmonises with that of his predecessors, even copying individual images though not whole pictures. His compositions are his own, and he appears to include rituals and events consistent with monastic life in his own time. His superior observation and depiction of human anatomy makes for a development of both semiotic male nudity and the depiction of female dress. Changes of female fashion are suggested by his drawings: an absence of the poncho-type cloak, more fitted gowns, the use of a hairnet, and the development of exaggerated sleeves. Artist F demonstrates that extended sleeves, which were to become fashionable for men as well as women in the twelfth century,[95] were already known as early as the first half of the 11th century.[96]

---

94 For a discussion of humeral veils see Elizabeth Coatsworth's account of the possible example from Maaseik in Coatsworth and Owen-Crocker, *Clothing the Past*, pp. 341–43.

95 Margaret Scott, *Medieval Dress and Fashion* (London (paperback edition), 2009), pp. 40–56.

96 They also appear in later eleventh-century Anglo-Saxon manuscript art and in the Anglo-Norman Bayeux Tapestry; Owen-Crocker, *Dress*, pp. 214–15; Gale R. Owen-Crocker, "The

Male dress in art continues to be driven by the conventions of 'classical' garments for holy figures, long garments for seated figures, and short tunics for others, but the artist shows cowled, poncho-type garments worn by recipients of charity, and the irregular appearance of the tonsure on his figures makes it uncertain whether these were monks or secular dependants of the monastery, or a mixture of both. Some of the recipients of benefit wear long undergarments beneath the poncho-type garment and this is not seen in conjunction with other clothing types. A V-necked style is depicted on different male garments and one female, accompanied by a roll collar, perhaps another innovation of the 11th century. Unusual variations are the tunic hitched up at only one side, different from the common double-hitched skirts that go with bare feet and vigorous physical effort, and a tunic with a jagged edge which might belong to an entertainer.

Although Artist F sometimes simply duplicated drawings of figures, distinguishing them only by colour (see for example the women, and the two rear men at Fig. 3.8), in other cases he used costume variation to distinguish them, as in the case of the three Marys (Fig. 3. 13) and the occasional figures in rolled collars among groups of men in different styles (Figs 3.5, 7, 12).

Some of his details may be unrealistic, mere artistic flourishes, particularly some of the 'tippets' (but perhaps not all of them) and the little curls at the back of a garment which are suggestive of a hood or cowl, but which may be misleading to the modern eye. Bareness to the point where genitalia were visible is surprising in a culture which did not celebrate nudity in art, and may be more semiotic than realistic, sometimes as indication of turpitude, sometimes showing social rank, but sometimes, as in the case of the ploughman, perhaps indicating that poverty did not mean a person was undeserving of God's favour.

However, in depicting anatomically vivid figures, and features of costume that were, perhaps taken from his own observation, Artist F brought the Harley Psalter up to date, suggesting that depiction of contemporary dress fashion was not incompatible with the use of a holy book used for worship, whether that was for learning, study, meditation, or for lections in church.

Acknowledgements

I am grateful to Sarah Anderson, Christopher Monk, and Jonathan Wilcox for reading a draft of this paper and making helpful suggestions, particularly appreciated since it was completed in lockdown conditions in 2020–21.

Significance of Dress in the Bayeux Tapestry," *Medieval Clothing and Textiles* 13 (2017), 1–30, at p. 26.

CHAPTER 4

Adorning Medieval Life: Domestic and Dress Textiles as Expressions of Worship in Early Medieval England

Maren Clegg Hyer

I had long quoted Betty Coatsworth's publications before, as a young graduate student, I met her one fateful morning at the International Congress on Medieval Studies, in Kalamazoo, Michigan. I expected to meet a great scholar, and I did, but also one generous and kind, from the cafeteria table to the conference session. Her contributions to scholarship have influenced my research at every turn; her friendship has been just as important a gift. It is a privilege to contribute to this collection in her honour.

∴

Introduction

In her 2007 article "Cushioning Medieval Life: Domestic Textiles in Early Medieval England," Elizabeth Coatsworth highlights the ubiquitous role of domestic textiles in dressing the early medieval English world in soft furnishings.[1] Textiles, both domestic and dress, played a similarly ubiquitous role as expressions of worship among the members of the early medieval English Church, in both expected and surprising ways. Expected expressions of worship might include donation of domestic and elaborate dress textiles either re-purposed or created for monastic and ecclesiastical use, donations attested widely in significant numbers within the period in wills, monastic and ecclesiastical inventories, and histories, as well as the archaeological record. Rejection of the same finery in the religious or secular context could prove an equally standard expression of worship, as hagiographical sources highlight. Surprisingly, however, a smaller number of worshippers found expression for their devotion in a celebration of textile finery, and not only when it decorated

---

[1] Elizabeth Coatsworth, "Cushioning Medieval Life: Domestic Textiles in Anglo-Saxon England," *Medieval Clothing and Textiles* (2007), 1–12.

altar, church, or priest. Two such examples occur in the works of Byrhtferth of Ramsey and William of Malmesbury. This chapter will first contextualize and offer examples of the more common expressions of worship through textile art, and then examine counterexamples in the works of these two authors.

Textiles as Expression of Worship

There may be some today who underestimate the profound need for textiles in a worship environment, but the early medieval English did not. Whether it be for the clerics, monks, or nuns who inhabited religious foundations, or the church and its worshippers, each religious group and space needed soft furnishings and fabrics for a variety of functions. Wills of early medieval English women (largely seculars) attest what kinds of textiles they collected for their homes: bedding, wall hangings, tablecloths, napkins, and cushions. In her will (written between 984 and 1016), for example, Wulfwaru leaves *anes heall-wahriftes. ꝿ anes beddreafes* ("a hall-hanging and some bed-clothing"), as well as *anes heallreafes. ꝿ anes burreafes, mid beodreafe. ꝿ mid eallum hræglum swa ðerto gebyreð*[2] ("a hall-hanging and a bedroom-hanging, with a tablecloth, and with all the cloths which belong with it") to her sons. Wills likewise mention clothing. In the will of Æthelgifu (written between 980 and 990) she leaves her *rotostan cyrtel* ("brightest gown") to one recipient, her *blæwenan cyrtel ... neaþene unrenod / ꝿ hire betstan heafodgewædo* ("blue gown ... unadorned at the bottom and her best head-dresses") to a second, *.iii. godwebbenan cyrtlas* ("three silk/purple gowns") to others, and to one less favored, *oðera hire dunnan cyrtla* ("some of her other, dun-coloured gowns").[3]

The same types of furnishings and textiles left to the families of early medieval English women could likewise decorate the ecclesiastical world, and in fact, the same wills reference just such bequests. Alongside the textiles left to her family, Wulfwaru leaves to St Peter's monastery at Bath *anes mæssereafes mid eallum þam ðe ðærto gebyreð. ꝿ anes hricghrægles þæs selestan þe ic hæbbe. ꝿ anes beddreafes mid wahryfte ꝿ mid hoppscytan. ꝿ mid eallum þam þe þærto gebyreð*[4] ("a mass-vestment with all that belongs with it, and the best mantle that I have, and bed-clothing with a hanging and a curtain and with all that

---

2   "The Will of Wulfwaru," *Anglo-Saxon Wills*, ed. D. Whitelock (New York: 1930; 1973), p. 64, ll. 16, 17. All translations are the author's, unless otherwise indicated.

3   *The Will of Æthelgifu*, ed. D. Whitelock and N. Ker (Oxford, 1968), ll. 7, 45, 47–49. Dorothy Whitelock argues that although *godwebbe* can also mean fine cloth such as silk or luxurious weaves of wool, it can also mean "purple" (note, *The Will of Æthelgifu*, p. 12).

4   "Will of Wulfwaru," pp. 62–63, ll. 20–23.

belongs with it"). In addition to the clothing listed above, Æthelgifu donates her *betste wahrift* ("best wall-hanging") and *betste setrægl* ("best seat-cover") to St Albans for the souls of herself and her husband.[5]

Considering that the celebration of the mass alone, according to the ninth-century *Collectanea pseudo-Bedae*, would require mass-vestments that could include an ephod or superhumeral (often identified as the amice), a tunic (often identified with the alb), a girdle, a maniple, a stole, a dalmatic, and a chasuble,[6] as well as an altar cloth, such textile donations from women to the Church would have been necessary and most welcome expressions of art and worship.

Early medieval English people, often women, as those most likely to be the means of production, answered the need with significant effort. Wulfwaru and Æthelgifu were not alone in their donations as worship; at Ely, for example, even after Norman depredations at the Conquest, the inventory of ecclesiastical textiles included forty chasubles, fifty-two albs, over fifty amices, five dalmatics, seven tunicles, seventeen stoles, thirty-three copes, eleven palls, forty-three cloaks, fifty hangings, fifty bench-covers, two altar tapestries, four other tapestries, and six sets of priestly vestments and seven deacons' vestments, many worked in gold, silver, and embroidered threads.[7] Ely's inventory is one of many, and so perhaps it is unsurprising that two of the very few sets

---

5   *Will of Æthelgifu*, l. 7.

6   *Collectanea Pseudo-Bedae* (Scriptores Latini Hiberniae 14), ed. Martha Bayless and Michael Lapidge (Dublin, 1998), pp. 174–77. In collections roughly contemporary to the *Collectanea*, Hrabanus Maurus and Amalarius of Metz expound on symbolism of priestly vestments in similar ways, Hrabanus identifying the tunic as the alb, and the ephod as the amice (see Maureen C. Miller, *Clothing the Clergy: Virtue and Power in Medieval Europe, c. 800–1200* (Ithaca, NY, 2014), pp. 56–59). For an extensive discussion of priestly vestments as they developed across early and later medieval Europe, with greater regulation and similarity by the later Middle Ages, see Miller, p. 15.

7   *Liber Eliensis: The History of the Isle of Ely*, 2.114, ed. and trans. Janet Fairweather (Woodbridge, 2005), pp. 234–35. Similar lists can be found in Thomas of Marlborough's *History of the Abbey of Evesham*, ed. Jane Sayers and Leslie Watkiss (Oxford, 2003), pp. 156–57. Although donors are not always listed in the lengthy inventories, and some textiles were likely to be produced locally in ecclesiastical foundations or associated workshops on their estates, some donations come with attributions. For example, the *Liber Eliensis* documents gifts made by Queen Ælfgifu shortly after her marriage to King Cnut (1017), with items donated *sanctis nostris* ("to our saints") such as *pannum sericum ... auro et gemmis intextum* ("silk cloth ... interwoven with gold and gems"); *Liber Eliensis*, ed. E.O. Blake (London, 1962), 2.79, p. 149. Translations mine. Fiona J. Griffiths traces the trend more widely across early and later medieval England and the Continent; "'Like the Sister of Aaron': Medieval Religious Women as Makers and Donors of Liturgical Textiles," in *Female "vita religiosa" between Late Antiquity and the High Middle Ages: Structures, Developments and Spatial Contexts*, ed. Gert Melville and Anne Müller (Vita regularis, Abhandlungen 47) (Berlin, 2011), pp. 343–74.

of textiles that survive from the period in the archaeological record mirror the inventories and include fine embroideries created, donated, and then used as religious clothing. The first set is comprised of composite textiles, a (so-called) *casula* ("chasuble") and a *velamen* ("veil" or "altar cloth") at Maaseik, Belgium. Associated traditionally (but improbably) with two eighth-century English sisters, St Harlindis and St Relindis, the textiles are comprised of multiple fragments of luxury fabrics and embroidered and tablet-woven strips, some of which, according to Mildred Budny and Dominic Tweddle, "originated in southern England and date from the late eighth century or the early ninth."[8] The early medieval English sections of embroidery were worked in gold and silk and adorned with blue and green glass beads, pearls, copper bosses, and threads of several colours: red, beige, green, yellow, light blue, and dark blue.[9] However the early medieval English fabrics ended up in the composite vestments (thought to have been assembled at a later point), it is clear they were products of early English hands; textiles used and reused for ecclesiastical worship, they later became themselves relics, object of worship, and highly studied works of art.

The second group of textiles are the Cuthbert embroideries at Durham. This group includes parts of a matching stole and maniple donated by King Athelstan to the shrine of St Cuthbert at Chester-le-Street in 934. Athelstan himself did not make or commission the majority of these embroidered textiles. Instead, a donation statement stitched on the back of both the maniple and the stole indicates that they were created between 909 and 916, either by the hands of, or more likely, at the commission of Athelstan's stepmother, Ælfflæd: *ÆLFFLÆD FIERI PRECEPIT ... PIO EPISCOPO FRIÐESTANO* ("Ælfflæd had this made / for holy Bishop Friðestan"). That both Ælfflæd and Athelstan considered donation of such luxury textiles a "high" form of worship is indicated in having commissioned and gifted (or re-gifted, if the textile was ever given and then taken back from Friðestan) the textiles as a "royal" donation to a powerful ecclesiast. They knew the gold-embroidered items would be considered impressive objects of art, as well as objects intended for worship. These factors made certain the donation was remembered and honoured, then

---

8   "The Early Medieval Textiles at Maaseik, Belgium," *The Antiquaries Journal* 65 (1985), 353–89 at p. 366.

9   M. Budny and D. Tweddle, "The Maaseik Embroideries," *Anglo-Saxon England* 13 (1984), 65–96. There is a third item often associated with the group, a later medieval *velamen* of indeterminate origin. I leave it out of the discussion for obvious reasons. I discuss these textiles in much greater detail in "Recycle, Reduce, Reuse: Imagined and Re-imagined Textiles in Anglo-Saxon England," *Medieval Clothing and Textiles* 8 (2012), 49–62 at pp. 53–55 and Figs 3.2 and 3.3.

and now. A third item in the group, commonly known as Maniple II, is also a repurposed and highly beautiful textile, as Elizabeth Coatworth's examination of its construction suggests: it is a long, reversible, gold-embroidered band cut in half and stitched into the shape of a maniple at a later date, deriving, as she argues, from a prior, luxury garment.[10] Whether the work of secular or religious women at home or in workshops, or the gift of secular or religious men and women, as all these options are both likely and possible,[11] the impact of such beautiful, colourful, and luminescent textile gifts on the experience of worship, whether the priest's or the congregation's, should also not be underestimated.

Stephen of Ripon, an early contemporary of Bede, speaks with appreciation in describing donations of Bishop Acca to the church at Ripon, with its *magnolia ornamenta huius multiplicis domus de auro et argento lapidibusque pretiosis*

10   See "Text and Textile," in *Text, Image, Interpretation: Studies in Anglo-Saxon Literature and its Insular Context in Honour of Éamonn Ó'Carragáin*, ed. A. Minnis and J. Roberts (Turnhout, 2007), pp. 187–207. I discuss this set of textiles in additional detail in "Recycle, Reduce, Reuse," pp. 49–51, 53, 57, and Figs 3.1 and 3.4. Hero Granger-Taylor argues that some of the fragments of braids and silk among the textiles found with Cuthbert may have formed part of a dalmatic. If so, the surviving Durham collection is comprised of even more repurposed and donated luxury ecclesiastical textiles, as early record of the donation suggests; see "The Weft-Patterned Silks and Their Braid: The Remains of an Anglo-Saxon Dalmatic of c. 800?", in *St. Cuthbert, His Cult and His Community to AD 1200*, ed. Gerald Bonner, David Rollason, and Clare Stancliffe (Woodbridge, 1989), pp. 303–27.

11   It is important to keep these options in mind, as donated textiles could have been made in workshops for religious monastic communities by women religious or by lay women who worked at estates that belonged to religious communities, or by women who worked as part of a secular estates, or by women who worked independently in any of these contexts. These women might have and probably did include all social classes, from slave to royalty, and had greater or lesser say in the end result of their labours. The commissioners of the donated textiles could range equally widely and include donors of any gender. For evidence of textile work among communities of women religious, see the analysis of relevant finds at the community at Whitby in Penelope Walton Rogers, "In Search of Hild: A Review of the Context of Abbess Hild's Life, her Religious Establishment, and the Relevance of Recent Archaeological Finds from Whitby Abbey," Chapter 5 in this volume. For examples of secular estate and town workshops, see the story of St Dunstan and Æthelwynn; Author B, in *Memorials of Saint Dunstan, Archbishop of Canterbury*, ed. William Stubbs (Rerum Britannicarum Medii Aevi Scriptores 63) (London, 1874; 1965), pp. 20–21; and the remarks of Byrhtferth in the life of St Oswald, respectively. In Byrhtferth's account, the death of the saint occasions calamitous interruption of the events of daily life, including merchants leaving the market and women their *colos et opus textrinum* ("distaffs and the work of the weaver's area/workshop"); *Byrhtferth of Ramsey: The Lives of St Oswald and St Ecgwine*, ed. and trans. Michael Lapidge (Oxford, 2009), pp. 194–95. Translations for Byrhtferth by Lapidge unless otherwise indicated. Here, the translation is mine. Additional evidence for workshops in both contexts is discussed in Alexandra Lester-Makin's magisterial *The Lost Art of the Anglo-Saxon World: The Sacred and Secular Power of Embroidery* (Oxford and Philadelphia, PA, 2019), pp. 119–20.

et quomodo altaria purpura et serico induta decoravit, quis ad explanandum sufficere potest? ("splendid ornaments of gold, silver, and precious stones; but of these and of the way he decorated the altars with purple and silk, who is sufficient to tell?").[12] Aldhelm shares a similar response to an altar cloth at the church of St Mary in Malmesbury, *Aurea contortis flavescunt pallia filis, / Quae sunt altaris sacri velamina pulchra* ("a golden cloth [which] glistens with its twisted threads and forms a beautiful covering for the sacred altar").[13] Such "purple," golden, and silken altar cloths, colourful and gleaming by candlelight, would clothe the central focal point of each worship space, the altar, inviting attention to, reverence for, and contemplation of heavenly glory for lay and ecclesiastical participants of services of worship.

Vestments worn while conducting the mass would play a similar role in the experience of worship, and they receive similar attention and reverence in descriptions of the period. In the eleventh century, Goscelin of St Bertin describes a white alb that had been attributed to the hands of St Edith (Eadgyth), a West-Saxon nun of the late tenth century. Waxing eloquent, he lauds the work as, *praestantissimam auro, gemmis, margaritis ac perulis Angligenis a summo contextam ... circa pedes aureas apostolorum ymagines Dominum circumstantes* ("the most excellent, with gold, gems, pearls, and small English pearls embroidered at the top ... [and] near the feet, golden images of the apostles standing around the Lord").[14] The language Goscelin uses to characterize the work of Eadgyth suggests that he considered "that the making of sacred vestments was itself a form of spirituality, a meditation on Christ and praise of him."[15]

The contrasts of white with gems, gold, and pearls on those celebrating and perhaps officiating during the mass would be striking, and just as the colourful and gold-adorned altars and altar cloths would do, such ecclesiastical clothing would rivet the attention of the celebrants on the host and priest alike in a moment of reverence and worship. It is not impossible to imagine what such an alb would look like; in many respects, Goscelin's description

---

12   *The Life of Bishop Wilfrid by Eddius Stephanus*, trans. Bertram Colgrave (Cambridge, 1985), pp. 46–47. Although Colgrave names the author as Eddius Stephanus, the more likely author is Stephen of Ripon.

13   Latin text from *Aldhelmi Opera*, ed. Rudolfus Ehwald (Monumenta Germaniae Historica, Auctorum Antiquissimorum 15) (Berlin, 1919), p. 18. Translation from Michael Lapidge and James L. Rosier, "Carmina Ecclesiastica," *Aldhelm: The Poetic Works* (Cambridge, 1985), p. 49.

14   *Le Légende de Sta. Edith en prose et verse par le moine Goscelin*, ed. André Wilmart (Analecta Bollandiana 56) (1938), p. 79. I am indebted to C.R. Dodwell, *Anglo-Saxon Art* (Ithaca, NY, 1982), pp. 261–62, n. 103, for this reference and others cited in the original in this section.

15   Miller, *Clothing the Clergy*, p. 149.

mirrors the pearl-adorned, heavily embroidered textiles of Maaseik and the gold-embroidered Durham vestments. The Durham vestments, in particular, retain enough of their original brightness and hue to give some sense of how they might have appeared, depicting Old Testament prophets and Christian symbols. Each figure was embroidered in brightly-coloured silks and gold-wrapped thread. Panels had matching tablet-woven braids made from the same materials, brocaded in "silver-gilt thread."[16] Though the colours have faded today, Mrs A.G.I. Christie describes the visual impact for its viewers in both tenth-century and twentieth-century Durham:

> Draperies were coloured purple-red and green, both tints occurring on the same vestment. Hair, usually worked in fawn striped with purple-red and green, was sometimes executed in blue and white lines. Faces were pale fawn, with the features outlined in a deeper tint. Some of the foliage was in purple-red, pink and sage green, a line of each colour being worked in succession ... The letters ... were in either myrtle green or pale purple-red ... These colours have now perished, and the embroidery is of a warm brown tint which varies slightly in depth in different parts of the design.[17]

Such beautiful textiles, without doubt, acted as both visual symbol of and invitation to worship for both priests and congregants. The textiles' presence at the altar at the celebration of mass might have carried additional significance in the worship of the women of early medieval England; though forbidden in some cases from approaching the altar, they might still approach and express reverence through the beautiful, glowing works of their hands, or works commissioned at their hands.[18]

---

16   Grace M. Crowfoot, "The Tablet-Woven Braids," in *The Relics of Saint Cuthbert*, ed. C.F. Battiscombe (Oxford, 1956), p. 433.

17   *English Medieval Embroidery* (Oxford, 1938), p. 47.

18   Miller, *Clothing the Clergy*, makes this point eloquently (see pp. 142–53). As she states, "From the ninth century, ecclesiastical legislation prohibited women from physically entering the church sanctuary and approaching the altar" (p. 145), and yet, women worked and donated many of the textiles, luxurious and otherwise, that clothed ecclesiastical environments, often as an expression of women's artistry and reverence. See powerful arguments about women's insertion of themselves at the altar through similar textile donations across the period in Griffiths, "Like the Sister of Aaron," pp. 343–34. The black stone line in Durham Cathedral (behind which medieval women were required to stand to worship) is a salient reminder of their absence near the centre points of worship, the textiles donated to Cuthbert, their presence.

Statues are another form of invitation to devotional worship that were clearly part of the early medieval English Church,[19] and here, textiles might also play an important role as expression of worship by donation.[20] One example is the offering of Gytha, the wife of Tovi, one of King Cnut's Anglo-Danish retainers, who dressed a life-size statue of Christ discovered at Waltham with her gem- and gold-encrusted girdle as an act of reverence before God when it was placed near the church's altar.[21] Similar adornment of statues of St Mary, St John, and local saints (see note 20) must have visually augmented other focal points of worship, as well, rendering conspicuous and enhancing the visual experience of worship and inviting veneration of the figure of God and other holy figures.

It is notable that these "high art" textiles as expressions of worship are accompanied by perhaps more prosaic textiles, as earlier referenced: used domestic wall hangings, napkins, and seat covers were also donated to church and abbey as expressions of worship, in the case of Æthelgifu, her very best textile hanging and seat cover being donated for the good of her soul and that of her husband.[22] How might such domestic textiles, as gifts produced by secular or ecclesiastical worshippers, have been considered an expression of worship? Just as mass vestments and altar cloths were quite obviously needed for purposes of the Church, so robes and other daily clothing for clerics, nuns, or monks; towels and blankets for ecclesiastical dormitories; and soft furnishings for a cold, stone or wood church structure would have eased the way of God's servants and paved the way for ecclesiastical work to continue. Byrhtferth certainly saw them in such a way, as I will discuss. All must have proven welcome

---

19   See Elizabeth Coatsworth, "Cloth-making and the Virgin Mary in Anglo-Saxon Literature and Art," in *Medieval Art: Recent Perspectives: A Memorial Tribute to C.R. Dodwell*, ed. Gale R. Owen-Crocker and Timothy Graham (Manchester and New York, 1998), pp. 8–25, for example, for a thorough discussion of sculpted Marian devotional items in the period, much of it associated with textile imagery.

20   For additional discussion of evidence for the phenomenon of devotional statues and associated textiles across early and late medieval England, see Maren Clegg Hyer, "Precious Offerings: Dressing Devotional Statues in Medieval England," in *Refashioning Dress, Medieval to Early Modern*, ed. Gale R. Owen-Crocker and Maren Clegg Hyer (Medieval and Renaissance Clothing and Textiles 4) (Woodbridge, 2019), pp. 17–26.

21   *The Waltham Chronicle: An Account of the Discovery of Our Holy Cross at Montacute and its Conveyance to Waltham*, ed. and trans. Leslie Watkiss and Marjorie Chibnall (Oxford, 1994), pp. xv, 22, and 84.

22   Her worship would also continue long after her death, as long as her offerings continued their existence in a church environment. For as long as anyone remembered their association with her, she would be memorialized. I am indebted to Gale R. Owen-Crocker for this insight.

and needful items, produced or donated in the name of worship, particularly for church foundations not staffed with workshops of their own.

These expressions of worship by domestic textile are honoured in textual sources, just as vestments and altar cloths are. Goscelin of St Bertin describes a room provided for him in the bishop's compound in Wiltshire, a room he had initially thought very poor indeed:

> *Repente omnis illuuies exstirpatur, parietes et laquearia sordentia purgan-tur, frondibus et iuncis uiridantibus herbisque flagrantibus gratificatur, parietes et superna cortinis et auleis, sedilia tapetiis contexuntur, cunctis-que solemniter paratis hospes inducor. Non illam putabam domum quam prius uideram.*[23]

All at once all the filth was rooted out, the walls and filthy beams were cleansed and strewn with foliage and green rushes and sweet-smelling grasses, the walls and ceilings were entwined with curtains and hangings, the seats with covers, and when all things had been prepared in a proper fashion, I was brought in as a guest. I did not believe it was the house I had first seen.[24]

The fabrics which turned a hovel into a home for Goscelin could have been produced at the nunnery at Wilton Abbey; they could also belong to the long tradition of donations of new or re-purposed furnishings from seculars to ecclesiastical institutions. Whatever the source, the donations of textile func-tioned as a practical devotional practice or expression of worship by those who produced and provided them to Goscelin.

Textile Rejection as Expression of Worship: Ecclesiastical and Hagiographical Attitude to Dress

It is perhaps ironic that, despite the perceived necessity for beautiful textiles for devotional, ecclesiastical purposes, the general opinion among the clergy was to lambast finery or refinement in textiles for all other purposes, ecclesi-astical or secular. This standard attitude towards dress derives in large meas-ure from biblical attitudes to luxury goods, including textiles: outside of the

---

23   "Liber Confortatorius of Goscelin of Saint Bertin," in *Analecta Monastica*, ed. C.H. Talbot (3rd ser., Studia Anselmiana 37) (Rome, 1955), p. 102.

24   Coatsworth, "Cushioning Medieval Life," p. 6. Translation is Coatsworth's.

furnishings of the Tabernacle, such matters were most often the province of the wicked and worldly. Thus, the prototypical rich man of the often-quoted parable in Luke 16 is distinguished as one who took pleasure in being "clothed in purple and fine linen," and faring "sumptuously every day" (verse 19), unlike the poor beggar at his gates.[25] The rich man, however, ends his days in hell, unsuccessfully begging for relief as the erstwhile beggar rests blissfully in "Abraham's bosom" (Luke 16:22–25). The message is clear: to have pleasure in heaven, one must reject luxury on earth, including luxurious textiles, outside those that adorn holy spaces.

The rejection of such luxury items becomes a *topos* identifying the prototypical saint, and that *topos* is evident from the outset of the hagiographical tradition of early medieval England. In Bede's prose *Vita* of St Cuthbert, for example, part of Cuthbert's sanctity is couched in his rejection of fine or colourful cloth and clothing:

> *Uestimentis utebatur communibus, ita temperanter agens, ut horum neque mundiciis neque sordibus esset notablis. Unde usque hodie in eodem monasterio exemplo eius obseruatur, ne quis uarii aut preciosi coloris habeat indumentum, sed ea maxime uestium specie sint contenti, quam naturalis ouium lana ministrat.*

> He wore ordinary garments and, keeping the middle path, he was not noteworthy either for their elegance or for their slovenliness. Hence his example is followed in the same monastery even to this day, so that no one has a garment of varied or costly colouring, but they are fully satisfied with that kind of garment which the natural wool of the sheep provides.[26]

The rejection of fine (and even comfortable) clothing as a form of devotional worship extends to female saints as well as male; one of the key signs of sanctity demonstrated by St Æthelthryth, according to Bede's *Historia Ecclesiastica*,

---

25   All biblical references are to the Vulgate and its translations at http://www.drbo.org/.

26   Bede, *Bedae Vita Sancti Cuthberti, Two Lives of Saint Cuthbert: A Life by an Anonymous Monk of Lindisfarne and Bede's Prose Life*, ed. and trans. Bertram Colgrave (New York, 1969), pp. 212–13. In Bede's *History of the Abbots of Wearmouth and Jarrow*, he similarly praises the sanctity of his teacher Ceolfrid, describing his moderation during his tenure as abbot of Wearmouth and Jarrow, as he practised *insolitam rectoribus et escae potusque parcitatem, et habitus vilitatem* ("an abstinence in food and drink and a poverty of dress rare among rulers"); Bede, *Vita Sanctorum Abbatum Monasterii in Uyramutha et Gyruum* (*History of the Abbots of Wearmouth and Jarrow*), in *Bede: Opera Historica*, ed. J.E. King (London, 1979), vol. 2, pp. 430–31.

is that *ex quo monasterium petiit, numquam lineis sed solum laneis uestimentis uti uoluerit* ("from the time she entered the monastery, she would never wear linen but only woollen garments").[27] She also bathed infrequently, which might have made her less welcome to her earthly counterparts, but clearly not to her heavenly bridegroom. Her rejection of pleasure in finery is similarly highlighted in her reaction to a large and painful tumor on her neck that appeared just before her death (perhaps from plague). Bede tells us she welcomed the affliction: she argued that she had worn too many necklaces as a young person, and the tumor was a just, purifying penance to rid her of the *reatu superuacuae leuitatis* ("guilt of my needless vanity").[28]

Bede argues that taking pleasure in beautiful clothing and other luxuries is actually unholy, as in the case of the nuns at Coldingham. In the *Historia Ecclesiastica*, Bede reminds his readers of the prophecy of the diligent and austere Irish monk Adamnan, who saw a vision regarding the nuns: an angel came to him and told him that during the angel's visit to Coldingham, he found none doing anything appropriate. Instead, he found all living in luxurious excess. Such excesses included that, *uirgines quoque Deo dicatae, contemta reuerentia suae professionis, quotiescumque uacant, texendis subtilioribus indumentis operam dant, quibus aut se ipsas ad uicem sponsarum in periculo sui status adornment, aut externorum sibi uirorum amicitiam conparent* ("even the virgins who are dedicated to God put aside all respect for their profession and, whenever they have leisure, spend their time weaving elaborate garments with which to adorn themselves as if they were brides, so imperiling their virginity, or else to make friends with strange men").[29] The warning of the vision is clear: fire will burn Coldingham shortly if they fail to repent of their pleasure in luxurious dress, and it does. Bede's contemporary Boniface states his opinion even more directly. After discussing worldly behaviors of laymen, Boniface pens his well-known criticisms of excess in dress, which he considers evidence of the coming of the Antichrist.[30] Considering how such love for dress might creep into ecclesiastical contexts, as well, he asserts that "Such attire shows the wickedness of their souls, giving proof of arrogance and pride, luxury, vanity."[31]

---

27   *Bede's Ecclesiastical History of the English People*, 4.19, ed. Bertram Colgrave and R.A.B. Mynors (Oxford, 1969), pp. 392–93.

28   Ibid., 4.19, pp. 396–97.

29   Ibid., 4.25, pp. 424–27.

30   His most often quoted lines of complaint are found in his letter to Lull, listed as number 78 in "S. Bonifatii et Lulli epistolae," *Monumenta Germaniae Historica Epistolae 3*, Merovingici et Karolini Aevi I (Berlin, 1892); see, for example, p. 355, lines 17–25.

31   Ibid., p. 134.

Such attitudes are not limited to eighth-century Northumbria. In the late tenth and early eleventh centuries during the Benedictine Reform, West Saxon abbot Ælfric makes the same connections between hagiographical *topoi* of sanctity and the rejection of pleasure in luxury items, including fine or colourful textiles. Among his many *Vitae*, Ælfric's female saints' lives are particularly associated with the rejection of pleasure in clothing as a form of worship. Thus, when St Eugenia is cleared of attempted seduction of the wicked Melantia, her family welcomes her with open arms, rejoicing and insisting that she don golden robes. However, she dislikes it: *Hi þá gefretewodon . þa fæmnan mid golde / hyre un-þances* ("They adorned her, the woman with gold / to her displeasure").[32] Similarly, Roman maiden St Agnes, despite her tender years, refuses marriage and luxury, although the kinsmen of her would-be husband *deorwurðe gyrlan . and deorwurðran behéton* ("offered costly and costlier garments").[33] Her response is unequivocal: she *þæt eall forseah* ("she despised all that"). When the young groom comes to plead his case in person, he brings her similar gifts and is similarly rejected. Agnes explains her rejection, arguing that her heavenly lover has promised her better gifts and heavenly wealth, including a promise to dress her *mid orle . of golde awefen* ("with garments woven from gold").[34] Agnes's response to her bridegroom is particularly interesting because she does not appear to reject pleasure in *heavenly* finery, only earthly. St Agatha is similarly tempted by the bawd Aphrodosia with all types of luxuries, including *gymmas . and gyrlan of golde* ("gems and garments of gold"), but like the other female saints, Agatha *eall forseah / on meoxes gelicnysse . þe lið under fotum* ("rejected it all as if it were dung which lies underfoot").[35]

An extreme example of rejection of worldly pleasure in clothing as a form of worship comes in Ælfric's story of St Mary of Egypt, who wore no clothing at all. Thus, when the elderly saint Zosimus encounters her in the desert, he finds that she loathed her old life of sin so greatly that she achieved sanctity and worshipped God by living in the wilderness *eallunga lichamlicum wæfelsum bereafod* ("utterly deprived of bodily clothing").[36] Her nudity presents quite a challenge to the two elderly saints, so she asks Zosimus to clothe her with his

---

32 "Natale Sancte Eugenie Uirginis," *Ælfric's Lives of Saints*, ed. Walter W. Skeat (Early English Text Society, original series 76, 82) (Oxford, 1881 and 1885; 1996), vol. 1, hom. 2, pp. 24–51 at 40. All translations of Ælfric are mine.

33 "Natale Sancte Agnetis Uirginis," *Ælfric's Lives*, vol. 1, hom. 7, pp. 170–95 at 170.

34 Ibid., p. 172.

35 "Natale Sancte Agathe Uirginis," *Ælfric's Lives*, vol. 1, hom. 8, pp. 194–209 at 196, 198.

36 "De Transitu Mariae Aegyptiace," *Ælfric's Lives of Saints*, ed. Walter W. Skeat (Early English Text Society, original series 94, 114) (Oxford, 1890 and 1900; 1996), vol. 2, hom. 33b, pp. 2–53 at 14.

scyccels "cloak." He unfastens it, and *gegyrede hire be þam dæle þe heo mæst mihte* ("she clothed herself to the extent which she was most able"),[37] making it possible for the two of them to converse for a time. She later explains to a concerned Zosimus that she doesn't really mind not having clothing, saying, *ic eom ofer-wrigen mid þam oferbrædelse godes wordes* ("I am clothed with the garment of God's word").[38] As she runs into the desert, and again when she is later found dead, we are told she continues to wear nothing *buton gewealdan þæs toslitenan rægeles* ("except the ragged protection of the garment") which Zosimus first gave her.[39]

Representative? General Attitudes towards Dress

The attitudes found in Bede, Ælfric, and the hagiographical and homiletic traditions more generally which reject pleasure in worldly dress as a form of devotional worship appear to reflect the "party line," so to speak, of ecclesiastical circles across the period. Indeed, the general perspective among ecclesiasts on the matter makes it somewhat difficult to gauge what non-ecclesiasts might have thought on the same subject. At the same time, one suspects that pleasure in worldly dress must have been common in both secular and ecclesiastical circles, given how frequently luxurious dress is mentioned (in wills and as made-over donations to religious institutions, in particular) as well as condemned. Early medieval English preference for luxury dress is similarly borne out in what archaeological evidence remains. Indeed, the finishing of secular as well as ecclesiastical dress with elaborate, possibly tablet-woven gold and silk borders seems to have been so commonplace a technique as to have identified "English work" and the "English people" more generally, as Goscelin or an eleventh-century contemporary remarks when describing King Edward's unusually sumptuous costume. He describes typical English cloaks as *auro supra paratos et huiusmodi uestes secundum morem gentis* ("designed with gold above and over-clothing of the same manner, according to the custom of the people").[40]

---

37   Ibid., p. 14.
38   Ibid., p. 40.
39   Ibid., p. 52.
40   Latin quoted from *The Life of King Edward Who Rests at Westminster*, ed. Frank Barlow (Oxford, 1992), p. 25. Translation is mine.

Outliers: Expressions of Worship through Textile Finery

It is interesting to see these distinct attitudes of pleasure and displeasure in luxury textiles converge in a few outliers in the hagiographical tradition. Late-tenth/early eleventh-century monk and writer Byrhtferth of Ramsey appears to embody unusually positive attitudes towards luxurious textiles for one of ecclesiastical background. In listing the positive characteristics of St Oswald, archbishop of York, in his *vita*, for example, rather than including the expected hagiographical distaste for luxurious dress, Byrhtferth describes Oswald quite differently:

> *Erat enim ualde | inclitus in omnibus operibus suis, amabilis et affabilis omnibus amicis suis. Fulgebat cotidie in sericis uestibus et epulabatur per singulos soles splendide; cui suppeditabant gaze terrestres necnon honores – quos seruauit Christo, non sibi, sicut postea rei probauit euentus.*

> For he was truly excellent in all his actions, lovable and affable to all his friends. He glistened each day in his silken garments and he dined lavishly every day; he was abundantly supplied with earthly treasure and distinctions: all of which he reserved for Christ, not himself, as the outcome of things subsequently proved.[41]

Although Byrhtferth is quick to suggest that Oswald's enjoyment of luxury is actually his gift to Christ and an act of worship, this set of attributes is the polar opposite of the expected hagiographical trope of intense dislike for finery that should occur at this moment in the description, and is therefore a very unusual feature. Michael Lapidge points out that Byrhtferth's description of Oswald's "silken finery" is also reminiscent of similar phrases from both Jerome and pseudo-Augustinian writing; however, "Whereas these patristic authors use the phrase contemptuously, Byrhtferth oddly uses it as a term of approbation."[42]

Perhaps recognizing the unusual nature of his praise, Byrthferth immediately contrasts Oswald's enjoyment of finery to similar enjoyment of goods by the secular clerics who were replaced, at times violently, by monks such as Oswald during the tenth-century Benedictine Reform. In the case of the clerics, such enjoyment is clearly not acceptable, as Byrthferth accuses them of giving these goods not to the Church or Christ, but to their *uxoribus* ("wives").[43]

---

41   *Byrhtferth of Ramsey*, pp. 34–35.
42   Ibid., p. 34, n. 14.
43   Ibid., pp. 34–35.

By his next reference to Oswald's attire, the silk has disappeared, and Oswald wears instead humble *ferrugineo* ("russet garments").[44] Were the beautiful silken garments simply vestments, under which Oswald wore humble robes? Perhaps so, in which case the luxurious textiles would have been considered appropriate aspects of worship and possessions of the church. But Byrhtferth's original linking of silken garments and lavish dining is suggestive that Oswald demonstrated an unusual enjoyment of finery in his ecclesiastical work, one often rejected within the hagiographical tradition.

In subsequent sections, Oswald is represented more traditionally as self-denying, but Byrhtferth's appreciation for "the finer things" reasserts itself in a section of Oswald's *vita* that describes his effectiveness as a leader of his monastic community at Westbury. Again, intending only praise, Byrhtferth states that

> *Tanta eis contulit ex secularibus rebus* (*in potu uidelicet et cibo necne uestimentis*), *"ut absque murmuratione seruire" Deo potuissent. Hii his contenti, iugiter parebant ante faciem saluatoris, ymnis et psalmis uacantes et lectionis studio operam dantes*

> Oswald granted to them such great benefactions in worldly possessions (that is, in drink and food as well as clothing) that they were able 'to serve God without grumbling.' Contented with these benefactions, the monks were always obedient before the face of the Saviour, occupying themselves with hymns and songs and busying themselves with the business of reading[45]

Byrhtferth alludes a second time to the happiness of the monks under Oswald's leadership, reflecting that they were *"cotidiano uictu" contenti* ("well content with their 'daily rations'").[46] What this quantity of "daily bread" was like, we do not know, but it is clear that food and clothing were bestowed liberally on Oswald's monks during his time as their ecclesiastical leader; Byrhtferth's Oswald seems to have known how to keep his community happy, perhaps providing the same bounty that he himself appears to have enjoyed. Byrhtferth's uncritical admiration and praise suggests that he found Oswald's appreciation

---

44   Ibid., pp. 36–37.

45   Ibid., pp. 70–71. Byrhtferth's quotation of *"ut absque murmuratione seruire"* comes from the Benedictine Rule (c. 53, see n. 85).

46   Ibid. In this instance, the quoted element is taken from James 2:15. The context is feeding the poor.

of the finer things in life a praiseworthy matter within the cloister where he shared them. Perhaps it could be argued that Oswald's sharing of bounty and creation of a happy life for God's servants were forms of worship, just as donations of textile hangings and seat covers that provided similar comfort in cold churches and cloisters were laudable expressions of worship.

In some ways, Byrhtferth's pleasure in bounty seems more consistent with attitudes of the secular court, whom he describes in ways similar to Oswald. Relating the coronation of King Edgar, he notes with great enthusiasm and detail the abundance of drink and the ecclesiastical and secular finery. Observing that everyone had plenty to drink, he also describes the abbots *niueis uestibus induti, ostro atque <peplo> cooperti* ("dressed in snow-white albs covered with purple")[47] and the king *coronatus lauro et roseo decoratus honore* ("crowned with laurel and decorated in roseate splendor"), the noblemen *gloriose fulserunt* ("gleaming attractively"), and the queen *uestita carbasea ueste ...<splendide> circumamicta, uarietate lapillorum et margaritarum suffulta elatius | <precellens> ceteris matronis* ("dressed in linen garments and robed splendidly, adorned with a variety of precious stones and pearls, she loftily surpassed the other ladies present").[48] The celebratory drinking and the brilliant company would not be likely to appeal to the tastes of St Æthelthryth or St Mary of Egypt, but it is clearly another type of bounty that pleased Byrhtferth, perhaps a glorious reflection of a bountiful heavenly kingdom represented through a resplendent earthly court honouring a righteous king. After all, passages in Exodus describe reverentially the lavish textiles embroidered in silk, brilliant colours, and gems that were devoted first to the Tabernacle and later to the temple by Israel's people and later kings as an expression of worship (cf. Exodus 36). Certainly, to take pleasure in such textiles was to take pleasure in what pleased God.

Elsewhere, Byrhtferth praises the donations to Ramsey of Bishop Ælfnoth, which include a wide variety of luxurious materials:

> *Qualibus illud monasterium ornamentis ditauit et gloriosis muneribus exornauit, quis expediet? Libros sancti euangelii concessit; uestes ad ministrandum Deo optulit; cuncta necessaria ecclesie dedit et, ut paucis concludam uerbis, calices, sciffos, manutergia, sexonica, cornua ad uinum fundendum, stragulas, tapetia, lectisternia, cortinas, cucullas fratrum, pellicia, sicque ut cum honore Domino parere potuerint.*

---

47   Ibid., pp. 106–07.
48   Ibid., pp. 110–11.

Who shall say with what adornments he enriched that monastery, and with what bounties he endowed it? He gave gospel books; he gave vestments for performing services to God; he gave all necessary church furniture including, if I may conclude in a few words, chalices, cups, towels, girdles (?), horns for pouring out wine, coverlets, tapestries, beds, curtains, monks' cowls, furs – and all so that they could obey the Lord with dignity.[49]

For Byrhtferth, the daily running of the church requires not only a Benedictine's single focus on the glory of God, but a great deal of earthly matter in order that such worship might proceed in a focused and "dignified" way. For him, that seems to include bedding, tapestries, and furs for the monks' use.

In some respects, the *Gesta Regum Anglorum* of William of Malmesbury suggests the opposite and perhaps more conventional attitude to finery, compared to Byrhtferth's. William repeats Boniface's criticism of luxurious dress in any context,[50] and he likewise blames the Norman Conquest, at least in part, on his early medieval English predecessors' excessive pleasure in dress, arguing *Monachi subtilibus indumentis et indifferenti genere ciborum regulam ludificabant* ("Monks, with their finely-woven garments and their undiscriminating diet, made nonsense of their Rule").[51] However, he also reports an interesting incident which suggests that Byrhtferth's attitude was not unique in its time.

William tells the story of one of the daughters of King Edgar, St Eadgyth (died *c.* 984), who spent her life at the convent of Wilton. He praises her for many of the usual virtues of the pious, her virginity and her vigils, as well as her humility. However, he also reports that

> *non mediocriter iuditium offendebat hominum, fallens uidelicet oculos eorum auratarum apparatu uestium; siquidem cultioribus indumentis iugiter ornata procederet quam illius professionis sanctitudo exposceret.*

> she used to give no small offence to public opinion (deceiving it, no doubt, by appearances), by the splendor of her gold-embroidered garments; for she always went about in more elegant clothes than were called for by the sanctity of her profession.[52]

---

49   Ibid., pp. 130–33.
50   *William of Malmesbury: GESTA REGVM ANGLORVM The History of the English Kings*, ed. R.A.B. Mynors with R.M. Thomson and M. Winterbottom (Oxford, 1998), vol. 1, pp. 118–19.
51   Ibid., pp. 458–59.
52   Ibid., pp. 402–03.

Assuming she took too much pleasure in her finery, her bishop reproved her:

> *Vnde a sancto Athelwoldo palam increpita respondisse fertur, nec inepte*
> *nec infacete: "Verax et irrefragabile iuditium Dei, sola mortalium operitur*
> *conscientia; nam et in sordibus luctuosis potest esse iactantia. Quapropter*
> *puto quod tam incorrupta mens potest esse sub istis uestibus quam sub tuis*
> *discissis pellibus."*

For this she was openly rebuked by St Æthelwold, and her reply, according to the story, was neither irrelevant nor without point: 'The judgment of God is true and irrefutable, while man's conscience, alone is hidden; for even in dismal mourning garb there can be an element of display. This makes me think that a pure heart may lie hid beneath these garments as easily as under your ragged sheepskin.'[53]

The bishop felt both *laetumque erubescens* ("abashed" and "delighted") at the *ueritatem dicti* ("truth of the saying") and left her alone. We are told that, subsequently, she was honoured in life by St Dunstan for her sanctity and distinguished after her death by miracles at her tomb.[54] This Eadgyth is, in fact, the same whose handiwork on a white alb was so lauded by Goscelin.[55]

In Eadgyth's case, as in St Oswald's, their biographers were left with a conundrum: each took pleasure in opulent dress (and plenty of food, in Oswald's case), in contradiction to the usual patterns of hagiographical piety, but each also demonstrated pious attitudes, deeds, and ultimately miracles. Therefore, such contradictions had to be mentioned, explained, and indeed, defended as alternate forms of worship, within the hagiographical tradition to which each belonged.

---

53   Ibid.

54   Ibid. In the latter instance (*ueritatem dicti*), translation is mine.

55   Lester-Makin, *Lost Art of the Anglo-Saxon World*, p. 118, Griffiths, "Like the Sister of Aaron," pp. 355–56, and Gale R. Owen-Crocker "Smelly Sheep, Shimmering Silk: The Sensual and Emotional Experience of Textiles," in *Sense and Feeling in Daily Living in the Early Medieval English World*, ed. Maren Clegg Hyer and Gale R. Owen-Crocker (Liverpool, 2020), pp. 197–218 comment on an additional detail about Goscelin's passage lauding the alb: Eadgyth herself is described as having depicted herself as a suppliant Mary at the feet of the Lord in the scene, as Owen-Crocker states, "a remarkable expression of Edith's simultaneous humility and arrogance!" (pp. 216–17). Eadgyth, in other words, seems to have had a penchant for the conspicuous in her forms of worship.

Diversity in Forms of Worship?

These outliers of the early medieval English hagiographical tradition invite interrogation of attitudes toward luxurious textiles in ecclesiastical use. When might appreciation of luxurious textile be read as a form of devotion or worship?

Certainly, appreciation and indulgence in textile finery in secular contexts appears to have been widespread and robustly criticised in ecclesiastical circles throughout the period. Use of textile finery in ecclesiastical contexts, however, appears much more complicated. In traditional ascetic style, displeasure in textiles and other luxury objects for personal ecclesiastical use is lauded and promulgated from the beginning to the end of the period as a traditional sign of worship. Pleasure in textiles, by contrast, is an unholy feeling that aligns wearers with the world of temptation and sin.

However, at the same time, enjoyment of luxurious textiles and other objects is clearly acceptable as a form of worship when the finery is donated to general ecclesiastical purpose or even repurposed from secular garment to ecclesiastical function for the glory and contemplation of God and the prevention of sin.[56] Or at least, that is the case in early medieval England. In her work, *Clothing the Clergy: Virtue and Power in Medieval Europe, c. 800–1200*, Maureen C. Miller documents the conflicting expectations and injunctions concerning luxury in ecclesiastical-use textiles across early medieval Europe and identifies an outlier, an originator of the "ornate style" that shifted tastes to more elaborate and luxurious vestments and accoutrements to the Continent by the ninth century; she situates that ornate style in early medieval England.[57] Such a difference in attitude could explain consistent tensions within and beyond England over early medieval English ecclesiastical attire.[58] It is probably not a fluke that the earliest textual and archaeological documentation of gold vestments in early medieval Europe is associated with early medieval England.[59] But as the pre-Conquest ecclesiasts may have found, such fine work serves practical purposes, as textiles, like other luxury objects, might decorate

---

56   Cf. Hyer, "Recycle, Reduce, Reuse," pp. 49–62.

57   Miller, *Clothing the Clergy*, pp. 11–35 and 238, respectively.

58   So, for example, Alcuin's warnings to visiting early medieval English clerics to dress more simply while visiting Charlemagne to avoid his censure of overly ornate dress (Miller, *Clothing the Clergy*, p. 115); William of Malmesbury's use of luxurious dress as one just cause of the pride and downfall of the early medieval English ecclesiastical hierarchy at the Conquest, as discussed above, seems a similar, if much later reaction.

59   See Miller, *Clothing the Clergy*, p. 131.

sacred spaces and inspire veneration and worship of God, churches, and church authorities, including the teachers of the people.

Key examples of such sanctioned and intentional uses of luxury "art" objects for devotional purposes can be found in the earliest days of the English church. In Bede's *Vita Sanctorum Abbatum Monasterii in Uyramutha et Gyruum* (*History of the Abbots of Wearmouth and Jarrow*), for example, Benedict Biscop brings back sacred images from Rome to adorn the church for an important purpose, as Bede points out,

> *quatenus intrantes ecclesiam omnes etiam literarum ignari, quaquaversum intenderent, vel semper amabilem Christi sanctorumque eius, quamvis in imagine, contemplarentur aspectum; vel Dominicae incarnationis gratiam vigilantiore mente recolerent; vel extremi discrimen examinis, quasi coram oculis habentes, districtius se ipsi examinare meminissent*

> in order that all men who entered the church, even if they might not read, should either look (whatsoever way they turned) upon the gracious countenance of Christ and His saints, though it were but in a picture; or might call to mind a more lively sense of the blessing of the Lord's incarnation, or having, as is were before their eyes, the peril of the last judgment might remember more closely to examine themselves.[60]

The viewers' pleasure or enjoyment in seeing scripture come alive before them is intended to serve a godly purpose, the purpose of contemplation and worship. Likewise, luxury objects might encourage missionary work, something Boniface attests as he asks Abbess Eadburga to copy scriptures for him *cum auro* ("in letters of gold") for the *honorem et reverentiam sanctarum scripturarum ante oculos carnalium in praedicando* ("honor and reverence of the Holy Scriptures before the eyes of the carnally minded to whom I preach"). Boniface lists a second purpose for these golden words: so that Boniface himself can reflect on *quia dicta eius, qui me in hoc iter direxit*[61] ("the words of him who guided me along this path").[62]

In this light, are the hagiographical outliers examples of worship through textiles devoted to ecclesiastical use? Perhaps. Oswald's luxurious dress, like

---

60   *Bede: Opera Historica*, vol. 2, pp. 404–07.

61   Latin text listed as number 35, "S. Bonifatii et Lulli epistolae," *Monumenta Germaniae Historica Epistolae 3*, Merovingici et Karolini Aevi 1 (Berlin, 1892), p. 286, lines 9–12.

62   Although influenced by C.H. Talbot, *The Anglo-Saxon Missionaries* (New York, 1954), p. 91, the translation is largely my own.

his peers' at the coronation, certainly inspires praise and respect for the office of godly priesthood. If Eadgyth's dress likewise demonstrates the honour that comes to those who dedicate their lives to Christ (along the lines of Ezekiel 16:10), then her dress would serve as an attraction and encouragement for others to worship in the same way. At the same time, William of Malmesbury's criticism of what he and earlier writers such as Boniface consider the early medieval English ecclesiasts' excessive pleasure in luxury dress suggests that a statement such as Byrhtferth's that Oswald's finery was "reserved for Christ, not himself" might be perpetually viewed with suspicion in ecclesiastical circles.

In the end, Eadgyth makes an excellent point: there can be an element of display, an ostentation, in all extreme forms of devotional worship, from her beautifully embroidered robes to St Mary of Egypt's startling nudism (itself rather less practical and more problematic in accomplishing the work of an ecclesiast). Either case can be a form of worship, and either is pleasure in unusual and notable dress, or in the latter case, undress.

CHAPTER 5

In Search of Hild: A Review of the Context of Abbess Hild's Life, Her Religious Establishment, and the Relevance of Recent Archaeological Finds from Whitby Abbey

Penelope Walton Rogers

The North-East of England has fostered an unusual number of young girls who grew up to specialise in the early medieval period. Elizabeth Coatsworth was one, from County Durham, and Leslie Webster, Susan Youngs, Gale Owen-Crocker, and the present author were all near-contemporaries, educated in the schools of Newcastle upon Tyne. None of us can recall being taught much of the subject in formal lessons, but perhaps our interest was activated by Sunday School, where Bede, Caedmon, Cuthbert, and Hild featured alongside Bible stories; or by the educational trips to Jarrow, ostensibly to learn about the 1936 Jarrow March, but inclusive of a visit to the church where Bede had worshipped. Or perhaps it was the annual St Aidan pilgrimage, when charabancs of working people from Tyneside were decanted at Beal, ready to cross over to Holy Island as the tide rolled out. Bishop Hugh striding barefoot across the sands in cope and mitre, crozier in hand, with the acolytes scampering behind; the service in the ruins of Lindisfarne priory, our voices whipped away by the wind; kittiwakes wheeling above and Bamburgh Castle emerging in the distance from behind the strands of a sea fret: these things leave a lasting impression on a young mind. Elizabeth (Betty) must have known all these places in her childhood.

It is no accident that these memories consistently tie the early history of Northumbria to the Church: the two were inextricably linked (Northumbria is used here in the Anglo-Saxon sense of the kingdom North of the Humber). When, therefore, it came to selecting a topic on the theme of Art and Worship, the finds from recent excavations at Whitby Abbey instantly came to mind. Here, craft equipment, garment accessories, and other artefacts have yielded material evidence for life in a Northumbrian religious community. The archaeology provides a physical context for the 7th- to 9th-century historical sources and especially for the life of the first abbess, Hild. Hild ruled this double, male and female, house at a time when Northumbria was starting to emerge from an agglomeration of smaller kingdoms, and while Christianity was still a new religion to the Anglo-Saxons. At *Streanæshalh* (Whitby) she established a place of stability, where she hosted a synod and introduced sound teaching practices.

© KONINKLIJKE BRILL NV, LEIDEN, 2021 | DOI:10.1163/9789004467514_007

As a prominent figure in an increasingly male-dominated world, her wisdom and kind-liness were recognised by her peers. Her influence lived on long after her death, in the abbesses who succeeded her and in the bishops whom she had guided as novices in her house. This archaeological-historical exploration of the context of Hild's life and the religious community she founded, together with a review of the most recent finds from the Whitby excavations, is offered as a token of respect for Elizabeth Coatsworth, in recognition of the scholarship and kindness which she herself has displayed in her long career.

∴

A Princess in Deira

Hild was born into the Deiran royal house in AD 614. She was the younger daughter of Hereric and Bregoswith and great-niece of Edwin, who was the son of Ælle, the first confidently identified king of Deira.[1] This was an Anglo-Saxon dynasty, whose ancestors are likely to have arrived in the region in the 5th cen-tury (as illustrated by the large cremation cemetery at Sancton),[2] either direct from the northern Continent, or by way of Lincolnshire or East Anglia.[3] They became rulers of an area that incorporated the North York Moors, the Vale of Pickering, the Yorkshire Wolds, and the Vale of York (Fig. 5.1). The ruins of the Roman regional capital at York lay inside Deira's western margin, but its own

---

1   *Prosopography of Anglo-Saxon England*, www.pase.ac.uk, HILD 1 (accessed 20 February 2020). Bede, *Historia Ecclesiastica Gentis Anglorum*, 4.23; *Venerabilis Bedae, Opera Historica*, ed. Charles Plummer, 2 vols (Oxford, 1896), 1, p. 252. Plummer's Latin-only edition was used by the author because the standard modern edition was not accessible during the COVID-19 lockdown. Since Plummer's detailed footnotes on the English MSS proved to be a particu-larly useful resource, references to his edition have been retained here. The reader may pre-fer to consult the more recent Latin-English edition, B. Colgrave and R.A.B. Mynors *Bede's Ecclesiastical History of the English People* (Oxford, 1969).

2   Jane Timby, "Sancton I Anglo-Saxon Cemetery: Excavations Carried Out Between 1976 and 1980," *Archaeological Journal* 150 (1993), 243–365. The new chronology of the Spong Hill, Norfolk, cremation cemetery has probably moved the start dates of cemeteries such as Sancton into the earlier part of the 5th century: Catherine Hills and Sam Lucy, *Spong Hill Part IX: Chronology and Synthesis* (MacDonald Institute Monograph) (Cambridge, 2013), pp. 229, 338–39.

3   Nicholas Higham, *The Kingdom of Northumbria: AD 350–1100* (Stroud, 1993), pp. 66–68; David Rollason, *Northumbria, 500–1000: Creation and Destruction of a Kingdom* (Cambridge, 2003), p. 47; Thomas Pickles, *Kingship, Society and the Church in Anglo-Saxon Yorkshire* (Oxford, 2018), pp. 16–24.

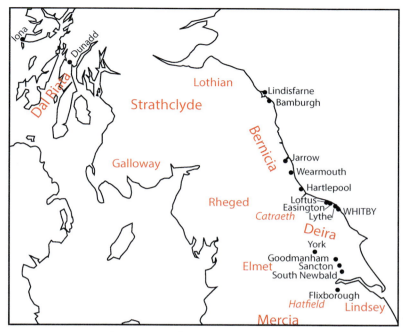

FIGURE 5.1   Seventh-century Northumbria: places mentioned in the text.
                © ASLab

earliest royal centre is likely to have been on the western edge of the Yorkshire
Wolds in the vicinity of Sancton and Goodmanham.[4] The burial rites of the
region were diverse and suggest that the Deirans were a mixed population,
with a variety of localised traditions and practices.[5]

   To the south of Deira lay the major power bloc of Mercia, to the west the
British (Brythonic-speaking) kingdoms of Rheged and Elmet, and to the north
Anglo-Saxon Bernicia, with a more shadowy entity, Catraeth, between Deira
and Bernicia, and Hatfield between Deira and Mercia.[6] These polities had been
jostling for power in the second half of the 6th century, but by the time of Hild's
birth, Deira had come under the control of the Bernician king, Æthelfrith, who
had also, through military campaigns, expanded the boundaries of Bernicia a

4   Higham, *The Kingdom of Northumbria*, pp. 66–67, 81; Pickles, *Anglo-Saxon Yorkshire*, p. 17.

5   Higham, *The Kingdom of Northumbria*, pp. 68–75; S.J. Lucy, "Early Medieval Burials in East
    Yorkshire: Reconsidering the Evidence," in *Early Deira: Archaeological Studies of the East
    Riding in the Fourth to Ninth Centuries AD*, ed. Helen Geake and Jonathan Kenny (Oxford,
    2000), pp. 11–18.

6   Higham, *The Kingdom of Northumbria*, pp. 82–89; Pickles, *Anglo-Saxon Yorkshire*, pp. 16–32;
    see also Rollason, *Northumbria, 500–1000*, pp. 28–53.

long way into northern British territory.[7] Edwin, the heir to the Deiran throne, was forced into exile at this point, but with the aid of Rædwald, King of the East Angles, he recovered his position and, as a result of Æthelfrith's defeat in AD 616, he acquired rulership over Bernicia and the newly conquered territories.[8] These lands became the foundation of the entity known to Bede as the "province of the Northumbrians,"[9] by which time it encompassed most of northern England and southern Scotland.

Hild's own father fell victim to these turbulent times. He too had gone into exile, but was killed by poisoning during his stay at the court of the king of Elmet, when Hild was still only an infant.[10] Once Edwin had reclaimed his kingdom, however, Hild seems to have been brought up in the relative security of her great-uncle's court. It was through Edwin's second wife, Æthelburg of Kent, that Christianity was introduced to the Deiran royal family and Hild herself was converted.

Christianity in Northumbria

The Anglo-Saxons of Deira and Bernicia followed the rituals and beliefs of Germanic pagans.[11] As described by Bede, the chief of Edwin's priests was Coifi and there was a sacred precinct with altars and shrines at Goodmanham.[12] The British kingdoms of the North and West, however, were led by Christian kings. Following the withdrawal of Roman rule, retained Roman practices had become a defining feature of royal authority, and in these regions Christianity was now bound up with the culture of the elite.[13] Here, monasteries were established, the most influential of which was the abbey on the island of Iona, off the west coast of Scotland. Founded by Columba with monks from Ireland in AD 563, the community was ruled by a succession of abbots who, unusually, held power above that of bishops.[14] Developing in isolation, they established among the Scots an ascetic monastic tradition that was often at variance with the practices of monasteries under closer supervision from Rome.

---

7   Higham, *The Kingdom of Northumbria*, pp. 108–13.

8   Higham, *The Kingdom of Northumbria*, pp. 113–19.

9   "Provincia Nordanhymbrorum," in Bede, *Historia Ecclesiastica, passim,* including 1.34, 3.22, 3.23. All translations from Latin and Old English in this chapter are by the author.

10   Bede, *Historia Ecclesiastica,* 4.23; Plummer, p. 255.

11   Gale R. Owen, *Rites and Religions of the Anglo-Saxons* (New York, 1981).

12   Bede, *Historia Ecclesiastica,* 2.13; Plummer, p. 113.

13   Higham, *The Kingdom of Northumbria,* 58–59.

14   Bede, *Historia Ecclesiastica,* 3.4; Plummer, p. 134.

Meanwhile in Kent, Bertha, the Frankish wife of King Æthelberht, was a practising Christian, and when in AD 597 Augustine's mission from Rome arrived, the re-introduction of Christianity into that region could begin in earnest.[15] Twenty-eight years later, when Edwin of Northumbria took as his second wife Æthelburg, the daughter of Æthelberht and Bertha, it was on the understanding that he himself would consider becoming a Christian.[16] It would appear that the leaders of the major Deiran kin groups and even Coifi the priest had already been moving towards conversion and it was agreed in council that they should all be baptised in one ceremony.[17] This took place at York in AD 627, at the hands of Paulinus, a bishop whom Queen Æthelburg had brought with her into the north. Hild's baptism at the age of 13, along with Edwin and his court,[18] was therefore into the Roman church, in what had been the Roman regional capital.

On Edwin's death in battle in 633, Æthelburg and Paulinus had to retreat to Kent, but after a brief period of apostasy, King Oswald (son of Edwin's sister, Acha, and therefore Hild's kinsman), re-established control.[19] Oswald, however, espoused the practices of Iona, having spent part of his youth in exile in the kingdom of Dál Riata. He arranged for a monk from Iona, Aidan, to become the founder of a religious community on Lindisfarne (Holy Island) and bishop of a new Lindisfarne see.[20] Other foundations in the Ionan style were to follow, including communities for women, such as the double house at Hartlepool (*Heruteu*) in AD 647.[21] This was the point at which the adult Hild stepped onto the stage.

Hild before *Streanæshalh* (Whitby)

Little is known of Hild's life between her baptism in AD 627 and the point at which she became a nun twenty years later. In the aftermath of Edwin's death, she could have taken refuge in East Anglia, Kent, or Gaul; or she may have

15   Bede, *Historia Ecclesiastica*, 1.25–1.26; Plummer, pp. 44–46.
16   Bede, *Historia Ecclesiastica*, 2.9; Plummer, p. 99.
17   Bede, *Historia Ecclesiastica*, 2.13–2.14; Pickles, *Kingship, Society*, pp. 59–68.
18   Bede, *Historia Ecclesiastica*, 2.14; Plummer, pp. 113–14; 4.23, p. 252.
19   Bede, *Historia Ecclesiastica*, 2.20–3.2; Plummer, pp. 124–31.
20   Bede, *Historia Ecclesiastica*, 3.3; Plummer, pp. 131–32.
21   Heiu, the founder of the Hartlepool house, is recorded as the first Northumbrian woman to become a nun: Bede, *Historia Ecclesiastica*, 4.23; Plummer, p. 253.

retreated to the royal stronghold at Bamburgh.[22] Nor do we know if she had been married, although the absence of any reference to her virginity in Bede's account may imply that she had.[23] All we know is that she spent those years "most nobly in a secular role."[24]

When she decided on a monastic life, her original plan had been to join her older sister, Hereswith, who was already a nun in Chelles, near Paris.[25] However, royal or not, Hild was now under the rule of her bishop, Aidan, who recalled her from a stay in East Anglia and persuaded her to found a small community at an unnamed spot on the north side of the Wear.[26] After a year of preparation there, she was appointed to succeed Heiu as abbess at Hartlepool, a role in which she was guided by Aidan. Finally, in AD 657, a property having been acquired at *Streanæshalh*, she built a *monasterium* there.[27] She will have taken with her to *Streanæshalh* Aidan's ideas of pastoral care of the lay population and the ascetic practices of the Ionan tradition.[28]

The Whitby (*Streanæshalh*) Synod and Its Aftermath

Tensions between the Scottish (Ionan) and Roman missions were now intensifying.[29] Although the dispute became focused on differences in tonsure and the date of Easter, there were other issues at stake. The greater power of the abbots and the stronger tradition of austerity among the Scots conflicted with the Romanists, who upheld the seniority of bishops within a diocesan structure, and who invested more in material possessions and stone buildings.[30]

22   Anne E. Inman, *Hild of Whitby and the Ministry of Women in the Anglo-Saxon World* (Lanham/Boulder/New York/London, 2019), pp. 15, 53.

23   Christine E. Fell, "Hild, Abbess of Streonæshalch," in *Hagiography and Medieval Literature, A Symposium*, ed. Hans Bekker-Nielsen, Peter Foote, Jørgen Højgaard Jørgensen and Tore Nyberg (Odense, 1981), pp. 76–99.
      Inman, *Hild*, pp. 16–17, 53.

24   "... *in saeculari habitu nobilissime* ... ": Bede, *Historia Ecclesiastica*, 4.23; Plummer, p. 252.

25   Chelles had gained a reputation for female learning under Abbess Bertila.

26   Bede *Historia Ecclesiastica*, 4.23; Plummer, p. 253. For a discussion of likely locations, see Fell, "Hild," pp. 81–82.

27   Bede *Historia Ecclesiastica*, 3.24; Plummer, p. 179 and 4.23, p. 254. See Peter Hunter Blair, "Whitby as a Centre of Learning in the Seventh Century," in *Learning and Literature in Anglo-Saxon England*, ed. Michael Lapidge and Helmut Gneuss (Cambridge, 1985), pp. 3–32 at pp. 8–9 for a discussion of Bede's meaning at this point.

28   Inman, *Hild*, p. 56.

29   Bede, *Historia Ecclesiastica*, 3.25; Plummer, pp. 181–88.

30   Higham, *The Kingdom of Northumbria*, pp. 132–50; Rollason, *Northumbria, 500–1000*, pp. 124–42; Pickles, *Anglo-Saxon Yorkshire*, pp. 106–07.

To resolve the issue, in AD 664 a synod was convened in Hild's establishment at *Streanœshalh*. King Oswiu (Oswald's brother and successor) presided and, although Hild herself supported the Scots, he decided in favour of the Roman faction.[31] Religious reasons were given for the decision, but the king must also have seen the political and economic advantages of aligning Northumbria with the powerful forces of Rome and Francia. Following the Synod, the episcopal see was restored in York and further monastic foundations such as Wearmouth (now Monkwearmouth) and Jarrow were established under the new conditions. From this point on the community at *Streanœshalh* will have had to follow the practices of the Roman church.

One major effect of this synod, perhaps unforeseen at the time, was its negative impact on the status of women in the Church. Targeted research has shown that, from Macrina in Cappadocia to Clotilde in Francia, women had been actively engaged in all aspects of Christianity.[32] In Britain, for example, Queens Bertha and Æthelburg had been instrumental in the conversion of the Anglo-Saxons. Most importantly, evidence has been produced that there were ordained women who celebrated mass and acted as confessors, and that there were abbesses with the status of bishop.[33] As Christianity had spread, different practices had sprung up and the Church in Rome was not unreasonably trying to introduce conformity and unity. This drive to uniformity, however, came from a patriarchal society, very different from that of the Anglo-Saxons.[34] Bit by bit, women's authority came to be eroded and even a conscientious scholar such as Bede, in his revision of the *Life of Cuthbert*, would make subtle adjustments which would downplay the role of the woman.[35] These shifts in the gender power-balance did not just apply to the monastic system. On the status of women in general, archaeology has much to contribute.

---

31   Bede, *Historia Ecclesiastica*, 3.25; Plummer, pp. 188–89.
32   Inman, *Hild*, pp. 19–28. Joan Morris, *Against Nature and God: The History of Women with Clerical Ordination and the Jurisdiction of Bishops* (London and Oxford, 1973); Stephanie Hollis, *Anglo-Saxon Women and the Church: Sharing a Common Fate* (Woodbridge, 1992); Gary Macy, *The Hidden History of Women's Ordination: Female Clergy in the Medieval West* (Oxford, 2008).
33   As Gary Macy has shown, early medieval "ordination" had a broader meaning than it did in later centuries; nevertheless, there existed women who officiated in roles later restricted to male clergy; Macy, *The Hidden History*, pp. 86–87.
34   Inman, *Hild*, pp. xiv, xxii, 3, 36–37, 50–51.
35   Hollis, *Anglo-Saxon Women and the Church*, pp. 199–207.

Early Anglo-Saxon Women

Double houses supervised by abbesses were an established feature of Anglo-Saxon England and the Frankish Continent, though a rarity elsewhere.[36] It can be argued that their origin lay in the greater degree of freedom exercised by women in early Germanic societies. Tacitus described the partnership between men and women of the Continental *Germani*[37] and in Anglo-Saxon cemeteries of the 5th and early 6th centuries, there is a strong sense of 'equal but different' in burial practices. The two genders are clearly differentiated, men by weaponry and women by brooches, necklaces, and textile craft equipment, but there is nothing in the sizes of the graves, their location, or the provision of extra elements such as coffins to suggest that one had dominance over the other.

In this early phase, women's age-related life events were marked in their clothing. There was considerable leeway for individual expression, but the underlying trend was for the peplos, the over-garment fastened on the shoulders, to be adopted at an age that corresponds with menarche; the head-veil and cloak were donned in the late teens and early twenties, probably the age of marriage, while the peplos would often disappear around the age of menopause.[38] Women's accessories included latch-lifters and symbolic keys, likely to represent control over household stores, and also textile craft equipment: the task of producing enough textiles to clothe and support a household, and its value to the farm's economy, cannot be overstated. The role of 'cunning women,' as herbalists and practitioners of magic, is also slowly emerging from the archaeology of the cemeteries.[39] Together, these imply that within the farmsteads, hamlets, and small villages of the Early Anglo-Saxon period, women were significant actors, conscious of their own identity, and, to judge

---

36   Sarah Foot, *Monastic Life in Anglo-Saxon England, c. 600–900* (Cambridge, 2006), p. 174; Barbara Yorke, *The Conversion of Britain: Religion, Politics and Society in Britain, 600–800* (Harlow, 2006), pp. 166–67.

37   Publius Cornelius Tacitus, *De Origine et Situ Germanorum liber*, ed. Alfred Holder (Leipzig, 1878), chapters 8 and 17–20, pp. 10, 14–16.

38   Penelope Walton Rogers, *Cloth and Clothing in Early Anglo-Saxon England, AD 450–700* (York, 2007), pp. 178–80. The final age-related threshold could perhaps represent widowhood.

39   Tania M. Dickinson, "An Anglo-Saxon 'cunning woman' from Bidford-on-Avon," in *In Search of Cult: Archaeological Investigations in Honour of Philip Rahtz*, ed. Martin Carver (Woodbridge, 1993), pp. 45–54. Penelope Walton Rogers, "Cunning Women," in *Circles and Cemeteries: Excavations at Flixton 1*, ed. Stuart Boulter and Penelope Walton Rogers (Bury St Edmunds, 2012), pp. 159, 172–75; Audrey Meaney, *Anglo-Saxon Amulets and Curing Stones* (British Archaeological Reports British Series 96) (Oxford, 1981), pp. 253–62.

from the quality and quantity of material goods in certain graves, the senior female in the household, the 'farm matron,' was a respected member of each small community.

There are signs of change in the gender balance in burials of the later 6th and 7th centuries. As new fashions arrived from the Continent, female life-transitions disappeared from the archaeological record and the head veil developed into a large lightweight cloth which covered most of the upper body and reached to below the hip.[40] If costume styles can be said to provide a commentary on social issues, then this speaks volumes. A suite of garments that honoured the significant events in a woman's life had been replaced with a large swathing garment, which – if it is correct to see the veil as an indicator of marriage[41] – shifted the woman's identity to her relationship with the male.

This change occurs at the same time as the relatively shallow social hierarchy of the early phase becomes vertically attenuated. Individual groups, probably kin groups, begin to rise above others and princely burials at Sutton Hoo, Taplow, and Prittlewell appear.[42] This in turn corresponds with historical evidence for the emergence of regional kings and their dynasties. The new elite included women, some of whom were accorded especially ostentatious burials in the mid-7th century. Outside the major kin-groups, however, a change in status is signalled by a lowering in women's life expectancy, increased levels of childhood nutritional stress and adult osteoarthritis, and evidence from teeth for diminished access to sweet foods.[43] This is mirrored in textiles, where prestige items such as gold-brocaded bands and patterned coverlets shift into the male domain.[44]

High-status female burials of the mid- to late 7th century still include textile craft equipment (unsurprising, since even Charlemagne's daughters were expected to learn to spin) but there are also indications of Christianity, most notably in the arrival of the 'collar cross,' a gold or gold-and-garnet cross worn centrally at the throat.[45] One impressive female-gender burial from this phase

40   Walton Rogers, *Cloth and Clothing*, pp. 126–27, 159–67, 187–89, 193.

41   Walton Rogers, *Cloth and Clothing*, pp. 242–44.

42   Helen Geake, "Burial Practice in Seventh- and Eighth-Century England," in *The Age of Sutton Hoo*, ed. M.O.H. Carver (Woodbridge 1992), pp. 83–94.

43   Nick Stoodley, *The Spindle and the Spear: A Critical Enquiry into the Construction and Meaning of Gender in the Early Anglo-Saxon Burial Rite* (Oxford, 1999), pp. 119–25.

44   Penelope Walton Rogers, "Cloth, Clothing and Anglo-Saxon Women," in *A Stitch in Time: Essays in Honour of Lise Bender Jørgensen*, ed. Sophie Bergerbrant and Sølvi Helene Fossøy (Gothenburg, 2014), pp. 262–63.

45   The collar cross worn at the throat by women has sometimes been confused with the pectoral cross worn over the heart by male priests; Sam Lucy, "The Trumpington Cross in Context," *Anglo-Saxon England* 45 (2016), 7–37.

has been located near Loftus, 14 miles along the coast from Whitby.[46] The woman had been buried with a bed in the centre of a square of mixed-gender graves, but instead of a collar cross she had a pendant incorporating a gemstone scallop shell. This the excavator equated with Christianity, although it also harks back to a pre-Christian symbol of female identity.[47]

Once written sources are available, men appear, on the face of it, to have become the primary decision-makers (though often taking counsel from women). The story of Oswiu dedicating his infant daughter to the Church in return for victory in battle[48] is an indication of the control a royal male might exercise over his family. Nevertheless, research into law codes has revealed how women's rights were protected in a variety of situations; and, most importantly, legal documents such as wills and charters show women inheriting and disposing of property, and retaining control of anything passed by the groom to the bride as the marital *morgengifu* or 'morning gift.'[49] The woman's kin group maintained an interest in her security and welfare throughout her life and all the indications are that women saw themselves as active agents on behalf of their birth-family. Then, as now, a relatively late age of marriage and economic independence strengthens a woman's position within her husband's family and makes her better able to assert her views and opinions.

We should not doubt the spiritual commitment of women such as Hild,[50] but for a mature woman from a royal or noble family, entering into the religious life must have also represented the chance to express her talents, by setting up her own establishment, acting as a guide to others, ministering to her community, and exerting influence in the outside world as advisor and diplomat. At the same time, it must not be forgotten that these women were only a few generations away from farming stock. In terms of administrative skills, one can draw a straight line back from the capable abbesses of the 7th century to the farm matrons of the 6th.

---

46   Stephen J. Sherlock, *A Royal Anglo-Saxon Cemetery at Street House, Loftus, North-East Yorkshire* (Hartlepool, 2012).

47   Adam Parker, "Fist-and-phallus Pendants from Roman Catterick," *Britannia* 46 (2015), 135–49.

48   Bede, *Historia Ecclesiastica*, 3.24; Plummer, p. 178.

49   Christine Fell, *Women in Anglo-Saxon England* (Oxford, 1984), pp. 56–81.

50   Fell, "Hild," p. 76.

Administration

Hild had established her first religious community with an endowment of a single hide and a handful of companions.[51] A hide (OE *hīd*, Latin *familia*, lit. 'family' or 'household') represented one farming household and, by inference, the land needed to sustain it.[52] When, in AD 655, King Oswiu granted twelve small estates (*possessiunculae*) for religious communities, six in Bernicia and six in Deira, he allocated to each estate ten hides. *Streanæshalh* (Whitby), appeared two years later, also with ten hides, and may have counted as one of the Deiran six (or it may have been a separate acquisition).[53] As the monastic system expanded, endowments became larger still, 70 hides to Wearmouth in AD 674 and 40 hides to Jarrow in AD 681,[54] while major houses could acquire satellite communities.[55] During Hild's lifetime, for example, *Streanæshalh* acquired a daughter house at Hackness and there is evidence for outposts at Lythe and Easington.[56]

In practical and economic terms these religious establishments are likely to have been organised in much the same way as secular ones, with a main estate centre, outlying farms, and a reeve to manage them.[57] When the duties of a reeve came to be written down in *c.* 1100, special emphasis was placed on the provision of textile-making equipment,[58] which, as we shall see, was an important feature of the Whitby archaeology. The community's income would include renders in kind from dependent households on the estates. If the records of Carolingian monasteries are any guide, these renders would generate a surplus which would then have to be processed.[59]

A number of the 7th-century Northumbrian foundations were, like *Streanæshalh*, located on headlands and, while their locations owed much to

51   Bede, *Historia Ecclesiastica*, 3.23; Plummer, p. 253.

52   Pickles, *Anglo-Saxon Yorkshire*, pp. 32–33.

53   Bede, *Historia Ecclesiastica*, 3.24; Plummer, p. 179; Fell, "Hild," pp. 85–86.

54   Rosemary J. Cramp, "Monastic Sites," in *The Archaeology of Anglo-Saxon England*, ed. David M. Wilson (Cambridge, 1976), pp. 201–52 at 229.

55   Pickles, *Anglo-Saxon Yorkshire*, p. 77.

56   Pickles, *Anglo-Saxon Yorkshire*, pp. 129, 161–62.

57   Foot, *Monastic Life*, pp. 5–6, 120–27; Pickles, *Anglo-Saxon Yorkshire*, p. 177; Hild's reeve appears in the story of Caedmon: *Historia Ecclesiastica*, 4.24, p. 260.

58   "*Be gesceadwisan gerefan*," in F. Liebermann, ed., *Die Gesetze der Angelsachsen 1: Text und Übersetzung* (Halle, 1903), pp. 453–55; Mark Gardiner, "Implements and Utensils in *Gerefa* and the Organization of Seigneurial Farmsteads in the High Middle Ages," *Medieval Archaeology* 50 (2006), 260–67.

59   Norman J.G. Pounds, *An Historical Geography of Europe, 450 B.C.–A.D. 1330* (Cambridge, 1973), pp. 201–14.

the Ionan practice of searching out isolated and elevated spots, it cannot be ignored that these places were also close to estuaries and harbours.[60] This was a period when coastal and riverine trading centres with contacts across the North Sea were springing up and the harbour at Whitby would have been useful for bringing in supplies and sending out any surpluses generated from renders, as well as maintaining contact with the rest of the monastic network in northern England and Francia. The evidence of coins has shown that Whitby, along with North Ferriby and the *wic* at York, was involved in local and overseas exchange in the earliest phase of monetisation, AD 680–710, and continued to be so until the mid-9th century.[61] Parallels can be drawn here with another double house at Minster-in-Thanet, Kent, also ruled by an abbess, which owned at least three ships in the 8th century and which received remission on tolls in certain ports.[62] By this means, houses such as *Streanæshalh* could exchange their agricultural and craft surpluses for commodities such as wine, oil, salt, and honey and also for precious items for the church and materials for the scriptorium. This was probably not seen as trade for its own sake, but rather as a sensible management of resources.

In terms of layout, the *Streanæshalh* establishment will have had a complex of buildings just as any secular estate centre would, with the addition of places specific to its function as a religious institution, such as the house for postulants "in a remote part of the monastery," the infirmary, the mausoleum, and the church dedicated to St Peter.[63] There was no standard layout for monasteries at this stage,[64] but the re-assessment of the archaeology has shown that the surviving early buildings were constructed in the native earth-fast timber tradition,[65] and the site has been described as "a big, rambling settlement with

---

60   David Petts, "Coastal Landscapes and Early Christianity in Anglo-Saxon Northumbria," *Estonian Journal of Archaeology* 13.2 (2009), 79–95; John Blair, *The Church in Anglo-Saxon Society* (Oxford, 2006), p. 150.

61   Pickles, *Anglo-Saxon Yorkshire*, pp. 118–20; Higham, *The Kingdom of Northumbria*, pp. 169–70; Richard G. Mason, *Whitby Abbey 1920s Clearance and Excavation; An Archaeological Reassessment* (unpublished, in archive at Historic England, 2018), pp. 83–84.

62   Susan Kelly, "Trading Privileges from Eighth-century England," *Early Medieval Europe* 1 part 1 (1982), 3–28; Gale R. Owen-Crocker, "Anglo-Saxon Women, Woman, Womanhood," in *New Readings on Women and Early Medieval English Literature and Culture: Cross Disciplinary Studies in Honour of Helen Damico*, ed. Helene Scheck and Christine E. Kozikowski (Leeds, 2019), pp. 23–41 at 26.

63   *Historia Ecclesiastica*, 3.24; 4.23; 4.24; Plummer, pp. 179, 156–57, 261–62.

64   Cramp, "Monastic Sites," pp. 217–41; Robin Daniels, *Anglo-Saxon Hartlepool and the Foundation of English Christianity: An Archaeology of the Anglo-Saxon Monastery* (Hartlepool, 2007); Rosemary Cramp, *Wearmouth and Jarrow Monastic Sites*, 2 vols (Swindon, 2005–06); Foot, *Monastic Life*, pp. 96–110.

65   Mason, *Whitby Abbey 1920s*, p. 74.

disparate activities going on in nooks and corners."[66] The original church has not been located, but at the heart of the community were funerary monuments likely to represent the mausoleum of Hild's kin group, the Deiran royal family.

All of this had to be administered. While the community was one of equals where everything was held in common,[67] it was necessarily under the supervision of the abbess.

Abbess Hild and Her Successors at *Streanæshalh* (Whitby)

Hild was abbess at *Streanæshalh* from AD 657 until her death in AD 680. She established regular observances there and to quote Bede, "She had so much wisdom that not only ordinary people in difficulties, but even kings and princes would sometimes seek advice from her, and take it."[68] Those under her direction were required to study the scriptures thoroughly and such was the comprehensive preparation provided at *Streanæshalh* in her time that five men trained there later became bishops.[69]

The next abbess was the daughter whom Oswiu had dedicated to the religious life, Ælfflæd. She had been placed as an infant in the Hartlepool house, under Hild's tutelage, and moved with Hild to *Streanæshalh*.[70] She was abbess from AD 680 until her death in AD 714, and for the first five years was co-abbess with her mother, Eanflæd, who had, while queen, been actively engaged in politics and the life of the Church. Ælfflæd continued in the same manner, and became another influential figure, "of the whole province the best consoler and advisor."[71] She is revealed as an educated woman in a letter to Abbess Adolana at Pfalzel,[72] and the anonymous *Life of Gregory* was composed at Whitby during her final years (indeed, the anonymous author could have been a *Streanæshalh* nun).[73]

---

66 Blair, *Church Anglo-Saxon Society*, p. 199.

67 Bede, *Historia Ecclesiastica*, 4.23; Plummer, p. 254.

68 *Tantae autem erat ipsa prudentiae, ut non solum mediocres quique in necessitatibus suis, sed etiam reges ac principes nonnumquam ab ea consilium quaererent, et inuenirent*; ibid.

69 Bede, *Historia Ecclesiastica*, 4.23; Plummer, p. 254; Hunter Blair, "Whitby," pp. 25–29.

70 Bede, *Historia Ecclesiastica*, 3.24; Plummer, pp. 178–79.

71 *semper totius provinciae consolatrix optimaque consiliatrix*: Eddius Stephanus, *Vita Sancti Wilfrithi*, ch. 60; Bertram Colgrave, ed. and trans., *The Life of Bishop Wilfrid by Eddius Stephanus* (Cambridge, 1927), pp. 128–29.

72 Pickles, *Anglo-Saxon Yorkshire*, pp. 84–85.

73 Switzerland, St Gallen, Stiftsbibliothek, Cod. Sang. 567; Bertram Colgrave, ed. and trans., *The Earliest Life of Gregory the Great: By an Anonymous Monk of Whitby* (Cambridge, 1985),

Less is known of the later community, but these early abbesses established a rule for later incumbents to follow and attached a sound reputation to the name of *Streanæshalh*.

The Meaning of the Name *Streanæshalh*

The town of Whitby did not acquire its current name until later,[74] when *Witebi* may have been the harbour settlement and *Prestebi* the headland area.[75] Bede, writing in the early 8th century, referred to Hild's establishment by its Anglo-Saxon name, *Streanæshal[c]h*,[76] although his supporting statement on the meaning of the name, *quod interpretatur sinus Fari*, has been the source of much debate.[77]

To take Bede's Latin first, *sinus* has often been translated as "bay," although it also has the meaning of "pocket" or "hidden place" and "inlet" would be a satisfactory alternative.[78] The mouth of the River Esk, which provides Whitby with its harbour, would fit his meaning here. *Farus* is derived from Φάρός, the island off Alexandria in Egypt, where stood a famous stone-built lighthouse, one of the 'seven wonders of the world.' Bede is likely to have known it from its appearance in the writings of classical authors and the 6th-century work of Gregory of Tours.[79] In the Roman period, there was a string of inter-visible

---

pp. 45–49; Andrew Breeze, "Did a Woman Write the Whitby Life of St Gregory?" *Northern History* 49.2 (2012), 345–50; Fell, "Hild," pp. 95–97.

74   A.D. Mills, *A Dictionary of English Place-names* (Oxford, 1991), p. 356.

75   Cramp, "Monastic Sites," p. 223.

76   Most commonly spelled *Streanæshal[c]h*, but also, *Streaneshalh, Streonaeshalch, Strenæshalc, Streneshalch, Streneshalh*; Bede, *Historia Ecclesiastica*, 3.24–25; 4.23–26; Plummer, pp. 179–83, 252–67. The spelling *Streon-* is found more often in the later 'King Alfred' version. According to Rahtz, one area of the headland was still identified on a map of 1794 as "The old Town of Streanshall"; Philip A. Rahtz, "Whitby 1958," *Yorkshire Archaeological Journal* 40 (1962), 604–18 at p. 607.

      For a summary of the arguments that identify *Streanæshalh* as Whitby, see Fell, "Hild," pp. 82–85; and Tony Wilmott, "The Anglian Abbey of *Streonæshalch*-Whitby: New Perspectives on Topography and Layout," in *Anglo-Saxon Studies in Archaeology and History, 20, Early Medieval Monasticism in the North Sea Zone: Recent Research and New Perspectives*, ed. Gabor Thomas and Alexandra Knox (2017), pp. 81–94 at 82.

77   Pickles, *Anglo-Saxon Yorkshire*, pp. 49, 143.

78   F.P. Leverett, ed., *A New and Copious Lexicon of the Latin Language, Compiled Chiefly from the Magnum Totius Latinitatis Lexicon of Facciolati and Forcellini, and the German Works of Scheller and Luenemann* (Boston, 1838), p. 830.

79   A.S. Elnashai, L. Di Sarno, and M.D. Carter, "New Light on an Ancient Illumination: The Pharos of Alexandria," *International Journal of Nonlinear Sciences and Numerical Simulation* 7.2 (2006), 137–48.

stone-built signal stations along the north-east coast and it has been argued on circumstantial evidence that there must have been one such on the headland at Whitby, before cliff erosion took it into the sea.[80] This is supported by the translation of the Latin word *farus/faros/fares* as Old English *torras*, "towers," at an earlier point in the text of the 'King Alfred' version of Bede.[81] For Bede, then, the Anglo-Saxon name with which he was familiar could be interpreted as "Tower-lighthouse Inlet."

To turn to the Old English, the final element *halh* is a word without a direct modern equivalent, although Patrick Stiles has demonstrated that its core meaning is something that diverges from a straight line or a flat plane and that it includes, *inter alia*, an angle, recess or nook.[82] In the case of *Streanæshalh*, the *halh* element can therefore be regarded as a straight translation of *sinus* or "inlet." The *streanæs* element is not so easily understood, but some authors derive it from *ge-stréon*, "gain," "wealth," "treasure," etc.[83] On this basis, it has been suggested that Bede was drawing a parallel with the story of Hild's birth, when her mother dreamt that she had found a jewel in the folds of her dress. Such a metaphor would not be unusual, given the Anglo-Saxon love of verbal puzzles and layered meanings, although this then presents the difficulty of the Latin *Fari* and the King Alfred translation of the word as "tower." If, instead of doubting Bede, we take his statement as correct, then *streanæs* should represent a tower-lighthouse. Re-using the idea that it is a metaphor, it might then be suggested that Bede was intentionally relating the 7th-century religious community to a safe harbour, a strong tower and a beacon of light.

The Excavations at Whitby Abbey

The standing ruins on the headland at Whitby belong to the 13th century. Little was known of the Anglo-Saxon foundation, until clearance and excavation of the site in 1920–28 uncovered, on the north side of the 13th-century church,

---

80   T.W. Bell, "A Roman Signal Station at Whitby," *Archaeological Journal* 155.1 (1998), 302–22; Wilmott, "The Anglian Abbey of *Streonæshalch*-Whitby," p. 86.

81   Compare *OE Historia Ecclesiastica*, 1.9 in Thomas Miller, ed., *The Old English Version of Bede's Ecclesiastical History of the English People* (Oxford, 1890), p. 46, with its Latin equivalent in *Historia Ecclesiastica*, 1.11; Plummer, p. 25.

82   Patrick Stiles, "Old English *Halh*, 'Slightly Raised Ground Isolated by a Marsh,'" in *Names, People and Places: An Onomastic Miscellany in Memory of John McNeal Dodgson*, ed. Alexander R. Rumble and A.D. Mills (Stamford, 1997), 330–44.

83   Hunter Blair, "Whitby," pp. 9–12; Stiles, "Old English *Halh*," p. 340; Pickles, *Anglo-Saxon Yorkshire*, p. 143.

built structures and a quantity of 'Saxon' artefacts.[84] As knowledge of Middle
Anglo-Saxon archaeology developed, this material came to be re-evaluated,
by Philip Rahtz,[85] Rosemary Cramp,[86] and, most recently, Richard Mason.[87]
Further small-scale archaeological investigations were conducted in 1958
and the 1980s, but substantial new evidence has since been added through
excavations carried out between 1993 and 2014 by Historic England (English
Heritage). These last have shown that Anglo-Saxon occupation covered a
much more extensive area of the headland than was previously realised. The
following summary, based on the research of Tony Wilmott, represents current
thinking on the layout of the Middle Anglo-Saxon features.[88]

The segmented remains of a boundary ditch appear to separate the headland from the surrounding countryside (Fig. 5.2). If the line has been correctly
surmised, it currently encloses an area of approximately 16 hectares, although
the northern edge has been subjected to so much erosion by the sea that a
further 16 hectares is likely to have been lost since Hild's time.[89] Originally,
therefore, the Anglo-Saxon structures will have been set on land overlooking
the River Esk, some 450 metres inland from the sea. If a Roman signal station
did exist here, it is likely to have been further out on the headland.[90]

The main areas of activity can be divided into four zones. In the north-west,
truncated by the present cliff edge, there was an occupation area, densely
filled with post-built structures, ditches, gullies, wells, and pits (Area Q). Finds
from this zone were mostly domestic, including loomweights, spindle whorls,
garment pins, and an iron trivet, although there was also a single fragment

---

84   Charles Peers and C.A. Ralegh Radford, "The Saxon Monastery of Whitby," *Archaeologia*
      89 (1943), 27–88.

85   Philip A. Rahtz, "Appendix C: The Building Plan of the Anglo-Saxon Monastery of Whitby
      Abbey," in Wilson, *The Archaeology of Anglo-Saxon England*, pp. 459–62.

86   Cramp, "Monastic Sites," pp. 201–52. Rosemary J. Cramp, "Appendix B: Analysis of
      the Finds Register and Location Plan of Whitby Abbey," in Wilson, *The Archaeology of
      Anglo-Saxon England*, pp. 453–57; Rosemary J. Cramp, "A Reconsideration of the Monastic
      Site at Whitby," in *The Age of Migrating Ideas: Early Medieval Art in Northern Britain and
      Ireland: Proceedings of the Second International Conference on Insular Art Held in the
      National Museums of Scotland in Edinburgh, 3–6 January 1991*, ed. R. Michael Spearman
      and John Higgitt (Edinburgh, 1993), pp. 64–73.

87   Mason, *Whitby Abbey 1920s*.

88   Wilmott, "The Anglian Abbey of *Streonæshalch*-Whitby"; and Wilmott in prep.

89   Calculations made in 1960 suggested that 300 metres of land had been lost to the sea
      since the Roman period; Bell, "Roman Signal Station," p. 313. More recent estimates indi-
      cate a distance of 450 metres; Wilmott, "The Anglian Abbey of *Streonæshalch*-Whitby,"
      p. 86.

90   A scatter of Roman finds, including late Roman pottery, lends credence to the idea that
      there was once a Roman signal station on the headland.

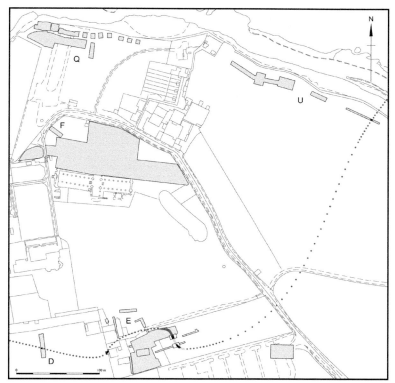

FIGURE 5.2   Map of the Whitby headland, showing the trenches that have
               produced Middle Anglo-Saxon archaeology and the projected line
               of the boundary ditch.
               Drawn by John Vallender, Historic England

of a funerary cross. Directly to the east of this there was a large hall-like,
post-in-trench building, 6 metres wide by at least 14 metres long (Area U).
Some slight evidence for glass-working was recovered in this area. The heart of
the religious establishment, however, is likely to have been in the centre of the
site. The church itself has not been located – it may have been directly below
the 13th-century church – but the central area uncovered in the 1920s has been
re-examined and extended to the west (Area F). Here there were graves and
memorial stones inscribed with names that, although no longer confidently
identified with individual members of the royal family,[91] may still represent

---

91   John Higgitt, "The Inscriptions," in *Corpus of Anglo-Stone Sculpture VI: Northern Yorkshire*,
       ed. James Lang (Oxford, 2002), allows Acha (sister of King Edwin) as a possible inter-
       pretation of Whitby 21 and perhaps Cyneburg (wife of King Oswald) for Whitby 49,

the dynastic burial ground described by Bede.[92] There was also an extensive range of valuable, high-status artefacts, alongside domestic material such as cooking pots and textile equipment.[93] A rutted cart track, with some small structures facing onto it, passed to the west of this zone. Finally, to the south there was a large, less prestigious, cemetery incorporating 225 graves for men, women, and juveniles, with a small stone-built structure, probably a mortuary chapel (Area E). This cemetery was tucked into a kink in the boundary ditch so that it was outside the perimeter, though possibly still on monastic land, and has been interpreted as a burial ground for lay people.

The artefacts to be reviewed below came from the 1993–2014 excavations,[94] but will be considered in relation to the finds recovered in the 1920s. The main focus will be on those topics and artefact groups which have seen substantial re-assessment in recent years, as a result of the excavation of other Middle Anglo-Saxon sites, the emergence of comparative material from the Portable Antiquities Scheme, and a renewed interest in material which sheds light on the lives of women. Where datable, their types and forms place them in the Middle Anglo-Saxon period, which means that they can be safely regarded as contemporary with the religious house established in AD 657 and destroyed in AD 867.[95]

Garment Pins

A short pin, usually less than 70 mm long, was adopted into women's dress in the late 6th century, when it coincided with the lengthening of the head-veil

---

but Ælfflæd is not accepted for Whitby 47; available online http://www.ascorpus.ac.uk/vol6_chap7.php; http://www.ascorpus.ac.uk/catvol6.php?pageNum_urls=422 (accessed 22 June 2020).

92   Bede, *Historia Ecclesiastica* 3.24; Plummer, p. 179.

93   Peers and Radford, "The Saxon Monastery."

94   Described in greater detail in Penelope Walton Rogers, *The Anglian Artefacts from Whitby Abbey Excavations, 1993–2014* ASLab Report to Historic England, 9 April 2019, to appear in Wilmott, in prep. Thanks are due to Tony Wilmott, Senior Archaeologist at Historic England, for permission to publish this material ahead of his own report, and to Susan Harrison at the English Heritage Helmsley store for information on the finds from the first excavation. The artefacts from the various excavations are either under the care of English Heritage, in their Helmsley store, or on display at Whitby Museum, or they are held by Whitby Museum itself.

95   Across the site there was a hiatus in pottery evidence between the 9th and 12th centuries; Wilmott, "The Anglian Abbey of *Streonæshalch*-Whitby," p. 86. For historical sources on the destruction of the abbey, see Fell, "Hild," pp. 88–89.

to below the hip (see above). In clothed burials it was often located on the shoulder or upper chest. The occasional rare example from a male grave usually proves to have been an *ad hoc* fastener, to fix a cloth wrapper on a spear, for example.[96] Short pins became even more common in occupation sites after the end of clothed burial and a variety of evidence demonstrates the continued use of the long veil.[97] It would appear from the comments of Aldhelm, who criticised those nuns whose head-coverings "fell freely to their ankles"[98] that women had taken this garment into their religious communities. Short pins from the Whitby excavations can therefore be taken as representatives of the veil worn by 'brides of Christ.' Although extremely common in a range of Middle Anglo-Saxon sites, pins are noticeably rare in the male religious houses of Wearmouth and Jarrow.[99]

There were seven short copper-alloy garment pins from the 1993–2014 excavations (Fig. 5.3), six from the occupation area at the northern cliff edge and one from the cemetery by the boundary ditch in the south.[100] The cemetery example came from a grave fill, but was thought to have originated on the body: if so, it probably indicates the practice of clothed-and-furnished burial, a ritual which came to an end in the late 7th century.[101] A single cremation burial, radiocarbon-dated to AD 610–680 (95% confidence), confirms a 7th-century element in this burial ground.[102]

These seven add to the 47 copper-alloy pins with identifiable head forms recovered in the 1920s from the centre of the site.[103] Taken together, the 54 have heads which can be polyhedral with inscribed ring-and-dot motifs (43%), biconical (24%), globular (13%), or flat, also with ring-and-dot (13%). These head forms had precursors in the Early cemeteries, but they were at their most

---

96   Walton Rogers, *Cloth and Clothing*, p. 126.

97   Walton Rogers, *Cloth and Clothing*, pp. 161–67. Gale R. Owen-Crocker, *Dress in Anglo-Saxon England: revised and enlarged edition* (Woodbridge, 2004), pp. 132–37, 157–59.

98   "*… talotenus prolixius dependunt*"; Aldhelm, *De Virginitate*, in R. Ehwald, ed., *Aldhelmi Opera* (Monumenta Germaniae Historica, Auctores Antiquissimi 15) (Berlin, 1919), p. 318.

99   A single example of a polyhedral pin from Jarrow draws parallels with the rare examples in 7th-century men's graves. Other pins from Wearmouth and Jarrow are from earlier and later periods; Seamus Ross, "Pins," in Cramp, *Wearmouth and Jarrow*, 2, pp. 236–42.

100   Walton Rogers, *The Anglian Artefacts*.

101   Alex Bayliss, John Hines, Karen Høilund Nielsen, Gerry McCormac, and Christopher Scull, *Anglo-Saxon Graves and Grave Goods of the Sixth and Seventh Centuries AD: A Chronological Framework* (Society for Medieval Archaeology Monograph Vol. 33) (Leeds, 2013), p. 479.

102   Wilmott, "The Anglian Abbey of *Streonæshalch*-Whitby," p. 90.

103   Peers and Radford, "The Saxon Monastery," pp. 61–64, along with two short bone pins, p. 70. The artefacts, records, and photographs are held in the English Heritage store at Helmsley.

a   b   c   d

e   f

FIGURE 5.3A–D   Copper-alloy pins from the 1993–2014 excavations: (a) Sf 31003,
                 polyhedral; (b) Sf 31009, rounded biconical; (c) Sf 24504, flat; (d) Sf
                 31004, lozenge-shaped.
                 Photos: Walton Rogers © ASLab
                 (e) The gilt copper-alloy bird pin from the 1920s excavation, accession
                 number W333.
                 © Whitby Museum
                 (f) The gold bird pin from the Balmaghie (Galloway) hoard.
                 © The Trustees of National Museums of Scotland

common in 8th- and 9th-century sites, declining only in the early Viking Age as
new shapes took hold. The main types are found throughout England, but have
an easterly bias and the greatest numbers reported to the Portable Antiquities
Scheme (PAS) have come from Yorkshire, Lincolnshire, and Norfolk.[104] Their
distribution can be extended north to Whithorn, a Northumbrian monastic
centre in south-west Scotland,[105] and across the North Sea to Domburg and
Dorestad in The Netherlands.[106] The many variations in moulded details and
metallurgical composition suggest that they were produced in several different

---

104   Walton Rogers, *The Anglian Artefacts*, Tables 1–2.
105   Peter Hill, *Whithorn and St Ninian: The Excavation of a Monastic Town 1984–91* (Stroud,
       1997), p. 363.
106   David A. Hinton and A.L. Parsons, "Pins," in *The Gold, Silver and Other Non-ferrous Alloy
       Objects from Hamwic, and the Non-ferrous Metalworking Evidence* (Southampton Finds
       Vol. 2), ed. David A. Hinton (Stroud, 1996), pp. 14–31 at 20, 25, 28.

workshops, and there may be diachronic changes not yet detected, but both the PAS and the excavated evidence show that polyhedral pins with ring-and-dot ornament were especially popular in Yorkshire as a whole, not just at Whitby.[107]

There was also a single example of a pin with a flat lozenge-shaped head (Fig. 5.3d). There have been five other examples from Yorkshire, and then a long gap until a further three examples in and around Hamwic.[108] There is no easy explanation for two clusters at opposite ends of the country, but the Yorkshire examples all fall within the boundaries of the former kingdom of Deira.[109] If this pattern continues to hold true with future finds, it will suggest that Deira retained a regional identity after it had been absorbed into Northumbria. Wool diamond twills with a particularly small pattern repeat found in two graves in the Early Anglo-Saxon cemetery at West Heslerton in the Vale of Pickering, and again in five examples from Anglo-Scandinavian York, are potentially also a Deiran tradition.[110]

These pins are all simple functional forms. The finely crafted silver and gilt pins with large flat ornamented heads found at other Middle Anglo-Saxon sites[111] are absent from Whitby. There is, however, a single gilded copper-alloy pin with a head in the form of a long-necked bird (Fig. 5.3e).[112] Moulded three-dimensional birds fit better in the Irish and Romano-British, rather than Anglo-Saxon, tradition,[113] although a copper-alloy pin with a folded-wing bird was metal-detected at South Newbald, East Yorkshire, and there are two other related examples, insecurely dated, from Richborough, Kent.[114] More recently a finely worked gold pin in 9th- or early 10th-century Anglo-Saxon style, with a head in the form of a long-necked, folded-wing bird, has emerged from the

---

107   Walton Rogers, *The Anglian Artefacts*, Table 2.

108   Walton Rogers, *The Anglian Artefacts*.

109   Walton Rogers, *The Anglian Artefacts*.

110   Penelope Walton Rogers, "Textile Networks in Viking-Age Towns of Britain and Ireland," in *Crafts and Social Networks in Viking Towns*, ed. Steven P. Ashby and Søren M. Sindbæk (Oxford, 2020), pp. 83–122 at 102.

111   Leslie Webster and Janet Backhouse, eds, *The Making of England: Anglo-Saxon Art and Culture AD 600–900* (London, 1991), pp. 82–85, 96–98; Kevin Leahy, "Middle Anglo-Saxon Metalwork from South Newbald and the Productive Site Phenomenon," in Geake and Kenny, *Early Deira*, pp. 51–82.

112   Cramp, "A Reconsideration of the Monastic Site," p. 67; Seamus Ross, "Dress Pins from Anglo-Saxon England: Their Production and Typo-Chronological Development," DPhil thesis, 2 vols (Oxford, 1991), 1, pp. 220–21; 2, p. 555.

113   Françoise Henry, *Irish Art in the Early Christian Period to AD 800* (2nd ed., London, 1947), plates 39b and I; Rupert Bruce-Mitford and Sheila Raven, *A Corpus of Late Celtic Hanging Bowls* (Oxford, 2005), *passim*.

114   Leahy, "Middle Anglo-Saxon Metalwork from South Newbald," pp. 56–57.

Balmaghie (Galloway) hoard (Fig. 5.3f).[115] The shapes of these birds' heads bear a resemblance to the bird-head terminals on the penannular brooches from Yorkshire which came to be produced in the 7th century in Dunadd, in Dál Riata.[116] Taking the evidence together, the Whitby bird pin is probably best interpreted as a product of the interchange of British/Scottish/Irish and Anglo-Saxon influences that typifies Northumbria.

Textile Production

The quantity of textile-making equipment recovered from the site is an even stronger indicator of the presence of women[117] and distinguishes this site from the all-male monastic houses, such as Jarrow and Wearmouth, where such items have been entirely absent.[118] They are a clear indication of cloth production within the Middle Anglo-Saxon precinct. Spinning and weaving equipment has been recovered from all parts of the site, in the central zone,[119] in the northern occupation area, and in the southern area close to the boundary ditch.

Spinning

The production of yarn is represented by spindle whorls, which were used to keep the spindle upright and maintain the momentum of spin during suspended-spindle spinning. There were five whorls from the recent excavations (three stone and two fired clay) (Fig. 5.4), and 15 from the 1920s excavations (nine stone, one probably clay, two jet, two bone, and one lead).[120] Most of the whorls were the typical plano-convex form (Walton Rogers Forms A1 and A2)[121] of eastern England in the 6th to 10th centuries, with a small number disc-shaped (Form B), possibly a Romano-British tradition. Most were plain and lathe-turned, although two had simple decoration and one had a runic inscription, possibly a personal name, LEU. Where the petrology has been

---

115 Martin Goldberg in prep.

116 Raghnall Ó Floinn, "The Anglo-Saxon Connection: Irish Metalwork, AD 400–800," in *Anglo-Saxon/Irish Relations before the Vikings*, ed. James Graham-Campbell and Michael Ryan (Oxford, 2009), pp. 231–51; Alan Lane and Ewan Campbell, *Dunadd: An Early Dalriadic Capital* (Oxford, 2000), pp. 114–18.

117 Walton Rogers, *Cloth and Clothing*, pp. 45–47.

118 Cramp, *Wearmouth and Jarrow*, 1, p. 345. The artefacts from the double house at Hartlepool were few, but included two loom weights; Daniels, *Anglo-Saxon Hartlepool*, p. 129.

119 Cramp "Analysis of Finds Register," p. 456; Mason, *Whitby Abbey 1920s*, pp. 76–77.

120 Peers and Radford, "The Saxon Monastery," pp. 68–74.

121 Walton Rogers, "Textile Networks," pp. 96–97.

FIGURE 5.4A–B   Spindle whorls from the 1993–2014 excavations, (a) stone, left to
right, Sf 24569, diameter 36 mm, Sf 10207, diameter 41 mm, Sf
42296 diameter 33 mm; (b) clay, left to right, Sf 42124, diameter
43 mm, Sf 31336, diameter 46 mm.
Photos Arabelle Barratt © ASLab

investigated, the stone has proved to be of local origin, as has the clay.[122] The
interest lies in their weights and sizes. Most Anglo-Saxon spindle whorls weigh
12–60g, but the majority of the Whitby whorls, at 11–29g, follow those from
the Middle Anglo-Saxon estate centre at Flixborough (7–33g, mainly 10–20g),
in being limited to the lower end of the range.[123] While there is no exact correlation between weight of whorl and quality of yarn, where light whorls are
associated with lightweight weaving equipment (see below) it is reasonable to
suppose that the fabrics being produced were relatively fine.

There are also two heavy clay whorls which stand out as different from the
rest (Fig. 5.4b). These are elliptical in side-view (Form C) and weigh 41g and
(estimated) 52g. No full survey of Anglo-Saxon spindle whorls has as yet been
conducted, but on the evidence available so far, in terms of size, shape, and
material, these two whorls would fit most naturally amongst the whorls of
Suffolk, Essex, and London. As women are likely to have retained the traditional spinning techniques learned in their youth, this raises the possibility
that the whorls represent women from southern East Anglia in the community. Since Hild was related to the royal house of East Anglia, which had its base
in south-east Suffolk, and women tended to enter the religious communities of
their kinswomen,[124] this would not be unlikely.

---

122   Personal communications from Mike Ridealgh and Gareth Perry.
123   Walton Rogers, *Cloth and Clothing*, p. 26. Penelope Walton Rogers, "Textile Production," in
Life and Economy at Early Medieval Flixborough, AD 600–1100, 2: The Artefact Evidence, ed.
D.H. Evans and Christopher Loveluck (Oxford, 2009), pp. 281–316 at 283–87.
124   Foot, *Monastic Life*, p. 150.

Weaving Equipment

Weaving on the warp-weighted loom was represented by clay loom weights, which were used to keep the warp under tension while work was in progress. There were eleven whole and 76 groups of fragments from the 1993–2014 excavations and thirty whole (or almost whole), with fragments of substantially more, from the 1920s. There was also a single example of a double-ended bone pin-beater, a multi-purpose hand-tool used with the same loom. The warp-weighted loom was the main cloth loom of the Anglo-Saxon period, in use with little alteration from the 5th to the 10th or 11th centuries.[125] There was no evidence for the specialist two-beam vertical loom at this site, nor for tablet-weaving.

The clay from which the loom weights were made matches the clay that can be gathered from the foot of the cliffs of the headland.[126] They have been made by shaping a gather of clay into a ball and pushing a hole through with the fingers: imprints of small finger-nails were preserved on at least one loom weight (Fig. 5.5a). The diameter of the perforation was usually just under a third of the overall diameter which is typical of the 'intermediate' loom weight, at its most common in the Middle Anglo-Saxon period (though continuing into the 9th/10th century).[127] One had an impressed mark in the form of a six-petal flower (Fig. 5.5b) and another had parallel rows of stab-marks.

The interest once more lies in the light nature of the weights (Fig. 5.6). Clay loom weights from farmsteads and villages of the Early period mostly fall within the range 150–550g, and a bimodal distribution was noted in the large collection from Mucking, Essex, with peaks at 200–300g and 400–450g.[128] The Whitby collection corresponds with the lighter group, as do the loom weights from high-status estate centres at Flixborough[129] and most of the Brandon collection,[130] while the heavier end of the spectrum is represented in the finds from the *wic* at Middle Anglo-Saxon London.[131] The slender pin-beater from Whitby, 6–7 mm in diameter, also corresponds with thin examples from

125   Walton Rogers, "Cloth, Clothing and Anglo-Saxon Women," pp. 254–55, 268.

126   Gareth Perry, in Walton Rogers, *The Anglian Artefacts*.

127   Walton Rogers, *Cloth and Clothing*, p. 30; Walton Rogers, "Textile Production," *Flixborough*, p. 283.

128   Helena Hamerow, *Excavations at Mucking vol 2: The Anglo-Saxon Settlement* (London, 1993), pp. 66–67.

129   Walton Rogers, "Textile Production," *Flixborough*, pp. 288–96.

130   Penelope Walton Rogers, "Textile Production and Treatment," in *Staunch Meadow, Brandon, Suffolk: A High Status Middle Saxon Settlement on the Fen Edge*, ed. Andrew Tester, Sue Anderson, Ian Riddler, and Robert Carr (Bury St Edmunds, 2014), pp. 285–94 at 288–90.

131   For sites and data sources, see Walton Rogers, *The Anglian Artefacts*.

FIGURE 5.5A–D   Clay loomweights from the 1993–2014 excavations. (a) Sf 42423,
                 intermediate, diameter 85 mm; (b) Sf 11687, intermediate, diameter 84
                 mm; (c) Sf 31151, bun-shaped, imprints fingernails, diameter 92 mm;
                 (d) Sf 3166, bun-shaped, stamped, diameter 81 mm.
                 Photo: Arabelle Barratt © ASLab

Flixborough, 6–8 mm in diameter, and contrasts with pin-beaters at other
sites, generally 8–12 mm thick.[132] The finds from the religious community at
Lyminge (another double house) and the *wic* at Ipswich have not yet been published, but if the sites described here are representative of the Middle period as
a whole, then they indicate a split in production at the end of the Early period.
This is most likely to represent the making of linen and fine wool textiles in the
estate centres and coarser cloths in larger centres of population.

The similarity between the Whitby collection and the Middle Anglo-Saxon
estate centres supports the historical evidence that the early religious

---

132   Walton Rogers, "Textile Production," *Flixborough*, pp. 287–89.

a

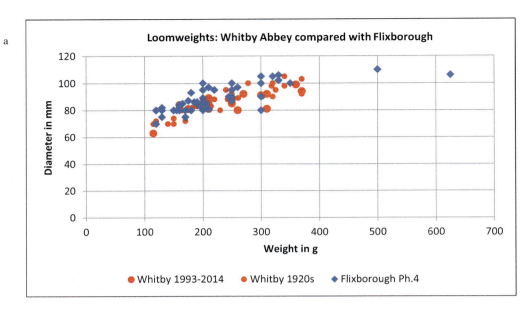

b

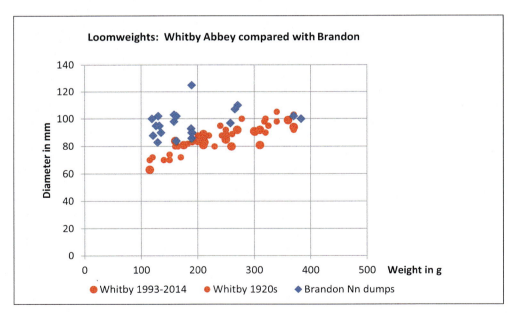

FIGURE 5.6A–C   Charts comparing the Whitby loomweights with loomweights from other Middle
                 Anglo-Saxon sites,
                 (a) Flixborough, Lincolnshire, (b) Brandon, Suffolk, and (c) Lundenwic (London).
                 © ASLab

communities were managed in much the same way as other estate centres. They suggest a concentration on good quality fabrics, but not the specialist weaves worked on a different loom (probably present at Brandon).[133]

A Wool Textile

Only one potential product of the Whitby looms was excavated, a single fragment of wool textile, 190 × 115 mm, recovered in the 1920s.[134] It is woven in plain 2/2 twill and is made from smooth combed-wool yarns, Z-spun in warp and weft, with a count of 24 × 16 threads per cm. The date of the piece is insecure, but its general characteristics would fit an Anglo-Saxon context that post-dated the introduction of wool combs in the late 6th or 7th century. Its

---

133 Walton Rogers, "Textile Production and Treatment," *Brandon*, p. 292.
134 Mrs J.W. Crowfoot [Grace M. Crowfoot], "A Textile from Whitby," in Peers and Radford, "The Saxon Monastery," pp. 86–88.

thread-count falls towards the higher end of the range for Anglo-Saxon wool twills.[135] It is a plain, good-quality, but not luxurious, fabric.

Counters

A series of black discs, 30–38 mm diameter, were recovered from the 1920s excavations, to which can be added a new example from 1993–2014. Some have a slightly domed top with an outer flange, some have a small central perforation, and several have either a single crossways groove or two grooves forming a cross on the flat face. In the most recent find, which is a fragment with only one complete face, the cross is broad and shallow and produced from repeated wear. The first group were defined as 'jet' but the recent find has been examined by a geologist who has identified it as 'soft jet' from the bituminous shale (Mulgrave shale), which is found in the Whitby Mudstone Formation above true jet.[136] Both true jet and soft jet were local materials. A flat perforated disc of copper alloy was found with one of the 'jet' examples and matched its diameter.

When discs of this nature have been found in 7th-century graves, they have often been classified as gaming counters, which is a reasonable conclusion when they are associated with dice.[137] In a monastic site, however, it is possible that they are counters from the kind of counting table, a relative of the abacus, which had been in use for computation since the Roman period.[138] The table was a portable board with lines that marked out columns for units, and the counters (*calculi*) were moved up, down, and sideways, to keep track of sums. As such they could have been used to teach arithmetic, or to make calculations for the estate's accounts. The 196 coins from the site (all excavations), ranging for the late 7th to the mid-9th century, bear witness to the economic activity of the community.[139]

This concludes the review of the new evidence, but a brief summary of the artefacts from earlier excavations can be included here.

---

135   Walton Rogers, *Cloth and Clothing*, pp. 70–73.
136   Personal communication from Mike Ridealgh.
137   Helen Geake, *The Use of Grave Goods in Conversion-Period England, c. 600–c. 850* (British Archaeological Reports British Series 261) (Oxford, 1997), pp. 100–01.
138   Harry L. Levy, "Catullus, 5, 7–11 and the Abacus," *The American Journal of Philology* 62.2 (1941), 222–24. For a late medieval illustration of a counting board in use, see figure 4 of Kevin Samoly, "The History of the Abacus," *Ohio Journal of School Mathematics* 65 (2012), 58–66.
139   Mason, *Whitby Abbey 1920s*, pp. 83–84; Pickles, *Anglo-Saxon Yorkshire*, pp. 118–20.

Artefacts Collected before 1993

As more comparative material has become available, the artefacts from the 1920s excavations have been re-evaluated and some of the less confidently identified objects have now been ascribed to other periods.[140] The pottery is also in the process of re-assessment.[141] Much of the core Middle Anglo-Saxon material, however, remains the same, though some items now have a closer dating and there is a better understanding of their function.

Literacy is indicated by the presence of styli, the tools used to write on wax tablets.[142] There are also at least two of the bone objects with metal points variously interpreted as parchment prickers or as styli.[143] Flat mounts for book covers or shrines include three openwork octofoil plates in gilded copper alloy, dated to the 8th century, and hinged fittings have also been noted.[144] Three imitation gemstones in green and blue glass, one cast with a bust in relief, and glass plaques and studs, including one square blue stud inlaid with gold and silver, are likely to have decorated similar items, or else chalices or altar crosses.[145] Some small casket keys in non-ferrous metals could have been used to keep valuables such as these secure.[146] Remains of six hooked escutcheons and two applied strips from hanging bowls have been dated to the second half of the 7th century and the 8th century.[147] Hanging bowls were prestige objects, most probably made in British or Irish workshops: their precise function is unknown, but they may have been associated with washing and in a monastic setting could have had a liturgical use.[148] Fragments of 8th-century glass vessels were also represented.[149]

---

140 Mason, *Whitby Abbey 1920s*, pp. 19–21.
141 Mason, *Whitby Abbey 1920s*, pp. 82, 99, citing Chris Cumberpatch, unpublished.
142 Peers and Radford, "The Saxon Monastery," pp. 64–65, 71; Webster and Backhouse, *The Making of England*, pp. 74, 142–43.
143 Peers and Radford, "The Saxon Monastery," p. 71, where described as "pegs"; Richard Gameson, "The Archaeology of the Anglo-Saxon Book," in *The Oxford Handbook of Anglo-Saxon Archaeology*, ed. Helena Hamerow, David A. Hinton and Sally Crawford (Oxford 2011), pp. 797–823, at pp. 799–802.
144 Peers and Radford, "The Saxon Monastery," pp. 50–55; Webster and Backhouse, *The Making of England*, p. 142. Cramp, "A Reconsideration of the Monastic Site," p. 67.
145 Webster and Backhouse, *The Making of England*, pp. 144–45.
146 Peers and Radford, "The Saxon Monastery," pp. 66–67.
147 Bruce-Mitford and Raven, *A Corpus of Late Celtic Hanging Bowls*, pp. 300–05.
148 Bruce-Mitford and Raven, *A Corpus of Late Celtic Hanging Bowls*, pp. 30–33.
149 Webster and Backhouse, *The Making of England*, pp. 143–44.

Garment accessories were originally thought to include brooches and buckles, although most of these can now be ascribed to earlier and later periods.[150] One penannular brooch, however, has been confidently identified with a type found in Early Christian Ireland (Fowler Type B),[151] which draws attention to the Irish influences on at least one hanging bowl mount and the square glass stud.[152] There were also three finger rings, of which two, one plain gold and the other copper-alloy with a coiled bezel, were, curiously, threaded on a Roman trumpet brooch, while a third has 9th-century ornament.[153] There were also 14 oval strap-ends of silver and copper alloy, with cast ornament, dated to the 9th century.[154] These are regarded as chapes for straps of different sorts, although their most common use was probably as pairs on the ends of knotted girdles.[155] Their decorative nature hints at a shift to greater ornamentation in the 9th-century clothing of the community. The plain triangular hooked tag[156] also had a range of uses, but the ornamented example is probably post-medieval.[157] Personal accessories included the remains of two bone combs, numerous metal tweezers, three small toiletry spoons, and a knife represented by a bone handle.[158] A copper-alloy comb, possibly of Frisian origin, was collected from the site in 1876.[159] Objects associated with domestic tasks were often omitted from the first report, although two copper-alloy skillets and needles were included,[160] to which can be added from the original finds register a millstone, a quern, pottery, a stone cresset, and shears.[161] Apart from the

---

150   A broad-banded annular brooch and most of the buckles illustrated in Peers and Radford, "The Saxon Monastery," Fig. 12 are late medieval forms. The safety-pin brooches and the second penannular brooch could be Anglo-Saxon or Romano-British.

151   Elizabeth Fowler, "Celtic Metalwork of the Fifth and Sixth Centuries A.D.: A Re-appraisal," *Archaeological Journal* 120.1 (1963), 98–160, at pp. 120, 147.

152   Susan Youngs, "Fine Metalwork to AD 650," in *"The Work of Angels": Masterpieces of Celtic Metalwork, 6th–9th centuries AD*, ed. Susan Youngs (London, 1989), pp. 20–71 at 60.

153   Mason, *Whitby Abbey 1920s*, p. 21. Gabor Thomas extends Trewhiddle Style in Northumbria into the 10th century: "Reflections on a '9th-century' Northumbrian Metalworking Tradition: A Silver Hoard from Poppleton, North Yorkshire," *Medieval Archaeology* 50.1 (2006), 143–64.

154   Peers and Radford, "The Saxon Monastery," pp. 55–57; Webster and Backhouse, *The Making of England*, pp. 142, 233–35.

155   Thomas, "Northumbrian Metalworking," pp. 158–59.

156   Peers and Radford, "The Saxon Monastery," pp. 59–60.

157   Mason, *Whitby Abbey 1920s*, pp. 19–20.

158   Peers and Radford, "The Saxon Monastery," pp. 61–63, 69–72.

159   A.J. White, "Copper-alloy Combs from Britain and Frisia," *Medieval Archaeology* 32 (1988), 212–13.

160   Peers and Radford, "The Saxon Monastery," pp. 66–68.

161   Cramp, "Finds Register," pp. 455–57.

textile-making equipment, there was little evidence for manufacturing, other than some sparse glass-working materials, including a millefiori rod and two fragments of tesserae.[162]

Finally, the stone sculpture must be mentioned.[163] This includes sparely decorated funerary crosses, some as early as the late 7th century, which find parallels in the Ile de France: Rosemary Cramp draws a connection with the religious community at Chelles.[164] Some later pieces are ornamented and include a naturalistic beast and an example of interlace.[165]

Review

Even if it had not been known that this was a double house, the presence of women at the Whitby site would have been promptly identified from the garment pins and the broad spread of textile equipment. The types and sizes of the equipment have proved to be typical of a well-managed estate centre. They are likely to have been used to transform raw materials, wool, flax, and hemp, brought in from the estates, into the good quality, but not luxurious, product seen in the single surviving (though undated) textile.

The men of the double house, on the other hand, are archaeologically invisible. In furnished burials weaponry is found with biological males, but weapons would not be expected in a religious community. They are present in estate centres such as Brandon[166] and Flixborough[167] but no examples securely dated to the Middle Anglo-Saxon period have been identified in the male houses at Wearmouth and Jarrow.[168] Metal-working crafts have some degree of association with men and metal-working was present at Jarrow[169] (and also at the

---

162 Webster and Backhouse, *The Making of England*, pp. 144–45. For some minor glass-working waste from the recent excavations, see Wilmott, "The Anglian Abbey of *Streonæshalch*-Whitby," p. 87.

163 Lang, *Corpus of Anglo-Stone Sculpture VI*.

164 Cramp, "A Reconsideration of the Monastic Site," pp. 68–71.

165 Lang, *Corpus of Anglo-Stone Sculpture VI*, Whitby 50, Whitby 36, and possibly Whitby 34.

166 Nicola Rogers and Patrick Ottaway, "Weaponry," in Tester *et al.*, *Staunch Meadow, Brandon*, pp. 265–67.

167 Patrick Ottaway, "Weapons and Armour," in Evans and Loveluck, *Life and Economy at Early Medieval Flixborough*, p. 123.

168 Cramp, *Wearmouth and Jarrow*, 1, p. 289.

169 Cramp, *Wearmouth and Jarrow*, 1, pp. 232–41, 304–05; 2, pp. 470–80.

double house at Hartlepool),[170] but the stone metal-working moulds from Whitby are from a later phase of the site.[171]

This different gender emphasis in the crafts was first noted by Rosemary Cramp, who has suggested that there could have been an exchange of metal-work for textiles within the monastic network.[172] There are certainly records of gifts between individuals, such as the linen cloth given by Verca, abbess of a Tyneside house, to Cuthbert at Lindisfarne.[173] It would be easy to imagine products of this nature leaving the Whitby harbour for transport to other communities along the coast or even across the North Sea. Other artefacts, likely to represent the movement of people as much as objects, have demonstrated connections with Ireland (or an Irish community), East Anglia, and Francia.

The second important feature to have emerged from the study of the artefacts is the contrast between the plain nature of the personal accessories of the 7th- and 8th-century group and the valuable objects associated with the celebration of the Christian religion. The simple ring-and-dot pattern on the pins has been shown to be standard for Yorkshire at this time and it would probably have been difficult for a nun to acquire anything else. These pins do not compare with the finely worked, individually crafted silver and gilt pins from sites such as Flixborough, Brandon, and South Newbald. The decorative plates and glass studs, on the other hand, will have been mounted on books and altar furniture such as crosses and chalices. This argues that the community at *Streanæshalh* had genuinely embraced the practice of equality and shared ownership described by Bede, and were saving their wealth for their religious practices.[174] It is only in the 9th century that more decorative ornament can be found in personal items.

This contrast between the two categories of artefact, together with the absence of weaponry, may help with the difficult archaeological problem of how to distinguish a secular estate centre from one used for religious purpose, where historical sources are silent. Given the vagaries of archaeological preservation, it would be risky to identify the function of a site solely from what is missing, but these two features – unornamented garment accessories and the absence of weapons – may at least be pointers to the kind of community resident at the site, to be considered with, for example, bio-archaeological evidence for a monastic diet.

---

170   Daniels, *Anglo-Saxon Hartlepool*, p. 127.

171   Lang, *Corpus of Anglo-Stone Sculpture VI*, Whitby 32.

172   Cramp, *Wearmouth and Jarrow*, 1, pp. 344–45.

173   Bede, Bertram Colgrave, trans., *Two Lives of Saint Cuthbert: A Life by an Anonymous Monk of Lindisfarne and Bede's Prose Life* (Cambridge, 1940), pp. 272 (Latin) and 273 (English).

174   Bede, *Historia Ecclesiastica*, 4.23; Plummer, p. 254.

Conclusion

Viewed from a modern perspective, the Anglo-Saxon period can resemble a slow downhill slide in the status of women. That women's rights and access to learning declined after the Norman Conquest was established some time ago,[175] but more recently the 9th century has come to be seen as a pivotal time for women in the Church, as abbesses became less prominent in public affairs and greater prestige and authority was accorded to their male counterparts – a process already begun in the 8th century.[176] The archaeological sources described above indicate that for some women it had begun earlier still. For Hild, however, born into the early 7th century, most of this was in an unknown future. She herself stood at the point where rulership dynasties were emerging and women who were lucky enough to be born into a royal or noble family could expect to be proactively engaged in their own lives, in the promotion of their kin group and in the spread of the new religion. Historians in recent years have been making significant advances in their investigation of the role of women in the early Church. Now, to this can be added the archaeological material from Whitby Abbey, which has usefully extended our knowledge of the physical context in which the early abbesses lived and of the practical, day-to-day management of religious communities such as *Streanæshalh*.

175   Doris Mary Stenton, *The English Woman in History* (London, 1957), pp. 29–37; Cecily Clarke and Elizabeth Williams, "The Impact of 1066," in Fell, *Women in Anglo-Saxon England*, pp. 148–93.
176   Hollis, *Women and the Church*.

CHAPTER 6

Embroidery on Spin-Patterned Linen in the 6th to 9th Centuries

Frances Pritchard

Anglo-Saxon embroidery has been a longstanding subject of interest for Elizabeth Coatsworth. It is therefore a pleasure to contribute a short paper in her honour on a neglected aspect of this skill, namely the choice of ground fabric, which is of fundamental importance to executing any needlework.

∴

The Linen

The particular ground fabric singled out here is a special type of linen. It is a high quality textile which it is argued was a prestige material in its own right and it was on account of this that it was chosen for a number of exceptional embroideries produced both in Britain and on the Continent in the early Middle Ages. The linen is unusual as, unlike most linen cloth produced throughout antiquity until the present day, the yarn is spun in both S and Z directions. Furthermore, the yarn is often inserted in either, or both, the warp and weft directions in certain sequences to create a shadow pattern in the form of a series of stripes or bands, or as small checks, which is often referred to as spin patterning. As Z-spun linen yarn was the norm in northern Europe, it begs the question why S-spun yarn was used as well, as it would have required a separate batch of yarn. This textile, therefore, required particular skills and labour-intensive production. In order to produce yarn suitable for this type of cloth it had to be evenly spun.[1] Also the textile required extensive finishing once removed from the loom, including washing, which caused the linen fibres to swell and close up the interspaces in the web, and flattening while the fabric was slightly damp on some form of smoothing board, or by use of a heavy roller, to bring out

---

1 I am very grateful to Lena Hammarlund for this, and other, technical observations.

© KONINKLIJKE BRILL NV, LEIDEN, 2021 | DOI:10.1163/9789004467514_008

FIGURE 6.1   Modern sample of spin-patterned linen woven by Lena Hammarlund, which
is in the process of being flattened with a glass smoother. The sample shows a
spin-pattern sequence in the warp of 2S, 2Z on the right and 4S, 4Z on the left
and has 15–16/12–13 threads per cm.
Photo: © Marie Wallenberg

the pattern (Fig. 6.1).[2] The shadow pattern is subtle and not always obvious,[3]
nevertheless, the textiles of this character would have been considered luxury

---

2   Boards of whalebone and reindeer antler were put to this use in the Viking world but it is
not known what was used in the Merovingian empire, although a wooden surface seems
probable.

3   This was observed in relation to the chequered pattern on the so-called 'mantle of Notre
Dame,' which was discovered in the reliquary said to be of St Florus in 1983 and is now pre-
served in the Musée municipal Alfred-Bonno, Chelles; Jean-Pierre Laporte, *Le Trésor des
Saints de Chelles* (Société Archéologique et Historique de Chelles) (Chelles, 1988), p. 92.

fabrics and this is borne out by the examples preserved, which were used for high status apparel and precious relics.

The production of this type of linen was relatively short lived in contrast to self-patterned linen such as diamond twills, herringbone twills, and subsequently bird's eye twill and diaper damasks. The earliest example recorded appears to be the linen lining used for a 'dalmatic' of St Ambrose, which is preserved in the church of Sant'Ambrogio, Milan, Italy, and probably dates to the late 4th century.[4] Unlike many other spin-patterned linens it is woven in warp-faced tabby with 48–54 threads per cm in the warp and 29–35 threads per cm in the weft, making it also the finest linen of this type.[5] The spin patterning is confined to the warp, with the spin contrasting every four ends, resulting in a pattern of narrow pin-stripes. Its quality suggests that more fabric of this type must have been produced at this period than is currently known. The latest so far recorded is the linen lining used for the embroidered garment which was recovered from Llangorse crannog, Wales, in the course of archaeological excavations in 1990. By chance the textile was preserved by being charred in a fire and deposited in waterlogged silt where it became attached to an off-cut of timber cleft from a quartered log of oak.[6] The garment, which showed signs of wear in the form of matted wads of silk between the embroidered panels and lining,[7] was already old by the time it was burnt, possibly when the island settlement was destroyed by Æthelflæd, Lady of the Mercians, in AD 916. In the linen cloth which was used as a garment lining, spin patterning is confined to occasional weft (?) bands of varying width with the spin differing every two threads.[8] The linen ground fabric on which the embroidery was worked, which belonged to the outer part of the same garment, is also unusual in having Z-spun yarn in one system and S-spun yarn in the other system and it is possible that some spin patterning may have been present which is now hidden under the heavily charred needlework.

A survey of textiles in northern Europe up to AD 1000 published by Lise Bender Jørgensen in 1992 singled out this cloth type as being concentrated

4   Hero Granger-Taylor, "The Two Dalmatics of Saint Ambrose?" *Bulletin de Liaison du CIETA* 58 (1983), 127–73 at pp. 144–45.

5   Granger-Taylor, "The Two Dalmatics," p. 145.

6   Alan Lane and Mark Redknap, *Llangorse Crannog: The Excavation of an Early Medieval Royal Site in the Kingdom of Brycheiniog* (Oxford, 2019), p. 276.

7   Hero Granger-Taylor and Frances Pritchard, "A Fine Quality Insular Embroidery from Llan-gors Crannog, near Brecon," in *Pattern and Purpose in Insular Art: Proceedings of the 4th International Conference on Insular Art*, ed. Mark Redknap, Nancy Edwards, Susan Youngs, Alan Lane, and Jeremy Knight (Oxford, 2002), pp. 91–99 at p. 97.

8   Louise Mumford and Mark Redknap, "Summary Catalogue of Textile Fragments," in Lane and Redknap, *Llangorse Crannog*, pp. 283–93 at 288–92.

in Alamannic Baden-Würtemberg, and a production centre in the southern Rhineland seems probable.[9] Unfortunately she grouped both linen and wool examples together in her survey, which diminishes its usefulness since S-spun wool, in contrast to S-spun linen, was commonplace and widely available in Europe. With respect to Britain, although linen was produced from locally grown flax,[10] documentary evidence indicates that linen textiles were sometimes acquired on the Continent, suggesting that certain special types of linen were not woven on looms in England. For example, Boniface sent towels (*villosam*) for wiping dry the feet of "the servants of God" to several bishops in England in the 740s in the course of his missionary work in Germany.[11] The lack of description means that such linen is difficult to identify, although a few years earlier Boniface sent Bishop Pehthelm of Whithorn a corporal patterned with white spots (*corporalę pallium albis stigmatibus variatum*), which could refer to a type of huckaback or honeycomb weave possibly similar to examples recovered from seventh- to ninth-century contexts (mainly burials) at Valsgärde (Sweden), Sievern (Germany), Ortes Alach (Germany), and York, all woven throughout from Z-spun yarn.[12]

As can be seen from the appendix (pp. 166–69), spin-patterned linen was not exclusively used as a ground fabric for needlework. Garments, particularly tunics and shirts, were made from it, although examples from many cemeteries throughout northern Europe are too fragmentary to convey much information. Nevertheless, they do indicate that the cloth had a wide distribution and was

---

9   Lise Bender Jørgensen, *North European Textiles until AD 1000* (Aarhus 1992), p. 142.

10   Penelope Walton Rogers, *Cloth and Clothing in Early Anglo-Saxon England, AD 450–700* (York, 2007), p. 14.

11   Michael Tangl, ed. *Die Briefe des heiligen Bonifatius* (Berlin, 1916), pp. 131 and 158 cited in Mildred Budny, "The Anglo-Saxon Embroideries at Maaseik: their Historical and Art-historical Context," *Academiae Analecta, Academie voor Wetenschappen, Letteren en Schone Kunsten van België, Klasse der Schone Kunsten* 45/2 (1984), 57–133 at pp. 89–90.

12   Greta Arwidsson, *Valsgärde 8. Die Gräberfunde von Valsgärde 2* (Uppsala, 1954), pp. 101–103; Anita Malmius, *Burial Textiles. Textile bits and pieces in central Sweden, AD 500–800* (Theses and Papers in Archaeology B13 [Stockholm University], (Stockholm, 2020)), pp. 88, 91–94, figs. 7.11 and 7.16; Hans-Jürgen Hundt, "Textilreste aus dem frühgeschichtlichen Kriegergrab von Sievern, Kr. Wesermunde, 1954," *Studien zur Sachsenforschung* 2, pp. 153–55; Heidemarie Farke, "Zur präparation und rekonstruktion archäologischer textilfunde aus dem Thüringer Raum," in *Archaeological Textiles in Northern Europe, NESAT IV* (Tidens Tand 5), ed. Lise Bender Jørgensen and Elisabeth Munksgaard (Copenhagen, 1992), pp. 208–17 at 210–11, abb. 2; Penelope Walton, *Textiles, Cordage and Raw Fibre from 16–22 Coppergate* (The Archaeology of York Small Finds 17/5) (London, 1989), pp. 353, 356–57.

associated with rich burials.[13] Examples preserved as relics in cathedrals and churches on the Continent provide more details about the cloth itself. Thus the Dress of the Virgin at Aachen Cathedral has a width selvedge to selvedge of 930 mm,[14] the width of the chemise of Bathilde at Chelles is 840 mm,[15] and *La grande robe* or 'mantle of Notre Dame' has a loomwidth of 850 mm.[16] As the latter was made from a 6.80 metre length of fabric, it must have been produced in a well-run workshop rather than in a modest domestic setting. An unusual feature of a rectangular fragment that was recycled as a relic wrapper and placed in a reliquary of St Candide at the abbey of St Maurice, Switzerland, is that S-plied yarn and Z-plied yarn was used to create spin-patterning in both systems,[17] which would have been an even more time-consuming process.

The whole range of surviving examples of spin-patterned linen is of medium to fine quality and, as well as balanced weaves, some of the cloth was warp-faced. However, only cloth with a balanced weave was selected for needlework, as it is easier to stitch. The embroideries that made use of this type of cloth share little in common with one another. What sets them apart is that they were made into garments associated with the elite or were claimed to be relics.

---

13   The production centre of the cloth in the southern Rhineland is disputed in Ulla Mannering and Irene Skals, "Textile News from Bornholm in Denmark: Recently Excavated Textiles from a Well-known Late Iron Age Cemetery," in *Archaeological Textiles – Links between Past and Present, NESAT XIII*, ed. Milena Bravermanová, Helena Březinová, and Jane Malcolm-Davies (Liberec and Prague, 2017), pp. 107–14 at 112. They consider that both wool and linen spin-patterned textiles could have been locally woven in imitation of the Alamannic/Frankish cloth but they thereby overlook the unusual character of the linen in combining S- and Z-spun yarn in the same textile.

14   Chris Verhecken-Lammens and Daniël De Jonghe, 'Technical Report,' in Monica Paredis-Vroon, Chris Verhecken-Lammens, and Daniël De Jonghe, "The Major Relics of Aachen Cathedral," *Bulletin du CIETA* 73 (1995–1996), 21–26, at p. 21.

15   Laporte, *Le Trésor*, p. 72; Anja Bayer and Caroline Vogt, "Neue textilkundliche Untersuchungen am sogenannten 'Hemd der Balthilde,'" *Zeitschrift für Archäologie des Mittelalters* 47 (2019), 31–52 at p. 37. The latter publication gives details of the selvedges which are reinforced with a series of linen cords, p. 36, abb. 5. I am very grateful to Caroline Vogt, Head of Studies, Abegg-Stiftung, Riggisberg, for allowing me to read the paper ahead of its actual publication in August 2020.

16   Laporte, *Le Trésor*, p. 92.

17   Regula Schorta, "Catalogue des tissus et enveloppes de reliques textiles," in *L'abbaye de Saint-Maurice d'Agaune 515–2015, Vol. 2 – Le trésor*, ed. Pierre Alain Mariaux (Bern, 2015), pp. 272–309 at 296. The wrapper is dated to the seventh to eighth centuries by an inscription handwritten on it in uncial script in black ink +*SALUA/TORIS*+. I am grateful to Caroline Vogt for this reference.

The Needlework

Probably the earliest of the embroideries worked on this type of cloth is the 'Dress of the Virgin' in Aachen Cathedral, an almost complete tunic which is normally kept folded as a holy relic, which has been dated to "not earlier than" the end of the fourth century (Fig. 6.2). It is decorated at the neck opening and side slits on the gores with geometric patterning worked in satin stitch in two-ply (Z-spun, S-ply) linen thread (Figs. 6.3 and 6.4).[18] Thus it is a notable early example of whitework, although the dress has now become yellow due to aging in the shrine.

The most fragmentary piece, measuring 25 × 15 mm, was recovered from a burial at Worthy Park, Hampshire, dating to the 6th or early 7th century.[19] Worked in stem stitch in two-ply (S-ply) thread, which was either wool or silk, the design is difficult to interpret although it has been suggested it may be part of an arcade or a vine scroll.[20] From its position on the left-hand side of the waist, the textile was possibly part of a pouch, or was contained within one, suggesting that it may have possessed a similarity to scraps of embroideries placed in relic-boxes, although the body was probably that of an adult male.[21] The person in question presumably had a certain status within the community as a wooden coffin was used for the burial and Elisabeth Crowfoot identified the textile as the finest from the cemetery.[22]

The best known of the embroideries is the chemise of Bathilde for which the spin-patterned ground fabric is described as being firm and glossy.[23] Bathilde (c.630–680) was Anglo-Saxon by birth and experienced a period of slavery before marrying the Frankish ruler, Clovis II. After his death in 657/658,

---

18   Verhecken-Lammens and De Jonghe, "Technical Report," p. 23 and figs. 2, 12, and 13. The dating, which is based on the spin-patterned fabric, is at p. 25.

19   Elisabeth Crowfoot, "The Textile Remains," in *The Anglo-Saxon Cemetery at Worthy Park, Kingsworthy near Winchester, Hampshire* (Oxford University School of Archaeology Monograph 59), ed. Sonia Chadwick Hawkes and Guy Grainger (Oxford, 2003), pp. 192–95. Two layers of cloth were recorded with the decoration being observed on the lower layer. The textile is now lost.

20   Walton Rogers, *Cloth and Clothing*, pp. 101–02, fig. 3.33d.

21   Relic boxes are associated with female graves in the transition period to Christianity, Catherine Hills, "Work Boxes or Reliquaries? Small Copper-alloy Containers in Seventh-century Anglo-Saxon Graves," in *Dying Gods: Religious Beliefs in Northern and Eastern Europe at the Time of Christianisation* (Neue Studien zur Sachsenforschung 5), ed. Christiane Ruhmann and Vera Brieske (Brunswick, 2015), pp. 51–61. It is unlikely that a man's pouch would have been made from a linen textile at this period.

22   Crowfoot, "The Textile Remains," p. 192.

23   Laporte, *Le Trésor*, p. 72.

FIGURE 6.2   Detail of the spin-patterned linen used for the Dress of the Virgin, Aachen
               Cathedral.
               Photo: Pit Siebags © Aachen Cathedral

FIGURE 6.3   Detail of the needlework at the neck of the Dress of the Virgin, Aachen
               Cathedral.
               Photo: Pit Siebags © Aachen Cathedral

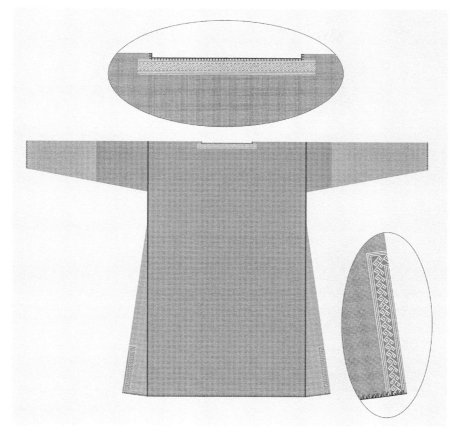

FIGURE 6.4   Diagram of the Dress of the Virgin at Aachen Cathedral showing the areas
of whitework at the neck and side gores and detail showing the needlework
patterning.
© Christina Unwin

she acted as regent for her son Clothar and then retired to an abbey at Chelles, which she had founded and where she died. The 'chemise,' first recorded in 1544,[24] has generally been believed to have been made for her burial but this has recently been disputed owing to its good condition.[25] It is stitched with a design of jewelled collars from one of which hangs a pectoral cross and a

24   Laporte, *Le Trésor*, p. 71.
25   Bayer and Vogt, "Hemd der Balthilde," p. 40 and 51.

FIGURE 6.5   Upper section of the spin-patterned chemise of Sainte Bathilde.
              Photo: © Musée municipal Alfred-Bonno, Chelles

festoon of pendant medallions imitating Byzantine originals (Fig. 6.5).[26] All
the stitching is carried out in silk thread and a recent study has identified that
this is of three types: silk with no appreciable twist; S-plied from two threads
without appreciable twist; and Z-plied from two S-twisted threads or threads
with very little appreciable twist. The first type is used in red, blue, and dark
blue hues, the second in white, ivory, greyish-beige, and light blue, and the
third in light blue.[27] There are no traces of a preliminary underdrawing and
both the outlines and fillings are worked in chain stitch with a very small
amount of split stitch.[28]

   It is perhaps worth mentioning that, although the renowned embroidered
panels forming part of the so-called chasuble of the two sisters, Sts Harlindis
and Relindis (now in the church of St Catherine, Maaseik), were worked on a
ground of plain Z-spun, tabby woven linen, the fine linen lining of the velamen

---

26   Hayo E.F. Vierck, "La 'chemise de Sainte-Bathilde' à Chelles et l'influence byzantine sur
      l'art de cour Mérovingien au VIIᵉ siècle," in *Centenaire de l'Abbé Cochet 1975. Actes du
      Colloque international d'archéologie* (Rouen, 1978), 521–64; Laporte, *Le Trésor*, pp. 71–85,
      pls. vi–viii.
27   Bayer and Vogt, "Hemd der Balthilde," p. 37.
28   Ibid., p. 37.

of St Harlindis, which was apparently added sometime after the velamen was first made, is characterized by spin-patterning.[29] The velamen or *palliolum*, which is over two metres in length, is considered to date to the eighth or early ninth centuries,[30] and its attribution is due to an attached vellum label inscribed in Gothic script, *Istud est velamen sancte harlindis abbatisse*.[31] St Harlindis (*c*.695–745) was the elder of the two sisters born into a Frankish aristocratic family. Educated at a monastery in Valenciennes (*Valencina*), she became the first abbess of Aldeneik, a small abbey in the Maas valley, which was founded in the first half of the eighth century and was, according to tradition, associated with the missionary work in the region of Sts Willibrord and Boniface.[32]

The most recent of the embroideries chronologically is that found during excavations at Llangorse crannog.[33] Through painstaking examination and analysis by the conservator, Louise Mumford, and curator, Mark Redknap; by illustrator, Tony Daly; and through specialist photographic enhancement by Cathy Treadaway, the design was established, with the overall scheme consisting of an upright stylized vine from which spring leaf scrolls enclosing various pairs of birds and animals; in addition, there are two border designs, one of pairs of lions and the other of diagonally opposed triangular acanthus leaves (Fig. 6.6).[34] It appears to have been worked in stem stitch on counted threads using silk thread with a slight S-twist for the background and two-ply (S-ply) linen thread for the figurative areas (Fig. 6.7)[35] and, although the ground fabric is hidden by the stitching, that does not mean a luxury fabric could not be used in these circumstances as a power statement. Illustrations and reconstructions of the needlework have implied that threads of different colours were used,[36] although this is hypothetical as the garment was so severely charred that no dye analysis is possible. However, it is worth considering whether the whole

---

29   Mildred Budny and Dominic Tweddle, "The Early Medieval Textiles at Maaseik, Belgium," *The Antiquaries Journal* 65 (1985), 353–89, at pp. 361, 379.

30   Budny and Tweddle, "The Early Medieval Textiles at Maaseik," p. 353.

31   Budny and Tweddle, "The Early Medieval Textiles at Maaseik," p. 355 and pl. LXVIIb. The writing is in a thirteenth-century hand.

32   Budny, "The Anglo-Saxon Embroideries at Maaseik," pp. 97–99 and 103. Much of the information derives from the anonymous Lotharingian *Vita Harlindis et Relindis*, compiled between *c*.855 and 881.

33   Lane and Redknap, *Llangorse Crannog*, pp. 276–77.

34   Mark Redknap and Tony Daly, "Interpreting the Motifs and Composition of the Llangorse Textile," in Lane and Redknap, *Llangorse Crannog*, pp. 294–300 at 294–98.

35   Louise Mumford, "Conserving and Recording the Textiles," in Lane and Redknap, *Llangorse Crannog*, pp. 277–83 at 278–79.

36   For example, Lane and Redknap, *Llangorse Crannog*, pp. 298–306.

FIGURE 6.6   Reconstruction of the overall embroidered schematic design present on
                either side of a gore on the garment from Llangorse crannog. The arrow
                indicates the position of the detail shown in Fig. 6.7.
                Drawing: Christina Unwin after Tony Daly © National Museum of Wales
                and Christina Unwin

item may have been worked in white on white with the texture and weight of the different single and plied silk and linen threads creating subtle effects, which was to some extent mimicked by the shadow-patterned linen lining. This makes better sense of the fact that a lot of the needlework, particularly the figurative motifs, was carried out in linen thread rather than being only silk thread as was initially thought.[37] White on white patterning was highly favoured in the production of late Roman and early medieval silk fabrics as shown by the figured damask silk patterned with a lion hunt used for one of the dalmatics of St Ambrose, the one lined with a spin-patterned linen.[38] Subsequently monochrome incised silks, proto-lampas and lampas fabrics, often worn by the ruling classes, leading prelates, and fashionable elite in the late tenth and eleventh centuries, were frequently produced in white or off-white.

Conclusion

Despite the rather limited amount of evidence, it is possible to assert that the spin-patterned linen textiles used for needlework in the sixth to ninth

37   Granger-Taylor and Pritchard, "A Fine Quality Insular Embroidery," p. 92.
38   Granger-Taylor, "The Two Dalmatics of Saint Ambrose?" pp. 141–44.

FIGURE 6.7   Detail of stitching showing a small lion motif worked in two-ply linen thread against a background of single silk thread with areas of wear revealing the tabby-woven linen ground.
Photo: © National Museum of Wales, © Amagueddfa Genedlaethol Cymru

centuries possessed a high prestige value. In contrast to silk fabrics, which were more obviously of exotic origin, and other artefacts such as certain types of jewelry, enamelwork, and illuminated manuscripts, fine linen, often now in an advanced state of mineralisation or in charred lumps, may not at first glance attract much attention or seem significant. It is, nevertheless, important to appreciate that this linen was considered highly desirable as a status symbol in early medieval Europe.

Appendix

TABLE 6.1   Spin-patterned linens[a]

Provenance	Date	Spin of warp	Spin of weft	Weave	Thread count	Spin pattern	Comment
Dalmatic lining, Sant'Ambrogio, Milan[b]	Late 4th century	Z & S	Z	tabby	48–54/ 29–35	warp 4S, 4Z throughout	
'Dress of Virgin,' Aachen cathedral[c]	Late 4th century or later	Z & S	Z & S	tabby	27–35/ 24–28	warp & weft 14S, 14Z throughout	
Child's grave 82, Harmignies, Belgium[d]	Late 5th to early 6th century	Z & S	Z & S	tabby	18/23	warp & weft 3S, 3Z in short sequences	on a metal attachment ring; fibre not positively ID
'Decapitation cloth of John the Baptist', Aachen cathedral[e]	5th century or later	Z & S	Z ?	tabby	28/19–22	spin changes in irregular sequences in only the warp	the spin direction of the weft remains to be identified

a   This table is not exhaustive. For example, Lise Bender Jørgensen mentions that 76 pieces have been found from 22 sites dating to the Merovingian period in Germany but unfortunately no distinction is made between those made from wool and those woven from linen, Jørgensen, *North European Textiles*, pp. 72–73. Further examples have been excavated from graves in Switzerland including tomb 64, Baar, Zug: Florence Carré, Antoinette Rast-Eicher, Bruno Bell, and Julien Boisson, "L'étude des matériaux organiques dans les tombes du haut Moyen Âge (France, Suisse et Allemagne occidentale): un apport majeur à la connaissance des pratiques funéraires et du vêtement," *Archéologie médiévale* 48 (2018), 37–99, at fig. 13b; and grave 47, Kallnach, Bergweg: Christiane Kissling and Antoinette Rast-Eicher, "Textilien," in *Kallnach-Bergweg: Das frühmittelalterliche Gräberfeld und das spätrömische Gebäude* ed. Christiane Kissling and Susi Ulrich-Bochsler (Bern, 2006), pp. 77–82 at 78.

b   Granger-Taylor, "The Two Dalmatics of Saint Ambrose?", pp. 144–45.

c   Monica Paredis-Vroon, Chris Verhecken-Lammens, and Daniël De Jonghe, "The Major Relics of Aachen Cathedral," *Bulletin du CIETA* 73 (1995–1996), 15–26, at p. 25.

d   Lisa Vanhaeke and Chris Verhecken-Lammens, "Textile Pseudomorphs from a Merovingian Burial Ground at Harmignies, Belgium," in *Northern Archaeological Textiles, NESAT VII*, ed. Frances Pritchard and John Peter Wild (Oxford, 2005), pp. 22–28 at 24.

e   Monica Paredis-Vroon, "Stoffweschel. Die vier grossen Aachener Heiligtümer aus textilrestauratorischer Sicht," in *Venite et videte. Kunstgeschictliche Dimensionen der Aachener Heiligtümsfahrt*, ed. Andreas Gormans and Alexander Markschies (Aachen, 2012), pp. 23–47 at 34 and 43, fig. 7.

TABLE 6.1   Spin-patterned linens (*cont.*)

Provenance	Date	Spin of warp	Spin of weft	Weave	Thread count	Spin pattern	Comment
Stöbnitz, Kr. Querfurt, Bezirk, Halle, Germany[f]	*c.*5th/6th century	Z & S	Z	tabby	20/14	warp 8S, 8Z throughout	on an iron belt buckle; fibre not positively ID
Adult burial (probably male) grave 75, Worthy Park, Hampshire[g]	*c.*6th/7th century	Z & S	Z & S	tabby	22/22	warp & weft have slightly irregular sequences of 4 to 6 threads S and Z	on an iron object; fibre not positively ID
Burial, Huinerveld, Putten, The Netherlands[h]	*c.*6th/7th century	Z & S	S	tabby	24/19	warp 4S, 4Z throughout	on back of a disc brooch
Burial, Huinerveld, Putten, The Netherlands[i]	*c.*6th/7th century	Z & S	Z	tabby	21/12	no details available	
Bedburg-Morken-Harff, Erftkreis, Germany[j]	*c.*600	Z & S	Z & S	tabby	24/15	spin changes in warp (?) after every 5 ends and in weft (?) after every 6 picks	fibre not positively ID
Ortes Alach, Germany[k]	7th century	Z & S	Z	tabby	18/14	warp 4S, 4Z throughout	
Boat grave 5, Valsgärde, Sweden[l]	*c.* mid 7th century	Z & S	Z	tabby	32/13	warp (?) 4S, 4Z throughout	on iron fragments; fibre not positively ID

---

f   Bender Jørgensen, *North European Textiles*, p. 238.
g   Crowfoot, "The Textile Remains," pp. 192–95.
h   Bender Jørgensen, *North European Textiles*, p. 223.
i   Ibid., p. 233.
j   Ibid., p. 240.
k   Heidemarie Farke, "Zur präparation und rekonstruktion archäologischer textilfunde aus dem Thüringer Raum," pp. 208–17 at 211.
l   Bender Jørgensen, *North European Textiles*, p. 262. Another spin-patterned textile was present in boat grave 6, which also dates to the seventh century, but no further details have been published, p. 160.

TABLE 6.1   Spin-patterned linens (*cont.*)

Provenance	Date	Spin of warp	Spin of weft	Weave	Thread count	Spin pattern	Comment
Chemise of Bathilde, Chelles[m]	mid to late 7th century	Z	Z & S	tabby	20/23	weft repeating sequences 4S, 8Z, 4S, 20 to 32Z	
Grave 36, Lembech, Kr. Recklinghausen, Germany[n]	7th–8th century	Z & S	Z	tabby	30/15	warp 4S, 4Z throughout	on back of brooch; fibre not positively ID
Grave 116, Lembech, Kr. Recklinghausen, Germany[o]	7th–8th century	Z & S	Z	tabby	16/16	warp 6S, 6Z throughout	associated with brooch; fibre not positively ID
Woman's grave 51, Nørre Sandegård Vest, Bornholm, Denmark[p]	7th–8th century	Z & S	Z	tabby	24/17	warp 4S, 4Z throughout	
Relic wrapper within the main reliquary of St Candide, abbey of St Maurice d'Agaume, Switzerland[q]	7th–8th century	S_2Z & Z_2S	S_2Z & Z_2S	tabby	25–26/ 23–25	warp & weft in repeating sequences of 4S-ply, 4Z-ply, 4S-ply, 4Z-ply, 4S-ply, 20–24Z-ply	
'Le manteaux Notre Dame,' Chelles[r]	*c.*8th century	Z & S	Z & S	tabby	28–30/ 18–20	warp 6S, 6Z; weft 4S, 4Z throughout	

m Laporte, *Le Trésor*, p. 72. The analysis was undertaken by Brigitte Oger. A recent re-examination of the textile gives a more variable thread count (18–27/25–29) and more irregular spin pattern sequence in the weft, Bayer and Vogt, "Hemd der Balthilde," pp. 34–36.

n Bender Jørgensen, *North European Textiles*, p. 241.

o Ibid., p. 242.

p Mannering and Skals, "Textile News from Bornholm in Denmark," p. 110.

q Schorta, "Catalogue des tissus et enveloppes de reliques textiles," p. 296.

r Laporte, *Le Trésor*, p. 92. The analysis was undertaken by Naomi Moore.

TABLE 6.1   Spin-patterned linens (*cont.*)

Provenance	Date	Spin of warp	Spin of weft	Weave	Thread count	Spin pattern	Comment
Looveen, Gem Beilen, The Netherlands[s]	AD 650–850	Z & S	Z	tabby	24/15	warp 4S, 4Z throughout	on iron mount; fibre not positively ID
Looveen, Gem Beilen, The Netherlands[t]	AD 650–850	Z & S	Z	tabby	18/12	warp 4S, 4Z throughout	on iron fragment; fibre not positively ID
Lining of the *velamen* of St Harlindis, church of St Catherine, Maaseik, Belgium[u]	c.800 (?)	Z & S	Z & S	tabby	36/36	spin changes in irregular sequences in warp and weft	
Garment lining, Llangorse crannog, Wales[v]	9th-early 10th century	Z	Z & S	tabby	23–25/ 23–25	spin changes in weft (?) after every two threads but limited to bands of 20, 16 and 8 threads	

s   Bender Jørgensen, *North European Textiles*, p. 222.
t   Ibid., p. 222.
u   Budny and Tweddle, "The Early Medieval Textiles at Maaseik, Belgium," p. 379.
v   Mumford and Redknap, "Summary Catalogue of Textile Fragments," pp. 289–92.

CHAPTER 7

The Embroidered Fragments from the Tomb of Bishop William of St Calais, Durham: An Analysis and Biography

Alexandra Lester-Makin

Dr Elizabeth (Betty) Coatsworth and I have known each other for 20 years, our mutual love of early medieval embroidery first bringing us together. Betty went on to co-supervise my PhD, "Embroidery and its Context in the British Isles and Ireland during the Early Medieval Period (AD 450–1100)," with Gale R. Owen-Crocker at the University of Manchester. During this time, we became firm friends and I am therefore very pleased to be able to contribute to this volume. I thought it was only fitting that I should write about the subject that is close to both of our hearts, early medieval embroidery, and pieces associated with a location that is important to Betty, Durham.

∴

Introduction

The two fragments of embroidery under discussion are extremely significant, thought to date to no later than 1096, when they were probably interred with the body of William of St Calais in Durham Cathedral (bishop of Durham from 1081 until his death). English embroidery rarely survives from this transitional period, between the Norman military conquest of 1066 to full Norman control of England, c.1100.[1] Despite this, the St Calais embroideries have been overlooked by scholars who focus on the tenth-century embroidered stole, maniple, and probable ribbons, which were re-discovered in the tomb of St Cuthbert in Durham Cathedral in 1827.[2] The St Calais embroideries appeared in the Victoria and Albert Museum's 1963 *Opus Anglicanum* exhibition but

---

1 See Alexandra Lester-Makin, *The Lost Art of the Anglo-Saxon World: the Sacred and Secular Power of Embroidery* (Oxford, 2019).

2 John Lingard, *Remarks on the "Saint Cuthbert" of the Rev. James Raine, M.A.* (Newcastle, 1828), pp. 5–6.

not in their 2016–17 exhibition, *Opus Anglicanum: Masters of English Medieval Embroidery*. The 1963 exhibition catalogue included a single, brief entry for both pieces, highlighting the similarities between the embroideries' motifs and those in the borders of the eleventh-century Bayeux Tapestry, and noting that eleventh-century inventories list religious vestments also decorated with lions and griffins.[3] A photograph, brief descriptions based on the catalogue entry, and an explanation of a single embroidery stitch, underside couching, appear in the souvenir guide, *Embroideries at Durham Cathedral*.[4] There has been no detailed analysis of the embroideries' materials and construction, nor any discussion about their original function. Elizabeth Coatsworth feels it is important that the technique, embroidery style, and iconography of both pieces should be given serious consideration to determine their relationship to other pre- and post-Conquest works.[5] This chapter aims to fulfil her wish.

Technical Analysis (Table 7.1)

Both pieces are stored at the Durham Conservation Studio, where the initial analysis took place in May 2017. It was possible to examine the front and back of the embroideries. Photographs and microscopic images were taken using a Nikon D320.0 Digital camera and a Veho Discovery VMS-0.04 USB microscope. Measurements were taken manually and a written record of observations was made.

Embroidery 1

Stylised foliage resting on a base, worked on a ground fabric of 1 × 2 weft-faced compound twill samite silk cloth with an S-diagonal to the twill (Fig. 7.1a and b, Table 7.2).[6] The foliage motif incorporates two complete and one partially surviving row of leaves. Each row consists of two leaves, one to the left and one to the right (Fig. 7.2). The small surviving section of the top row indicates the same layout. The inner edges of the leaves on the right overlap those to the left, suggesting leaves unfurling from a central stem. Each row is also slightly overlapped by the one below, mimicking newer growth towards the top of the

---

3   Donald King, *Opus Anglicanum: English Medieval Embroidery* (London, 1963), p. 13.
4   Jill Ivy, *Embroideries at Durham Cathedral* (Sunderland, 1998), pp. 16–18.
5   Elizabeth Coatsworth, "Stitches in Time: Establishing a History of Anglo-Saxon Embroidery," *Medieval Clothing and Textiles* 1 (2005), 1–27 at p. 23.
6   I would like to thank Frances Pritchard for identifying the ground fabric of both embroideries.

TABLE 7.1   Terminology

Term	Meaning
Design	The embroidered picture or pattern.
Element	Component part of a motif.
Ground fabric	The fabric on which the embroidery is worked.
Motif	Component part of a design.
	A basic flower is constructed from three different motifs: petals, leaves and a stem.
Order of work / working order	The order in which elements and / or motifs are completed.
Ply	When two or more threads are spun together.
S-twist / S-ply	When the direction of spun fibres mimics the central bar of the letter S.
Stitch direction	The direction in which stitches are worked for example, left-to-right, top-to-bottom and *vice versa*.
Twist	When a thread is spun around its central axis.
Warp threads	Fixed threads within a ground fabric. Conventionally depicted vertically.
Weft threads	Threads that are woven under and over the warp threads in set patterns. Conventionally depicted horizontally.
Z-twist / Z-ply	When the direction of spun fibres mimics the central bar of the letter Z.

TABLE 7.2   Measurements of Embroidery 1

Constituent parts	Measurements in mm
Textile	Width: top – 83, stand – 19, base – 41
	Height: left – 30, middle – 74, right – 31
Embroidery	Width: 9–64
	Height: 24–67
Outlines and dividing lines	Width: 3.5–5.5

FIGURE 7.1A   The foliage embroidery discovered in the tomb of
Bishop William of St Calais, front (measures 83 mm
wide by 74 mm high at the largest points).
Photo: Durham Cathedral. With the kind permission
of Durham Cathedral

FIGURE 7.1B   The foliage embroidery discovered in the tomb of
Bishop William of St Calais, reverse.
Photo: Durham Cathedral. With the kind permission
of Durham Cathedral

FIGURE 7.2   Line drawing of the foliage motifs of Embroidery 1.
             © Alexandra Lester-Makin

plant motif. The foliage rests on a base reminiscent of a chalice's stand, giving the whole of the surviving design a chalice-like appearance.

The embroidery is worked in silver-gilt metal and silk threads. The metal thread was made by wrapping narrow thin strips of the metal round a silk thread which has an S-twist. Most of the metal has disappeared leaving stains in its place. Surviving metal is tarnished, indicating it is silver-gilt not gold, which does not generally blemish.[7] All the silk threads, except those used for outlines which are red-gold in colour, have faded to pale gold/fawn and have been worked in both untwisted and S-twisted forms (see below).

The stitching is not underside couching but surface couching, as well as laid-work, satin stitch, and split stitch. All lines are worked in surface couching constructed from metal threads couched (held) in place with silk thread, which survive well in many areas. The metal thread is couched in twos, not singly which was the more common practice during the early medieval period (Fig. 7.3a and b). The majority of the couching was worked in double bricking

---

7   J.M. Cronyn, *The Elements of Archaeological Conservation* (1990; repr. London, 2001), pp. 230–32; E. Pye, "Conservation and Storage: Archaeological Material," in *Manual of Curatorship: a Guide to Museum Practice*, 2nd ed., ed. J.M.A. Thompson (1992; repr. Oxford, 1994), pp. 392–426 at 411.

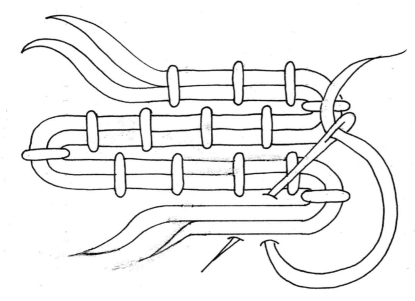

FIGURE 7.3A   Line drawing depicting the double brick couching method.
               © Alexandra Lester-Makin

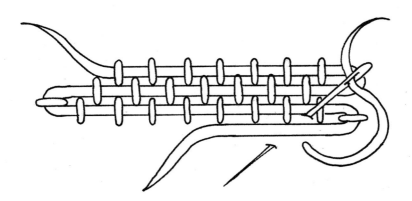

FIGURE 7.3B   Line drawing depicting the single brick couching method.
               © Alexandra Lester-Makin

FIGURE 7.4   Microscopic image showing an example of a pair of silver-gilt
              threads that does not continue to follow its original line but is
              used to outline another part of the motif as well (x 210).
              © Alexandra Lester-Makin

although there are places where the pattern is not consistent, particularly on
deep curves and sharp angles. The lines are generally constructed from four
pairs of metal threads couched next to each other, creating the broad width of
each row. However, each pair of metal threads does not necessarily complete a
full row, starting on one but swapping to another part way, resulting in sections
of some rows being constructed from three pairs of metal threads instead of
the more usual four (Fig. 7.4).

The embroidery has been used to create the illusion of leaves folded along
their length, with the chosen stitches creating areas of light and shade that
mimic the upper facing and up-turned underneath surfaces of each leaf, respectively. The underneath section, that is the lower half of each leaf as one views
it, has been completely infilled with laid-work, which is constructed from three
layers of stitching: first, a base layer worked in long stitches covers the whole
of the element in question; second, another layer of long individual stitches
which lie over the top of the base layer at intervals of 2.5 mm; and third, one
small couching stitch per long individual stitch, sewn through the base layer,

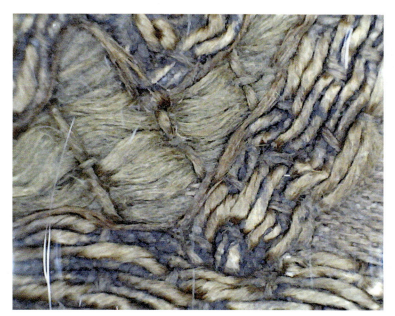

FIGURE 7.5   Microscopic image showing a detail of the laid-work
embroidered on the leaves of embroidery 1 (x 210).
© Alexandra Lester-Makin

over the long individual stitch and back through the base layer, thus holding
all the stitches in place at regular intervals (Fig. 7.5). This version of laid-work
is stitched in exactly the same way as that used on the Bayeux Tapestry but in
silk thread instead of wool. There are a number of later examples of laid-work
stitched in silk threads, such as details of leaves on the late thirteenth-century
Clare Chasuble.[8] The base layer of long stitches on the St Calais embroidery is
worked in untwisted silk, while all the second layer and couching stitches are
worked in a silk thread with a varying S-twist. The variation in the amount of
twist suggests that the same thread was used for all three layers of the stitch,
but that used to create the long stitches and the holding stitches was manually
twisted by the worker as needed. An outline stitch partially survives around
the laid-work. The type of stitch is difficult to decipher but it appears to be
split stitch.

---

8   Clare Browne, Glyn Davis, and M.A. Michael (eds.), *English Medieval Embroidery: Opus
Anglicanum* (London, 2016), p. 8, fig. 6.

FIGURE 7.6   Microscopic image showing three of the dots embroidered on
the leaves of embroidery 1 (x 210).
© Alexandra Lester-Makin

The top half of each leaf is not so densely embroidered, with only a line of five or six dots stitched across the space (Fig. 7.6). The lack of embroidery creates the illusion of lightness in this section, indicating that it is the upper facing part of the leaf. The number of dots is determined by the amount of space available. Embroidered in untwisted silk thread and incorporating three satin stitches, each dot measures 1.5 mm wide by *c.* 1 mm long. On the reverse of the embroidery it can be seen that a single length of silk was used to stitch each row of dots, which were secured at the start with a knot. Once the dots were complete, the thread was sometimes used to embroider another element within the motif or it was caught beneath other stitches, holding it secure.

The lines of the base stand are also stitched in surface couching in silver-gilt and silk threads. Only the triangle at the base of the motif has been infilled with silk thread, which is most likely the same as that used for the laid-work on the leaves. The stitching has not survived well and there is a small triangular area where it has completely disappeared, leaving the ground fabric visible (circled in Fig. 7.7). The embroidery appears to be satin stitch worked both horizontally

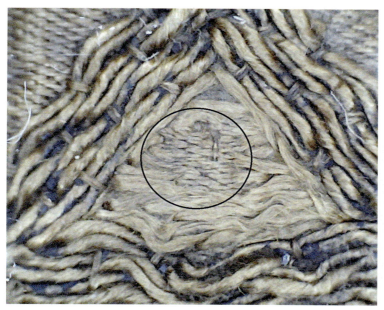

FIGURE 7.7   Microscopic image showing the infilled triangle of the
chalice-like stand with the ground fabric showing through a gap
in the infill, circled (x 210).
© Alexandra Lester-Makin

and at a slight diagonal. Each stitch measures 1 mm–3 mm long. The infill was also outlined with a single silk thread worked in long split stitches.

The edges of the ground fabric are frayed, but some areas, particularly on either side of the base, appear to have been cut or trimmed at some point during the object's history. The ground fabric has been turned under, forming a hem along the upper and lower edges. These hems were made after the embroidery was completed, evidenced on the upper hem by embroidery continuing over the turned edge to the back of the fragment. On the reverse, the hem edges have been left raw, indicating that priority was given to the front of the embroidery; the reverse was not intended to be seen. The hems were probably held in place with functional stitching, holes for which can be seen on the reverse side of the lower hem. Covering the functional stitch lines on the front of the embroidery are three couched threads, two at the top and one surviving at the bottom, effectively hiding the functional stitching from view (Fig. 7.8). Although it is difficult to distinguish the threads' fibres, they are S-twisted and

FIGURE 7.8   Microscopic image showing a detail of the couched threads
              positioned along the top edge of Embroidery 1 (x 210).
              © Alexandra Lester-Makin

tightly 2-plied in a Z direction which gives them a different quality from the
rest of the embroidery. The couching stitches, probably worked in silk thread,
survive intermittently. In some areas they are evenly spaced but the stitching
technique is not as accurate as that used to couch the silver-gilt metal threads.
Decoratively covering functional areas of stitching, including hems and seams,
with embroidery and braids was popular during the medieval period.[9]

Embroidery 2

Four roundels, each encircling a lion or a griffin *passant*, embroidered on a 1 × 2
weft-faced compound twill samite silk cloth with an S-diagonal to the twill
(Fig. 7.9a and b, Table 7.3).

---

9 See Coatsworth, "Stitches in Time," pp. 5–7; Alexandra Lester-Makin, "Looped Stitch: the
   Travels and Development of an Embroidery Stitch," in *The Daily Lives of the Anglo-Saxons*,
   ed. Carole Biggam, Carole Hough, and Daria Izdebska (Medieval and Renaissance Texts and
   Studies 519 and Essays in Anglo-Saxon Studies 8) (Tempe, AZ, 2017), pp. 119–36.

TABLE 7.3   Measurements of Embroidery 2

Constituent parts	Measurements in mm
Textile	Width: top – 111, middle – 94, base – 17
	Height: left – 86, right – 66
Embroidery excluding border	Width: 16–93
	Height: 36–71
Border: horizontal line	Width: 2–3
	Height: 90 long
Border: vertical line	Width: 2–3
	Height: 70
Roundel: top left	External diameter: 34
	Internal diameter: 26.5
	Width of band: 2.5
	Lion: 21 wide by 23 high
Roundel: bottom left	External diameter: 34
	Internal diameter: 26
	Width of band: 3–3.5
	Griffin: 25 wide by 24 high
Roundel: bottom right	External diameter: 34
	Internal diameter: 27
	Width of band: 2.5–4
	Lion: 25 wide by 22 high
Vines	Width: 2–3
Crossed bands	Width: 3.5
Trefoil: top	Width: 7
	Height: 19
Trefoil: bottom	Width: 13
	Height: 9

FIGURE 7.9A   The roundel embroidery discovered in the tomb of Bishop
William of St Calais, front (measures 111 mm wide by 93 mm
high at the largest points).
Photo: Durham Cathedral. With the kind permission of
Durham Cathedral

FIGURE 7.9B   The roundel embroidery discovered in the tomb of Bishop
William of St Calais, reverse.
Photo: Durham Cathedral. With the kind permission of
Durham Cathedral

FIGURE 7.10   Line drawing of the animals, roundels and foliage motifs of
Embroidery 2.
© Alexandra Lester-Makin

Two rows of inhabited roundels survive; the bottom row is in better condition than the top where the left roundel is approximately two thirds complete and only the bottom part of the roundel on the right is extant (Fig. 7.10). In the lower left roundel stands a griffin confronting a lion within its own roundel to the right. These two roundels are joined by a simple vine-like band, off which spring two trefoils. Mirroring trefoils also sprout from each roundel and a stylised swirl can be seen emerging from the roundel on the right. On the row above, on the left a second lion stands in its partially surviving roundel, facing the fragmentary fourth roundel to its right. Here the claws and legs of another griffin are just visible. These measure 20 mm wide by 11 mm high, leading to the conclusion that this motif would have been similar in size to the extant griffin to the bottom left. The vine which would presumably have joined these two roundels has not survived; however, the top of what may have been the lower trefoil can just be seen at the top edge of the remaining ground fabric between the roundels (circled in Fig. 7.11). The upper and lower rows of roundels are connected by crossing vine-like bands, from which a trefoil can be seen growing to the right. Two hemmed edges and an embroidered borderline worked in a feather/chevron pattern survive to the right and along the base of the design.

Evidence strongly suggests the roundel design repeated and mirrored itself across the width of the original object, to the left of surviving embroidery: at the top left there are fragments of what was most likely a vine stem which

FIGURE 7.11   The roundel embroidery with areas that evidence the original larger
design circled.
Photo: Durham Cathedral. With the kind permission of Durham
Cathedral

ended in a trefoil, similar to the one that sprouts from the left side of the roundel to the bottom right (circled in Fig. 7.11). The lower left roundel has two
interesting features: on the ground fabric at the top left is a mark indicating
a vine-like band projected from the roundel at this point (circled in Fig. 7.11);
at the bottom left is the extremely fragmented end of another probable vine
band (circled in Fig. 7.11). Below this, at the very edge of the ground fabric
at the bottom left corner is what appears to be the tip of either a trefoil or spiral
that probably sprouted from the fragmented vine band just described or from
the side of a now lost roundel to the left (circled in Fig. 7.11).

The embroidery is now discoloured but it is still possible to identify the
embroidery threads – silver-gilt and silk. The microscopic images clearly show
the silver-gilt thread was made by wrapping thin narrow strips of metal around
a core of silk with an S-twist. The majority of the metal has disappeared and
that which remains is discoloured or tarnished. Silk thread, with a slight
Z-twist and 2 S-ply, was used as an outline. The extant threads demonstrate
that the environmental conditions within the tomb were more conducive to

the survival of animal fibres, rather than plant fibres. This, combined with evidence from later examples of underside couching, suggests the silver-gilt threads were held in place with linen threads, which did not survive.[10]

The couple of published accounts state the piece is worked in underside couching. Close examination reveals that this is not the only stitch, with a second, stem stitch also being utilized. Certainly, all the metal thread work is underside couching, which can be determined by the pattern of indentations in the metal threads on the front of the embroidery and the tiny loops of metal thread on the reverse, created when the couching thread pulled small loops of the metal thread to the reverse of the work (Fig. 7.12a and b). The couching thread passed through the loops, thus holding the metal thread in place. By pulling the metal thread through the ground fabric at set points, indented patterns can be created on the front of the embroidery. This design, except for two very narrow bands and the frame that survives along the original edges of the ground fabric, has been stitched as single bricking with a distance of 1 mm–1.5 mm between each indentation (see Fig. 7.12a).

Stem stitch was used as an outline and survives around the majority of the roundels, bands and trefoils, and in a number of small sections around the lion on the bottom row (Fig. 7.13a and b). It was not worked in the 'traditional' manner: at the start of each stitch the thread is brought to the front of the ground fabric through the hole created when the thread was taken to the reverse of the ground fabric when completing the penultimate stitch, which creates a rope-like effect on the front and a seemingly continuous line of small straight stitches on the reverse (Fig. 7.14a). Instead, in this variation, the stitch was brought to the front of the ground fabric slightly behind where it had previously been taken to the reverse of the textile, creating a rope-like effect that can appear disjointed on the front and a broken line of small individual stitches on the reverse (Fig. 7.14b). It would be interesting to see if this variation of stem stitch was used on other embroideries of this period. It may be that this was a preferred technique or it could represent the working style of a particular embroiderer.

Although it is difficult to analyse the order of work, the positioning of the stitches on the reverse of the embroidery indicates the underside couching was completed first and the outline afterwards. This would make sense from a practical perspective as underside couching needs a lot of manipulation which

10   For discussion on these variables see Lester-Makin, *The Lost Art of the Anglo-Saxon World*, pp. 33–38; Lisa Monnas, "The Making of Medieval Embroidery," in *English Medieval Embroidery: Opus Anglicanum*, pp. 7–23 at 14.

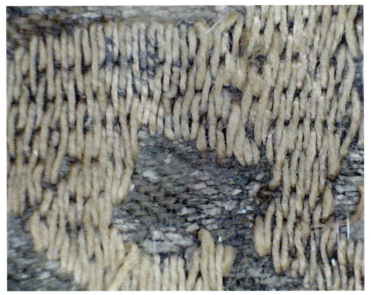

FIGURE 7.12A   Microscopic image showing a detail of underside couching
                on Embroidery 2 from the front (x 210).
                © Alexandra Lester-Makin

FIGURE 7.12B   Microscopic image showing a detail of underside couching
                on Embroidery 2 from the reverse (x 210).
                © Alexandra Lester-Makin

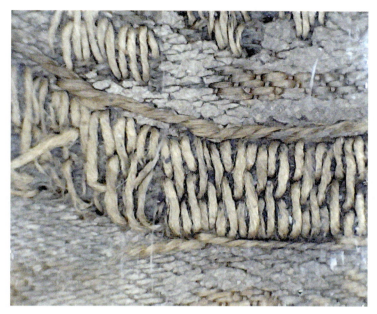

FIGURE 7.13A   Microscopic image showing a detail of the stem stitch outline
around a roundel on Embroidery 2 (x 210).
© Alexandra Lester-Makin

FIGURE 7.13B   Microscopic image showing a detail of the stem stitch outline
around a lion on Embroidery 2 (x 210).
© Alexandra Lester-Makin

FIGURE 7.14A   Line drawing depicting stem stitch worked the traditional
way. Side view showing the stitch as it pierces the ground
fabric.
© Alexandra Lester-Makin

FIGURE 7.14B   Line drawing depicting stem stitch as worked on Embroidery 2. Side
view showing the stitch as it pierces the ground fabric.
© Alexandra Lester-Makin

might distort or split the stitches of the finer silk outline, if it had been completed first.

The design was almost certainly drawn onto the ground fabric before
embroidering commenced. The precision with which these small motifs were
rendered, particularly the detailed animals and those elements with curves,
confirms this idea. Without under-drawing there is a greater potential for
stitches to be inaccurately positioned and the design to become skewed as
work progresses. These issues are particularly relevant with underside couching because once the stitch has been created it is difficult to unpick; the metal
thread buckles and gaps can appear between the strips of wrapped metal, leaving the core thread visible. The hole in the ground fabric, created by passing a
metal thread through to the reverse, would potentially break some of the warp
and weft threads, meaning that individual threads of the ground fabric cannot
be smoothed back into their original positions, thus leaving a hole visible.

Running along the two surviving edges to the right and along the base of the
textile is a border also worked in silver-gilt thread (see Fig. 7.9a). This line was

worked along two original edges. At the top right of the textile the vertical line of stitching turns slightly, demonstrating that the border originally continued diagonally from bottom right to top left. It can therefore be assumed that the border originally encompassed the whole design, following the shape of the object to be made from the completed embroidery. The border is stitched in underside couching but manipulated to look like a continuous row of feathers, a technique seen on the twelfth-century Worcester fragments and later examples of *Opus Anglicanum*.[11] The fabric along both edges was turned under to form a hem. Analysis of the reverse shows that the vertical hem was created first and the embroidered border was stitched through it, effectively holding the turned-under fabric in place. However, the embroiderer stitched the border along the base of the design and after the turning point at the top of the vertical line, before the hems were turned under along these edges. To complicate matters, all three border lines were stitched together. The vertical hem must have been stitched along an exposed edge of ground fabric that could be turned under during the embroidery process, while the other hems could not be turned under until the ground fabric had been cut to shape.

Although these two edges are original, the fragment has at some point in its history become detached from a larger piece. Most of the edges appear to have been trimmed but there are a number of places, at the top middle and left side of the textile, where the fabric appears frayed, indicating the ground fabric may have broken away from the rest of the textile at these points.

Discovery and Museum Contexts

The St Calais fragments are first mentioned in a footnote of Reverend James Raine's 1852 publication about Auckland Castle, in which he stated that when the Chapter House of Durham Cathedral was partially demolished in 1795, the workmen opened the grave of Bishop William of St Calais. In the tomb the men, "found the bones of a tall man, portions of a pair of sandals, fragments of a robe richly embroidered in gold, ornamented with griffin *passant*, and other quaint devices."[12] Embroidery 2 does incorporate a standing griffin with a raised tail, so this may be the textile Raine refers to, although there is no mention of the two lions. It is interesting that the workmen specifically stated

---

11   Lester-Makin, *The Lost Art of the Anglo-Saxon World*, pp. 133–36, Pl. 27. For later examples see Browne, Davis, and Michael, *English Medieval Embroidery: Opus Anglicanum*, p. 114ff.

12   James Raine, *A Brief Historical Account of the Episcopal Castle, or Palace of Auckland* (Durham, 1852), p. 8, n. 1.

that the embroidery was worked in gold thread. There are a number of possible explanations: that the silver-gilt thread had survived in the grave in better condition that it does today, giving the impression that is was actually gold thread; that the workmen were mistaken in their description; or that there was another now lost embroidery that incorporated griffins worked in gold thread.

There is only one mention of the embroideries between their discovery and their appearance in the Victoria and Albert Museum's 1963 exhibition. In an article dating to 1880, Rev. J.T. Fowler reports on excavations undertaken on the site of the Chapter House in 1874. As part of his discussion he states that, "some fragments with still more elaborate patterns, which came from the grave of Bp. De St Carileph, opened in 1795, have been preserved, together with the sole of one and the upper-leather of another plain shoe from the same grave."[13] Presumably, then, the two fragments must have been stored within Durham Cathedral. They were probably on display in the Cathedral Library in 1977, when Martin Carver noted single thong flip flops, supposedly from St Calais' tomb, were on display.[14] Today both embroideries are housed in the store of the Durham University Conservation Studio, which is based at Palace Green Library in Durham. During the early 2000s the fragments were hermetically sealed and stored while a new exhibition gallery was being created in the Cathedral. At this time both embroideries were set in one frame together with a small piece of braid, also found in the tomb. In 2016 the two embroideries were re-framed without the braid. Each embroidery now sits in a Perspex cavity cut to its exact shape, thus giving each piece maximum support and relief from any stress the fibres were under. This layer is sandwiched between two other layers of Perspex, encasing and protecting the embroideries from the outside environment and human touch. This form of casing means both the front and reverse of each piece is visible to scholars wishing to analyse them (Fig. 7.15).

William of St Calais

William of St Calais is a somewhat enigmatic figure. W.M. Aird points out that although St Calais is regarded as the founder of the Anglo-Norman cathedral

---

13   [Rev.] J.T. Fowler, "An Account of Excavations Made on the Site of the Chapter-house of Durham Cathedral in 1874," *Archaeologia* 45.2 (1880), 385–404 at p. 403.

14   Martin Carver, "Early Medieval Durham: the Archaeological Evidence," in *Medieval Art and Architecture at Durham Cathedral: British Archaeological Association Conference Transactions for the year 1977*, ed. Nicola Coldstream and Peter Draper (Leeds, 1980), pp. 11–19 at 12.

FIGURE 7.15   Both embroideries in their perspex case.
With the kind permission of Durham Cathedral

in Durham and the instigator for restructuring its clergy from secular clerics to Benedictine monks, he actually spent little time there because his secular duties kept him at court.[15] We know little of his early life except that he was a member of the clergy at the church in Bayeux before joining the monastery of St Calais, where he eventually became prior. In *c.*1078 he became abbot of St Vincent's monastery at Le Mans. During this period St Calais was often involved in secular affairs and it may be at these sessions that he met William of Normandy, later William I of England. William nominated St Calais for the episcopal position at Durham and he was duly ordained bishop in January 1081.[16]

According to Meg Bernstein, St Calais appears uninterested in integrating into his new homeland. She states that while the public cathedral displays, "Norman-derived monumental scale and elevation composition," and "places visual priority on Anglo-Saxon surface decoration and arcading," his private chapel, which was built at the same time, prioritises Norman styles. He

---

15   W.M. Aird, "An Absent Friend: the Career of Bishop William of St Calais," in *Anglo-Norman Durham 1093–1193*, ed. David Rollason, Margaret Harvey, and Michael Prestwich (1994, repr. Woodbridge, 1998), pp. 283–97 at 283–84.

16   Symeon of Durham, *Libellus de Exordio Atque Procursu Istius, hoc est Dunhelmensis, Ecclesie: Tract on the Origins and Progress of this the Church of Durham*, ed. David Rollason (Oxford, 2000), bk. 4, ch. 1; Aird, "Absent Friend," p. 290.

evidently considered Norman visual culture to be superior to native English art.[17] This is an important point because if true, it is probable that St Calais chose designs for his ecclesiastical vestments that aligned him with the Norman institutions he was associated with. This attitude probably deepened during his three-year exile from England between 1088 and 1091, when he was forced to live in Normandy after taking part in a failed coup to put Robert Curthose on the English throne. While there he took on the role of chief administrator on behalf of Curthose.[18] According to Symeon of Durham, when St Calais returned from Normandy, he took care to send ahead of him many gifts for the church at Durham, including altar vessels worked in gold and silver, other ornaments and books.[19] Although vestments are not mentioned, St Calais may have brought back decorative ideas not only for the new cathedral and private chapel but also for their soft furnishings and his episcopal robes. Indeed, the mortuary[20] of St Calais tells us that when he died the monks took a number of items from "the chapel," possibly St Calais' private chapel, including five copes, three white and black; three chasubles, two white and one black; with a great stole and maniple embroidered merely on the ends, and a white cloth for the altar.[21] Symeon of Durham records that upon St Calais' death his body was "wrapped in episcopal vestments as is customary" and he was buried in the Chapter House of the cathedral.[22] Although the documentary evidence is not as detailed as some early medieval inventories, only listing the number of vestments and their colours, it indicates that St Calais possessed numerous textiles, some of which may have come from or been inspired by his time in Normandy.

---

17   Meg Bernstein, "A Bishop of Two Peoples: William of St Calais and the Hybridization of Architecture in Eleventh-century Durham," *Journal of the Society of Architectural Historians* 77.3 (2018), 267–84 at pp. 268, 269.

18   Aird, "An Absent Friend," pp. 293–94.

19   *... sed non pauca ex auro et argento sacra altaris uasa et diuersa ornamenta, sed et libros plurimos ad ecclesiam premittere curauit*, Symeon of Durham, *Libellus*, bk. 4, ch. 8.

20   An account of his funeral and the items he left at Durham.

21   *... et de ejusdem Capellâ habuit Ecclesia plurima ornamenta, videlicet v capas, quarum iij albæ et negræ; iij casulas, quarum ij albæ et una nigra, cum stolâ et manipulo magnis, in fine tantum brudatis; unum pannum album pro altari*, in *Medieval Dress and Textiles in Britain: a Multilingual Sourcebook*, ed. Louise M. Sylvester, Mark C. Chambers, and Gale R. Owen-Crocker (Woodbridge, 2014), pp. 22, 23. I would like to thank Peter Lester for help with translating the Latin text.

22   *"Placuit ergo illis ut in capitulo tumulari deberet, quatinus in loco quo fratres cotidie congregarentur, uiso eius sepulchre carissimo patris memoria in eorum cordibus cotidie renouaretur"*, and *"Cuius corpus pontificalibus secundum morem uestimentis obuolutum fratres, qui cum eo fuerant, Dunhelmum transtulerunt ..."*, Symeon of Durham, *Libellus*, bk. 4, ch. 10.

Materials and Production

The embroidery on both fragments is worked on samite silk. Whether the fragments of cloth are from the same silk textile needs further analysis to ascertain. Anna Muthesius has argued that weft-faced compound twill samite silk was, "arguably the most important weave in Byzantium." Up to the twelfth century Byzantine silk was used as a political tool within royal circles, the members of which had tight control over the production of the highest quality textiles.[23] Through multiple gift exchange and diplomatic networks samite silk found its way into north European courts and religious settings. It is probably through such networks that St Calais acquired the silk that was used as the embroideries' ground fabric. The religious institutions of Bayeux, St Calais, and Le Mans, where William spent his early vocation, are known to have been main centres for the distribution of Byzantine silks,[24] so it is not unlikely that St Calais saw and used such fabrics in all three establishments. As he rose through the monastic ranks, he was probably able to obtain pieces for himself and he would also have had the opportunity to obtain silk during his three-year exile.

By 1000 raw silk that could be made into thread was obtainable from a number of sources but not Byzantium or Byzantine Sicily, due to the large quantities needed in Byzantium's silk weaving industry. Raw silk could be sourced from Muslim Sicily and Spain but the main purchasing centre in the Mediterranean was Fustat in Egypt.[25] It was also likely raw silk or silk thread was traded through river-based networks that reached the Silk Road.[26] Silver-gilt thread is produced by coating a thin strip of silver with a layer of gold, which is then wrapped round a core thread, in this case of silk. The methods for making this type of metal thread were known in Europe from the tenth century[27] and, according to Elizabeth Plenderleith, there was a considerable debasement in the metal used to make metal threads from the eleventh century.[28] Flax to make linen threads and fabric had been grown in England throughout the early medieval period and it would, presumably, have been relatively easy

---

23   Anna Muthesius, "Silk in the Medieval World," in *The Cambridge History of Western Textiles 1*, ed. David Jenkins (Cambridge, 2003), pp. 325–54 at 326, 343.

24   Anna Muthesius, *Byzantine Silk Weaving AD 400 to AD 1200*, ed. Ewald Kislinger and Johannes Koder (Vienna, 1997), pp. 140–42.

25   Muthesius, "Silk in the Medieval World," p. 326.

26   Marianne Vedeler, *Silk for the Vikings* (Oxford, 2014), pp. 58–60.

27   Paul Garside, "Gold and Silver Metal Thread," in *Encyclopedia of Medieval Dress and Textiles of the British Isles c. 450–1450*, ed. Gale R. Owen-Crocker, Elizabeth Coatsworth, and Maria Hayward (Leiden, 2012), pp. 237–39 at 238.

28   Elizabeth Plenderleith, "The Stole and Maniples: (a) the technique," in *The Relics of St Cuthbert*, ed. C.F. Battiscombe (Oxford, 1956), p. 378.

to obtain, for those who could afford it. The complex production process and amount of man/woman power needed to convert the plant fibres into useable thread would have made linen affordable only to those within higher ranking circles.[29] The evidence therefore suggests that the materials utilized in making the two St Calais embroideries came from a wide cultural and geographical range. They all had in common the concept of prestige and incorporated a visual message of far reaching and influential networks.

While the Normans often destroyed native art in an attempt to eradicate Anglo-Saxon culture or sent it to their other territories, embroidery appears to have been somewhat exempt, with native professional embroiderers being commissioned to produce and decorate numerous items.[30] The will of Queen Matilda (c.1031–1083), wife of William the Conqueror (c.1028–1087), is a typical example, stating that a chasuble being made by one Aldret of Winchester's wife and another robe being embroidered in England should go to the Church of the Holy Trinity in Caen.[31] In fact, one Leofgyth is named in Domesday Book as having embroidered items for the previous regime and the new Norman rulers.[32] C.R. Dodwell has noted that although the Normans admired embroidery, there appears to be no evidence of it being undertaken on a professional level within Normandy itself.[33] It is therefore likely that the St Calais embroideries were made in England by professional embroidery workers.[34] During this period there are two possibilities for professionally commissioning and creating embroideries. The first is through the independent worker system: as Matilda commissioned Aldret's wife to make her a chasuble, so St Calais could commission and provide the materials. The second option would be to commission embroideries through a workshop. In this instance St Calais could provide all or some of the materials and the workshop may have provided the

---

29   Lester-Makin, *The Lost Art of the Anglo-Saxon World*, p. 46.

30   C.R. Dodwell, *Anglo-Saxon Art: a new perspective* (Manchester, 1982), pp. 216–19.

31   *Ego Mathildis Regina do Sancte Trinitati Cadomi casulam quam apud Wintoniam operator uxor Aldereti et clamidem operatam ex auro que est in camera mea ad cappam faciendam ... ac vestimentum quod operator in Anglia ...*, in *Les Actes de Guillaume le Conquérant et de la Reine Mathilde pour les Abbayes Caennaises*, ed. L. Musset (Caen, 1967), pp. 112–13.

32   *Leuiede fecit 7 facit aurifrifiŭ regis 7 reginæ*, trans. C. Thorn and F. Thorn, "6: Wiltshire," in *Domesday Book*, ed. J. Morris (Chichester, 1979), p. 74b.

33   Dodwell, *Anglo-Saxon Art*, p. 139; for discussions about embroidery workers in other Norman territories see Alexandra Lester-Makin, "The Bayeux Tapestry as an Artefact of Culture Transfer," in *Cultural Transfers in the Norman Medieval Worlds (8–12th Cent.): Objects, Actors and Mediators*, ed. Pierre Bauduin, Luc Bourgeois, and Simon Lebouteiller (Turnhout, forthcoming).

34   For a detailed discussion of early medieval English embroiderers see Lester-Makin, *The Lost Art of the Anglo-Saxon World*, pp. 101–40.

rest.[35] It is possible that St Calais designed the embroideries himself, incorporating motifs he particularly wanted to include. There is evidence from the tenth century that St Dunstan (craftsman, monk, and Archbishop of Canterbury between 960–978), was commissioned by Æthelwynn to design a stole for her and her girls to embroider,[36] so it is possible that St Calais did something similar, or at least specified the motifs he required. Due to the paucity of extant embroideries from the period, it is not possible to identify stylistic trends which would indicate cultural or geographical locales and places of production. However, as St Calais was often away from Durham at the king's court, it is likely that he commissioned the embroideries from someone who was known at court such as Leofgyth or Aldret's wife, or a workshop situated in one of the royal centres.

The embroideries themselves can tell us about the women who made them. The technical analysis shows that each piece utilizes different stitches, thus creating contrasting finishes. Although informed patrons may have discussed the embroideries' technical attributes with workers, in this instance it is likely these choices were left to the embroiderers, St Calais being preoccupied with his secular duties, rather than the minutiae of embroidery production. Embroidery 2 appears much finer than Embroidery 1 but this is a visual misconception. Embroidery 1's design is larger and the method used to create the surface couching, sewing over two metal threads at a time and using three or four rows of double threads to create one line, creates a bulkier finish. The metal threads on both embroideries are c.0.2 mm in diameter, which suggests the same type of thread was used on both pieces; this could be confirmed with more detailed analysis.

Due to the fragmentary nature and small size of Embroidery 1 it is impossible to suggest whether more than one worker created the original piece. It is likely that Embroidery 2 was completed by a single worker (see below). The

---

35   For a detailed discussion about embroidery production in early medieval England see Lester-Makin, *The Lost Art of the Anglo-Saxon World*, pp. 101–40; for the production of the Bayeux Tapestry see Alexandra Lester-Makin, "The Front Tells the Story, the Back Tells the History: a Technical Discussion of the Embroidering of the Bayeux Tapestry," in *Making Sense of the Bayeux Tapestry: Readings and Reworkings*, ed. Anna C. Henderson with Gale R. Owen-Crocker (Manchester, 2016), pp. 23–40.

36   *Rogatus est Dunstanus a quadam matron Ethelwinna nomine domum suam uenire, quatinus in casual sacerdotali faceret picturam, unde puellae suae insuendi auri traherent formam. Opus plumarium uocant Latini, William of Malmesbury Saints' Lives: Lives of SS. Wulfstan, Dunstan, Patrick, Benignus and Indract*, ed. M. Winterbottom and R.M. Thomson (Oxford, 2002), pp. 182, 183. We know very little about Æthelwynn/Ethelwinna, except that she was a married woman who had a circle of young women or girls living within her household. See Lester-Makin, *The Lost Art of the Anglo-Saxon World*, p. 119.

consistency of stitchwork on both pieces demonstrates the worker(s) were well trained. Indeed, the underside couching of Embroidery 2 demonstrates the worker was trained to a high technical standard. The embroiderers had knowledge of the materials' properties and how to manipulate them to achieve the required results, using a variety of stitches, some of which are technically challenging. This evidence demonstrates the worker(s) were practiced in both silk and silver-gilt metal thread work, and in traditional stitches – satin, stem, laid-work and surface couching – and the newer variation of underside couching.

Design

There are no known surviving embroidery designs comparable to the foliage and base of Embroidery 1, and there are few parallels in other art forms. Although King stated there were comparable motifs in the borders of the Bayeux Tapestry,[37] a close inspection of the foliage motifs within these areas reveals that this is not actually the case. There are a number of foliage motifs that incorporate a stand of one triangle and a circular ring but none have an upper triangle. There are a number of these motifs where the leaves 'grow' from a central stem and the row above is partially covered by the row below. However, all have a *visible* central stem and none of the leaves are divided in two along their length.

The closest embroidered parallel to Embroidery 1's foliage motif appears in the border of the early eleventh-century Blue Mantle of St Kunigunde, housed in the Bamberg Diocesan Museum in Germany (Fig. 7.16). This motif appears at least four times around the edge of the mantle where it sprouts from the spiral that curls around it, ostensibly encasing the foliage within a roundel. The compound leaves sprout,[38] one to the left and one to the right on each row, from a central point but they do not overlap each other. Each leaf is divided along its length with a sinuous line that appears to represent leaflets, unlike the undulating dividing lines on the leaves of Embroidery 1, which probably represent the outer edge of the folded over leaf, thus the underside of the leaf is seen in the lower half. The lower half of each leaf is infilled in surfacing couching worked in gold thread while the upper half appears to be free of embroidery. There are only two rows of leaves with what appears to be the bud of a flower

---

37   King, *Opus Anglicanum*, p. 13.
38   I would like to thank Gale R. Owen-Crocker for bringing the compound leaf shape to my attention.

FIGURE 7.16   Detail from St Kunugunde's cope showing the embroidered foliage motif at
the bottom right, Diözesanmuseum Bamberg.
Photo: Uwe Gaasch

growing from the central point of the upper row, unlike Embroidery 1, which
originally had a third row of leaves, if not more.

Another design parallel is the eighth- to ninth-century Annunciation Silk,
a weft-faced compound twill samite silk housed in the Vatican Museums,
Vatican City (Fig. 7.17).[39] Situated along the lower edge of the surviving textile
are three lotus flower motifs. The central flower incorporates four leaves of
which the two on the upper row and towards the rear are clearly woven in
the same style as those of the St Calais embroidery. Each is divided along its
length with an undulating line. The lower half of the leaves are woven in a dark
colour representing the turned-over underside of the leaf, while the upper half
incorporate a line of six or seven dots. There are also similar leaves positioned
in the corners of the textile. These have the same internal elements, dark lower
half, undulating dividing line, and a row of dots, but here the left leaf overlaps
the right leaf, mirroring the right-over-left overlap of the embroidery. Similar
leaf designs are also evident on the eighth-century St Servatius Amazon Silk at
Maastricht (Fig. 7.18). However, on this piece the infill elements are reversed

---

39   I would like to thank Hero Granger-Taylor for bringing this textile and the lotus flower
motif to my attention, and to Clare Vernon for referencing sources relating to palmette
motifs during this period.

FIGURE 7.17   The Annunciation Silk with the lotus flower and leaves positioned in the
               centre and two corners of the lower edge of the textile.
               Photo: © Governorate of the Vatican City State-Directorate of the Vatican
               Museums

with the darker turnover at the top and the line of dots along the bottom of
each leaf. There are also a number of surviving 'Hunter Silks' with similar
scenes woven into them.[40] One ninth-century example is associated with the
relics of St Calais, so it is possible William saw and was influenced by these
types of silk during his time at Le Mans.

Embroidery 1's foliage motif appears to originate in earlier lotus flower
patterns woven into Byzantine samite silks. The use of laid-work on the
turned-over underside of leaves appears to echo that of the slightly earlier
St Kunigunde mantle, but this may simply be a coincidence of the workers'
knowledge of the properties of silk and metal threads and the finished effect
the commissioners required.

Embroidery 2's vine-like bands with spirals and trefoils, and roundels inhabited by lions and griffins are a development of similar motifs found throughout
the medieval period and across artistic genera. From the late eighth to ninth
century are two roundel strips from Maaseik, which were probably inspired
by illuminated manuscripts and stone sculpture.[41] The borders of the Bayeux
Tapestry incorporate a number of lions and griffins *passant* with heads and

---

40   Muthesius, *Byzantine Silk Weaving*, pp. 67–69, pl. 79B.
41   See Mildred Budny and Martin Tweddle, "The Maaseik Embroideries," *Anglo-Saxon
      England* 13 (1984), 78–80.

FIGURE 7.18   The St Servatius Amazon Silk with the woven leaves
positioned in corners of the textile.
Photo: Sjoerd Aarts, Treasury of the Basilica of Saint
Servatius, Maastricht. With thanks to the Treasury of the
Basilica of Saint Servatius

tails in the same position. The lions in particular are stylistically similar enough to suggest the designer of Embroidery 2 was familiar with Canterbury art, the style which influenced the Bayeux Tapestry. Church inventories also list vestments embroidered with inhabited roundels; for example, Christ Church, Canterbury, lists a black tunicle owned by Lanfranc (d. 1089), who was also a monk in Normandy before becoming Archbishop of Canterbury, decorated with these designs worked in gold.[42]

One type of episcopal vestment provides a parallel not only in design and stitching but also in shape, the liturgical sandal which is, in fact, a slipper-like shoe.[43] From the eleventh century, sandals and stockings (buskins) became markers of episcopal status with bishops regularly wearing them.[44] There are three early examples of silk-embroidered liturgical sandals, all dating to the twelfth to thirteenth centuries, which share similarities with the St Calais embroidery. A twelfth-century example discovered in the tomb of Bishop William in Périgueux Cathedral, France, is thought to be English embroidery. Worked on samite silk cloth, the design incorporates griffins and lions inhabiting a scrolling vine that ends in trefoils and spirals embroidered in underside couching in silver-gilt metal threads and outlined in red silk thread, worked in split or stem stitch (Fig. 7.19a–b).[45] From the late twelfth-century are the sandals of Hubert Walter, Archbishop of Canterbury. The design embroidered around the sides and back of the sandals is also similar to the St Calais fragment (Fig. 7.20), incorporating a lion *passant*, among other creatures, which inhabit roundels from which sprout spirals and foliage. The embroidery is also worked in underside couching in silver-gilt metal and outlined in stem stitch with silk threads on samite silk.[46] Around the edges of the design, forming a border between it and a narrow-embroidered band above, is a line of feather-like stitching, the same as the border on the St Calais textile. It is particularly noticeable on these sandals that the stitched border follows the shape of different parts of the sandal. One corner at the front, just to the side of the throat opening, turns from the vertical at a similar angle to the border at the top right of the St Calais fragment. In Fig. 7.20 it can be seen that Hubert Walter's

---

42   *cum stellis et bestijs aureis in circuli brudata*, *Inventories of Christchurch Canterbury*, ed. J. Wickham Legg and W.H. St John Hope (London, 1902), p. 57.

43   Pauline Johnstone, *High Fashion in the Church* (Leeds, 2002), p. 15.

44   Maureen C. Miller, *Clothing the Clergy: Virtue and Power in Medieval Europe, c. 800–1200* (London, 2014), p. 199.

45   Christine Descatoire, *L'Art en Broderie au Moyen Âge: autour des collections du musée de Cluny* (Paris, 2019), p. 51.

46   Coatsworth and Owen-Crocker, *Clothing the Past: Surviving Garments from Early Medieval to Early Modern Western Europe* (Leiden, 2018), pp. 386–88.

sandals incorporate an embroidered border along the curve of the side seam, also called the closing seam, which is also similar to that on the St Calais piece. The third example was discovered in the tomb of Bishop John II in Basel cathedral, Switzerland, and dates to either the twelfth or early thirteenth century. These shoes also incorporate spiralling bands which end in trefoils worked in either gold or silver-gilt metal thread in underside couching with stem stitch outlines worked in a dark red-brown silk thread on a (plain) samite silk. The surviving embroidery is fragmentary, so an exact comparison of stitched borders and shape around the throat and side seam cannot be made. However, these sandals are interesting because the embroidery formed an outer layer that was attached to a leather base and sole.[47] This helps make sense of the leather shoes supposedly discovered in St Calais' tomb.

Marquita Volken has analysed photographs of the shoes and although she clarifies that the fragments need to be correctly examined in person, she has stated that while the piece on the left of Figure 7.21 is more likely to date to the fourteenth or early fifteenth centuries, the sole on the right appears to have the correct shape and stitches for a mid to late eleventh-century turn shoe.[48] Although these observations throw into doubt the assumption that the shoes are from St Calais' grave, it is possible to suggest that the sole, on the right of Figure 7.21, formed the base of an episcopal sandal that was covered by Embroidery 2. We can take this hypothesis further by mapping how the embroidery would have fitted around such a shoe: the right edge of the surviving fragment would have been positioned at the front centre of the sandal, forming the lower part of the throat seam and the start of the vamp line; the textile would wrap around the left side of the sandal towards the back, forming the quarter area and positioning the curved edge of the embroidery on the outside of the sandal along the side seam line. The St Calais fragment, along with the leather sole, could very well be an even earlier example of an episcopal sandal than other extant examples. These are the only episcopal vestment types that conform to the unusual shape of this embroidery and although the workmen who discovered the tomb described a robe embroidered with a griffin, it is possible that the textile was found in a position near the ankle, and the workmen mistook it for part of a long robe.

---

47   Hans-Rudolf Meir and Peter-Andrew Schwarz (eds.), *Die Grabfunde des 12. Bis 19. Jahrhunderts aus dem Basler Münster* (Basel-Stadt, 2013), p. 114. I am grateful to Marquita Volken for bringing this work to my attention.

48   I would like to thank Marquita Volken for her analysis.

FIGURE 7.19   The embroidered episcopal sandals discovered in the tomb
of Bishop William in Périgueux Cathedral, France. The
embroidered animals and stitchwork are similar to that on the
St Calais roundel fragment.
© RMN-Grand Palais (musée de Cluny – musée national du
Moyen Âge) / Michel Urtado

FIGURE 7.20   Detail of one of Archbishop Hubert Walter's sandals. The lion, roundels,
foliage and spirals, and stitchwork are similar to that of the St Calais roundel
fragment. This shoe also has a border line that follows a similar shape to the
one on the St Calais embroidery.
Reproduced courtesy of the Chapter of Canterbury

Conclusion: The Biographies of the William St Calais Embroideries

Object Biography Theory, originally developed by Igor Kopytoff,[49] has been
adopted by archaeologists as a means of telling the 'life stories' of objects,
particularly from cultures that leave little or no written record; it has also
been successfully used within the study of dress, textiles, and early medieval
embroideries.[50] Both the surviving St Calais embroideries are small and lack

49   Igor Kopytoff, "The Cultural Biography of Things: Commoditization as Process," in *The
Social Life of Things: Commodities in Cultural Perspective*, ed. Arjun Appadurai (Cambridge,
1986), pp. 64–91.

50   See Elizabeth Coatsworth and Gale R. Owen-Crocker, *Clothing the Past*; Alexandra Knox,
"Middle Anglo-Saxon Dress Accessories in Life and Death: Expressions of a Worldview,"
in *Dress and Society: Contributions from Archaeology*, ed. Toby F. Martin and Rosie Weetch
(Oxford, 2017), pp. 114–29; Alexandra Lester-Makin, *The Lost Art of the Anglo-Saxon
World*, pp. 57–76; Alexandra M. Makin, "Embroidery and its Context in the British Isles

FIGURE 7.21   Fragments of two shoes that were thought to have come from Bishop William
               of St Calais' tomb. However, the piece on the left probably dates to the 14th or
               early 15th century. The sole on the right has the correct shape and stitches for a
               turn shoe dating to the mid- to late 11th century.
               With the kind permission of Durham Cathedral

a detailed report of their discovery, therefore the 'object biography' approach, drawing on details deducible from the artefacts themselves, is a useful one.

Embroidery 1 was inspired by lotus leaves woven into the eighth- to ninth-century Annunciation Silk, an example of the highest quality samite silks to come from Byzantium. A 'Hunter Silk' housed with the relics of St Calais himself indicates that William was aware of these prestigious textiles and their imperial and religious connotations. Thus, he used a samite silk as the ground fabric on which he commissioned the embroidering of motifs that displayed his artistic tastes and religious and secular ambitions. The lines of couched threads along the upper and lower edges of the fragment indicate this may have been a border incorporating foliage motifs like those on the St Kunigunde mantle. However, because the stitchwork continues underneath the upper border-line and over the edge of the hem, it is likely the embroidery

and Ireland during the Early Medieval Period (AD 450–110.0)," PhD dissertation, The University of Manchester, 2016, pp. 40–45.

was originally made for one purpose and then recycled, cut from one item and turned into a border that was attached as an appliqué to another. Although we cannot say when this occurred, it is not an unlikely scenario as embroideries were precious and accordingly recycled until they were no longer of any use,[51] but it does leave unanswered questions: did St Calais commission and later recycle the embroidery or was it a gift which he recycled? If so, who and where did the embroidery come from and what meaning did it have for St Calais?

Embroidery 2 is finely worked in underside couching and stem stitch. The design depicts motifs seen throughout the period and on many types of textile. Its design, shape, and size give credence to the idea that it was part of a sandal, a vestment particularly associated with bishops and other high-ranking clergy from the eleventh century. Due to his secular commitments St Calais was away from Durham much of the time, so it is likely he commissioned the embroidery while at court. As the designer(s) was aware of wider artistic styles such as the Canterbury style of art, the technical attributes of the embroideries demonstrate the embroiderer was well versed in the use of metal and silk threads, and the stitches utilized. This person may have worked as an independent concern or part of a larger workshop and was probably known to other members of the court who could have recommended her to St Calais.

The materials and designs incorporated into the embroideries give us an insight into St Calais' mindset. He was using the best materials and workmanship available to express his artistic ideals which harked back to Normandy, and to create clothing that conveyed his power and influence within both the Church and State. These objects brought together far flung cultures and artistic styles in the most up-to-date ecclesiastical fashions to express the attitudes and ambition of one man. When St Calais was buried in them, he was proclaiming his worldly and religious status in both this world and the next.

Today the embroideries are not seen as political or religious messages. They are precious artefacts kept hidden from general view in order to protect them for future audiences. Their biographies are not over, continuing into a future when scholars will be able to reveal more about their past lives.

---

51   See Maren Clegg Hyer, "Reduce, Reuse, Recycle: Imagined and Reimagined Textiles in Anglo-Saxon England," *Medieval Clothing and Textiles* 8 (2012), 49–62.

PART 2

In Their Contexts: Art and Worship through Sculpture, Carving, and Manuscript

∴

Framing Fragmentation: (Re)Constructing Anglo-Saxon Sculpture

Jane Hawkes

When I first began my doctorate on the non-Crucifixion iconography of pre-Viking sculpture in the north of England, the only significant study to-date on the subject was that of Betty Coatsworth, whose doctorate on the Crucifixion iconography of Anglo-Saxon sculpture was the inspiration for my own work and provided much of the foundational scholarship on which I was lucky enough to be able to draw. This has remained the case, and decades on it is a considerable privilege to dedicate this essay to a scholar whose studies into Anglo-Saxon sculpture (and art generally), remain inspirational and required reading.

∵

Introducing the Fragmented

With only three of the high crosses produced during the early medieval period still standing *in situ* in England, it is something of a truism to say that the once monumental Anglo-Saxon sculptures encountered today exist as nothing more than fragments:[1] fragments recovered from church walls and excavated from church floors and foundations.[2] Two pieces of the late eighth-century Rothbury cross, for instance, the top of the shaft and the remains of the cross-head, were recovered from the fabric of the Norman tower of the parish church in Rothbury in 1849–1850 and subsequently donated to the Society of

---

1   The three Anglo-Saxon crosses still standing *in situ* in England are those at Bewcastle, Irton, and Gosforth (all in Cumbria); the monuments at Bewcastle and Irton have been dated to the eighth century. That at Gosforth dates to the tenth. See Richard N. Bailey and Rosemary Cramp, *Corpus of Anglo-Saxon Stone Sculpture Volume II. Cumberland, Westmoreland and Lancashire North-of-the-Sands* (Oxford, 1988), pp. 61–72, 115–17, 100–04, illus. 90–119, 355–64 and 367–68, 288–308, respectively.

2   The catalogue entries in all the volumes produced for the Corpus of Anglo-Saxon Stone Sculpture provide details of evidence of such discoveries.

© KONINKLIJKE BRILL NV, LEIDEN, 2021 | DOI:10.1163/9789004467514_010

Antiquaries of Newcastle upon Tyne.[3] The many fragments now preserved in the south porch and at the west end of the north aisle in the parish church of Bakewell (Derbyshire), were likewise recovered (in 1843–1846), during refurbishment of the tower, but as rubble from the foundations (Fig. 8.1).[4] As is clear at Bakewell, such fragments now lie in places removed from their original context in the churches: the shaft fragment at Cundall in North Yorkshire, for instance, lies behind the church organ.[5]

Increasingly, however, ecclesiastical collections are being brought together for display with more consideration. At Lythe in North Yorkshire, many of the over forty fragments recovered from the walls and foundations of the eighteenth-century church tower, which was taken down and rebuilt in 1910,[6] are now on show under that tower in a carefully designed Heritage Lottery funded display, as are those in the parish church at Burnsall, in West Yorkshire,[7] the design for which involved scholarly advice and input from Betty Coatsworth. In museums they are displayed as collections in the regional institutions – such as those excavated from St Alkmund's, Derby, and Repton (Derbyshire),[8] which are on display in the Derby City Art Gallery and Museum – but it is another story entirely in the national arena. In the British Museum, only two of the dozens of fragments preserved in its stores are displayed in the early medieval gallery, one – a late eighth-century cross-head from Lancaster – being set high up against the wall so that only one side (displaying an inscription) is visible (Fig. 8.2a).[9] This setting, of course, attempts to convey its original relationship with the human viewer, but it is too high to see properly, the other side is invisible (Fig. 8.2b), and the decision to prioritise the inscription is one embedded

---

3   Elizabeth Coatsworth, "The Iconography of the Crucifixion in Pre-Conquest Sculpture in England," PhD thesis, 2 vols, University of Durham, 1979, 1, 200–07; 2, 42–43, pls. 27, 81–82, 101; Rosemary Cramp, *Corpus of Anglo-Saxon Stone Sculpture Volume 1. County Durham and Northumberland* (Oxford, 1984), pp. 217–21, fig. 20, illus. 1206–24; Jane Hawkes, "The Rothbury Cross: An Iconographic Bricolage," *Gesta* 35.1 (1996), 73–90.

4   Jane Hawkes and Philip Sidebottom, *Corpus of Anglo-Saxon Stone Sculpture Volume XIII. Derbyshire and Staffordshire* (Oxford, 2018), p. 113, illus. 16, 64.

5   James Lang, *Corpus of Anglo-Saxon Stone Sculpture Volume VI. Northern Yorkshire* (Oxford, 2002), pp. 93–97, illus. 159–78.

6   Ibid., pp. 153–292, illus. 463–596.

7   Elizabeth Coatsworth, *Corpus of Anglo-Saxon Stone Sculpture Volume VIII. Western Yorkshire* (Oxford, 2008), pp. 107–14, illus. 79–138.

8   Hawkes and Sidebottom, *Corpus Volume XIII*, pp. 162–75, 198–218 and 227–28, illus. 147–88, 247–346, 406–07.

9   Richard N. Bailey, *Corpus of Anglo-Saxon Stone Sculpture Volume IX. Cheshire and Lancashire* (Oxford, 2010), pp. 215–18, illus. 562–67; London, British Museum, acc. no. M&LA 1868, 10–43.

FIGURE 8.1 Fragments of Anglo-Saxon sculpture, South Porch, All Saints' Church, Bakewell, Derbyshire.
Photo: Jane Hawkes

a   b

FIGURE 8.2A–B   Cross-head from St Mary's Priory, Lancaster, Lancashire, late eighth
century; (a) as currently displayed in British Museum showing inscription;
(b) as previously displayed in British Museum showing reverse with incised
lozenges and hole for central inset.
Photos: Jane Hawkes

in the earliest antiquarian interests of the sixteenth century.[10] In this respect
it would appear that we have not advanced very far in our national focus of
interest in Anglo-Saxon sculpture.

Most of the carved fragments were recovered during the massive rebuilding
of medieval churches undertaken by the 'established' Church in the nineteenth
century, following the full emancipation of the Churches that did not conform

10   Jane Hawkes, "Creating a View: Anglo-Saxon Sculpture in the Sixteenth Century," in
Making Histories: Proceedings of the Sixth International Conference on Insular Art, ed. Jane
Hawkes (Donington, 2013), pp. 372–84; Jane Hawkes, *Creating a Scholarship: Perceptions
of Anglo-Saxon Sculpture, c.1550–c.1950* (forthcoming).

to it. Yet, ironically, it was during the process of establishing the Anglican Church during the so-called Reformation in the sixteenth and seventeenth centuries that most of the sculptures were initially broken up. As is well known, following the Act promulgated by the General Assembly of the Church of Scotland held in Aberdeen in 1640, which was directed at all churches where "Idolatrous Monuments, made and erected for Religious worship, are yet extant,"[11] a further Assembly was called in 1642 in response to the Commissioners' Report on the 1640 Act. This brought attention to monuments, "such as Crucifixes, Images of Christ, Mary, and Saints Departed," that had not been "taken down, demolished, and destroyed,"[12] including the "idolatrous monuments in the Kirk of Ruthw[ell]," which were identified with the requirement that the previous Act "be put to execution."[13] As a result, the cross at Ruthwell was broken up and its fragments scattered: one piece was used as a bench in the church; another was reused as a gate-post; and a third was buried, only to be recovered by grave-diggers in 1823. At this point, the local minister gathered the fragments together and reconstructed the cross in the garden of the manse, before it was eventually moved into the parish church. Less well known are the destructive activities carried out earlier in the century at Sandbach, in Cheshire, where the Anglo-Saxon crosses became the focus of local, popular iconoclastic attention. In 1614 a group of Reformers had been brought before the Court of the Star Chamber and charged with destroying monuments, particularly crosses, in the Sandbach area. Their plea, that they were merely protesting the idolatrous worship of crosses, secured their freedom, leaving them free to return and "undertake other missions of destruction."[14]

Clearly, the Anglo-Saxon sculptures that we view today are fragmentary; they are broken, piecemeal, worn and removed from their original contexts.

---

11   *The Acts of the General Assemblies of the Church of Scotland from the Year 1638 to the Year 1649. Inclusive. Printed in the year 1682. To Which are now added the index of the unprinted Acts of these Assemblies; and the Acts of the General Assembly 1690* (Edinburgh, 1691), pp. 92–93; see Fred Orton and Ian Wood with Clare A. Lees, *Fragments of History: Rethinking the Ruthwell and Bewcastle Monuments* (Manchester, 2007), pp. 32–33.

12   Ibid.

13   *Acts (1638–1649)*, p. 4; see Orton *et al.*, *Fragments*, pp. 32–33.

14   A.C.F. Tait, "The Sandbach Crosses," *Transactions of the Historical Society of Lancashire and Cheshire* 98 (1946), 1–20 at p. 8. See also Bailey, *Corpus Volume IX*, pp. 99–120. It is generally accepted that as the crosses are not mentioned in William Webb's account of Sandbach, made some thirty-six years after that of William Smith, in *c*.1621 – which did mention the crosses – they had been dismantled during the iconoclastic activities in the area during 1614. See Daniel King, *The Vale-Royall of England, or Countie Palatine of Chester* (London, 1656), reprinted in G. Ormerod, *The History of the County Palatine and City of Chester*, 3 vols, 2nd ed. (London, 1882), 2, pp. 1–239.

a

b

c

FIGURE 8.3A–C   Museum displays of early sculptures: (a) Early Medieval Gallery, British
Museum; (b) Parthenon Marbles Hall, British Museum, with fragments
from Athens, Greece; (c) Main Gallery, Paestum Museum, Paestum, Italy,
with fragments from temple site.
Photos: Jane Hawkes

Even those that remain *in situ*, stand in landscapes vastly altered from those in which they were originally erected. Needless to say, signs of early medieval habitation have long been lost, and with current interest in deforestation on a planetary scale, it has not gone unobserved that the island of Britain is one of the most denuded of tree-cover in the world: a phenomenon that post-dates the early medieval period. Added to this is the fact that no documentation survives to facilitate our recreation of the original motives informing the commission, production and expectations of these artworks, unique to the Insular world until at least the twelfth century. Our receptions and perceptions are, therefore, as fragmented, our understandings as incomplete, as the original works themselves.

Encountering the Sculptural Fragment

The resulting fragmentation of the sculpture and the means of its recovery have certainly informed its display: as archaeological remains. This, however, is not the only explanation for the presentation of the carvings as excavated artefacts. For, implicit in the decisions made about displaying the carvings are perceptions of Britain's national heritage. To take the examples presented by the British Museum: the two fragments of Anglo-Saxon sculpture on display in the early medieval gallery (above eye level and between two columns separating one area of the gallery from another) are lost in the wealth of gold, silver, and ivory artefacts (Fig. 8.3a). They are thus passed by, barely noticed. And yet recovered fragments of ancient Greek sculptures are displayed on their own in a purpose-built gallery and presented – not as archaeology – but as paintings hung at eye-level along the walls, in total denial of their original setting and function, and in stark contrast to their display in museums elsewhere (Fig. 8.3b). In Paestum (southern Italy), for example, the remains of the Greek temple carving are set above head-height in a manner replicating their original setting on the outer walls of the temple *cella*, and can be viewed through windows on the upper galleries looking down on to the central space of the museum (Fig. 8.3c). An analogous display is presented in the Acropolis Museum in Athens where the counterparts of the pieces from the temple of Athena on the Acropolis held in the British Museum, can be seen, exhibited as archaeological remains that attempt to re-present their original setting. In the British Museum, however, the viewer is encouraged to interrogate, examine, and marvel at each fragment in its own right as if it were a painted canvas hung in an art gallery. Given the manner in which the 'Fine Arts' are dominated by painting, this display presents a clear attempt to elevate sculpture (albeit

great 'Paulinus' Cross, known to have existed there in the time of Henry VIII. The animals and figures of the Masham shaft are of the best Anglian work; on the highest tier are Our Lord and the Apostles; below them two tiers of illustrations from the life of a saint, possibly St Cuthbert; and below is a series of animal forms gracefully though fancifully drawn. The column can hardly have been an architectural feature, but as the foot of a round-shafted cross, more ambitious than the Collingham shaft, and carrying a large head represented by the fragment still in evidence, its meaning is cleared up. For the restoration of the Paulinus cross at Dewsbury we have convincing data. A number of pieces, which could only find a place on a cylindrical column, suggest something like the Masham shaft. Of these pieces one shows the junction of the round shaft with the upper flat panels, including the 'swag' which finishes them below as at Gosforth. Higher up the cross are figure-subjects in the same style of drawing and carving as those below; the Miracle of the Loaves and Fishes, the Miracle of Cana, and adjacent to the scroll-panel over the last a Madonna and Child (not seen in this view but given in Fig. 91). The peculiar cable-edging shows that all these fragments belong to one monument. Over the scroll-panel are the feet of two figures which must have filled a panel bringing the shaft up to the size required to meet a head of which the angel and votary formed the topmost arm. The restoration therefore is not fanciful, but built up from careful measurements and the consideration of

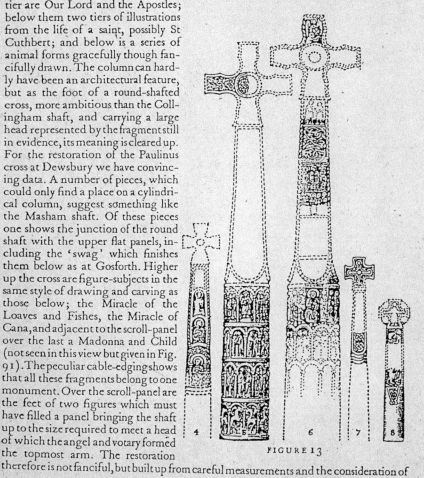

FIGURE 13

FIGURE 8.4   W.G. Collingwood's reconstruction of Anglo-Saxon monumental stone columns as crosses, including that at Masham (his Fig. 13.5).
W.G. Collingwood, *Northumbrian Crosses of the pre-Norman Age* (London, 1927)

fragmentary) to equal status. It demonstrates quite clearly that the sculptural heritage valued and claimed by Britain is not the early medieval; indeed, it is not even its own heritage. The irony of this in the context of Britain's decision to 'exit Europe' is interesting to say the least.

Visually Reconstructing the Fragmented

Despite these issues, however, the fragmentation of Anglo-Saxon sculpture does have its advantages. It allows us, for instance, to reconstruct the types of monuments that were originally set up across the landscape. These generally took the form of the high cross: the tall tapering monolith surmounted by a cross-head.[15] This can now be understood to reflect the influence of the late antique form of the obelisk, the obelisk being surmounted by a cross-head in its Christianised incarnation.[16] Familiarity with the obelisk that stood next to Old St Peter's in Rome would have rendered the squared tapering form of the high-cross particularly emotive.[17]

But in addition to the high cross was the monumental column, erected (uniquely in early medieval Europe) across England in the early ninth century. These originally stood over 3 m high with diameters of 60 cm or more and were surmounted by a cross-head. Initially, in the belief that all Anglo-Saxon monuments were high crosses, the columns were imagined as the bases of such crosses. But it is clear from Collingwood's drawing of the column at Masham, North Yorkshire,[18] that these monumental columnar crosses existed only in the mind of the draftsman (Fig. 8.4).

As monumental columns, however, they can be associated with late antique and early Christian columns, such as that surmounted by a cross and erected by Constantine next to the Holy Sepulchre in Jerusalem. Although this was unlikely to have been seen by Anglo-Saxons (other than Willibald whose travels to Jerusalem were recorded in the eighth century by Hygeburg at

---

15   See, e.g., Elizabeth Coatsworth, "Landmarks of Faith: Crosses and Other Free-standing Stones," in *The Material Culture of the Built Environment in the Anglo-Saxon World*, ed. Maren Clegg Hyer and Gale R. Owen-Crocker (Liverpool, 2015), pp. 117–36; Jane Hawkes, "Planting the Cross in Anglo-Saxon England," in *Place and Space in the Medieval World*, ed. Meg Boulton, Jane Hawkes, and Heidi Stoner (New York, 2018), pp. 47–62.

16   For summary, see Jane Hawkes, "'Iuxta Morem Romanorum': Stone and Sculpture in Anglo-Saxon England," in *Anglo-Saxon Styles*, ed. Catherine E. Karkov and George Hardin Brown (Albany, New York, 2003), pp. 69–100.

17   Hawkes, "'Iuxta Morem Romanorum,'" pp. 79–80.

18   W.G. Collingwood, *Northumbrian Crosses of the Pre-Norman Age* (London, 1927), fig. 13.5.

FIGURE 8.5
Polychrome Angel of the Annunciation,
early ninth century, Lichfield Cathedral,
Staffordshire.
Photo: Jane Hawkes

Heidenheim),[19] it was known through written accounts, and the late antique triumphal and Jupiter columns which informed Constantine's monument would have been familiar to Anglo-Saxons. Together, associations and encounters with the columns of antiquity are likely to have informed the columns supporting cross-heads that were set up across the region. Thus, the sculptural fragments have enabled us to reconstruct carved stone monuments that originally presented – in public settings – the imperium of the Church.[20]

The fragmented condition of these monuments and their preservation within the fabric of ecclesiastical structures has also ensured the survival of the gesso, paint, and, in some cases, the metal and paste-glass insets with which the carvings were originally enhanced. Traces of paint have been noted on many of carved fragments, but those recovered from under the nave of Lichfield cathedral in 2003 reveal the sophisticated nature of such colouration (Fig. 8.5).

---

19   *Vita Willibaldi episcopi Eichstetensis*, ed. O. Holder-Egger (Monumenta Germania Historicae Scriptores 15.1) (Hanover, 1887), pp. 86–106; trans. C.H. Talbot, *The Anglo-Saxon Missionaries in Germany: Being the Lives of SS. Willibrord (by Alcuin), Boniface (by Willibald), Sturm (by Eigil, Abbot of Fulda), Leoba (by Rudolf, Monk of Fulda) and Lebuin (by an anonymous writer), together with the* Hodeoporicon *of St. Willibald (by Huneberc of Heidenheim) and a Selection from the Correspondence of St. Boniface* (London and New York, 1954), pp. 153–80.

20   See summary of scholarship in Jane Hawkes, "The Church Triumphant: the Figural Columns of Early Ninth-century Anglo-Saxon England," in *Form and Order in the Anglo-Saxon World, AD 600–1100*, ed. Sally Crawford and Helena Hamerow with Leslie Webster (Oxford, 2009), pp. 29–42.

The three pieces unearthed at this time are carved with the figure of an arch-angel set against a plain background that was painted white and framed in red, with the angel wearing a yellow robe under-painted with red to replicate the red-gold so prized by Anglo-Saxons. The wings are also rendered in a sophisticated painterly manner: each feather painted red, shaded through pink to white. Gold foil decorated the halo.[21] Many of the fragmented sculptures also preserve the small holes made to contain insets. One of the pieces from the early ninth-century column that once stood in the church at Reculver (which preserves traces of red and blue paint along with white gesso), also retains holes drilled to affix a metal staff-cross held by Christ as he ascends into heaven; the central boss in the cross-head of the early ninth-century North Cross standing in the market-place at Sandbach, likewise preserves rivet holes drilled to attach a metal collar or cover over the boss; while the Lancaster cross-head, in addition to the bosses bearing holes intended to hold insets, also displays, on the face now hidden from view in the British Museum, a rivet-hole that once held a metal inset contained within incised centrally-placed lozenges understood to refer to the universal nature of the salvation made available through Christ's crucifixion (Fig. 8.2b).[22] Elsewhere, the deeply drilled pupils of the eyes of the Virgin preserved in the south aisle at Breedon-on-the-Hill in Leicestershire, were, like many other examples, most likely intended to hold insets of paste-glass. Indeed, the recent restoration of a cross-shaft fragment from Aberlady, East Lothian, undertaken by the National Museums of Scotland, has revealed the tin casings used to hold such insets in place – in this case, in the eyes of one of the interlacing birds filling the surface of the piece.[23]

From such fragments it is clear that the carved stone monuments erected across the landscape of Anglo-Saxon England, and even the panels and friezes used to decorate churches – as is probably the case with the Breedon Virgin – were colourful, eye-catching monuments, glittering in the sunshine and the flickering light of candles and lamps inside the churches. Indeed here, it is worth noting the deformed figures of the Damned eternally struggling

21   Warwick Rodwell, Jane Hawkes, Emily Howe, and Rosemary Cramp, "The Lichfield Angel: A Spectacular Anglo-Saxon Painted Sculpture," *The Antiquaries Journal* 88 (2008): 48–108.

22   Reculver 1a, see Dominic Tweddle, Martin Biddle, and Birthe Kjølby-Biddle, *Corpus of Anglo-Saxon Sculpture Volume IV. South-East England* (Oxford, 1995), p. 151, illus. 116; Sandbach see Hawkes, *Sandbach Crosses*, fig. 6.3; Lancaster (Priory) 1, see Bailey, *Corpus Volume IX*, pp. 99–113, illus. 250; 215–18, illus. 564. On the significance of the lozenge, see Jennifer O'Reilly, "Patristic and Insular Traditions of the Evangelists: Exegesis and Iconography," in *Le isole Britanniche e Roma in età romanobarbarica*, ed. A.M. Luiselli Fadda and Éamonn Ó Carragáin (Rome, 1998), pp. 49–94.

23   For the Breedon Virgin, see Rodwell et al., "The Lichfield Angel," fig. 11; for the Aberlady insets, see Alice Blackwell, "Bright Eyes: Recreating Medieval Sculpture," https://blog.nms .ac.uk/2012/06/05/bright-eyes-recreating-medieval-sculpture/ (accessed 6 February 2020).

within and threatened by the sinuous zoomorphs that fill the panel at the base of the cross-shaft from Rothbury, which also featured a crowd of the Blessed peering down from Heaven at the top of the cross-shaft, immediately beneath the cross-head that preserves in its arms holes intended to hold floating wicks or candles, indicating that it originally stood within the church rather than in the landscape.[24] The crosses can thus be considered in terms of the escatological *crux gemmata*, "the sign of the Son of man" (*signum filii hominis*), mentioned in the 'Little Apocalypse' of Matthew 24:30 as appearing in the heavens at the time of the Second Coming.[25] But they are also understood to have inhabited a complex matrix of associations surrounding the jewel-encrusted crosses encased in precious metals that were familiar in church processions and on altars,[26] objects that the monumental stone crosses are thought to have referenced in their employment as permanent stone versions of these more portable objects, erected to sacralise the landscape of Anglo-Saxon England.[27]

Understanding the Monumental

Understanding the nature of the motifs and figural schemes carved in relief on these fragmented/fragmentary monuments, however, has raised significant problems: largely due to the expectations of those attempting to interpret the subjects depicted.

---

24   Rothbury 1; Cramp, *Corpus Volume 1*, pp. 217–21; Jane Hawkes, "The Road to Hell: The Art of Damnation in Anglo-Saxon Sculpture," in *Listen, O Isles, unto Me: Studies in Medieval Word and Image in Honour of Jennifer O'Reilly*, ed. Elizabeth Mullins and Diarmuid Scully (Cork, 2011), pp. 230–242 at 236–38.

25   See also "the sign of the living God" (*signum Dei vivi*) of Revelation 7:2. Éamonn Ó Carragáin, "Sources or Analogues? Using Liturgical Evidence to Date *The Dream of the Rood*," in *Cross and Cruciform in the Anglo-Saxon World: Studies to Honor the Memory of Timothy Reuter*, ed. Sarah Larratt Keefer, Karen Louise Jolly, and Catherine E. Karkov (Medieval European Studies 11) (Morgantown, WV, 2010), pp. 135–65; Brandon W. Hawk, "'Id est, crux Christi': Tracing the Old English Motif of the Celestial Rood," *Anglo-Saxon England* 40 (2011), 43–73.

26   Ilse A. Schweitzer Van Donkelaar, "The *Crux Gemmata* and Shifting Significances of the Cross in Insular Art," *Marginalia: The Journal of the Medieval Reading Group at the University of Cambridge* 3 (2006), available at http://merg.soc.srcf.net/journal/06illumi nation/schweitzer.php (accessed 30 April 2020). See also, Barbara C. Raw, "*The Dream of the Rood* and its Connections with Early Christian Art," *Medium Aevum* 39 (1970), 239–56; Elizabeth Coatsworth, "The Pectoral Cross and Portable Altar from the Tomb of St Cuthbert," in *St Cuthbert, his Cult and his Community, ed. Gerald Bonner, David Rollason, and Clare Stancliffe* (Woodbridge, 1989), pp. 287–301; Richard N. Bailey, *England's Earliest Sculptors* (Toronto, 1996), pp. 46, 122–23; Hawkes, *Sandbach Crosses*, p. 143.

27   Bailey, *England's Earliest Sculptors*, pp. 7–8; Hawkes, "'Iuxta Morem Romanorum'," p. 87.

a   b

FIGURE 8.6A-B   Remains of cross-shaft and cross-head, early ninth century, All Saints'
                 churchyard, Bakewell, Derbyshire: (a) east face showing rider, inhabited
                 plant-scroll and bow of archer at base; (b) west face showing incomplete
                 Crucifixion in cross-head and figures below venerating the cross/
                 crucifixion.
                 Photos: Jane Hawkes

In the case of those who consider them to have functioned as 'Preaching Crosses' the carvings are considered to relate a clear chronological biblical narrative. The panel above the crucifixion at Sandbach has thus been interpreted as depicting Christ standing before Pilate sitting on the left. It is easy to miss Christ in the series of profile busts holding out scroll-shaped objects (who are more accurately identified as the three Magi), but hard to confuse Pilate with a female figure with a child on her lap who reaches up to her breast (the Virgin and Child receiving the Magi). The figures flanking the cross of the crucifixion have likewise been confusedly interpreted: as the Virgin and Mary Magdalene – despite the fact that one has a pointed beard, in keeping with the figural style used across the monument which distinguishes between clean-shaven and bearded male figures. The scene below the Crucifixion is also disconcertingly interpreted: as the Annunciation to the Virgin. All three figures in this panel, however, are neatly bearded and the putative angel, who is presumed to be the centrally enthroned figure, has lost his wings, leaving the figures more clearly identifiable as Christ flanked by Moses and Elijah at the Transfiguration. To round it all off, the figures in the lowermost circular frame have been identified as the Visitation depicting (unnervingly) the adult John the Baptist with his mother Elizabeth and the Virgin. Uniquely in Christian art, the Virgin and Elizabeth hold keys and a book, and all three are again bearded; in fact, the three figures should be identified as Christ, flanked by Peter and Paul in one of the earliest versions of the *Traditio Legis cum Clavis*.[28]

This example offers an extreme, but salutary reminder of the need to observe the details of the images and the pitfalls of deciding *a priori* what they must depict, something that also holds true for another group of scholars: those who wish to consider Anglo-Saxon sculpture as dating to the Viking Age. To take just one example: the incomplete cross at Bakewell has recently been interpreted in the light of tenth-century political activities in the region when lands at Hope and Ashford which had previously been in the hands of Danish settlers were purchased by Ealdorman Uhtred and confirmed by Athelstan of

28   Ethel Egerton, *The Saxon Crosses, Sandbach, Cheshire: an Illustrated Description and History* (Sandbach, 1930). This was reprinted by The Rotary Club of Sandbach in December 1986 and the views reiterated to the author in a personal communication from John Minshull, Vice-President and Secretary of the Sandbach Historical Society (24 August 1996). For full discussion, see Jane Hawkes, "Reading Stone," in *Theorizing Anglo-Saxon Stone Sculpture*, ed. Catherine E. Karkov and Fred Orton (Morgantown, WV, 2003), pp. 5–30 at 7–10; Hawkes, *Sandbach Crosses*, pp. 56–62. The contemporary currency of the view of the crosses as performing a 'preaching' function can be seen in the signage of the recent redisplay of the collection of Anglo-Saxon sculpture at Durham Cathedral in the Monks' Dormitory.

Wessex and Edward the Elder, sometime before 911.[29] Ignoring the remains of the bowman at the foot of the east face of the shaft (Fig. 8.6a), the other motifs are explained in keeping with later Icelandic myth: the rider is identified as Odin/Woden on his horse Sleipnir, the plant-scroll with its bunches of berries as Yggdrasil, the world tree, and the quadruped as the squirrel who runs between the eagle at the top of Yggdrasil and the worm or serpent eating its roots. Together, these are argued to present "a visual means of assisting the preaching of the gospel to the pagans."[30]

Apart from the problems of explaining the belief systems of tenth-century Anglo-Scandinavians in the light of thirteenth-century Icelandic texts, close observation of the carvings makes it difficult to substantiate such readings. Sleipnir, for instance, is never depicted in the Scandinavian-period art of Britain and Ireland, and in early medieval Scandinavian art he is always illustrated as having eight legs (rather than four), as on the Tjängvide picture stone from Gotland in Sweden.[31] Then there is the problem of identifying the plant-scroll as Yggdrasil which, in both versions of Snorri Sturlusson's *Edda*, is understood to be an ash tree. It is also unclear that the quadruped at the top of the plant-scroll can be identified specifically as a squirrel, particularly in the absence of an eagle and a *wyrm*/serpent. *Grímnismál* (one of the poems of the poetic *Edda*),[32] identifies a number of beings living within Yggdrasill, but primary among them is Níðhǫggr, the serpent who tears at the roots of the tree, and Ratatoskr, a squirrel who carries messages between Níðhǫggr and an eagle who lives at the top of the tree. Without any evidence that the eagle or serpent/*wyrm* are present in the plant-scroll at Bakewell – a rider being depicted at the top of the plant-scroll and a bowman at its base – the interpretation of the quadruped as the squirrel Ratatoskr is fraught at best. It is, furthermore, currently accepted that most creatures depicted in Anglo-Saxon art are deliberately ambiguous, making the specific identification of a species (or in this case, the quadruped in the plant-scroll at Bakewell as a squirrel)

29   *Charters of Burton Abbey* (British Academy Anglo-Saxon Charters 2), ed. Peter H. Sawyer (Oxford, 1979), pp. 5–7; Barbara Yorke, "Historical Background," in Hawkes and Sidebottom, *Corpus Volume XIII*, p. 40.

30   A. Mora-Ottomano, K. Mapplethorpe, and P. Flintoft, "The High Cross at Bakewell Churchyard, Derbyshire: Archaeological Excavations" (Archaeological Research Services Ltd. Unpublished Report 2012/27), p. 7.

31   Jörn Staecker, "Heroes, Kings and Gods," in *Old Norse Religion in Long-Term Perspectives: Origins, Changes, and Interactions*, ed. Anders Andrén, Kristina Jennbert, and Catharina Raudvere (Lund, 2006), pp. 363–68 at 365, fig. 3. https://en.wikipedia.org/wiki/Tj%C3% A4ngvide_image_stone#/media/File:Tj%C3%A4ngvide.jpg (accessed 1 May 2020).

32   Codex Regis: Reykjavik, Árni Magnússon Institute for Icelandic Studies, GKS 2365 4°, fols 16–21.

impossible, and probably unnecessary – if not redundant.[33] Overall, therefore, it seems unlikely that the plant-scroll depicted on the cross at Bakewell was intended to depict episodes recorded in thirteenth-century Icelandic poetry (or prose), making it difficult to assume that the monument as a whole can be associated with events otherwise recorded as occurring in the region in the tenth century.[34]

In fact, early medieval schemes featuring a bowman shooting up into an inhabited plant-scroll are common in early Christian and Anglo-Saxon art, particularly, but not exclusively, in Psalters. Clearly these do not replicate the carving at Bakewell, but they do present a set of motifs found frequently in Anglo-Saxon sculpture which have been considered in terms of early exegesis on the "sharp arrows of the mighty" (*sagittae potentis acutae*), of Psalm 119:4. These were understood to refer to the words of God shot from the bow of the preacher, the idea deriving from the "burning coals" (*carbonibus desolatoriis*) in the second part of the verse, and from their perceived connection with visions of the apocalypse: these include four horsemen, the first of which is armed with a bow (Revelation 6:2). Like the archer of Psalm 119, this apocalyptic rider was associated with the words of God – specifically, the preaching mission of the Church.

Considered together in the context of a monumental cross, therefore, the archer at the base of the Bakewell shaft and the rider in the cross-head could be regarded as signifying a common set of references concerned with the themes of preaching and the Church, which, in the exegetical tradition, were linked (through the bowman and rider) with the psalms and the Second Coming. These references are also consistent with the plant-scroll. This motif conveys ideas (based on John 15) involving Christ, his Church, and the sacraments, while creatures feeding off its fruit signify those receiving spiritual sustenance.

Furthermore, viewing the monument as a whole, the sacramental references are made clear on the other side of the cross (Fig. 8.6b). Here, the incomplete Crucifixion shows the cross inserted into the Hill of Golgotha, a detail which, by the early ninth century, was intended to highlight the association

---

33   See, for example, Leslie Webster, *Anglo-Saxon Art: a New History* (London, 2012), pp. 34–40; Melissa Herman, "Something More than 'Man': Re-examining the Human Figure in Early Anglo-Saxon Art," in *The Art, Literature and Material Culture of the Medieval World: Transition, Transformation and Taxonomy*, ed. Meg Boulton and Jane Hawkes, with Melissa Herman (Dublin, 2015), pp. 278–92; Leslie Webster, "*Wundorsmiþa geweorc*: A Mercian Sword-pommel from the Beckley Area, Oxfordshire," in *Crossing Boundaries. Interdisciplinary Approaches to the Art, Material Culture, Language and Literature of the Early Medieval World*, ed. Eric Cambridge and Jane Hawkes (Oxford, 2017), pp. 97–111.

34   See Hawkes and Sidebottom, *Corpus Volume XIII*, p. 112.

between the cross and Golgotha: that being the geographical point of Christ's return at the Final Judgement.[35] Other features, such as the loincloth and the spear- and sponge-bearers, were intended to highlight the Christ's humanity and suffering at his sacrifice.

At another level, the spear-bearer also served to refer to the Old Testament prophecy of Zechariah (12:10) about the piercing of the Messiah: "and they shall look upon me, whom they have pierced" (et aspicient ad me quem confixerunt). In early exegesis this was commonly associated with the Christ of Revelation. Augustine, for instance, linked Christ as Judge with the prophecy, claiming he would return at the Second Coming – as foretold at his Ascension (Acts 1:10–11):

> The Son alone will be apparent to the good and the bad in the judgement in the form in which he suffered and rose again and ascended into heaven […]. That is, in the form of man in which he was judged, [he] will be judge in order that also that prophetic utterance may be fulfilled, "They shall look upon him whom they pierced."[36]

The association was also made in discussions of baptism in that the wound from the spear was regarded as a source of life shared by the baptised. Thus, in another homily, Augustine argued that:

> "One of the soldiers with a spear laid open his side and forthwith came thereout blood and water." A suggestive word was made use of by the evangelist in not saying […] pierced […] but "opened" that thereby, in a sense, the gate of life might be thrown open from whence have flowed forth the sacraments of the Church without which there is no entrance to the true life.[37]

---

35   Gertrud Schiller, Iconography of Christian Art, trans. Janet Seligman, 2 vols (London, 1971–72), 1, pp. 95–97.

36   Augustine, Tractate XXXVI.12 in Iohan. 8.16–18: sed quoniam bonis et malis in iudicio solus Filius appareabit, in ea forma in qua passus est, et resurrexit, et adscendit in caelum … id est, in forma hominis in qua iudicatus est iudicabit, ut etiam illud propheticum impleatur: "Videbunt in quem pupugerunt;" Sancti Avrelii Avgvstini in Iohannis Evangelivm tractatvs CXXIV, ed. A. Mayer (Corpus Christianorum Series Latina 36) (Turnhout, 1954), p. 331; trans. Philip Schaff, A Select Library of the Nicene and Post-Nicene Fathers of the Christian Church, 14 vols (1819–93, repr. Grand Rapids, MI, 1978), 7, p. 213. See also Tractate XX1.13 in Mayer, Sancti Aurelii Augustini, pp. 219–20.

37   Augustine, Tractate CXX.2 in Iohann.19.31–35: "Sed unus militum lancea latus eius aperuit, et continuo exiuit sanguis et aqua". Vigilanti uerbo euangelista usus est, ut non diceret: […] percussit […] sed: "aperuit"; ut illic quodammodo uitae ostium panderetur, unde sacramenta

Thus, the scene at Bakewell, although incomplete, yet displays elements pointing to a complex set of references incorporating the human and redemptive aspects of the Crucifixion, the mysteries of the two sacraments, and the General Resurrection at the Last Judgment within the context of ninth-century iconographic developments and exegetical thinking.[38]

Further emphasising this is the pair of figures below, whose pose identifies them as venerating the Crucifixion above. Figures adoring the cross in this way are not common in early medieval art, for when the liturgical ritual of the *adoratio crucis* was illustrated the adoring figures were shown kneeling, as required in the Good Friday liturgy.[39] From the turn of the ninth century, however, figures were depicted standing by the cross with their arms extended towards it in exaggerated gestures indicating their role as witnesses – rather than the more common poses of mourning.[40] It is an attitude that illustrated contemporary interest in venerating the cross as the sign of the redemptive nature of the Crucifixion.[41]

The presence of a pair of figures with their arms upraised, and their heads upturned towards the Crucifixion at Bakewell, therefore, can be understood to reflect the iconographies of the *adoratio crucis* (with the figures standing rather than kneeling in adoration), and/or bearing witness to the salvific nature of the cross and the Crucifixion. Furthermore, the two figures force the viewer to look up, in imitation, at the cross-head, encouraging the viewer to contemplate the form of the cross and its varied significations.

With this in mind, it is worth turning, briefly, to consider the ways in which the viewer might have been further encouraged in their contemplation. As noted, the carvings tended to be brightly coloured and decorated with insets, and so would have had an immediate impact on those encountering them.

---

ecclesiae manauerunt, sine quibus ad uitam quae uera uita est, non intratur. (Mayer, *Sancti Aurelii Augustini*, p. 661; trans. Schaff, *Nicene and Post-Nicene Fathers*, p. 434).

38   Celia Chazelle, *The Crucified God in the Carolingian Era: Theology and the Art of Christ's Passion* (Cambridge, 2001), pp. 85–95.

39   E.g., San Vincenzo al Volturno, Italy, 826–843 (Schiller, *Iconography*, fig. 346); Prayerbook of Charles the Bald, 846–869, Munich, Residenz, Schatzkammer, fols 38v–39r (Schiller, *Iconography*, fig. 354); see also John Mitchell, "The High Cross and Monastic Strategies in Eighth-century Northumbria," in *New Offerings, Ancient Treasures: Studies in Medieval Art for George Henderson*, ed. Paul Binski and William Noel (Cambridge, 2001), pp. 88–114, fig. 7:15; Chazelle, *The Crucified Christ*, pp. 155–58.

40   E.g., Stuttgart Psalter, 820–839, Stuttgart, Württemburgische Landesbibliothek, Bibl. Fol. 23 (Schiller, *Iconography*, fig. 355); engraved crystal, mid-ninth century (Schiller, *Iconography*, fig. 361); Otto von Weissenburg Gospel Harmony, c.868, Vienna, Österreichische Nationalbibliothek (Schiller, *Iconography*, fig. 363).

41   Chazelle, *The Crucified Christ*, p. 124.

They were moreover, arranged in panels.[42] This suggests that they probably functioned like the painted wooden panels we call 'icons,'[43] which would have been encountered by those visiting Rome and entering churches more locally, as at Wearmouth and Jarrow.[44] In fact, Bede, resident at Jarrow, associates painted wooden panels with sculptural panels in his commentary on the Temple,[45] where he asks, rhetorically:

> if it was not contrary to that same law to make the historiated panels why should it be contrary to the law *to sculpture or to paint as panels* the stories of the saints and martyrs of Christ?[46] (italics added).

For Bede painted wood and carved stone were clearly interchangeable. Indeed, he went on to argue that if it was permissible to create elaborate visuals in the Temple, it was also permissible to display images in a church because "their sight is wont to produce a feeling of great *compunction* in the beholder."[47] Here he was writing within the tradition articulated by Gregory the Great a century earlier.[48]

---

42   Mitchell, "The High Cross," p. 95.

43   Jane Hawkes, "Stones of the North: Sculpture in the North in the 'Age of Bede,'" in *Newcastle and Northumberland: Roman and Medieval Art and Architecture*, ed. Jeremy Ashbee and Julian Luxford (British Archaeological Association Conference Transactions 36) (Leeds, 2013), pp. 34–53 at 45–50.

44   Bede, *Historia Ecclesiastica* 1.25; in *Bede's Ecclesiastical History of the English People*, ed. and trans. Bertram Colgrave and R.A.B. Mynors (Oxford, 1969), pp. 75–77; Bede, *Historia Abbatum* 7, in *Abbots of Wearmouth and Jarrow*, ed. and trans. Christopher Grocock and I.N. Wood (Oxford, 2013), pp. 36–39.

45   Paul Meyvaert, "Bede and the Church Paintings at Wearmouth-Jarrow," *Anglo-Saxon England* 8 (1979): 63–77.

46   Bede, *De Templo* 2.824–43: *Si eidem legi contrarium non fuit in eodem mari scalpturas histriatas [...] quomodo legi contrarium putabatur si historias sanctorum ac martyrum Christi sculpamus siue pingamus in tabulis qui per custodiam diuinae legis ad gloriam meruerunt aeternae retributionis attingere*; ed. David Hurst, *Bedae Venerabilis Opera, Pars II. Opera Exigetica. 2A* (Corpus Christianorum Series Latina 119A) (Turnhout, 1969), pp. 212–13; translation based on Seán Connolly, *Bede: On the Temple* (Liverpool, 1995), 91–92.

47   Bede, *De Templo* 2.832–33: *horum aspectus multum saepe compunctionis soleat praestare contuentibus.* Hurst, *Bedae Venerabilis Opera*, p. 212; trans. Connolly, *Bede*, p. 91.

48   Gregory I, *Sereno episcopi Massiliensi: Et si quis imagines facere voluerit, minime prohibe, adorare vero imagines omnimodis devita. Sed hoc sollicite fraternitas tuo ammoneat, ut ex visione rei gestae ardorem compunctionis percipant et in adoratione solius omnipotentis sanctae trinitatis humiliter prosternantur; Gregorii I papae registrum epistolarum*, ed. Paul Ewald and Ludwig M. Hartmann (Monumenta Germaniae Historica: Epistolae 2) (Berlin, 1899), p. 271; trans. John R.C. Martyn, *The Letters of Gregory the Great*, vol. 3 (Toronto, 2004), p. 746: "And if someone should want to paint images, do not prohibit him at all, but

This tells us that panel paintings of any medium were expected to induce compunction – the attitude deemed necessary to achieve understanding of salvation. As part of this process the act of viewing enabled imagined movement between the tangible and the intangible, the human and the Divine. In fact, being in relief the carvings could be understood to *enact* the processes of viewing imagery. For Bede, the relief carvings of the Temple appeared "as if they were coming out of the wall," (*prominentes quasi de pariete*) with the result that the viewer did not learn "the words and works of truth extrinsically from others" (*exeunt quia uerba et opera ueritatis non adhuc ab aliis extrinsecus discunt*), but rather, had them "deeply rooted within themselves, holding them in readiness [so that they] can bring forth from their hearts the things that ought to be done" (*sed ut sibimet infixa radicitus parata semper ab intimis cordis quae sunt agenda siue docenda proferunt*).[49] It is, perhaps, no accident that much of the figural sculpture preserved in such fragmentary form defies the limits of the panels that frame them. As I have demonstrated elsewhere, the halo of the figure of Christ at Ruthwell, for instance, extends over the moulding that outlines and emphasises the confines of the panel, fracturing its shape, crossing boundaries, and extending beyond planar surfaces to bring the divine into the realm of the human viewer.[50] Similar phenomena can be seen on the late eighth-century cross-head from Rothbury, as well as the early ninth-century cross from Easby, North Yorkshire, now in the Victoria and Albert Museum – to name but a few.[51]

At Rothbury, the angel, enclosed in the inner moulding framing the upper cross-arm, grasps the upper rim of the deeply dished cruciform halo of Christ that extrudes over the upper intersection of the frames at the centre of the cross-head so that it extends almost to the outer edge of the stone. The result is such that the cross of the crucifixion itself recedes, while the figure of the Crucified is thrust forward as Christ resurrected, crowned with the halo of

---

in every way avoid worshipping the images. But let your Fraternity give this advice with concern that from the portrait of a past event they may receive a strong feeling of compunction and they should bow down humble, only worshipping the almighty Holy Trinity."

49   Bede, *De Templo* 1.1509–15; Hurst, *Bedae Venerabilis Opera*, pp. 184–85; trans. Connolly, *Bede* 1.14.2, p. 54, following Peter Darby, "Bede, Iconoclasm and the Temple of Solomon," *Early Medieval Europe* 21.4 (2013), 390–421 at p. 419.

50   Jane Hawkes, "East Meets West in Anglo-Saxon Sculpture," in *England, Ireland, and the Insular World: Textual and Material Connections in the Early Middle Ages*, ed. Mary Clayton, Alice Jorgensen, and Juliet Mullins (Tempe, AZ, 2017), fig. 3.2b for the Ruthwell figure of Christ, and pp. 58–60 for further discussion of the phenomenon.

51   See Cramp, *Corpus Volume I*, illus. 1206 (for the Rothbury cross-head, Rothbury 01), and Lang, *Corpus Volume VI*, illus. 194–96, 201–03 (for Easby 01a–d).

divine majesty.[52] In effect, cross and crucifixion recede into the past, while Christ is resurrected in Majesty in a notional future, enacted in the present.[53] In an analogous manner, groups of three and six apostles cluster in panels on one face of the Easby cross-shaft in such a way that each apostle is portrayed as a bust emerging from the frame containing the group, or from 'behind' the halo of the apostle 'in front.' At the base, the haloes of the lowermost row of figures cross over one another and on each side stand proud of the spiral columns supporting the arch containing the panel, while being cut off by the inner roll-moulding running the length of the shaft. Above them two further figures emerge from behind the lower row of haloes, and, although theirs too cross over one another, both are contained by the spiral columns. This has the effect of apparently crowding the apostles into a confined space, while placing two of them coherently behind the other three. Such coherence is broken, however, with the figure surmounting the group who logically could be considered as standing 'behind' the others in perspectival space. Yet this expectation is denied by the fact that his halo, unlike those of the apostles 'before' him, obtrudes over the upper arch enclosing the group, and by the fact that the twisted strands of plant scroll emerge from 'behind' his shoulders and pass behind the arch. Illogically he is thus placed on the same plane as the three figures at the 'front' of the group. Here, the relief carving has been exploited to contradict the expected means of expressing depth and varied planes of existence which were well established in late antique and early Christian carving. Here, the artifice exploited in the relief carving presents figures that exist both in a receding plane and on the same planar level.[54]

Summary

While Anglo-Saxon sculpture has survived only in fragments, it is clear that these will continue to reward close examination. Although, for the most part, lying disregarded in out-of-the-way places within parish churches their very fragmentation, resulting in their reuse as building fabric, preserves valuable

---

52   See Hawkes, "The Rothbury Cross," pp. 77–80.

53   For full discussion, see Jane Hawkes, "Stones of the North: Sculpture in Northumbria in the 'Age of Bede'," in *Newcastle and Northumberland. Roman and Medieval Architecture and Art*, ed. Jeremy Ashbee and Julian Luxford (British Archaeological Association Conference Transactions 36), (Leeds, 2013), pp. 34–53.

54   Lang, *Corpus Volume VI*, illus. 196; see further discussion in Jane Hawkes, "A Sculptural Legacy: Stones of the North from the 'Age of Wilfrid'," in *Wilfrid: Abbot, Bishop and Saint. Papers from the 1300th anniversary conferences*, ed. N.J. Higham (Donington, 2013), pp. 124–35.

insights into their original appearance as brightly coloured monuments bearing insets that would have glittered in sunshine and lamp light, rendering their carvings forever shifting and fluid as the light moved across them, enhancing, in some cases, the visceral nature of their subject-matter. While imagined reconstructions of both the original monumental forms and significances represented by the surviving fragments have produced, and continue to produce, some puzzling results, the response to George Forrest Browne's despairing cry in 1889 of "What mean these stones?" (echoing Joshua 4:6),[55] would nevertheless now elicit a number of responses shedding increasing light on the extraordinary complexity and sophistication of the original sculptures and their interactive role in the various acts of encounter enjoyed in the churches and landscapes of Anglo-Saxon England.

---

55   George F. Browne, *The Anglian Sculptured Stones of Pre-Norman Type: Disney Lectures, Lent Term 1889* (private circulation).

CHAPTER 9

The Thread of Ornament

Catherine E. Karkov

Betty Coatsworth's work on sculpture, textiles, and metalwork has informed a generation of scholarship on the art of early medieval England. I offer this essay in her honour in the hopes that it brings together ideas that work across her three areas of interest and expertise.

∵

In the early Middle Ages ornament was rarely without meaning of some sort. The mounts for gems on metalwork crosses and book covers could be turned into tiny churches or shrines creating miniature representations of the heavenly Jerusalem, as they are on the cover of the ninth-century Carolingian Codex Aureus of St Emmeram (Munich, Bayerische Staatsbibliothek, Clm 14000), or the Lothair Cross made in Ottonian Germany *c*.1000, and now in the treasury of Aachen Cathedral. The religious symbolism of this type of ornament is obvious, in part because it is indisputably representational (and 'representation' is always assumed to have more meaning than 'ornament'), in part because of the well-known and traditional meanings attached to gemstones, and in part because of the sacred or liturgical nature of the types of objects on which such ornament occurs.

Early medieval English art is often far less literal and far more ambiguous than that of either the Carolingians or Ottonians, both in its narrative imagery and in its abstract or ornamental patterns or images. For example, the stepped bezel on the tenth- or eleventh-century gold and garnet ring, possibly a bishop's ring, from the West Yorkshire Hoard is quite architectural in profile (Fig. 9.1), with the granules rising from their settings to form what look like miniature domed buildings. It too may have been intended to represent the kingdom of heaven, inhabited in this case by Christ and/or the Trinity, which may be symbolised by the three nested lozenge shapes. Within, yet simultaneously supporting the lozenges, are crosses formed by the larger of the raised granules. In this context, the red garnet at the centre could also be a Christological symbol,

FIGURE 9.1   Tenth- or eleventh-century gold and garnet ring
from the West Yorkshire Hoard.
© Leeds Museums and Galleries

a reference to the blood of Christ and his sacrifice on the cross. Garnet, or 'car-
buncle' as the English would have known it prior to the Norman Conquest,
was traditionally associated with blood, but it is also one of the fire stones, and
Isidore of Seville describes it as glowing like the embers of a coal, and casting
rays of light out into the eyes of the viewer.[1] The garnet in the West Yorkshire
Hoard ring glows with heavenly fire like the divine light emanating from the
heavenly kingdom, or the ever-watchful eye of Christ; but such an interpretation of this ornament is not obvious. You have to be aware that the diamond (or
lozenge) shape was a symbol of Christ in the art of the early medieval Insular
world,[2] you have to be familiar with the practice in this same art of hiding symbols within patterns that at first glance might appear to be 'mere' ornament,

---

1   Isidore of Seville, *The Etymologies of Isidore of Seville*, ed. and trans. Stephen A. Barney,
    W.J. Lewis, J.A. Beach, and Oliver Berghof (Cambridge, 2006), p. 326. See also Karen Eileen
    Overbey, "Passing Time with the Staffordshire Hoard," *postmedieval: a journal of medieval
    cultural studies* 7 (2016), 378–87.
2   See, for example, the use of the shape within both text and ornament in the Book of Kells
    (Dublin, Trinity College 58), fols 34r, 188r, and 290v.

and of embedding crosses within crosses.[3] This is an art that makes you work for or puzzle out meaning.

The Old English language had several words to describe ornament or ornamented objects, including *fætan, fah/fag*, and *geatwe*. *Fætan*, a verb, meant 'to adorn or ornament.' It is most often used in poetry, and is generally taken to refer to adorning with gold or precious metals as it is most often used to refer to the decoration of metalwork such as the West Yorkshire Hoard ring, or the gold-adorned or plated treasure that Beowulf receives after he defeats Grendel: *fættan golde fela leanode* ("many gifts adorned with gold").[4] In phrases such as *fætte scyldas* or *fædde beagas*[5] it could simply mean ornamented rather than golden or gilded, so "ornamented shields" and "ornamented rings," respectively. *Fætan* could also mean "to load, put, or burden" and is used to describe, for example, a "draught horse."[6] Although 'the burden of ornament' could be a productive notion for thinking through all those heavily ornamented armed and armoured warriors, or even the gold- and gem-covered works of art themselves, I am not going to pursue that idea in the present essay. Suffice it to say that *fæt* was beautiful ornament, but it also did work. Similarly, *fah* or *fag* could have two different meanings. It could mean "parti-coloured" or "variegated" in terms of colour, material, or pattern, and is used to describe things as diverse as the multi-coloured plumage of the phoenix and the serpentine or damascened patterns of a warrior's sword.[7] But *fah/fag* could also mean "hostile" or "enemy."[8] Both senses of the word are captured in the description of the sword Hrunting in *Beowulf*:

---

3   The classic study is Robert B.K. Stevenson, "Aspects of Ambiguity in Crosses and Interlace," *Ulster Journal of Archaeology* 44/45 (1981–82), 1–27.

4   *Beowulf*, line 2102; *Beowulf and Judith*, ed. Elliott van Kirk Dobbie (Anglo-Saxon Poetic Records 4) (New York, 1953), p. 65. All quotations are taken from this edition. All translations are my own unless otherwise stated. For the range of meanings of *fætan* see *Dictionary of Old English*, s.v. *fætan*: https://tapor.library.utoronto.ca/doe/. Hereafter *DOE*.

5   *Beowulf*, lines 333, 1750; Dobbie, *Beowulf and Judith*, pp. 12, 54.

6   *Fæthengest*, Exeter Book *Riddle 22*, line 14; *The Exeter Book*, ed. George Philip Krapp and Elliott van Kirk Dobbie (Anglo-Saxon Poetic Records 3) (New York, 1936), p. 192.

7   *Bleobrygdum fag, The Phoenix*, line 292; Krapp and Dobbie, *The Exeter Book*, p. 102. *Fagum swyrdum, Judith*, line 264; Dobbie, *Beowulf and Judith*, p. 106.

8   *DOE*, s.v. *fag, fāh*: https://tapor.library.utoronto.ca/doe/. It could also mean stained, and specifically stained with blood, which often lends ambiguity to translating *Beowulf* (see *DOE*, *fāh*[2], *fāg*[2], meaning number 2).

wæs þæm hæftmece   Hrunting nama.
Þæt wæs an foran   ealdgestreona;
ecg wæs iren,   atertanum fah,
ahyrded heaþoswate

That hilted sword was named Hrunting. It was one of the foremost of heirlooms; the blade was iron decorated with adder-twigs [or hostile with adder-twigs].[9]

Ornament in this case is deadly, it can also fool or betray. It has the appearance of venomous serpents and thus gives the object on which it appears the bite of a venomous serpent – and swords, of course, could fail in battle, as did Hrunting, they could betray. *Geatwe*, again a word which occurs most commonly in poetry, could mean "decoration," "ornament," "adornment," "precious objects," "trappings," or "military garments" – warriors clothed in ornament then, at least in the case of the *Beowulf* poem, in which Beowulf and his men enter Heorot *in hyra gryregeatwum*, their horror- or terror-ornaments.[10] They are beautiful and they are deadly, echoing the *fah/fag* duality, or duplicity, of meaning. As a Simon Mittman and Patricia MacCormack have recently explored the implications of horror- or terror-ornaments for our understanding of the Staffordshire Hoard, the gold and garnet work that adorns most of the armour and weapons in the hoard covering the warriors with gleaming blood and fire, and casting their awesome flames into the eyes of their opponents. These ornaments, they argue, turned the men who wore them into "fabulated" warriors, part man, part animal, part god-like being, part metal killing-machine.[11] Thinking of ornament in this way suggests that what might appear at first to be simply precious decoration actually has the power to transform in more than one sense of the word. It can transform a mundane object into treasure, it can transform a pendant into a protective breastplate, and it can also transform one type of being into quite another.

Ornament has the power to transform things as well as people, and I want to think more about the power of ornament both to transform stone sculpture and to transform and direct our experience of that sculpture. Women and men in early medieval England did not write about sculpture. They might mention

---

9   *Beowulf*, lines 1457–60a; Dobbie, *Beowulf and Judith*, p. 45.
10   *Beowulf*, line 324; Dobbie, *Beowulf and Judith*, p. 12.
11   Asa Simon Mittman and Patricia MacCormack, "Rebuilding the Fabulated Bodies of the Hoard-warriors," *postmedieval: a journal of medieval cultural studies* 7 (2016), 356–68.

its existence, but they certainly did not describe it with the attention to detail that they devoted to metalwork or books or even architecture, even though in some cases sculpture was meant to look like metalwork, and in some cases it had all the word and image complexity of an illuminated manuscript – the Ruthwell Cross, for example – and in some cases it was meant to house a body, or at least appear to do so.[12] On the other hand, they do seem to have had a sense that, as a material, stone was a living thing. Isidore of Seville had written that stone had the ability to capture and imitate the sound of the human voice. This type of stone he called *icon*, although his source, Pliny, called it *echo*.[13] And in the poem *The Ruin* we do get a sense of stone as an enduring witness to the rise and fall of kingdoms:

> *Oft þæs wag gebad*
> *ræghar ond readfah   rice æfter oþrum,*
> *ofstonden under stormum;   steap geap gedreas.*

Often this wall endured covered with moss and red-stained [or ornamented] (*readfah*), endured one kingdom after another, withstood the storm, the steep arch has now fallen.[14]

The building described in *The Ruin* has a life: it endures, it witnesses, it dies. In fact its death is paralleled with that of its former inhabitants. Just as death takes away all of the brave men (*swylt eall fornom secgrofa wera*),[15] so the building's high roof shed its tiles and fell to the earth (*tigelum sceadeð | hrostbeages hrof. Hryre wong gecrong ...*).[16]

The Ruin is preserved in the c.1000 Exeter Book of poetry, so it is later than the eighth-century Bewcastle Cross, nevertheless it speaks of an environment very like that of Bewcastle. *The Ruin* is about a city, a city often thought to be Bath – or at least an old Roman city like Bath – but the sort of life cycles that it envisions are now more readily visible, perhaps, in places like Bewcastle

---

12   Howard Williams, "Hogbacks: The Materiality of Solid Spaces," in *Early Medieval Stone Monuments: Materiality, Biography, Landscape*, ed. Howard Williams, Joanne Kirton, and Meggen Gondek (Woodbridge, 2015), pp. 241–68.

13   Barney, et al., *Etymologies*, p. 319.

14   *The Ruin*, lines 9b–11; Krapp and Dobbie, *The Exeter Book*, p. 227.

15   *The Ruin*, line 26; Krapp and Dobbie, *The Exeter Book*, p. 228.

16   *The Ruin*, lines 30b–31; Krapp and Dobbie, *The Exeter Book*, p. 228.

(Fig. 9.2), now in Cumbria but once part of the kingdom of Northumbria.[17] At Bewcastle, time, earth, stone, and the endless cycles of life and death were in the early medieval period, and remain today, crucial material elements of the site and its monuments, its progression of ruins, which include a dying cross that is in some ways similar to, though much less verbal than, the Ruthwell Cross. The eighth-century presence at Bewcastle was built in and from the ruins of the Roman frontier fort of Fanum Cocidii, which was itself built on what seems to have been a prehistoric cult site. There are the ruins of Bronze Age tombs nearby, and it is possible that Kirk Beck, the small stream that flows just to the west and south of the site, was used for votive deposits. The Roman fort was begun in the early AD 120s, its name, Fanum Cocidii, bearing witness to the continued life of the British deity Cocidius, who remained popular all along the line of Hadrian's Wall. The fort eventually covered an area of about six acres and underwent four primary structural phases between the second and the mid-fourth centuries. Stones from its ruined structures can still be seen sticking out of the fort's ramparts, down which they have slid over the centuries. Some were reused in later buildings, including the Norman Castle and its fourteenth-century rebuilding, the late-thirteenth century church that once stood where the present church stands now, and many of the houses and other buildings still in use in the area. The Bewcastle Cross was erected in the eighth century in what had been British territory but had recently been claimed by the expanding kingdom of Northumbria. It stood on the terrace in front of the old Roman bath house, the ruins of which are believed to have been still partially standing at the time it was erected: high arches shedding their trappings similar to the decaying structures of *The Ruin*.

The intricate knot-work, interlace, and geometric patterns that appear on the narrow sides of the Bewcastle Cross (Figs. 9.3 and 9.4) are often compared to those used to decorate gold and bejewelled book covers and processional or altar crosses. The comparison is certainly valid, and similar designs do occur in sculpture and metalwork – and manuscript illumination as well – but we should be cautious in simply equating ornament in one medium with that in another. No surviving piece of metalwork carries the same patterns or combination of patterns that appear at Bewcastle. It is important to be aware of the shared language of forms and styles across media and across cultures, but it is equally important that we approach each work of art as a unique creation,

---

17   A complete set of images of the cross is available at: http://www.ascorpus.ac.uk/catvol2 .php?pageNum_urls=30 (accessed 6 March 2020). The cross is catalogued as Bewcastle 1, and the west side face 1A and the east as face 1C.

FIGURE 9.2   Bewcastle Church and Cross.
                Photo: Catherine E. Karkov

being aware that ornament might have carried meanings and functions specific to individual works and the circumstances in which they were produced
and/or displayed, and being aware also that materials and materiality matter.

One crucial difference between Bewcastle (or any of the monumental free-
standing sculpted stone crosses) and its metalwork counterparts is that it is
not manipulable. It is impossible physically to spin the cross around, to turn
it over in one's hands, or to see all four of its sides lined up neatly together
at the same time without the aid of technology. This is part of both its material stoniness and its sculptural nature. As a material, stone demands things
of the viewer. It makes you work for meaning physically as well as mentally. It
demands above all that *you* move around *it*, and at Bewcastle, ornament acts as
a kind of guide up, down, and around the monument. It does not really matter
where you start, the ornament serves as a kind of thread that you follow as you
move from side to side. In this movement, alternation and rhythm are both
vitally important – the alternation between sides or panels decorated entirely
with representational ornament (human figures, animals, growing plants) and
those decorated with combinations of foliate and geometric or knot-work
patterns, and the measured alternations of the asymmetrical up-and-down
rhythm of the differently sized panels. These alternations and differences
influence the rhythm and speed of the movement of the viewer around the

FIGURE 9.3
The Bewcastle Cross, north side.
Photo: Catherine E. Karkov

FIGURE 9.4
The Bewcastle Cross, south side.
Photo: Catherine E. Karkov

cross, although they are likely to influence each individual viewer differently. Most analyses start with the west and east faces, the so-called primary faces, but I am going to start with the narrow sides, the "ornamental" sides, which have received much less attention.

At Bewcastle the ornament on the narrow sides, the north and south sides, includes different types of knot-work and a chequerboard pattern. A similar, though far from identical arrangement of knot-work and abstract patterns covers the narrow sides of the Rupertus (or Bischofshofen) Cross, made in the second half of the eighth century and preserved in the Cathedral Treasury in Salzburg.[18] At Bewcastle these panels are combined with panels of foliate ornament, the basic elements of which can also be found on metalwork, including the Rupertus Cross, although I am not going to pursue that comparison any further in this paper, largely because Bewcastle is ultimately made of stone, not metalwork, and material matters both to design and function as well as to overall meaning, but also because, as I stated above, it is important to consider the ways in which ornament works specifically on individual monuments and in specific locations.

The arrangement of the panels at Bewcastle is different on each side, and very different from that on the sides of the Rupertus Cross. The panels create a different rhythm to the way we experience each side of Bewcastle, as well as directing the viewer's eyes to focus on the two narrow sides and their individual panels differently. Ornament here works as a thread, guiding our experience of the cross, as well as carrying meaning in its own right. On the north side (Fig. 9.3) panels of foliate ornament frame or contain the panels of knot-work and the chequerboard pattern, their fruits and flowers hanging downwards. The overall effect is one of containment that focuses the viewer's attention inwards and downwards. No matter where the original eighth-century church stood in relation to the cross, and no matter what its size and height, this side of the cross would never have been lit by the sun to the extent that the other sides would have been, and this relative shade would have heightened the impression of calm and inward focus of this side.[19] Everything about it is quiet and contained. The chequerboard pattern at the centre is the largest of the panels as well as the panel most different from all the other ornament on the cross. It becomes the centre of attention, with its quiet and regular repetition

---

18   See Elizabeth Coatsworth and Michael Pinder, *The Art of the Anglo-Saxon Goldsmith: Fine Metalwork in Anglo-Saxon England: its Practice and Practitioners* (Woodbridge, 2002), pp. 161, 259; Leslie Webster and Janet Backhouse, eds, *The Making of England: Anglo-Saxon Art and Culture AD 600–900* (London, 1991), pp. 170–72.

19   To a certain degree it still does, although the fire damage to this side of the cross, as well as the agricultural landscape around the site detract from its peacefulness.

of pattern. But it is mesmerising; it draws you in, and once immersed in the pattern there is no up or down, right or left. It is the simplest field of ornament on the monument, yet also perhaps the most complex once you really start looking at it. Its seemingly unending field of crosses and the larger pattern of crosses within crosses which that field constructs make it a particularly fitting focus for the viewer's attention on this side. The panels of knot-work on the south side of the Bewcastle Cross are perhaps best known for their use of crosses within crosses, but the fact that one has to search for them within its panels creates an entirely different visual rhythm and viewing experience. If the cross was originally painted, as most agree that it was, the panel on the north side may well have been painted in a combination of alternating red and yellow squares similar to those which cover the body of the evangelist Matthew in the seventh-century Book of Durrow,[20] or those that we see worked in the sixth- or seventh-century Sutton Hoo shoulder clasps with their stamped gold foils showing from beneath the red of the garnets.[21] If this was the case, the intricacy of the pattern would have been even more apparent – as of course would the monument's reference to the great gold and jewelled crosses. There is also a spatial element to the panel, with crosses formed by the squares carved into the stone, and crosses formed by the squares that are left standing in reserve, that furthers our attention inward on the panel and into the materiality of the cross. It presents an ever-shifting field, or troop of crosses embedded in and emerging from the stone – sometimes in neat horizontal rows, sometimes appearing one behind the other, depending on where the viewer looks and how long they look at it.[22] The panel is both *fag* and *fah*, both shifting and variegated in its ornament, and a dangerous weapon, a troop of defensive crosses standing guard around the dead.

On the south side (Fig. 9.4) of the cross, panels of foliate ornament are framed within alternating panels of knot-work. In contrast to the north side, the fruits and flowers that grow from the stems of the scrolling plants all rise upward towards the sun as if responding to its light. The sundial, the gnomon of which once projected from the centre of the uppermost panel of foliate ornament, is a clear sign of just how important the sun and its movement across the sky were to the conception and design of this side of the cross. The movement of the carved plants helps to draw our attention to its importance

---

20   Dublin, Trinity College, 57, fol. 21v.

21   See: https://research.britishmuseum.org/research/collection_online/collection_object
      _details/collection_image_gallery.aspx?partid=1&assetid=722929001&objectid=86906
      (accessed 6 March 2020).

22   If the squares carved into the surface were originally inlaid with glass, the alternation of
      translucency and flat colour, and of texture, would have achieved a similar effect.

within the larger programme of the cross. The sundial is also a sign that time was as important as light, since the purpose of the dial – whether it was actually functional or not – was to indicate time. In this context, the movement of the viewer around the cross echoes the celestial movement through time and space mapped by the sundial, bringing heaven and earth together.[23] Each of the knot-work panels once again contains embedded cross patterns that it has taken modern eyes some time to puzzle out, but which would have been much more evident to the eyes of the monument's original audience. If painted, colour could have helped these hidden crosses to stand out more clearly. At the centre of this side is a panel of knot-work, the threads and interstices of which form multiple cross shapes, directing the viewer inwards towards a meditation on the meaning of the cross itself; but this panel is small, and the primary sense of motion on the south side is upwards towards the sun rather than inwards towards the central panel. If, as has been suggested, glass or metalwork fittings were used to fill in elements of the hidden crosses, the shining jewel-like quality, and upward and outward movement of the ornament on this side could have been remarkable – the whole side glittering in the sun, in contrast to the relative shade, and focus down and in towards the centre of the cross on the north side of the monument. It is important to remember that light at Bewcastle would have had an aesthetic value and appeal as well as a symbolic value and a liturgical function, as did light playing across the shimmering surfaces of the gilded crosses. It may also have had other meanings, and I will turn to a consideration of those at the end of this essay. Suffice it to say here, that, as Éamonn Ó Carragáin has shown in great detail, light and shadow are vital parts of the liturgical symbolism of the Bewcastle Cross,[24] but the play of light and shadow across its surfaces would also have increased the appeal of its ornament, perhaps even have been understood as part of its ornament, as it would have been an integral part of the sort of variegated or colourful surfaces that Old English texts so often described as *fah*, or of the gleaming troop of warriors in *Beowulf*.

The asymmetrical balance (or what might also be called the play of symmetry and asymmetry) created by the two narrow sides of the Bewcastle Cross is complemented by the balance of its two broad faces. On the west face are standing figures contained within discrete niched panels. In the lowest panel

23   On the sundial see Fred Orton and Ian Wood with Clare A. Lees, *Fragments of History: Rethinking the Ruthwell and Bewcastle Monuments* (Manchester, 2007), pp. 131–43.

24   Éamonn Ó Carragáin, 'A Liturgical Interpretation of the Bewcastle Cross,' in *Medieval Literature and Antiquities: Studies in Honour of Basil Cottle*, ed. Myra Stokes and Tom Burton (Cambridge, 1987), pp. 15–42.

is a layman holding a bird of prey, above that is a commemorative inscription, above that is Christ recognised by beasts in the desert, and at the top is John the Baptist holding the lamb of God. There is little, if any sense of motion, and all three figures face out at us demanding that the viewer pause and approach them as one would the painted icons on which they are partially modelled. The stillness of the figures focuses the viewer's attention inward to contemplating the meaning of the individual panels, the relationship of the carved figure to the viewer, and the way in which the three figures fit together. The east face is carved with a continuous inhabited vine-scroll, the motion of which is upwards towards the sun, and this is highlighted by the little animal at the bottom of the vine who leaps from the stone base of the cross into its curling branches. The lively animals who cling to the vine and bite at its fruit balance the still figural ornament on the west face. Symbolically, the scroll turns this side of the monument into a tree of life rising naturalistically from the stone and soil of this place, and complementing the architectural structure of the niched panels in which the figures on the west face stand. As we move around the cross, then, it is constantly changing. It shifts from a space inhabited by humans, an architectural space of stone, the stone of which this place was built, but also the stone on which the Church was built, to a living, growing tree rising up out of the earth.[25] On this monument stone also remembers, much as it did in *The Ruin*. Standing on the terrace in front of the ruined bath house, it is a remnant and reminder of the Roman past, the ruined fort in which Bewcastle was built, and the passing of time from civilisation to civilisation. The sundial secured within the ornament of the south side makes that abundantly clear, as do the names of the men and women recorded in the cross's inscriptions whose bodies have decayed along with the site's monuments.[26]

---

25   Its shifting nature is similar to, though less obvious than, that of the Ruthwell Cross, on which see Benjamin C. Tilghman, "On the Enigmatic Nature of Things in Anglo-Saxon Art," *Different Visions: a Journal of New Perspectives on Medieval Art* 4 (2014), 1–43 at pp. 25–36: http://differentvisions.org/articles-pdf/four/tilghman-enigma-anglo-saxon-art.pdf (accessed 6 March 2020). As Tilghman notes, the cross becomes two different things at once as do objects and concepts in early English poetry; see Sarah Larratt Keefer, "'Either/ And' as 'Style' in Anglo-Christian Poetry," in *Anglo-Saxon Styles*, ed. Catherine E. Karkov and George Brown (Albany, NY, 2003), pp. 179–200.

26   There is the nobleman, Alcfrith, or a name something like that, who is commemorated in the main inscription preserved on the west face of the cross (discussed further below), and the woman Kynibur*g, whose name is carved in the border just above the lowest panel of ornament on the north face. There are traces of the names of other men and women in the borders between other of the panels but they are now too worn to be legible.

It is the two narrow sides that weave these shifting visions of the cross together. Their foliate ornament echoes the vine-scroll of the east face, but without its lively creatures, while the names inscribed in the borders between the panels recall the figural panels and inscriptions of the west face, though in a different form – and inscribed into rather than emerging from form. The knot-work panels focus our attention inward on the, again, multiple forms of the cross, but they also add yet another layer of meaning. It is these panels that turn the monument into a stone version of a *crux gemmata* like the Rupertus Cross – there is nothing on either of the two broad faces to suggest that form of the cross. And it is these panels that, in their alternation and different patterns, convey the notion that the cross is an ever-present yet eternally shifting thing, something that cannot be reduced to or confined within a single human form of representation. Their alternation with the vine-scroll panels reveals the cross as both a static object of meditation and a living tree, while the different shapes of the cross within the knot-work and chequerboard panels reveal that even when static the cross emerges in multiple forms. The knot-work panels suggest the cross as simultaneously within and tied to this place, made of this stone, into which they draw our attention, and as the eternal *crux gemmata*, a sign of both Jerusalem and the foundation of the Church, and of the heavenly Jerusalem. The passage between the earthly and the heavenly cities, like the passage of life and the growing cycle of a tree, is marked by the sundial on the south face.

Material is also important, and this is where Bewcastle's ornament is very different from that of the metalwork crosses. This ornament is carved out of stone; it both emerges from it and directs our attention into it, as opposed to being ornament attached to a surface, a covering over of wood. In this respect, Bewcastle (as well as many other of the free-standing stone crosses that covered the landscape of early medieval England) is also very different from the high crosses of early medieval Ireland, on which the panels of figural ornament are also carved out of the stone but are planned and designed as if they were metalwork plaques attached to a wooden core, complete with borders carved to resemble twisted wire around their figural panels, and carved hinges and clasps that hold them to the moulded borders.[27] Bewcastle and other of the English crosses are also different from the early medieval Scottish and Pictish crosses and cross-slabs which are decorated with carved bosses resembling

---

27   Carved clasps or hinges survive on the mouldings of the tenth-century Muiredach's Cross
      at Monasterboice (Louth) and the cross at Durrow (Offaly), which may be the product of
      the same sculptor. For Muiredach's Cross, see Peter Harbison, *The High Crosses of Ireland*,
      3 vols (Bonn, 1992), 2, *Photographic Survey*, figs. 472–87; and for Durrow, ibid., figs. 247–62.

those that covered the surfaces of Insular metalwork, concealing the rivets, nails, and joints that held their different components together.[28]

Ornament is also something that un-knots the Bewcastle Cross from the contemporary Ruthwell Cross (Dumfries and Galloway), with which it has so often been linked.[29] There is no knot-work, or interlace, or any form of non-representational ornament of any kind on the Ruthwell Cross. If we identify it at all with a great heavenly jewelled cross, it is only by reading it backwards through the much later poem *The Dream of the Rood* preserved in the *c.*1000 Vercelli Book,[30] and/or the eleventh-century Brussels reliquary cross now in the Treasury of the Cathedral of St Michael and St Gudula in Brussels.[31] The visionary cross that the dreamer sees is described in the poem as a wooden cross simultaneously covered in gold and gems (*mid since gegyrwed*) and soaked with blood (*hwilum hit wæs mid wætan bestemed, / beswyled mid swates gang*),[32] and the latter is a wooden altar cross that was originally covered with gold and jewels. The runic poem on the Ruthwell Cross says nothing about treasure, only blood. It is also the runic poem, and really only the runic poem, that makes us aware that the cross is meant to be equated with the True Cross, the fragments of which were believed to be contained in reliquaries like the Brussels Cross, and that translates the long-ago events of the crucifixion and the far-away place of Jerusalem into the present and onto Northumbrian soil (at least in the eighth century it was Northumbrian soil). The poem reads:

On the north side:

> [+*ond*]*geredæ hinæ god almeittig·*
> *þa he walde on galgu gistiga*
> *modig f*[*ore*] [*allæ*] *men*
> [*b*]*ug ...*
> [*ahof*] *ic riicnæ kyninc·*
> *heafunæs hlafard*

---

28   See George and Isabel Henderson, *The Art of the Picts: Sculpture and Metalwork in Early Medieval Scotland* (London, 2011).

29   See e.g. Orton *et al.*, *Fragments of History*; Éamonn Ó Carragáin, *Ritual and the Rood: Liturgical Images and the Old English Poems of the* Dream of the Rood *Tradition* (London, 2005).

30   Italy, Vercelli, Biblioteca Capitolare, CXVII.

31   On both the poem and the reliquary cross, see Ó Carragáin, *Ritual and the Rood*.

32   *The Dream of the Rood*, line 23b, lines 22b–23a, respectively; *The Vercelli Book*, ed. George Philip Krapp (Anglo-Saxon Poetic Records 2) (New York, 1932), p. 61.

> *hælda ic ni dorstæ*
> *[b]ismærædu uŋket men ba æt[g]ad[re*
> *i]c [wæs] miþ blodi bist[e]mi[d]*
> *bi[got][en of]* ...

and on the south:

> *[+k]ris[t] wæs on rodi*
> *hwepræ per fusæ fearran kwomu*
> *æppilæ til anum ic pæt al bi[h][eald]*
> *s[aræ] ic w[æ]s· mi[þ] so[r]gu[m] gi[d]ræ[fi]d*
> *h[n]a[g]* ...
> *miþ s[t]re[l]um giwundad*
> *alegdun hiæ [h]inæ limwærignæ· gistoddu[n*
> *h]im [æt] [his] [li][c]æs [hea]f[du]m*
> *[bih]ea[ld]u[n h]i[æ þ]e[r]* ...[33]

[and] Almighty God stripped himself when he wished to mount the gallows, brave in the sight of all men. [I dared not] bow. I [raised aloft] a powerful king. The Lord of heaven I dared not tilt. Men insulted the pair of us together. I was drenched with blood [begotten from that man's side]. Christ was on the cross. But eager ones came hither from afar. Noble ones came together. I beheld all that. I was terribly afflicted with sorrows. I bowed [to the hands of men], wounded with arrows. They laid him down, limb-weary; they stood at the shoulders of the corpse. They looked upon the Lord [of heaven].

Both the first-person voice of that poem and the inhabited vine-scroll of the cross's narrow sides reveal the cross as a living thing, and is both the stone that we see and the wood that is speaking in the voice of the True Cross. The Bewcastle vine-scroll suggests that it too is a living thing and that it too could be seen simultaneously as wood (via the vine-scroll) and as stone, but it is a different sort of living thing, one without voice.

The lengthy runic commemorative inscription on the west face of the Bewcastle Cross also makes it clear that it had a very different function and meaning from Ruthwell. It is, most obviously, a memorial monument and Ruthwell is not, but the Ruthwell Cross is also not the shining victory beacon

---

33   Square brackets indicate letters that have been supplied or restored based on the text of *The Dream of the Rood*. Ó Carragáin, *Ritual and the Rood*, pp. xxii–xxiii.

that we encounter at Bewcastle. I want to conclude by suggesting some ways in which the ornament of the cross relates to ideas of a shining beacon and of victory as stated in the inscription, helping to materialise these aspects of the cross before the eyes of the viewer. The inscription takes up a whole panel, so its importance was clearly considered to be on a par with that of the figural panels on the same side. It has been reconstructed as:

[+] *þis sigb[e]c[n] *[.]setton hwætre[d . .]þgær a[.]w[.]wo[.] *[æ]ft[.[lcfri *m[.]n[g]u[.]ŋcb[...]u/ŋ[.] gebid[.] [..]so[.]o ...³⁴*

This victory beacon Hwætred ... thgar and ... set up in memory (after) .lcfri ... (and perhaps others) pray for his soul (or for their souls).

It tells us that the cross is a *sige-beacen,* a "victory beacon," a sign that someone has engaged in battle and triumphed, or perhaps may still be engaged in battle but will triumph. Within the context of the figural panels above and beneath it, the inscription suggests the simultaneous and eternal victory of Christ and the Cross over death, the spiritual victory of those who recognise and believe in Christ, and the hoped for victory over death of the man commemorated by the cross in this world. It may also be understood as a sign of the victory of the Northumbrians as they expanded their kingdom north and west into the former British kingdom of Rheged, the territory in which the cross stood at the time it was erected. With its ornamental panels carved and painted with motifs that would have been familiar from metalwork, the Bewcastle Cross helps to convey the idea both of victory and of a beacon shining out over the land. The panels would also have linked it to battle gear, the shining, gem-encrusted terror ornaments of the Staffordshire Hoard. The filigree scrollwork of the pectoral cross from the hoard can be read as a simplified and abstracted version of the scrolling plants in the panels on Bewcastle's south side, while the leafy terminals of its famous folded great cross conjure the same sort of imagery.³⁵ And, of course, the pressed gold leaf panels beneath the cloisonné garnets

---

34 The square brackets indicate characters that are no longer legible. The text of the inscription is available at: http://www.ascorpus.ac.uk/catvol2.php?pageNum_urls=30 (accessed 6 March 2020).

35 Although the two crosses are religious objects they are also part of an assemblage otherwise consisting entirely of weapons and armour, and should therefore also be considered as weapons or armour, even if only spiritual weapons or armour themselves. For an excellent discussion of the hoard, see Chris Fern, Tania Dickinson, and Leslie Webster (eds.), *The Staffordshire Hoard: An Anglo-Saxon Treasure* (London, 2019). See also: https://www.staffordshirehoard.org.uk (accessed 6 March 2020).

that decorate so many of the sword fittings carry patterns similar to that of the chequerboard panel on Bewcastle's south side.

Like the warriors who wore the Staffordshire Hoard gear, the Bewcastle Cross becomes a fabulated thing, an ordinary piece of stone decked out in ornamented garments that transform it into a supernaturally powerful, beaming weapon in multiple battles, and thus a warrior in its own right. It had a double nature, it could exclude and defeat those who refused to believe in Christ, and it could be a beacon to those who might wish to convert, to be included and saved by its powers. But the Bewcastle Cross is made of stone, the stone of a particular place and, as the poem *The Ruin* and Isidore of Seville's comments about stone make clear, stone remembers and echoes in a way that metalwork simply does not. The cross sits on what was once a terrace in front of what was once the bath house of a Roman fort dedicated to the British god Cocidius, a god of war and hunting. It sits at the end of the Maiden Way that ran north from one of Hadrian's Wall's most important forts, Banna, or Birdoswald. The remains of the Roman fort at Bewcastle were still partially standing when the cross was erected. There is, then, a history of war, battle, and death to this place that stretches back well beyond the coming of the Northumbrians in the eighth century. Historically, the Christian Church sprang from the remains of imperial Rome, the Northumbrian Church spreading from those roots to establish itself on British land, land which also in this case carried the remains of imperial Rome. The cross's materials and materiality can then, in addition to their other meanings, be understood as visual statements of the decay of one empire and the rise of a new Christian empire – just as the building in *The Ruin* bears witness to the rise and fall of one kingdom after another. The Cross is also a statement about the defeat of the Britons who inhabited the area before it became Northumbrian territory, and whom Bede so frequently portrayed as barbaric and polytheistic peoples whether that was actually the case or not. It speaks of the origins of both Church and empire in the Roman world, and the presence, even dominance, the fighting presence of both in the here and now of the Bewcastle landscape.

The Bewcastle Cross can never be pinned down to a single monolithic meaning – liturgical, memorial, or political. It has layers and knots of meaning that cross and interlace and shine out in multiple ways across and from its surfaces, as well as backwards and forwards across time. Perhaps, in the end, this is the primary reason that knot-work and ornament make up such a high proportion of its carved decoration. It was meant to be puzzled over, meditated on, its multiple and shifting meanings rising to the surface one after the other. Ornament is the thread that we pick up and follow around the four sides of the cross, weaving them together to reveal its full meaning and power.

CHAPTER 10

A Newly Identified Anglo-Saxon Sculpture in Great Chalfield Church, Wiltshire

David A. Hinton

One of Betty Coatsworth's interests has been Anglo-Saxon sculpture, and in the south of England her work on the great roods in churches in Hampshire and Wiltshire has been of particular importance. I hope that the paper offered here, although about a carving of less obvious interest than those, will be a sufficient reflection of that aspect of the honorand's career.

∴

A carving set into the sill of the north window in the nave of the small church of All Saints, Great Chalfield, Wiltshire (Number 1 on the location map, Fig. 10.1; present position in the church, Fig. 10.2), was described by Pevsner as "a Norman stone re-used with a column and some leaf in the spandrel."[1] It was characteristic of Pevsner to have observed something widely overlooked, and to have recognized architectural form in what at first glance looks beyond interpretation. Nevertheless, his dating was questioned during the Summer Meeting of the Royal Archaeological Institute in 2016, and an earlier, Anglo-Saxon date was proposed.

The carving is not a single slab, but is in two unequal parts (Fig. 10.3): the larger is now in three pieces, but with no gaps between the joins; it is 0.67 m long overall and between 0.165 and 0.18 m deep; on it is the column noted by Pevsner, with the beginnings of an arch springing from it, and a leaf or frond above, as he also observed. The smaller piece, 0.295 m long, also has a frond, now placed so as to touch the other, and slightly more of an arch, but without any part of a column surviving. The stones do not have their original edges, both having been cut back to give flat surfaces, so they may have been reused as walling before being set in the sill; a small chamfered stone in the left end may be of the same date, or be a filler. Great Chalfield is in an area with high-quality

---

1 N. Pevsner, *The Buildings of England. Wiltshire* (Harmondsworth, 1963), p. 229.

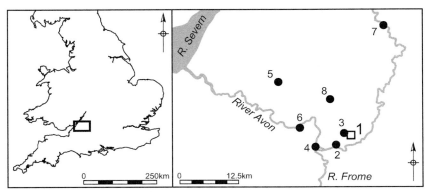

FIGURE 10.1   Location map: 1, Great Chalfield; 2, Bradford-on-Avon; 3, Little Chalfield; 4,
                Limpley Stoke; 5, Abson; 6, Bath; 7, Malmesbury; 8, Colerne.

limestone – indeed, it gives its name to one of the strata – and the carving seems to be from the same bed as a large carved stone now built into the altar in the Anglo-Saxon chapel at Bradford-on-Avon, Wiltshire, about three miles away (Fig. 10.1); that slab has been described as "Bradford Stone, Ancliffe Oolite, Member of Forest Marble formation, Great Oolite Group, Middle Jurassic" and is attributable to the eighth century.[2]

On the larger of the two Great Chalfield fragments, the column's base has two shallow steps. Its shaft has a long central carved panel between two plain framing bands; all are very worn and damaged, so that the pattern in the central panel is extremely difficult to interpret. It seems to consist of geometric lines, sharply angled, but it looks different under different lights and photographic scans (Figs. 10.4 and 10.5). It may consist of a series of discrete knots with fillers to look like interlace, but may be continuous strands; the Bradford slab has a border of that sort. The column has a rectangular capital, within which is a carved panel, again too worn for certain identification but seemingly different from the panel in the column, perhaps having flowers or buds. The arch springs from the capital and has outer borders and the beginning of a framed pattern. The leaf carving in the spandrel noted by Pevsner has three elements, curled and with hollowed-out centres. The mirror image of a similar leaf is on the smaller stone, also with a portion of an arch, a little better preserved and with a pattern that may be the same as in the column panel; no part of a capital has survived. Neither stone has visible traces of plaster or paint.

2   Rosemary Cramp, *Corpus of Anglo-Saxon Stone Sculpture Volume VII. South-West England*
    (Oxford, 2006), p. 205 and illus. 407–09.

FIGURE 10.2   The east end of the north wall of the nave, Great Chalfield.
               Photo: Penny Copeland

FIGURE 10.3   Sculptural fragments set in the window sill.
                       Photo: Penny Copeland

FIGURE 10.4   Sculptural fragments set in the window sill, horizontal view.
                       Photo: Penny Copeland

It is likely that the two stones were originally from the opposite sides of a single arch (reconstructed in Fig. 10.6). The leaves are not exactly the same size, and the diameters of the remaining fragments of the arch seem to be slightly different, but this may not indicate that they came from two different arches, rather that the sculptor made slight adjustments while working; subsequent wear may also have affected the lines. The carving could notionally have been the surround of a small window or other opening, but nothing like that is known in any medieval English setting. The probability is that the arch was part of a single panel, framing a figure: Christ, Mary, an evangelist, King David or an angel are all possible. Such a composition is unusual in sculpture, but one of the figural wall-panels at Breedon, Leicestershire, is analogous; it has a half-length figure set in an archway with rounded columns and is taken to be Mary because of the headdress, although the blessing hand and the book that is being held in the other would be more appropriate to an apostle.[3] Another Breedon figure in an archway is a full-length archangel,[4] and one panel at Breedon has a pattern apparently not dissimilar to, though less tightly compressed, than that at Great Chalfield. The recently discovered free-standing shrine panel at Lichfield, Staffordshire, has a figure, but does not feature an arch (Fig. 8.5).[5] Also recently recognized as Anglo-Saxon are figures in arcades from Upton Bishop, Herefordshire.[6] The half-length female figure on a grave-marker at Whitchurch, Hampshire, is set in the outline of an arch.[7] Single figures in archways do not seem to feature in sculpture after the ninth century, with the possible exceptions of the cross-shaft at Yetminster, Dorset,[8] and the surviving pieces at Congresbury, Somerset.[9]

Details of the Great Chalfield carving include the fronds in the spandrels of the arch; their form is not closely paralleled in Anglo-Saxon sculpture, but their position can be compared on the font in Wells Cathedral, Somerset, for

3 Illustrated in Leslie Webster and Janet Backhouse (eds), *The Making of England: Anglo-Saxon Art and Culture A.D. 600–900* (London, 1991), p. 240, fig. 22, with other figures in archways shown in figs. 23–24, and (p. 241) 26, and no. 210 (p. 245), all attributed to the ninth century.
4 Leslie Webster, *Anglo-Saxon Art* (London, 2012), p. 131.
5 Warwick Rodwell, Jane Hawkes, Emily Howe, and Rosemary Cramp, "The Lichfield Angel: a Spectacular Anglo-Saxon Painted Sculpture," *Antiquaries Journal* 88 (2008), 48–108.
6 John Hunt, "A Figure Sculpture at Upton Bishop, Herefordshire," *Antiquaries Journal* 89 (2009), 179–204.
7 Dominic Tweddle, *Corpus of Anglo-Saxon Stone Sculpture Volume IV. South-East England* (Oxford, 1995), illus. 483.
8 Cramp, *Corpus Volume VII*, p. 127 and illus. 149–51.
9 Catherine M. Oates and Michael Costen, "The Congresbury Carving – an Eleventh-century Saint's Shrine," *Antiquaries Journal* 83 (2003), 281–309; Cramp, *Corpus Volume VII*, pp. 149–51.

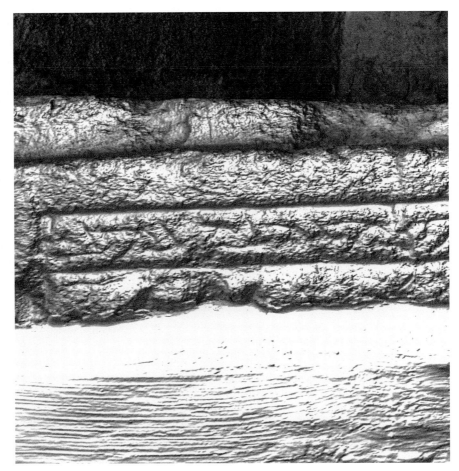

FIGURE 10.5   Reflectance Transformation Imagery detail of the panel on the larger stone, by
                Penny Copeland.

instance.[10] The pattern in the column panel is too worn for proper comparison
with other sculpture, but two fragments at Berkeley, Gloucestershire,[11] and one
from Glastonbury, Somerset,[12] have different versions of fret- or knot-work. The

---

10   Cramp, *Corpus Volume VII*, p. 177 and illus. 328–36.
11   Richard Bryant, *Corpus of Anglo-Saxon Stone Sculpture Volume X. The Western Midlands*
      (Oxford, 2012), pp. 129 and 132, illus. 10–12 and 21–24.
12   Cramp, *Corpus Volume VII*, pp. 157–58 and illus. 251.

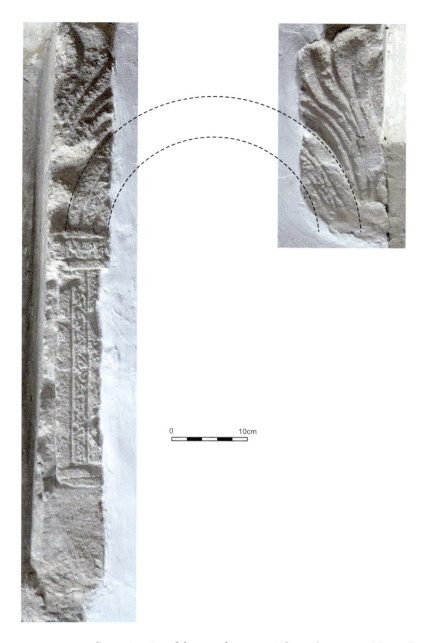

FIGURE 10.6   Reconstruction of the carved stones to indicate the suggested form of
the original composition.
Created by Penny Copeland

Bradford slab has a border of running interlace knots.[13] All those are attributed eighth-/ninth-century dates, except for the Wells font, which is tenth-/eleventh-century.

Partly because the south of England (except for Kent) has many fewer mid-Anglo-Saxon sculptures than Mercia or Northumbria, manuscript illustrations may be more useful for comparative purposes, in particular the painting of King David in the Vespasian Psalter because of the patterns within its columns, and in its bottom border.[14] Columns and arches were also used for canon tables, such as those in the Lindisfarne Gospels, which has steps at the bottom of the columns like those on the Great Chalfield sculpture, and is also attributed to the early eighth century;[15] steps at the bottom of pilaster strips continued to feature not only in manuscripts such as the ninth-century Royal Bible,[16] but also on buildings such as the early eleventh-century chapel at Bradford-on-Avon, Wiltshire.[17] Figures within archways were also painted in later centuries, the early eleventh-century Eadui Psalter and Codex both having flat tripartite columns that are reminiscent of the Great Chalfield arrangement, though neither has similar patterns in the panels.[18]

Placing the two leaves in an art-historical context is not straightforward. Plants in the spandrels of an arch are present in the surviving evangelist portrait in the St Augustine Gospels, brought to England from Italy at an early date, and used as an exemplar for many years;[19] in that case, they actually grow out of the beam of the arch. In the Vespasian Psalter, the plants are detached. The other manuscripts cited above do not have them at all. The shape of the leaves, ribbed and curved but not with curling or serrated ends, also bears some similarity to the Vespasian Psalter plants, specifically to those growing on the insides of the downward-turned lower shoots. There is some similarity also to leaves in the early tenth-century Junius Psalter,[20] but not to the acanthine forms that dominated in manuscripts from then onwards. Anglo-Saxon sculptures do not provide any close parallels, although a stone attributed to

---

13   Cramp, *Corpus Volume VII*, illus. 407.

14   London, British Library, Cotton Vespasian A. i; Michelle P. Brown, *Manuscripts from the Anglo-Saxon Age* (London, 2007), p. 70, attributed therein to Kent, 720s–30s.

15   London, British Library, Cotton Nero D. iv; Brown, *Manuscripts*, p. 4.

16   London, British Library, Royal 1. E. vi; Brown, *Manuscripts*, p. 74.

17   H.M. Taylor, "J.T. Irvine's work at Bradford-on-Avon," *Archaeological Journal* 129 (1972), 89–118, pls. IX–XIII.

18   London, British Library, Arundel 155 and *Hanover*, Kestner Museum, WMXXIa 36, respectively; Brown, *Manuscripts*, pp. 154–55.

19   Cambridge, Corpus Christi College, 286; Brown, *Manuscripts*, p. 22.

20   Oxford, Bodleian Library, Junius 27 (S.C. 5139): Elżbieta Temple, *Anglo-Saxon Manuscripts, 900–1066* (London, 1976), cat. no. 7 and illus. 1.

the tenth century from Shaftesbury Abbey, Dorset, has something of the same sort,[21] as do the belfry openings at Langford, Oxfordshire, attributed to the mid-eleventh century.[22] A tenth-century date is advanced for the leaf fragment at the Old Minster, Winchester,[23] although the suggested similarity to the *Benedictional of St Æthelwold* does not seem to allow for the straightness of the leaf ends.[24] There are earlier examples in metalwork, such as on panels 14 and 18 on the probably mid- to late ninth-century Abingdon sword,[25] or on the ninth-/tenth-century Seine sword-pommel.[26] Norman and later medieval work do not seem to offer closer parallels, so a date in the eighth or ninth century seems the most likely for the Great Chalfield pieces.

A panel of high quality may seem out of place in a small church that is not thought to have Anglo-Saxon fabric; quoins in the north-west corner of the nave might possibly be earlier than the rest of the building, but they are not obviously different. The manor may in the mid-Anglo-Saxon period have been within the parochial territory of a minster at Bradford-on-Avon (Fig. 10.1); the medieval Hundred of Bradford usually included both Great and Little Chalfield, and a correlation between hundreds and *parochiae* was the norm in Wiltshire.[27] The Chalfields were not included within the large estate given to Shaftesbury Abbey in 1001, but the boundaries given in the charter ran "along Alnothe's boundary to Aethelwine's boundary at Chaldefelde, then ... to the boundary of Aelfwine," terminology that implies that those bounds formed the eastern edge of the Bradford estate.[28] In Domesday Book, two Chalfield manors were recorded, each having had a different Anglo-Saxon owner and each paying geld for two and a half hides.[29] The entry for the second manor may be unique – "As much is recorded as is contained in the above," presumably

---

21   Cramp, *Corpus Volume VII*, pp. 110–11 and illus. 97.

22   Tweddle, *Corpus Volume IV*, p. 215 and illus. 298–303.

23   Martin Biddle and Birthe Kjølbye-Biddle, "The Excavated Sculptures from Winchester," pp. 96–107 and 273–327 in Tweddle, *Corpus Volume IV*, p. 305, illus. 606 (also in the online catalogue, Winchester (Old Minster), no. 67).

24   London, British Library, Additional 49598.

25   David A. Hinton, *Catalogue of the Anglo-Saxon Ornamental Metalwork, 700–1100, in the Department of Antiquities, Ashmolean Museum* (Oxford, 1974), no. 1.

26   David M. Wilson, *Catalogue of Antiquities of the Later Saxon Period, I. Anglo-Saxon Ornamental Metalwork 700–1100* (London, 1964), no. 65.

27   J. Pitt, "Malmesbury Abbey and Late Saxon Parochial Development in Wiltshire," *Wiltshire Archaeological and Natural History Magazine* 96 (2003), 77–88 at p. 77.

28   J.H.P. Pafford, "Bradford-on-Avon, the Saxon Boundaries of Ethelred's Charter of 1001 A.D.," *Wiltshire Archaeological and Natural History Magazine* 54 (1951), 210–18 at p. 214.

29   *Domesday Book: Wiltshire*, ed. Caroline and Frank Thorn (Chichester, 1979), p. 25, nos. 8 and 9.

because an equal division of a five-hide unit had only recently occurred (the first manor had half a mill, so the other half presumably belonged to the other manor). The owner of a five-hide estate was regarded as 'thegn-worthy,' and was therefore expected to have a residence that included a *belhus*, implying a chapel.[30] The proximity of the church to the manor-house today at Great Chalfield is certainly a commonly observed Anglo-Saxon feature, though the present arrangement places it within the overall manorial enclosure, which is less usual; that could have happened as a result of the diversion of a stream to create a moat in the thirteenth century, when it seems that the Percy family walled their property.[31]

The first ecclesiastical reference to Great Chalfield was in 1316, and then as a chapel, but it was called a church when next mentioned in 1349; Little Chalfield was also a chapel, in 1308, and a church in 1362 (Fig. 10.1).[32] References to them as 'chapels' may have reflected their sizes rather than their parochial responsibilities, as both had small medieval parish territories, not amalgamated until long after the Reformation. In the fifteenth century, they were recorded as having values below the taxation threshold, which would explain their absence from the 1291 Taxation list, rather than that they were two of the anonymous chapels that contributed to Bradford's income at that time.[33] The font now in Great Chalfield church seems likely to be thirteenth-century and indicative of parochial responsibility, there being no record of its having been brought from elsewhere.

No mention of the carving has been found prior to a sentence in a leaflet about the parish church written in 1924 by the owner and restorer of the adjacent manor-house, Robert Fuller, who also contributed substantially to restoration of the church. This describes the north window "and under it an interesting piece of stone carving of Runic design thought probably to have come from the earlier chancel." Fuller's phrase "Runic design" may imply that he thought the carving pre-Norman, and perhaps had been told so by a visiting authority. 'Runic' seems only ever to have been applied to letters and inscriptions, so someone may have thought that the pattern within the column was actually a series of letters; alternatively, Fuller misheard his visitor to say that the sculpture was 'rude,' a word often applied in the nineteenth century to

---

30   John Blair, *The Church in Anglo-Saxon Society* (Oxford, 2005), pp. 385–96.

31   Anthony Emery, *Greater Medieval Houses of England and Wales 1300–1500. Volume 3, Southern England* (Cambridge, 2006), p. 569.

32   R.B. Pugh and Elizabeth Crittall (eds), *Victoria History of the Counties of England: Wiltshire, Vol. 7* (Oxford, 1953), pp. 62–64.

33   *Taxatio Ecclesiastica Angliae et Walliae auctoritate P. Nicholai IV, circa A.D. 1291*, ed. T. Astle (Record Commission Publications 49) (London, 1802), p. 180b.

pre-Norman sculpture.[34] By 1964 he had reconsidered and thought them early Norman, perhaps influenced by Pevsner.[35]

The medieval church had a nave and chancel, with a chantry chapel added in the late fifteenth century by Thomas Tropenell, who is also credited with rebuilding the chancel. The Parish Register records work on the fabric in 1719 which included a buttress on the north side,[36] which seems an addition alongside a pre-existing one. If the 1719 buttress involved renovating the north window, and if the carved fragments were found at that time, they may have been set in the sill then. The internal window jambs look as if they have been restored more recently, but this work could have been done without disturbing the sill. The chancel was repaired again in 1722, 1747, and 1765, but those works seem to have involved the roof and the floor, so would probably not have revealed a sculptural fragment, although some rebuilding done in 1775 might have done so. If the sculpture was set in the window in 1719 rather than by Tropenel in the fifteenth century, it was not considered worth mentioning either in the Register or by the Rev. John Lewis, incumbent 1718–61, whose voluminous papers include a daily diary that disappointingly reveals no interest in antiquities.[37]

The carvings were not included among the records and detailed drawings done in the early 1830s by Larkins Walker, although he showed the north window and the buttress added in 1719, which he labelled 'Modern.'[38] That could suggest that they were brought to the church later in the nineteenth century, although clearly there was no local memory of that by the 1920s. It may seem unlikely that they would have been reset with some care in 1719 only to be hidden from view within the next hundred years, but the church was white-limed and painted in 1765, when a canopy was placed over the pulpit,[39] next to the window (Fig. 10.2), so perhaps the carvings were obscured then, although they now show no obvious trace of having been painted over and subsequently cleaned. They could have been covered by panelling, or Larkins Walker may have thought them too 'rude' to be worthy of record; he also did

---

34   This sometimes led to such phrases as "it is a puzzling question whether they [the Sandbach crosses] are of early rudeness or late rudeness," G.F. Browne, "Brief Precis of the Description of the Sculptured Stones of Cheshire," *Archaeological Journal* 44 (1887), 146–56 at p. 155.

35   R.F. Fuller and C. Floyd, *Great Chalfield Manor, Wiltshire* (London, 1964), p. 14.

36   Steven Hobbs (ed.), *Gleanings from Wiltshire Parish Registers* (Wiltshire Record Society 63) (Chippenham, 2010), pp. 132–35.

37   Oxford, Bodleian, Eng. misc. e23.

38   Thomas Larkins Walker, *The History and Antiquities of the Manor House and Church at Great Chalfield, Wiltshire* (London, 1837), Pl. 2.

39   Hobbs, *Gleanings*, p. 114.

not mention or draw a curious stone that projects prokrossos-like from the centre of the external north wall of the nave. It is very weathered, but may have been a beast's head, as two drilled eyes seem to survive, and possibly traces of a jaw. It is unlikely to be a reset gargoyle, as it is narrow and is curved at the back. J.C. Buckler, in 1820s pictures of the manor complex that include the church's north side, did not show the projecting head, but such work would not necessarily be accurate in details; it is shown quite clearly in a print taken from a painting by John Le Keux, ironically used as the frontispiece to Larkins Walker's book.

But even though there may well have been a tenth-/eleventh-century manor-house in Great Chalfield on the same site as the present one, would there have been one in the eighth-/ninth-century middle period, and would it have had a sculpture of the quality that seems indicated by the carving? One of the very few instances of Anglo-Saxon workmanship including a sculptural element in an ecclesiastical building that is of comparable status is Limpley Stoke, three miles west of Bradford-on-Avon and part of its medieval parish (Fig. 10.1); there, the very worn animal-headed door-stops have been attributed most recently to the mid-tenth to mid-eleventh century,[40] but the comparison to the larger examples at Deerhurst, Gloucestershire, would allow the ninth century as a possibility. A little further away is Abson, also Gloucestershire, where there is a cross-shaft fragment attributed to the ninth century (Fig. 10.1); the church there had the status only of a chapel-at-ease in the Middle Ages.[41]

There are examples of sculpture on limestone from the mid-Anglo-Saxon Bath area fifty miles and more away at Winchester[42] and Romsey,[43] both in Hampshire, as well as at the more local sites mentioned above.[44] Clearly there were limestone quarries active, if only intermittently, during the seventh to ninth centuries, as well as later, even though only a few broken fragments of interlace survive from the period at Bath,[45] and nothing of such early date from the other major minster in the area, Malmesbury. The role of the Great Chalfield fragment as a teaching aid during Christian worship, the other theme of this Festschrift, cannot be addressed without knowing its exact composition

40   Cramp, *Corpus Volume VII*, pp. 220–21.

41   Bryant, *Corpus Volume X*, p. 125.

42   Biddle and Kjølbye-Biddle, "The Excavated Sculptures from Winchester," pp. 291–314; several of the Winchester pieces are thought earlier than no. 606, cited above.

43   Ian R. Scott, *Romsey Abbey. Report on the Excavations 1973–1991* (Hampshire Field Club and Archaeological Society Monograph 8) (Winchester, 1996), p. 111, no. 21.

44   C. Roger Bristow and Bernard C. Worssam, "Regional Geology," pp. 13–24 in Cramp, *Corpus Volume VII* for general discussion.

45   Cramp, *Corpus Volume VII*, pp. 139–42.

and location, but it may serve to show that there was a sculptural tradition in the area pre-dating the well-known series of sculptures typified by the inter-laced and other beasts on the Colerne cross-shaft and others.[46]

Acknowledgements

I am very grateful to Richard Bryant, who visited Great Chalfield to see the sculpture and who provided me with a number of useful ideas and references; his reconstruction of the putative arch helped to give confidence to the one in Fig. 10.6. Mr Robert Floyd of Great Chalfield arranged access and kindly supplied the reference to the sculpture in his grand-father's 1924 pamphlet. Isobel Geddes and Gilbert Green, members of the Wiltshire Geology Group, generously gave their time to visit both Great Chalfield and Bradford-on-Avon to compare the stones. The illustrations are by my University of Southampton colleague Penny Copeland, and her discussions have also been of great benefit.

46   Cramp, *Corpus Volume VII*, pp. 42–48.

CHAPTER 11

The Company They Keep: Scholarly Discussion, 2005–2020 of the Original Settings for the Poems in the *Dream of the Rood* Tradition

Éamonn Ó Carragáin

Fig. 11.1 Betty Coatsworth has produced a rich body of scholarship, across a wide variety of specialised fields. My most vivid memory of Betty in action is when she and Gale closely examined a glorious thirteenth-century *Opus Anglicanum* cope at the Lateran Cloister museum in September 2009. We all looked on, fascinated, as we also had that same morning, when we heard Betty explain the mosaic images of beautiful seventh-century vestments in the Chapel of San Venanzio, also part of the Lateran complex. The secret of Betty's achievement as an interdisciplinary scholar is her generosity and her talent for friendship. She is a shining exemplar of how to work with others, and how to inspire others by good humour, energy, intelligence, and deep commitment to the project in hand.

∵

Three Old English poems in the *Dream of the Rood* tradition survive. They are best appreciated as independent poems.[1] The longest, which gives the tradition its name, is preserved in an anthology of English vernacular religious prose and verse, in the Capitular Library of Vercelli Cathedral, where the relics of St Eusebius of Vercelli (the patron saint of canons regular) are enshrined. The other two poems are each integrated into the design of a major work of art: the eleventh-century reliquary cross at Brussels Cathedral; and the great high cross at Ruthwell, which may possibly also have been understood as a reliquary

---

1   Peter Orton provided an interesting hypothesis on the origins of the tradition in his *Writing in a Speaking World: the Pragmatics of Literacy in Anglo-Saxon Inscriptions and Old English Poetry* (Tempe, AZ, 2014), pp. 132–37: that it began when the Ruthwell poem was independently composed for inscription on the Ruthwell Cross; and that the Ruthwell song was then elaborated in various oral versions, one of which survives, reworked, in the Vercelli *Dream*.

© KONINKLIJKE BRILL NV, LEIDEN, 2021 | DOI:10.1163/9789004467514_013

FIGURE 11.1   Elizabeth (Betty) Coatsworth pictured in the Theodotus Chapel, Sancta Maria
                 Antiqua, Forum Romanum, September 2009.
                 Photo: Eric Kentley, by kind permission

cross.[2] In all three cases, the immediate context or setting helps us to appreciate the structure, themes, and early reception history of that poem. In the last
fifteen years, the earliest poem, at Ruthwell, has been fiercely debated. Major
new scholarship on the contexts of the Vercelli and Brussels poems will be
noted first, but most of this survey will concentrate on the setting and reception of the Ruthwell poem.

---

2   The hole at the centre of the Annunciation panel at Ruthwell may have been inserted to
    hold a relic of the Cross, perhaps in the ninth century when the panel was also adorned
    by placing a Crucifixion panel just below it, on the base of the cross; Éamonn Ó Carragáin,
    "Liturgical Innovations Associated with Pope Sergius and the Iconography of the Ruthwell
    and Bewcastle Crosses," in *Bede and Anglo-Saxon England*, ed. Robert T. Farrell (British
    Archaeological Reports 46) (Oxford, 1978), pp. 131–47, at 131–34.

I published a book on the settings of the poems in 2005.[3] From 2007, in retirement, I published on the subject only when invited. Each publication was adapted to the themes of the occasion and, in the case of a festschrift, to the interests of the scholar being honoured. These occasional publications were unified by four concerns: first, filling gaps in the 2005 book; second, correcting its errors; third, restating its central ideas briefly and clearly, in terms adapted to the interests of scholars with different specialisations, and students with general interests;[4] fourth, the reporting of relevant new discoveries and approaches in ecclesiastical history, liturgy, Christology, and epigraphy. *Ritual and the Rood* was written to challenge what in 2005 seemed about to become a new orthodoxy: that the Ruthwell poem had nothing to do with the iconography of the monument, and that the Ruthwell monument was not a cross. To oppose this emerging consensus, the book necessarily included much specialized information about the intense interest that some clerics from Britain and Ireland had in Rome, how they made their own epitomes of its diverse traditions, and adapted those traditions (and prestigious customs they found on their way there and back, for example in Gaul) to their own needs.[5]

Late Anglo-Saxon Contexts: The Vercelli Book and the Brussels Cross

Ritual and the Rood had a major lacuna. While providing accounts of the epigraphic settings, at Ruthwell and Brussels, discussion of how the *Dream of the Rood* fitted in with the concerns of the Vercelli compiler was postponed

---

3   Éamonn Ó Carragáin, *Ritual and the Rood: Liturgical Images and the Old English Poems of the* Dream of the Rood *Tradition* (London, 2005).

4   See, for example, Éamonn Ó Carragáin, "Christian Inculturation in Eighth-Century Northumbria: the Bewcastle and Ruthwell Crosses," *Yale Institute of Sacred Music, Colloquium Magazine* 4 (2007), on line at https://web.archive.org/web/20100406002248/http://www .yale.edu/ism/colloq_journal/vol4/carragain1.html (accessed 28 September 2020).

5   On the importance of "*imitatio Romae*" in the period, see the set of three essays on "The Translation of the 'Roman' Liturgy North of the Alps": Éamonn Ó Carragáin, "The Periphery Rethinks the Centre: Inculturation, 'Roman' Liturgy and the Ruthwell Cross," pp. 63–83; Jesse D. Billett, "The Liturgy of the 'Roman' Office in England from the Conversion to the Conquest," pp. 84–110; and Yitzhak Hen, "The Romanization of the Frankish Liturgy: Ideal, Reality, and the Rhetoric of Reform," pp. 111–23, in *Rome Across Time and Space, c. 500–1400: Cultural Transmission and the Exchange of Ideas*, ed. Claudia Bolgia, Rosamond McKitterick, and John Osborne (Cambridge, 2011); and the "Introduction" to *Roma Felix – Formation and Reflections of Medieval Rome*, ed. Carol Neuman de Vegvar and Éamonn Ó Carragáin (Aldershot, 2007), pp. 1–10.

for reasons of length.[6] A symposium in Rome on the 'Soul and Body' theme (April 2004), enabled me to show how 'Soul and Body' material, which recurs throughout the Vercelli Book (including the first two of the three verse lections which directly precede the *Dream*) has an important structural role to play in that compilation.[7] The 2012 Toller Lecture at the University of Manchester again addressed the question of the immediate context of the *Dream*.[8] Meanwhile, understanding of the Vercelli Book had been transformed by Samantha Zacher's *Preaching the Converted*, and the complementary volume of essays, showing that the poetry of the Vercelli Book should be read as a seamless unity with the prose items and helping to abolish the tendency to think of religious poetry and homiletic prose as inhabiting separate worlds; a similar approach was later taken by Francis Leneghan.[9] In 2005–2020 a consensus emerged that the Vercelli collection was compiled at a centre where the Benedictine Reform had not yet taken hold, accounting for the personal, though coherent, ways the texts are arranged, so that one text can complement, or even correct, another: personal collections point towards canons, rather than monks.[10]

---

6   In April 2008, the generous online review of the book by M. Jane Toswell (*The Medieval Review*, TMR 08.04.19), rightly pointed out the contrast in the book between the great attention devoted to Ruthwell and the single "episodic" chapter on *The Dream of the Rood*.

7   Éamonn Ó Carragáin, "'Soul and Body' Texts and the Structure of the Vercelli Book," in *Studi su Anima e Corpo: Lessico, Idee, Figurazioni Letterarie e Iconografiche nell'Antichità e nell'alto Medioevo* (*Romanobarbarica* 20) ed. Anna Maria Luiselli Fadda and Paolo Vaciago (Rome, 2011), pp. 109–27. See now the magisterial chapter by Samantha Zacher, appropriately titled "The 'Body and Soul' of the Vercelli Book: The Heart of the Corpus," in her *Preaching the Converted: the Style and Rhetoric of the Vercelli Book Homilies* (Toronto, 2009), pp. 140–78.

8   Éamonn Ó Carragáin, "The Vercelli Book as a Context for *The Dream of the Rood*," in *Transformation in Anglo-Saxon Culture: Toller Lectures on Art, Archaeology and Text*, ed. Charles Insley and Gale R. Owen-Crocker (Oxford, 2017), pp. 105–28.

9   Zacher, *Preaching the Converted*; see also *New Readings in the Vercelli Book*, ed. Samantha Zacher and Andy Orchard (Toronto, 2009); and Francis Leneghan, "Teaching the Teachers: the Vercelli Book and the Mixed Life," *English Studies* 94 (2013), 627–58.

10   For a strong contrary argument that the Vercelli Book belonged to a prelate of the Benedictine Reform, from a major monastic centre such as Canterbury, see Elaine Treharne, "The Form and Function of the Vercelli Book," in *Text, Image, Interpretation: Studies in Anglo-Saxon Literature and its Insular Context in Honour of Éamonn Ó Carragáin*, ed. Alastair Minnis and Jane Roberts (Turnhout, 2007), pp. 253–66; Francis Leneghan provides good evidence for a reader (and collector) who is also a preacher: "Teaching the Teachers," p. 632; for an argument that the Vercelli collector was a canon, not a monk, see my Toller lecture, "The Vercelli Book as a Context," pp. 123–25. One of the most interesting pieces of scribal editing in the Vercelli Book is the way in which the Guthlac excerpt (Homily XXIII) was included to counterbalance the over-strict regime of fasting central to *Elene* (see my Toller Lecture, pp. 115–17), and the way in which St Bartholomew brings Guthlac straight to heaven (a theme that homily shares with the *Dream*). Our

Griffin Murray's beautifully produced study of the twelfth-century Irish reliquary Cross of Cong is important for study of the Brussels Cross and its distych.[11] Murray demonstrates that the inscriptions on the two reliquaries are laid out in a strikingly similar manner. Both reliquaries can be read "by lowering the front of [either] down toward the viewer so that it is horizontal." Both inscriptions contain verse, followed by details of patronage and requests for prayers. Murray concludes, convincingly, that "[t]he layout of the inscription on the Brussels Cross is so similar to that on the Cross of Cong that it seems probable, considering that they are both True Cross reliquaries, that either the former directly influenced the latter, or that both are based upon an earlier reliquary cross that is now lost."[12]

Variation and Envelope Patterns: Rethinking the Upper Stone at Ruthwell

Analysis of the upper stone at Ruthwell in *Ritual and the Rood* contained a serious mistake. In Chapter Two of the book, I had analysed the Visitation panel on the first broad side of the upper stone, but had left to Chapter Three the cross-head, including the archer represented just above the Visitation.[13] But study of the Mass chants for the Nativity of John the Baptist (24 June) made it clear that on the first broad side, the image of the Archer was intended to help onlookers interpret the Visitation panel immediately below: the first side of the upper stone needed to be studied as a unity.[14] I published the corrected analysis in 2009.[15] The Archer wears, around his neck, a highly unusual quiver: a book satchel, in which the upper part of a book can be seen clearly (Fig. 11.2):

---

understanding of the Guthlac cult, and of St Bartholomew's place within it, has now been transformed by *Guthlac: Crowland's Saint*, ed. Jane Roberts and Alan Thacker (Donington, 2020).

11   Griffin Murray, *The Cross of Cong: a Masterpiece of Medieval Irish Art* (Dublin, 2014), especially pp. 151–52.

12   Murray, *The Cross of Cong*, p. 152.

13   Ó Carragáin, *Ritual and the Rood*, pp. 99–106 (Visitation) and pp. 141–43 (Archer).

14   Thesis supervision in 2004 led me to study, with my student, the liturgical texts for the cult of St John the Baptist: Elizabeth Raggi-Killorin, "Angelus Domini: the Representation of John the Baptist in Anglo-Saxon England" (Minor MA Thesis, University College Cork, October 2004). The Archer panel is discussed at pp. 22–23.

15   Éamonn Ó Carragáin, "Chosen Arrows, First Hidden then Revealed: the Visitation-Archer Sequence as a Key to the Unity of the Ruthwell Cross," in *Early Medieval Studies in Memory of Patrick Wormald*, ed. Stephen Baxter, Catherine Karkov, Janet L. Nelson, and David Pelteret (Studies in Early Medieval Britain) (Farnham, 2009), pp. 185–204.

FIGURE 11.2   Ruthwell Cross, first side of upper stone The Archer
with the Book in his book satchel.
Photo: Catherine E. Karkov, by kind permission

this Archer takes his ammunition from scripture.[16] The Introit or opening chant
of the day-Mass on 24 June recalled the way in which, at the Visitation, John
the Baptist, leaping in his mother's womb, performed his first act of prophecy
by acclaiming the divine presence of Christ within Mary's womb:

> *Ant. De ventre matris meae vocavit me Dominus nomini meo & posuit os
> meum ut gladium acutum sub tegumentum manus suae protexit me posuit
> me quasi sagittam electam. Psalm. XCmo 1. [Bonum est confiteri Domino].
> AD REPET. Justus ut palma [Psalm 91:13].*[17]

---

16   On the archer as preacher, and the imagery of the upper stone at Ruthwell, the fundamen-
      tal article is Barbara Raw, "The Archer, the Eagle and the Lamb," *Journal of the Warburg
      and Courtauld Institutes* 30 (1967), 391–94. Earlier scholarly discussion of the Archer
      image is surveyed in Éamonn Ó Carragáin, "Sacralised Secular Images on the Ruthwell
      Cross: the Archer Panel and Christ 'miþ strelum giwundad,'" in "Percepta Reprendere
      Dona": *Studi di filologia per Anna Maria Luiselli Fadda*, ed. Corrado Bologna, Mira Mocan,
      and Paolo Vaciago (Florence, 2010), pp. 241–55.
17   René-Jean Hesbert, *Antiphonale Missarum Sextuplex* (Brussels, 1935), pp. 134–35, No. 119,
      as quoted in Ó Carragáin, "Chosen Arrows," p. 191.

From my mother's womb the Lord has called me by my name: he has made my mouth like a sharp sword; he has protected me under the covering of his hand, and placed me like a chosen arrow. [Psalm 91:1] It is good to give praise to the Lord. [For the repetition:] The just shall flourish like the palm tree [Psalm 91:13][18]

The anonymous liturgist who first assigned this Introit chant to the birthday of John the Baptist had been daringly original, for early Christian writers had insisted that the Trinity produced only one "chosen arrow": Christ.[19] Jerome had summed up the unanimous tradition:

When he says "chosen arrow," he shows God to have many arrows which are not chosen: these arrows are the prophets and apostles, who hasten over the earth [...]. Christ, however, is the single chosen arrow, [chosen] from many arrows; and the only-begotten son, chosen from many sons. [God] hid him in his quiver, that is, in a human body, so that in him the fullness of divinity should live bodily.[20]

In the Introit chant for his birthday, John the Baptist was given Christ's unique title. The Old Testament reading intoned at the same Mass for 24 June was Isaiah 49:1–7, which included the verses from which the Introit's libretto had been taken. In one of the rare annotations the monks at Wearmouth made to the Codex Amiatinus, they indicated that Isaiah 49 was the lection they intoned "on the Feast of John the Baptist." They then, in 716, sent off their great manuscript to Rome. Their gift to the Pope made it clear that Wearmouth, though Northumbria had been converted recently, was fully aware of universal Christian traditions:[21]

Listen, you islands, and give ear, you people from far off
[*Audite insulae et adtendite popule de longe*]
The Lord has called me from the womb:

---

18   Ó Carragáin, "Chosen Arrows," p. 191.
19   See Jerome, *Commentariorum in Esaiam Libri XIII–XVIII*, ed. M. Andrieu (Corpus Christianorum Series Latina (hereafter CCSL) 76A (Turnhout, 1963)), pp. 534–35.
20   Jerome, *In Esaiam*, p. 534, as quoted in Ó Carragáin, "Chosen Arrows," p. 194.
21   Annotation to the opening of Isaiah 49 in the Codex Amiatinus, fol. 526r: "in s[an]c[t]i ioh[annis] bap[tistae]." Discussion in Richard Marsden, *The Text of the Old Testament in Anglo-Saxon England* (Cambridge, 1995), p. 180. See now Celia Chazelle, *The Codex Amiatinus and its "Sister" Bibles: Scripture, Liturgy, and Art in the Milieu of the Venerable Bede* (Leiden, 2019), pp. 160, 282–83, 396–97, and colour plate XVII on p. 578.

FIGURE 11.3   Ruthwell Cross, first side of upper stone: The Archer and the Visitation.
                 Photo: Catherine E. Karkov, by kind permission

from my mother's womb he has remembered my name,
and made my mouth like a sharp sword:
in the shadow of his hand he has protected me
and has made me like a chosen arrow [*et posuit me sicut sagittam
    electam*]:
in his quiver he has hidden me [*in faretra sua abscondit me*] ...²²

The liturgy, creatively adapting scripture, on 24 June presented the two children in their mothers' wombs as a unique pair of "chosen arrows." John, as yet unborn, is already a prophet, acclaiming his younger cousin (in Mary's womb) by leaping in the womb of his mother Elizabeth. We may suppose that in the weeks before and after the midsummer solstice, near the Nativity of John the Baptist, members of the Ruthwell community who were attentive to their liturgy would give special attention to the figure of the pregnant Elizabeth, the figure on the right in the panel (Fig. 11.3). After the summer solstice came the "lessening days" of late summer and autumn.²³ During the weeks of midwinter, before and after Christ's nativity, such an audience would give special attention to Mary (the figure on the left). The emphasis and significance of this panel changed as the sun ran its yearly course.

The sculptors of the upper stone emphasized the intense physicality of the Visitation (Fig. 11.4). On the right of the panel, Elizabeth gazes intently at the mother of her Lord, who has come to visit and help her, an old woman, in her childbirth. The panel seems to represent the very moment when John leaps in her womb: in reaction, Elizabeth stretches out to touch, on Mary's body, the reality of the Incarnation. Mary's head is partially turned towards the spectator: it is the very moment when she prepares to intone her Magnificat (the canticle which a community at Ruthwell would have sung at Vespers each evening).²⁴ Her right hand, fingers outstretched, embraces Elizabeth's upper arm, as though to encourage her to appreciate the reality that God has taken on flesh, become a human being. Above the women, the Archer with the book-satchel, his arrow ready to shoot, implies that the Incarnation, as yet hidden, will lead to great things.²⁵

---

22   Isaiah 49:1–2.

23   On the solar Incarnation-cycle which associated the "growing days" with Christ and the "lessening days" with John the Baptist, see Ó Carragáin, "Chosen Arrows," pp. 188–90.

24   On this iconographic detail and its significance, see Jane Hawkes and Éamonn Ó Carragáin, with Ross Trench-Jellicoe, "John the Baptist and the *Agnus Dei*: Ruthwell (and Bewcastle) Revisited," *The Antiquaries Journal* 81 (2001), 131–53, at p. 147.

25   The archer aims at something on the transom of the cross (not at the eagle at the top of this first side). In *Ritual and the Rood* (pp. 142–47 and figs. 30(a)–(c)) and in "Chosen

FIGURE 11.4   Ruthwell Cross, The Visitation, showing
gestures of Elizabeth (right) and Mary (left).
Photo: Catherine E. Karkov, by kind
permission

On this first broad side of the upper stone, all the inscriptions are in runes: any Northumbrian or Irish onlooker, once told that the inscriptions on this side of the upper stone were in runes, even if they could not read them, would have understood the essential message: that, like the two "chosen arrows" still hidden in their mothers' wombs, the writing on this side of the upper stone was mysterious, its meaning hidden.[26] The designer of the upper stone uses the two scripts, runic and Roman, as a central part of the iconographic pro-gramme. The upper stone was placed so high (about 12 feet high at the bottom, 18 feet at the top) that any script on it would have been difficult to read. But as

Arrows" (pp. 201–04 and plate 6b) I suggested that that the archer may be aiming the words of scripture at the figure of a catechumen or penitent, on the lost transom. Such figures are represented on the transoms of fragmentary cross-heads at Durham. The cross-heads are late, but have other features in common with the Ruthwell Cross, and may, like Ruthwell Church, be associated with the early cult of St Cuthbert.

26   The loanword rún ("a secret") is found in Irish from AD 800. See the Royal Irish Academy *Dictionary of the Irish Language* (*DIL*), s.v. For a good recent discussion of the ways in which runes were understood as ancient, Germanic and mysterious (while being also of interest to learned Christian audiences), see Tom Birkett, *Reading the Runes in Old English and Old Norse Poetry* (London, 2017), especially 13–49.

a symbol for "hidden mystery," the runic inscriptions would have intrigued all who looked at the cross, literate or not.[27]

On the second broad side of the upper stone, the equivalent large panel provides a number of striking contrasts with the Visitation scene. What was hidden in the Visitation panel is now openly revealed: John the Baptist points across his body to acclaim the *Agnus Dei*. The iconographic use of scripts is here completed: all the inscriptions on this side are in Latin and in Roman capitals: the language of public worship and the epigraphic style of Northumbrian monks and clergy (Figs. 11.5, 11.6).

The upper stone has been badly damaged, presumably by iconoclasts in 1641. John the Baptist appears at Ruthwell, as at Bewcastle, as a standing figure, but the loss of up to eight inches at his waist makes him look as if he is seated. Around his neck and hanging down both sides of his chest he wears a broad pallium or scarf, a sign of authority.[28] Across his body, the index finger of his right hand pointed at the lamb; but a single blow, perhaps from a hammer, has broken his index finger off at the upper knuckle. It also broke off the left foreleg of the lamb, which was sculpted in three dimensions, with space between it and John's pallium. John stands on two small globes.

The Ruthwell monument was an obelisk that became a cross, in the sense that the lower stone was probably erected first, then the upper stone placed on top.[29] We do not know whether much time, if any, separated the completion of the lower stone and the placing of the upper. But, although the cross was evidently completed in two stages, perhaps in successive seasons and possibly by different sculptors, it is likely that the upper stone was from the beginning part of the design. Anybody who had sung, or listened to, Old English vernacular poetry was familiar both with techniques of variation, and with envelope patterns.[30] The lower stone was already divided into two contrasting but complementary halves. The designer made the divisions of the upper stone a

27   See Elisabeth Okasha, "Script-mixing in Anglo-Saxon Inscriptions," in *Writing and Texts in Anglo-Saxon England*, ed. Alexander R. Rumble (Cambridge, 2006), pp. 62–70, at 67.

28   The pallium on John's right shoulder (at the left side of the panel) has sometimes been mistaken for a book. For a spirited but unconvincing defence of this interpretation, see Paul Meyvaert, "Reclaiming the *Apocalypse Majestas* Panel for the Ruthwell Cross," in *Insular and Anglo-Saxon Art and Thought in the Early Medieval Period*, ed. Colum Hourihane (Princeton, 2011), pp. 109–32.

29   See the books discussed in the next Section.

30   On envelope patterns, see Adeline Courtney Bartlett, *The Larger Rhetorical Patterns in Anglo-Saxon Poetry* (New York, 1935; reprint, 1966), pp. 9–29; on techniques of variation, see Daniel Donoghue, "Poetic Technique, OE," in *The Blackwell Encyclopaedia of Anglo-Saxon England*, ed. Michael Lapidge, John Blair, Simon Keynes and Donald Scragg (Oxford, 1999), p. 373.

FIGURE 11.5   Ruthwell Cross, second side of upper stone: John the Baptist and the
Agnus Dei.
Photo: Catherine E. Karkov, by kind permission

FIGURE 11.6   Ruthwell Cross, John the Baptist and the *Agnus Dei*, close up showing
                 damage to John's index finger and to the left foreleg of the Lamb.
                 Photo: Catherine E. Karkov, by kind permission

significant variation on those of the lower. All the broad sides of the lower
stone are inscribed in Roman capitals. Runes appeared only on its narrow sides,
where the poem, in four columns, enhanced and explained the vinescrolls. The
poem was an outstanding example of prosopopoeia: the Cross spoke in person of itself; it was also ekphrastic: the speaking Cross retold its experience on
Good Friday. The runic verses on the first narrow side (facing the inauspicious
north), told how the cross was mocked by its enemies; it could not bow. It had
to bear its Lord to his freely-chosen death. On the second narrow side (facing
the auspicious south), the Cross told how Christ's followers came to it. It could
now bow and (in a unique narrative detail) hand on Christ's dead body, emptied even of its blood, to them. The four columns, read (by the few?) or heard
sung (by the many?) in sequence, gently nudged people into a realisation
(which could have taken months, or even years for slow learners)[31] that the
dilemma and mockery of the first half of the poem led to the images of growth

---

31   A monastic vocation involved a commitment to slow (lifelong) and profound learning. See
     Catherine E. Karkov's fine meditation, "Thinking about Stone: An Elemental Encounter
     with the Ruthwell Cross," in *Slow Scholarship: Medieval Research and the Neoliberal
     University*, ed. Catherine E. Karkov (Cambridge, 2019), pp. 99–124.

in faith and repentance on the first broad side; and that the handing on of Christ's dead body to his followers in the second half of the poem led naturally to the Eucharistic images of recognition on the second broad side. The complementary halves of the upper stone (from hidden to revealed, from runes to Roman letters) are a significant variant on the design of the lower stone.

In addition, each broad side of the upper stone completes an envelope pattern which spans the whole of that side of the shaft. On the first broad side, the Visitation forms an "envelope" with the Annunciation at the foot of the shaft. These two Marian panels enclose the panels of the blind man (enlightenment by faith) and the female sinner (penitence and love). Both lections were intoned during Lent, when a monastic or clerical community would surely have understood that communal growth in faith and repentance was analogous to the growth of Christ in Mary's womb. After all, during Lent those preparing for baptism, or engaged in Lenten repentance, were told (in the persons of their godparents) that "already, having conceived you, the pregnant Church rejoices" (*iam uobis conceptis prignans gloriatur ecclesia*).[32] As Pope Leo I saw it, Christ "placed in the font of Baptism that very origin which he had assumed in the Virgin's womb. He gave to the water what he had given to his Mother. For, the same power of the Most High and overshadowing of the Holy Spirit (Luke 1:35) that caused Mary to hear the Saviour makes the water regenerate the believer."[33]

The equally powerful "envelope pattern" of the second broad side is formed by the Return from (or perhaps Flight into) Egypt, at the foot of the shaft, and the John the Baptist panel on the upper stone. The Egypt panel is the third and final panel of the Marian sequence. The Virgin is seated like a queen on the ass which brings Christ across the desert. Mary gestures across her body to acclaim the Christ-child, seated in majesty on her lap. Jane Hawkes has argued convincingly that the scene has elements of an *adventus* (the solemn entry of an emperor into his kingdom), and that it (like the liturgy of the Advent season) has overtones of the Second Coming of Christ in glory.[34] In the "envelope

---

32   Gelasian Sacramentary, admonition to the catechumens: trans. Edmund Charles Whitaker, *Documents of the Baptismal Liturgy*, 2nd edn (London, 1970), p. 174; Ó Carragáin, *Ritual and the Rood*, p. 137.

33   Sermon 25, Section 5; CCSL 138, p. 123: see *Sermons (Fathers of the Church 93) St Leo the Great*, trans. Jane Patricia Freeland and Agnes Josephine Conway (Washington, DC, 1995), p. 103; Ó Carragáin, *Ritual and the Rood*, p. 139.

34   Jane Hawkes, "'Hail the conquering hero': Coming and Going at Ruthwell: *Adventus* and Transition," in *The Art, Literature and Material Culture of the Medieval World: Transition, Transformation and Taxonomy*, ed. Meg Boulton and Jane Hawkes, with Melissa Herman (Dublin, 2015), pp. 80–96.

pattern" of the second broad side Christ is acclaimed by Mary his mother (at the foot of the shaft) and, on the upper stone, by John his cousin who, in a gesture which recalls Mary's, acclaims him as the *Agnus Dei* who takes away the sins of the world.

These "envelope" panels enclose two panels, as in the pattern of the first broad side. In each panel, a pair of creatures recognize Christ. Above the "Egypt" panel, the pair are human: the *titulus* explains that the hermits Paul and Anthony broke the loaf in the desert (*fregervnt panem in deserto*). The inscription (with its echo of the *fractio panis* rite, breaking of the loaf before Communion), combined with the flowing robes, imply this is a scene with Eucharistic overtones: by breaking the loaf between them, the hermits recognize Christ. At the top of the lower stone, just under the *Agnus Dei* panel, the *titulus* proclaims that beasts and dragons recognized Christ in the desert. But if these beasts were once evil beasts and dragons, they are now converted. They acclaim Christ by crossing their inner paws to form the first Greek letter of his messianic title, "Christ." At the top of the panel, the Latin *titulus*, beginning with the sacred name *Ihs XPs*, explains the animals' gesture. In each of these two "enclosed" panels, Christ is recognized by, and between, two living creatures. The scriptural phrase "you will be known in the midst of two living beings" (*in medio duorum animalium cognosceris*) was part of a canticle, sung every Friday at Lauds, and also on Good Friday, at the moment of Christ's death,[35] a particularly important usage. Jerome saw many dimensions of meaning in the phrase. Here are just a few of them:

> [The two living beings] are interpreted as the two Seraphim in Isaiah [6:2], and the [two] cherubim described in Exodus [28:18] [...] [Good interpreters] say that the Saviour is to be understood and believed in [the midst of] the primitive Church, which was called together from the circumcision [i.e. from the Jews] and from the foreskin [i.e. from the gentiles], [Christ] surrounding himself on this side and on that by two

---

35   Ó Carragáin, *Ritual and the Rood*, pp. 201–08. Though they dwell in the desert, the Ruthwell animals are reminiscent of the two otters who warmed Cuthbert after his nightlong vigil in the sea: see Richard N. Bailey, "*In Medio Duorum Animalium*: Habbakuk, the Ruthwell Cross, and Bede's Life of St Cuthbert," in *"Listen, O Isles, unto Me": Studies in Medieval Word and Image in Honour of Jennifer O'Reilly*, ed. Elizabeth Mullins and Diarmuid Scully (Cork, 2011), 243–52; for the influence of the Old Latin canticle on early Christian art, see Éamonn Ó Carragáin, "The Santa Sabina Crucifixion Panel: 'between two living creatures you will be known' on Good Friday at 'Hierusalem' in Fifth-century Rome," in *Crossing Boundaries: Interdisciplinary Approaches to the Art, Material Culture, Language and Literature of the Early Medieval World*, ed. Eric Cambridge and Jane Hawkes (Oxford, 2017), pp. 69–77.

peoples. There are those who understand the two living creatures as the two Testaments, Old and New, who are truly living and full of life, who [can be said to] breathe [the Spirit], and in the midst of which the Lord may be known.[36]

The relevance of the *in medio duorum* [...] *cognosceris* theme to several panels on the cross (upper and lower stones) contextualises the two globes under the feet of John the Baptist. The globes provide a visual link between this panel and the paired figures of the two "enclosed" panels below. To use Jerome's terms, John stood between "the two Testaments, Old and New, in the midst of which the Lord may be known." Augustine also singled out John: "to the prophets who went before, it was given to announce beforehand the things that were to come to pass concerning Christ: but to this man it was given to point him out with his finger."[37] The globes also provide a visual reminder of the first side of the upper stone, where a pair of women, Mary and Elizabeth, respond to the still hidden Incarnation.

The *Agnus Dei* panel has a fragmentary inscription: *ADORAMVS VT NON CVM*.[38] In April 2007 I searched the relevant databases, but failed to find a parallel for the whole phrase. The unusual connecting phrase *VT NON CVM*, however, occurs three times in the Letters of St Paul, and nowhere else in Scripture. One occurrence (1 Corinthians 11:32) is highly relevant to the *Agnus Dei* panel: it forms part of the earliest description of how a Christian community (in Corinth, about AD 54) gathered to celebrate the Eucharist. It was natural to intone this passage on Holy Thursday, as the Epistle for the Mass of the Lord's Supper (*Missa in Caena Domini*), which commemorated the day and the hour in which Christ instituted the Eucharist. The lection (1 Corinthians 11:20–32) begins by emphasizing that this involved a community: *Fratres, convenientibus vobis in unum* [...] ("Brothers, when you gather together [...]"). At the end of the lection, St Paul emphasizes the importance of reverence when celebrating the Eucharist, which was a pledge that Christ would soon come again to judge the world. It would go hard with those who failed to recognise Christ in the breaking of bread:

---

36   Jerome, *In Abakuk* II, iii, 2, in *S. Hieronymi Presbyteri Opera*, ed. M. Adriaen (CCSL 76A) (Turnhout, 1970), pp. 620–21. For a translation of the full passage, see Ó Carragáin, "The Santa Sabina Crucifixion Panel," pp. 71–72.

37   Augustine, *In Iohannis Evangelium*, IV, 1, ed. Radbod Willems (CCSL 36), 2nd edn (Turnhout, 1990), p. 31.

38   There is a photograph and a careful drawing of the surviving inscription by Ross Trench-Jellicoe in Hawkes *et al.*, "John the Baptist and the *Agnus Dei*," at pp. 134–35.

For as often as you shall eat this bread, and drink the cup, you shall show the death of the Lord, until he come. Therefore whosoever shall eat this bread, or drink the blood of the Lord unworthily, shall be guilty of the body and of the blood of the Lord. [...] But whilst we are judged, we are chastised by the Lord; that we be not condemned with this world (*dum iudicamur autem a Domino corripimur **ut non cum** hoc mundo damnemur* (emphasis added)).

I speculated that, while the Pauline sentence ended with *hoc mundo damnemur*, the Ruthwell commissioner may have preferred to omit these grim final words. Any cleric would have recalled St Paul's description of the Eucharist, and the unusual connecting phrase would be enough to remind them that those who participated unworthily risked damnation. The combination of *adoramus* ("we adore") with the enigmatic note of warning strengthens the Eucharistic connotations of the panel. An abbess or abbot might have felt that to spell out the enigma would have conflicted with the *Agnus Dei* rite for the breaking of bread: that was all about mercy. The celebrating priest in silence broke the loaf so that it could be divided among the community. Breaking the loaf (the body of Christ) was a solemn activity, and could take some time.[39] While this went on, the other members of the community sang in Latin, as often as was necessary, "Lamb of God, who takes away the sins of the world, have mercy on us" (not yet schematized into just three repetitions).[40] The laity could easily have been schooled to respond at the *miserere nobis* phrase, perhaps with a vernacular equivalent. When compared with other vivid accounts and images of damnation and punishment from Northumbria in the age of Bede,[41] the second broad side of the Ruthwell Cross shows a remarkable faith in Christ as just and merciful. Its iconography preserves some of the atmosphere of early Christian apses in Rome, where the Second Coming of Christ was desired, not feared.[42]

---

39   Tom O'Loughlin, "The Praxis and Explanation of Eucharistic Fraction in the Ninth Century: the Insular Evidence," *Archiv für Liturgiewissenschaft* 45 (2003), 1–20.

40   *"Agnus Dei, qui tollis peccata mundi: miserere nobis"*: for discussion of how the *Agnus Dei* chant was performed in the eighth century, see Ó Carragáin, *Ritual and the Rood*, p. 163.

41   Such as the demons on the Rothbury Cross, or the story Bishop Pehthelm told Bede, of the evil-living thane of King Cenred of Mercia (reigned 704–709) who died in despair soon after seeing (in a vision) the pamphlet of his good deeds and the large volume listing his evil acts.

42   Éamonn Ó Carragáin, "Conversion, Justice, and Mercy at the Parousia: Liturgical Apocalypses, from Eighth-Century Northumbria, on the Bewcastle and Ruthwell Crosses," in *Apocalypse Now and Then*, ed. Kathryn Banks (Literature and Theology 26.4) (Oxford,

But Is the Ruthwell Monument a Cross?

Within two years of my book's publication, two very different books denied that the Ruthwell monument was designed as a cross. The first, by Pamela O'Neill, is written in a clear, witty, and detached style.[43] It is a beautifully structured argument. It has a careful survey of how the early antiquaries described the cross, but, influenced by the theories of Fred Orton (see below) is unconvincingly dismissive of the sixteenth-century antiquarian Reginald Bainbrigg's description of "the cross of wonderful height which is in the church at Ruthwell." O'Neill argues that more than one sculptor or team worked on the cross, and that its construction may have taken several seasons.[44] O'Neill's treatment of the poem on the lower stone is weak, however. Seeing the monument as a pillar, she denies that the cross is the speaker of the runic verses, suggesting instead that the speaker is a follower of Christ standing by the cross.[45]

Two years after O'Neill's book, the eagerly-awaited synthesis by Fred Orton, Ian Wood, and Clare A. Lees was published.[46] Behind it lay years of examination of the Ruthwell and Bewcastle monuments, and also years of lively debate, especially at the 1995 and 1998 Medieval Congresses at the University of Leeds. Orton, Wood and Lees felt some early antiquarians, and some modern scholars too, saw crosses where in fact there were pillars or obelisks. As I was interested in Rome, city of many obelisks, this was fascinating. I suggested to Fred Orton and Ian Wood that they might consider, as an inspiration for Ruthwell and other insular monuments, the Vatican obelisk, which survived the Middle Ages still standing.[47] They accepted this idea. Orton participated in the University College Cork Rome seminar at the British School at Rome in September 1999, where we not only studied the Vatican obelisk, but other relevant works of art.

2012), pp. 367–83; and Rosemary Cramp, *Bede and Judgement*, Wearmouth Lecture (Monkwearmouth, 2009).

43   Pamela O'Neill, *"A pillar curiously engraven; with some inscription upon it": What Is the Ruthwell Cross?* (British Archaeological Reports, British Series 397) (Oxford, 2005).

44   O'Neill, *A pillar*, pp. 41, 75, 81.

45   O'Neill, *A pillar*, pp. 63–64.

46   Fred Orton and Ian Wood with Clare A. Lees, *Fragments of History: Rethinking the Ruthwell and Bewcastle Monuments* (Manchester, 2007).

47   Éamonn Ó Carragáin, "Between Annunciation and Visitation: Spiritual Birth and the Cycles of the Sun on the Ruthwell Cross: a Response to Fred Orton," in *Theorizing Anglo-Saxon Stone Sculpture*, ed. Catherine E. Karkov and Fred Orton (Morgantown, WV, 2003), pp. 131–87, at 181–87. On the Vatican obelisk in the Middle Ages, see now John Osborne, *"Plus Cesare Petrus*: the Vatican Obelisk and the Approach to St Peter's," in *Old Saint Peter's, Rome*, ed. Rosamond McKitterick, John Osborne, Carol M. Richardson, and Joanna Story (Cambridge, 2013), pp. 274–86.

However, as Richard Bailey pointed out in his review of the book, Orton, Wood and Lees dismiss too lightly the testimony of Richard Bainbrigg that he saw "a cross of wonderful height" in Ruthwell Church;[48] and since 2005, we have come to understand far better why early antiquarians used terms like "pyramid," "obelisk," or "cross," and what they meant by them.[49]

Fragments of History has many strengths. There are detailed descriptions of the landscape surrounding both Ruthwell and Bewcastle, and of the political situation in the early and mid-eighth century: the Anglo-Saxon push westward, along Solway Firth, towards Whithorn. There is a good discussion of the stylistic and iconographic differences between Ruthwell and Bewcastle, and a particularly informative examination of the Bewcastle sundial. *Fragments* places a refreshing emphasis on the differences of theme and structure between the Ruthwell poem and the Vercelli *Dream*. These strengths should be set against a reductive reluctance to admit liturgical and Christological influences. Orton, Wood and Lees understood the runic poem to be part of the design of the lower stone from the beginning. They put a welcome emphasis on the poem's materiality: that its layout encourages the reader to move around the monument in order to read it, or while hearing it sung or chanted.

Is the Poem Integral to the Monument, or a Later "Secondary" Addition?

In contrast to Orton, Wood and Lees, several scholars had followed Paul Meyvaert in denying the relevance of the poem to the cross. In the period being surveyed, Paul Meyvaert published the last two of his four articles on the monument. Paul's first two papers were, as was proper, influential. They put

---

48   Richard Bailey, review of *Fragments of History*, in *Journal of Ecclesiastical History* 59 (2008), 537–38.

49   Carol Neuman de Vegvar pointed out that from Anglo-Saxon England not a single pointed apex, as for an obelisk, has been found, while many cross-heads survive: "Converting the Anglo-Saxon Landscape: Crosses and their Audiences," in Minnis and Roberts, *Text, Image, Interpretation*, pp. 407–29 (at 409–10). While inspired by the tall narrow shape of obelisks, Anglo-Saxon Christians converted them into crosses. Derek Craig reminded us how ubiquitous was the cross-head, as an ideal (inscribed) shape, at Hoddom, ten miles from Ruthwell: "The Later Carved Stone Assemblage," in Christopher Lowe, *Excavations at Hoddom, Dumfriesshire: an Early Ecclesiastical Site in South-West Scotland* (Edinburgh, 2006), pp. 123–33. On the terms used by early antiquaries, see Jane Hawkes, "Creating a View: Anglo-Saxon Sculpture in the Sixteenth Century," in *Making Histories: Proceedings of the Sixth International Conference on Insular Art, York, 2011*, ed. Jane Hawkes (Donington, 2013), pp. 372–84.

forward four theses: first, that the upper stone should be reversed; second, that on the upper stone the male figure holding the lamb was not John the Baptist, but a portrait of God the Father in Majesty. Paul argued that this *Majestas* held a book, and was seated as though enthroned. Third, that the runic poem was added later, and had nothing to do with the rest of the cross: in this, Paul developed the ideas of Ray Page.[50] Fourth, that talk of the Roman liturgy was irrelevant. Paul's approach was immediately acclaimed by Eric Stanley, who teased out the implications of Paul's theories, and published them in his collected papers of 1987.[51] Stanley, rejoicing that Meyvaert had "set the poem free of the cross," proposed a series of late dates for the poem. In 2008, Pat Conner built on these opinions to argue that the poem, now floating as a text without a context, might have been influenced by the *Regularis Concordia* (a Winchester document promulgated in AD 970).[52]

I kept in friendly touch with Paul Meyvaert, visiting him at Harvard in July 2007. To explain his alienation from Roman Catholicism and its liturgy, he later kindly forwarded me his autobiography, *Jeffrey's Story*.[53] I naturally sent him my chapter for the Wormald *Gedenkschrift* as soon as it appeared.[54] Richard Bailey had been in contact with Meyvaert since 1980; our email correspondence with Paul soon widened to include Jane Hawkes.

Meyvaert's third article, in 2011, made no reference to his recent email discussions of iconography with Richard Bailey and Jane Hawkes.[55] He stuck to his "Majestas" theory, bringing forward new evidence from the Princeton Index of Christian art. He proposed, as if it were a new discovery, that 1 Corinthians 11:32 was the inspiration for the *ADORAMVS VT NON CVM* inscription.[56] But,

---

50   Meyvaert's correspondence with Page is discussed in his "Necessity Mother of Invention: a Fresh Look at the Rune Verses on the Ruthwell Cross," *Anglo-Saxon England* 41 (2013), 407–16.

51   Eric Gerald Stanley, "The Ruthwell Cross Inscription: Some Linguistic and Literary Implications of Paul Meyvaert's Paper 'An Apocalypse Panel on the Ruthwell Cross'" in Stanley, *A Collection of Papers with Emphasis on Old English Literature* (Publications of the Dictionary of Old English 3) (Toronto, 1987), p. xiii and pp. 384–99.

52   Patrick W. Conner, "The Ruthwell Monument Runic Poem in a Tenth-Century Context," *Review of English Studies* n.s. 59.238 (2008), 25–51.

53   *Jeffrey's Story: the Autobiography of Paul J. Meyvaert* (Tempe, AZ, 2005).

54   E-mail from Paul thanking me for the chapter, 16 August 2009.

55   Paul Meyvaert, "Reclaiming the Apocalypse *Majestas* Panel for the Ruthwell Cross," in *Insular and Anglo-Saxon Art and Thought in the Early Medieval Period*, ed. Colum Hourihane (Princeton, 2011), pp. 109–32.

56   Compare Ó Carragáin, "Chosen Arrows" (2009), pp. 200–01, with Meyvaert, "Reclaiming" (2011), pp. 118–22. This is all the more remarkable, as in "Chosen Arrows" (p. 186, note 5) I had had occasion to chide him gently for not referring to Barbara Raw's fundamental work on the Archer panel. Less cautious than I, Paul argued that the inscription may have

while I had stressed that that verse was part of the earliest extant description of a Christian community gathering to celebrate the Eucharist, and that it was therefore universally used as a Mass lection on Holy Thursday, when adopting my discovery Paul omitted these facts. This was methodologically odd. The intonation of the lection on Holy Thursday evening is an important part of the medieval reception history of that passage. Something very deep in Paul prevented him from acknowledging evidence as having a liturgical dimension. Paul's interpretations of the monument were learned, deeply literary, and indoor: he held that the cross stood from the beginning within the church at Ruthwell. He had no interest in whether the cross originally stood outside a church, as the Bewcastle Cross still does.

Meyvaert hinted in the third article that he was beginning to abandon his theory that the upper stone should be reversed.[57] But his most remarkable reversal came in his final article in 2013.[58] Here he looked back to his 1975–76 correspondence with Ray Page. He recounts that he was in the course of writing a fourth and last statement of his opinion that the layout of the poem was "daft,"[59] when a friend pointed out that, by laying out the poem in four columns, the Ruthwell designer got far more text into each column. Meyvaert now acknowledged that the poem was likely to be an integral part of the cross's original design. This abandonment of long-held opinions had negative implications for Stanley and Conner: their late datings, inspired by Meyvaert, now lacked any solid foundation. The members of the long-term project, "Runische Schriftlichkeit in den germanischen Sprachen (RuneS)" will publish their conclusions in 2021 and the following years.[60] These will demonstrate that the Ruthwell epigraphic poem, which they date to the eighth century (with a preference for mid-century), formed an integral part of the cross.

---

continued with *hoc mundo damnemur*, reading upward along the right-hand border. He provided a speculative reconstruction of the whole inscription, p. 121.

57   Meyvaert, "Reclaiming," pp. 122 and 124.

58   Meyvaert, "Necessity."

59   The expression is Page's (letter to Meyvaert, 1976), as printed in Meyvaert, "Necessity", p. 408.

60   I am grateful to Alfred Bammesberger, Gaby Waxenberger, and Kerstin Majewski for sending me advance copies of their forthcoming publications. The first volume is to be G. Waxenberger, *A Phonology of Old English Runic Inscriptions with a Concise Edition of the Old English Inscriptions and an Analysis of Graphemes* (Ergänzungsbände zum Reallexikon der Germanischen Altertumskunde) (Berlin: de Gruyter, 2021).

The Ruthwell Cross as a Tree of Life

Apart from the German RuneS project, the scholars discussed in the last two sections emphasized fragmentation. But in 2003 a great scholar, Jennifer O'Reilly, took a different view. She saw the vinescrolls and their *tituli* as the heart of the cross:

> In a single unifying image the sculptural decoration of the narrow sides reveals Christ to be the Tree of Life, that is, the axis at the centre of the world joining heaven and earth and providing spiritual food and healing for all. The Tree rises the height of the towering shaft on both sides and is shown in the form of a rooted vine-scroll filled with diverse creatures feeding on its fruit [...] The form and iconography of the Ruthwell Cross, its Christology and use of the written word show the Anglo-Saxons to be a people engrafted into the universal Church and familiar with its Romanised culture but also highly creative in adapting its conventions and integrating elements from their own tradition.[61]

Richard North had already emphasized how images of the Tree of Life helped the transition from Anglo-Saxon paganism to Christianity. His insights have recently been developed in an important book by Michael Bintley.[62]

Readers, Listeners and Onlookers: The Audiences of the Ruthwell Cross

The corpus of surviving runic inscriptions contains nothing like the four-column configuration of runes at Ruthwell. However, Ute Schwab had pointed out in 1978 that Roman and Byzantine inscriptions provided analogues for the Ruthwell layout.[63] Rosemary Cramp has always defended the Ruthwell poem

---

61   Jennifer O'Reilly, "The Art of Authority," in *After Rome*, ed. Thomas Charles-Edwards (Oxford, 2003), pp. 141–89 (at 152), as reprinted in *Jennifer O'Reilly: Early Medieval Text and Image* 2, ed. Carol A. Farr and Elizabeth Mullins (Variorum Collected Studies Series) (London, 2019), pp. 50–91, at 59.

62   Richard North, *Heathen Gods in Old English Literature* (Cambridge, 1997); Éamonn Ó Carragáin and Richard North, "The Dream of the Rood and Anglo-Saxon Northumbria," in *'Beowulf' and Other Stories: a New Introduction to Old English, Old Icelandic, and Anglo-Norman Literatures*, ed. Richard North and Joe Allard (Harlow, 2007), pp. 160–88; Michael D.J. Bintley, *Trees in the Religions of Early Medieval England* (Woodbridge, 2015).

63   Ute Schwab, "Das Traumgesicht von Kreuzesbaum. Ein ikonologischer Interpretatationsansatz zu dem ags. 'Dream of the Rood'", in *Philologische Studien. Gedenkschrift für Richard Kienast*, ed. Ute Schwab and Elfriede Stutz (Heidelberg, 1978), pp. 131–92.

as an integral part of the cross; in a paper in her honour, I argued that early Christian epigraphers often gave their inscriptions an element of difficulty or riddling. The time and effort needed to decipher the inscriptions encouraged readers to meditate more deeply on their significance.[64] Sean V. Leatherbury has now fully documented this early Christian epigraphic tradition.[65] Among the many strengths of his book is his demonstration that epigraphic planners often encouraged their readers to move around, in order to understand, and properly appreciate, their *tituli.*

Several scholars have explored the ways in which the Ruthwell Cross would have made sense to illiterate as well as literate onlookers. Carol Neuman de Vegvar demonstrated that, while educated clerics, monks, or nuns would value vine-scrolls as images of the Tree of Life, the unschooled laity may have valued such vegetal designs as being practically useful, to keep off demons or assure good weather.[66] I also argued that the Ruthwell Cross was designed to appeal to uneducated audiences, calling the poem "a perfect example of unobtrusive yet effective catechesis."[67]

Is the Liturgy Relevant to the Ruthwell Cross?

Richard W. Pfaff, who began his introduction to English Medieval Liturgy with a discussion of sources, correctly decided not to use my work as evidence of what kind of Divine Office was performed at Ruthwell: from there, "no textual evidence that would help us decide remains."[68] I fully agree. The early eighth century is the period of the mixed Rule: the abbess or abbot could and usually did make a selection of the preferred practices they had come across on their travels and through clerical contacts. If we know nothing about the abbess or abbot (or indeed whether there was one), we know less than nothing about the *consuetudines* or *ordines* they composed or followed.

---

64   Éamonn Ó Carragáin, "Who then Read the Ruthwell Poem in the Eighth Century?", in *Aedificia Nova: Studies in Honor of Rosemary Cramp*, ed. Catherine E. Karkov and Helen Damico (Kalamazoo, MI, 2008), pp. 43–75.

65   Sean V. Leatherbury, *Inscribing Faith in Late Antiquity: between Reading and Seeing* (London, 2020).

66   Neuman de Vegvar, "Converting the Anglo-Saxon Landscape," especially pp. 422–26.

67   Éamonn Ó Carragáin, "At once Elitist and Popular: the Audiences of the Bewcastle and Ruthwell Crosses," in *Elite and Popular Religion* (Studies in Church History 42), ed. Kate Cooper and Jeremy Gregory (Woodbridge, 2006), pp. 18–40.

68   Richard W. Pfaff, *The Liturgy in Medieval England: a History* (Cambridge, 2009), p. 52; see now also the splendid study by Jesse D. Billett, *The Divine Office in Anglo-Saxon England 597–c. 1000* (Henry Bradshaw Society, Subsidia 7) (London, 2014).

The Ruthwell Cross does not provide direct evidence of the liturgical customs of the Ruthwell community. I have long ago rejected the naïve idea that Mass would often (if ever) be celebrated out of doors, facing the Eucharistic west faces of Bewcastle or Ruthwell.[69] Instead, the cross is the most profound sculptural meditation on aspects of the liturgy to survive from Anglo-Saxon England: in particular on the Lenten rites of initiation, which always culminated in reception of the Eucharist. The designer seems to have been aware of new chants at Mass, and the new Marian feasts at Rome. The poet has the cross present Christ's dead body to his followers (southern narrow side), a unique and disturbing image. The Ruthwell community would have more easily accepted it if on Good Friday afternoon they had begun, like other eighth-century communities, to combine the Adoration of the Cross with reception of the Eucharist. It is quite possible that this new custom had not yet reached Ruthwell, except in the poet's memory and imagination: that their poet was relying on what he or she knew was being done elsewhere. But the whole programme of the cross (including its poem) suggests that commissioner, designer, and poet (who might possibly be one and the same person) had meditated deeply on the significance of what they had seen, or heard about, at Rome or some other greater liturgical centre.[70] Hubertus Lutterbach has demonstrated that rites of reception into monastic communities, male and female, were usually modelled on the Lenten and Easter rites of Christian initiation: Lenten scrutinies, acquisition of a new habit and name, culminating in reception of Communion.[71] Thus the Ruthwell Cross seems to be simultaneously a meditation on what it might mean to become a Christian, and also to become a nun or monk. It is pleasing to think that we have arrived back at Paul Meyvaert's description of

---

69   For a cautious statement of the early theory, see Éamonn Ó Carragáin, "Christ over the Beasts and the Agnus Dei: Two Multivalent Panels on the Ruthwell and Bewcastle Crosses," in *Sources of Anglo-Saxon Culture*, ed. Paul E. Szarmach with Virginia Darrow Oggins (Kalamazoo, 1986), pp. 377–403 (at 390); for later scepticism about such a theory, see Éamonn Ó Carragáin and Tomás Ó Carragáin, "Singing in the Rain on Hinba? Archaeology and Liturgical Fictions, Ancient and Modern (Adomnan, *Vita Columbae* 3.17)," in *"Listen, O Isles, unto Me,"* pp. 204–15.

70   I would still stand over the cautious use of liturgical evidence to date the Ruthwell Cross after the beginning and before the end of the eighth century, as summarized in Éamonn Ó Carragáin, "The Necessary Distance: *Imitatio Romae* and the Ruthwell Cross," in *Northumbria's Golden Age*, ed. Jane Hawkes and Susan Mills (Stroud, 1999), pp. 191–203.

71   Hubertus Lutterbach, *Monachus factus est: Die Mönchwerdung im frühen Mittelalter, zugleich ein Beitrag zur Frömmigkeits- und Liturgiegeschichte* (Münster, 1995); also Lutterbach, "Der Mönch – das besondere Gotteskind. Zur Genese und Prägekraft einer Metapher für christliche Klosterleben," *Revue d'histoire ecclésiastique* 99 (2004), 5–34. See Ó Carragáin, *Ritual and the Rood*, pp. 294–96. I am grateful to Sister Parousia Clemens and Jesse Billett for help with this matter.

the programme of the cross as "*Ecclesia* and *Vita Monastica*" via the liturgical evidence he was reluctant to acknowledge.

From the 670s onwards, the basilica of St Peter's in Rome uniquely celebrated 25 March as "The Annunciation of the Lord and his Passion." The Vatican Mass for 25 March was probably composed by the Abbot John the "Archcantor": as his title indicates, he was in charge of the choir and liturgy of St Peter's.[72] In Northumbria, where Irish and Roman traditions disputed the date of Easter, it may have been wise as well as eirenic to emphasize a learned tradition which everyone in Europe accepted. That the Passion took place on the anniversary of the Annunciation had long been a familiar idea at the monastery of St Martin's at Tours: each 27 March they held a vigil for the anniversary of the first Easter. John the Archcantor was abbot of another St Martin's monastery, just outside the apse of St Peter's on the Vatican: as abbot, he naturally was devoted to St Martin of Tours. He and Benedict Biscop, founder-abbot of Wearmouth, visited Tours on their way to Northumbria in AD 679, and Abbot John's body was returned to Tours when he died in Gaul on his way back from Wearmouth to Rome. At Wearmouth, also dedicated to St Peter, John had taught the Vatican liturgy of St Peter's to the monks: cantors flocked to him from all over Northumbria to learn these Vatican traditions *viva voce* from him.

In the Ruthwell runic poem, the Cross is confronted with the courage of God, "brave before all men," who chooses to die upon it. At the Annunciation, Mary had already encountered the courage of God who chose to take on flesh, in her encounter with the angel: Gabriel's name was interpreted as The Courage or Strength of God (*Fortitudo Dei*).[73] The Ruthwell poem, dramatizing the confrontation between the Cross and Christ, remodels the Crucifixion narrative on the Annunciation; then the great "envelope pattern" of the first broad side emphasizes the growth of Christ in Mary's womb, from Annunciation to Visitation, as the Lenten model for spiritual growth. Behind poem and cross at Ruthwell there lies a remarkable intellectual lineage: an eirenic tradition taught at Wearmouth by John the Archcantor. This tradition originated in the Gallican customs of St Martin's at Tours and the unusual Mass "of the Annunciation of the Lord and his Passion" at St Peter's on the Vatican.[74]

---

72   Éamonn Ó Carragáin, "Interactions between Liturgy and Politics in Old Saint Peter's, 670–741: John the Archcantor, Sergius I and Gregory III," in *Old Saint Peter's, Rome*, ed. Rosamond McKitterick, John Osborne, Carol M. Richardson, and Joanna Story (Cambridge, 2013), pp. 177–89.

73   See Ó Carragáin, *Ritual and the Rood*, pp. 83–94.

74   25 March was the anniversary of Christ's two great acts of kenosis or self-giving: Incarnation and Crucifixion. Máirín MacCarron has demonstrated that while, in his

We now understand better the origin of the feast of the Exaltation of the Cross (14 September).[75] Pope Sergius publicized his finding of the lost reliquary of the True Cross in St Peter's on the Vatican, even though he would himself celebrate the feast, not at the Vatican, but at his cathedral at the Lateran, on the other side of the city. His rediscovery of the ancient reliquary made it clear that Rome, and the Western Church, did not need to imitate imperial Constantinople in adopting the new feast, but simply to follow the ancient Roman traditions of St Peter's.

Christology: Is the Debate about Monotheletism Relevant to the Ruthwell Cross?

The relevance of the monothelete controversy to the Ruthwell Cross has been strongly opposed. In a review, Eric Stanley objected as follows:

> É. Ó Carragáin's entry for the Ruthwell Cross produces the translation "he willed to mount the gallows" a rendering of *walde* + infinitive with heightened volition, leading to an unwarranted anti-monotheletic interpretation. A less-forced rendering would be "He wished to mount the gallows," or "he willingly mounted the gallows," in line with the Latin hymn that may well underlie this use; for he might have done better to guide our understanding with reference to the *volens* of "Auctor salutis unicus" stanza 2, *Tu ascenderas crucem volens*, as we have been guided by earlier editors of and commentators on *The Dream of the Rood*. [a footnote reference follows to A.S. Cook, ed., *The Dream of the Rood* (1905), p. 23].[76]

I agree with Stanley that "willed" is a forced translation of *walde*. I chose it because I felt it necessary to emphasize the 'heightened volition' involved in a hero's choosing his own death. However, Stanley's alternative, "wished," is feeble: my current preference is for the more heroic "resolved": "when he resolved to ascend the gallows." Stanley was wrong to see the hymn "Auctor salutis unicus" as a possible source for the Ruthwell verb "walde." "Auctor salutis unicus"

early writings, Bede considered the Incarnation to have taken place at the Nativity (25 December), towards the end of his life he came to the conclusion that the Incarnation took place at the moment of the Annunciation, on 25 March; MacCarron, *Bede and Time: Computus, Theology and History in the Early Medieval World* (London, 2020), pp. 117–35.

75   "Interactions between Liturgy and Politics," pp. 184–88.

76   E.G. Stanley, review of the first edition of *The Blackwell Encyclopaedia of Anglo-Saxon England*, *Notes and Queries* 47.4 (2000), 490.

comes from the New Hymnal, compiled on the Continent in the mid-ninth century, which reached England only in the late tenth century. It is far too late to be a source for the Ruthwell poem.[77] Nor need "Auctor salutis unicus" be a source for *The Dream of the Rood*: that poem is more likely to have taken its *wolde* directly from an intermediate poem descended from the *walde* of the Ruthwell runic poem.

The danger in describing the ecclesiastical debates which form the intellectual background to a great work of art is that the reader may get the impression that the monument is itself polemical, designed as part of an ongoing argument. I tried to avoid giving this impression: *Ritual and the Rood* contains a section headed "Controversies subordinated to contemplation: the images on the Ruthwell Cross."[78] There, I pointed out that "the Ruthwell community's remoteness from major controversies gave them a great opportunity. In their relative isolation, they used images which had their origins in controversy, in new ways for contemplative purposes [...]"; and "[b]y a unique fusion of visual images with verbal images in two languages and two scripts, the Ruthwell designer transmuted controversial issues into food for joyful rumination on what it meant for the Ruthwell community to be members of, and partake in, the Body of Christ."[79]

Scholarship on the monothelete controversy has moved on a lot in the last fifteen years. We now have a good translation of the acts of the Lateran Synod of AD 649, with an excellent introduction; and two further books.[80] The orthodox opponents of monotheletism argued that Christ's human will could never be in conflict with his divine will because he was born of a Virgin: therefore the cult of the Virgin gained a new importance in liturgy and in art. The icon of the Virgin which Benedict Biscop, in the company of John the Archcantor of Saint Peter's, brought to St Peter's, Wearmouth, in AD 679, is best understood

---

77   Helmut Gneuss, *Hymnar und Hymnen im Englischen Mittelalter: Studien zur Überlieferung, Glossierung und Übersetzung lateinischer Hymnen in England. Mit einer Textausgabe der lateinisch-altenglischen Expositio Hymnorum* (Tübingen, 1968): New Hymnal no. 68, p. 353; also pp. 55–56, 77, and 102. Stanley, of course, thought that Paul Meyvaert had "set the poem free of the cross" so that it could be dated as late as the tenth century. In his article on the "Implications of Paul Meyvaert's Paper" (see note 51), Stanley makes it clear that A.S. Cook was also (like himself and Pat Conner) a convinced "late dater."

78   Ó Carragáin, *Ritual and the Rood*, pp. 259–61.

79   Ó Carragáin, *Ritual and the Rood*, pp. 260 and 261.

80   *The Acts of the Lateran Synod of 649*, trans. Richard Price with Phil Booth and Catherine Cubitt (Translated Texts for Historians 61) (Liverpool University Press, 2014); Cyril Hovorun, *Will, Action and Freedom: Christological Controversies in the Seventh Century* (Leiden, 2008); Phil Booth, *Crisis of Empire: Doctrine and Dissent at the End of Late Antiquity* (Berkeley, CA, 2014).

as one of the earliest consequences of the controversy for Christian visual culture in Northumbria.[81] As Anna Gannon has shown, the iconography of coins would be another.[82] Jennifer O'Reilly, in the article she was working on at the time of her sudden death, demonstrated that Bede saw the controversy as still important.[83] She concludes, significantly, that

> [Bede] was not concerned primarily with the historical details and contexts of past heresies, nor was he attempting to stem the mass conversion of Northumbria to monotheletism. Rather he made use of the way in which heresy and heretics can readily represent or encapsulate *continuing* challenges to the faith, understanding and behaviour of the teaching Church and its individual members. Like the fathers, he knew that the refutation of heresy can, by contradistinction, illuminate orthodox belief and practice.[84]

O'Reilly's balanced statement provides a corrective to the denial, by Orton, Wood and Lees, that the monothelete controversy was relevant to the Ruthwell Cross:

> The images of the Ruthwell monument can certainly be read as presenting Christ both as God and incarnate as a human being, but this scarcely amounts to an anti-monothelete statement: rather it reflects Chalcedonian orthodoxy, that Christ has two natures. The vernacular runic inscriptions, however, only draw attention to one and not two wills, in the phrase 'he wished to climb the gallows'. Since Christ is explicitly

---

81   Éamonn Ó Carragáin, "The Wearmouth Icon of the Virgin (A.D.679): Christological, Liturgical, and Iconographic Contexts," in *Poetry, Place and Gender: Studies in Medieval Culture in Honor of Helen Damico* (Kalamazoo, MI, 2009), pp. 13–37. Visual expressions of the Roman and Papal cult of the Virgin are surveyed by Eileen Rubery, "The Papacy and Maria Regina Imagery in Roman Churches between the Sixth and the Twelfth Centuries", in *The Oxford Handbook of Mary*, ed. Chris Maunder (Oxford, 2019), pp. 265–88.

82   Anna Gannon, "Firmly I believe and truly: Religious Iconography on Early Anglo-Saxon Coins," in *Divina Moneta – Coins in Religion and Ritual*, ed. Nanouschka Myrberg Burström and Gitte Tarnow Ingvardson (London, 2017) pp. 125–41.

83   Jennifer O'Reilly, "Bede and Monotheletism," in her *History, Hagiography and Biblical Exegesis: Essays on Bede, Adomnán and Thomas Becket*, ed. Máirín MacCarron and Diarmuid Scully (Variorum Collected Studies Series) (London, 2019), pp. 145–66. This article was written in honour of Alan Thacker, and can now also be found in *Cities, Saints, and Communities in Early Medieval Europe: Essays in Honour of Alan Thacker*, ed. Scott di Gregorio and Paul Kershaw (Turnhout, 2020), pp. 105–27.

84   O'Reilly, "Bede and Monotheletism," p. 166.

described as Almighty God, only his divine will is in question: his human will is not being considered. [...] The runic inscriptions actually come nearer to presenting a monothelete statement than a contradiction of the heresy. We can probably conclude that the monothelete debate had no significant bearing on the iconography of Ruthwell.[85]

This passage is partly convincing. Nothing on the Ruthwell Cross should be read as an "anti-monothelete statement": the commissioner, in the relatively remote Solway Firth, was not interested in polemics. Instead, she or he made an original synthesis of the devotional riches the anti-monothelete debate, and other contemporary controversies, had secured for the Western Church: a new interest in how Christ's growth in the Virgin's womb provided a model for growth in spiritual maturity; a new awareness of how human will operated; and a heightened awareness of Christ's real humanity, including a new three-dimensional concern with his weight.[86] Of course, the opening of the Ruthwell Poem "reflects Chalcedonian orthodoxy." O'Reilly demonstrated that, for Bede, each new heresy involved aspects of older ones; each debate involved returning, as it were, to first principles. Orton, Wood and Lees proposed a reductive and oversimplified reading of the poem's first two sentences:

> [+ond]geredæ hinæ ǧod ælmeittig . þa he walde on ǧalǧu gistiǧa
> modig f[ore] [allæ] men
> [b]uǧa {ic ni dorstæ} [...]

> God almighty stripped himself. When he resolved to ascend the gallows brave before all men
> [I dared not] bow [...]

The opening verb refers to stripping, not willing. The most original feature of the poem is its fusion of kenosis (stripping, pouring forth, self-giving) and courage.[87] This is no ordinary hero who kills his enemies, but a new kind of hero who gives himself until he is *limwoerig*, "brought to death by [the wounds in] his limbs," emptied even of his blood. Only in the Ruthwell poem is the

---

85   *Fragments*, p. 190.

86   On the question of Christ's weight, see O'Reilly, "Bede and Monotheletism," pp. 151–56. The importance to Bede and others of such issues might help to explain why the Ruthwell community commissioned such startlingly three-dimensional sculpture.

87   The fundamental text for understanding kenosis is Philippians 2:5–11. This was intoned at Mass on the Sunday that began Holy Week (the sixth Sunday of Lent, later to be called Palm Sunday): see Ó Carragáin, *Ritual and the Rood*, pp. 164–66.

fusion of kenosis and courage a major concern. These themes are present in the Vercelli *Dream*, but kenosis is not central to the narrative of that poem. At Ruthwell, however, both themes are central, and inseparable: Christ's heroic resolve to ascend the gallows is not simply an act of bravery, but determination to complete his courageous act of self-giving that had begun at the Annunciation. This resolve is not merely a divine act: it is equally an act of human courage. The phrase "brave before all men" can mean "braver than all other men" and also "brave in the sight of all men." Orton, Wood and Lees (like Stanley before them) failed to do justice to the paratactic nature of Old English verse: in this sentence "brave before all men" is a variation on "almighty God." If the first verb (*ongyrede*) refers to God's divine kenosis in Christ, the second verb, *walde* refers to the act that completed that kenosis: Christ's heroic human resolution to choose his death. Here the sophisticated Ruthwell poet took possession of the theological riches gained in the previous eighty years, to produce a new and startling image: not a polemical image, but a contemplative one. As O'Reilly saw, doctrinal controversies were remembered to enrich Christian tradition, both intellectual and spiritual. So successful was the enrichment that by the Carolingian period (and in tenth-century England) it had become no longer startling but normal to see that Christ "ascends the Cross willingly" (*tu ascenderas crucem volens*), as the New Hymnal has it.[88]

Is the Ruthwell Cross Roman or Celtic or Both?

In 2017, Clare Stancliffe published an excellent paper arguing that Ruthwell is the result of collaboration between Lindisfarne and Wearmouth.[89] Though the Ruthwell runes show that the community spoke Anglian, it may have included some local Britons. The churches at Ruthwell and Bewcastle were dedicated to Cuthbert of Lindisfarne.[90] Stancliffe argued that their cross shows the Ruthwell community engaged in a "charm offensive" towards the Britons of the locality. She suggested Æthelwald, bishop of Lindisfarne from *c*.724–40, as a possible commissioner of the cross.

I would cautiously propose a variant of her theory: a threefold cooperation between Wearmouth, Æthelwald of Lindisfarne, and Bishop Acca of Hexham

---

88 Gneuss, *Hymnar und Hymnen*, p. 353.

89 Clare Stancliffe, "The Riddle of the Ruthwell Cross: Audience, Intention and Originator Reconsidered," in Cambridge and Hawkes, *Crossing Boundaries*, pp. 3–14.

90 Meyvaert, "Reclaiming," p. 124.

(who died, like Æthelwald, in 740). He had been to Rome in 703–705 as Wilfrid's chaplain, but he was also Bede's friend (as well as his bishop). St Michael the Archangel himself told Wilfrid, fallen sick at Meaux in early 705 on his way back to Northumbria, that the Virgin Mary had procured for him some extra years of life, which he must use to build a church in her honour. Wilfrid was thus commissioned to strengthen in the diocese of Hexham the Marian devotion that Benedict Biscop (and John the Archcantor) had emphasized at Wearmouth a generation before.[91] When he woke up, Wilfrid called out "where is Acca, our priest": it seems likely that Acca provided Wilfrid's hagiographer with an authoritative account of the episode.[92] Probably for political reasons, Acca had to flee his cathedral at Hexham in 731. One of the best parlour-games in early Northumbrian studies is "Where was Acca hiding out from 731?" Surely Ruthwell, as well as Whithorn, should be added to the list of possible places. It is satisfying to imagine interesting people living for a while near that great cross, and perhaps even working out its theological programme with the local community. This adds another to the solutions listed by Richard Bailey on pp. 171–194, p. 297 of this volume.[93]

The Ruthwell Cross is an eirenic and welcoming monument. The iconographic programme of the second broad side balances an *Agnus Dei* panel, recalling the new Roman "*Agnus Dei*" chant sung "by the clerics and the people," against a panel in which the two hermits break the loaf between them, in the desert. The implications of the encounter between the famous abbot Anthony and the unknown hermit Paul fascinated at least two Irish monastic writers. In his life of Columba, Adomnán made it clear that at Iona they re-enacted a tableau inspired by it when an ordained cleric or monk visited the monastery. To invite a visitor to break the Eucharistic loaf with their abbot was a vivid and moving way of saying "you are welcome to share in our community." We know of the custom only because Adomnán tells us that St Columba

---

91   Éamonn Ó Carragáin with Alan Thacker, "Wilfrid in Rome," in *Wilfrid: Abbot, Bishop, Saint: Papers from the 1300th Anniversary Conference*, ed. N.J. Higham (Donington, 2013), pp. 212–30. Wilfrid was to fulfil this commission by building a chapel dedicated to Mary at Hexham. For Wilfrid, the all-important context was the election of a new Pope, John VII (705–707) who called himself "the slave of St Mary." Wilfrid would have understood, as the popes did, that "slaves of Mary" did not need to be slaves of anyone else. On John VII and his significance, see now John Osborne, *Rome in the Eighth Century: a History in Art* (Cambridge, 2020), pp. 22–66.

92   See now Clare Stancliffe, "Bede and Bishop Acca" in di Gregorio and Kershaw, *Cities, Saints, and Communities*, pp. 171–94.

93   Richard N. Bailey, "Bishop Acca's Portable Altar: Authentic Relic or Twelfth-century Hexham Fiction?" pp. 295–316 in this volume.

once refused to break the loaf with a visitor. He had discerned that the visitor (a humble man from Munster in Ireland, travelling incognito) was a bishop. Columba insisted that the bishop have the honour of breaking the loaf solo. Though Columba was the powerful abbot of a family of monasteries, he was only a priest. This was his unforgettable way to affirm the dignity of bishops. Only bishops were liturgical celebrants *ex officio*: priests could only celebrate when ordained and licensed by a bishop.[94]

The author of the *Navigatio Sancti Brendani* goes so far as to invent a brand-new Irish Paul the Spiritual Hermit, directed by St Patrick himself to seek out the stony hermitage, far out at sea, where he would pray until his death. This Irish spiritual hermit reenacts a new variant of the Paul and Anthony tableau with the abbot St Brendan, when that Kerry saint and his crew visit his hermitage. Instead of breaking bread, they face each other across a brimming pool of living water: man does not live on bread alone. Once more, rank is emphasized, but the tensions associated with rank are overcome: abbot and hermit gracefully acknowledge the validity of each other's way of life. The theme-song of the chapter might be, "Oh, the abbot and the hermit should be friends."[95]

The graceful Ruthwell panel presents yet another variant on the tableau. In effect, the status of St Anthony, as Abbot, is ignored: both saints are labelled *eremitae*. Richard Bailey showed that the Ruthwell Paul and Anthony panel is unusual in comparison with the many surviving Irish sculptural examples. By omitting the raven which brought the loaf from heaven, the panel concentrates our attention on the courteous act of breaking the loaf.[96] The Ruthwell sculptors provided us with a unique image of the importance of sharing, in liturgy, scholarship, and life.

---

94   The episode (Adomnán, *Vita Columbae*, Book 1 chapter 44), is analysed in Éamonn Ó Carragáin, "Ruthwell and Iona: The Meeting of St Paul and St Anthony Revisited," in *The Modern Traveller to our Past: Festschrift in Honour of Ann Hamlin*, ed. Marion Meek (Southport, 2006), pp. 138–44.

95   Éamonn Ó Carragáin, "Not by Bread Alone: St Brendan meets Paul, the Irish Spiritual Hermit (*Navigatio Sancti Brendani*, Chapter xxvi)," in *Prayer and Thought in Monastic Tradition: Essays in Honour of Benedicta Ward, SLG*, ed. Santha Bhattacharji, Rowan Williams, and Dominic Mattos (London, 2014), pp. 17–29: Rodgers and Hammerstein are given due acknowledgement at p. 18.

96   Richard Bailey, *England's Earliest Sculptors* (Toronto, 1996), p. 64.

Acknowledgements

The first part of my title I owe to Malcolm Parkes, who encouraged me to think that poems could, to some extent, be better understood "by the company they keep" in manuscript, monument, or reliquary. A special thanks to Rosemary Cramp, who has inspired and encouraged my research ever since we first met in 1975. Thanks to Catherine Karkov and Eric Kentley for the plates. Thanks also to Jane Roberts, Richard Bailey, Jesse Billett, Tom Birkett, Sister Parousia Clemens, Helen Gittos, Jane Hawkes, Anna Maria Luiselli Fadda, and Elisabeth Okasha.

CHAPTER 12

Bishop Acca's Portable Altar: Authentic Relic or Twelfth-Century Hexham Fiction?

Richard N. Bailey

Early in our careers Betty Coatsworth and I were both involved in the launch of the Corpus of Anglo-Saxon Stone Sculpture and I have benefitted from her advice and scholarship over many subsequent years. In cowardly fashion I have avoided commentary here on her specialist area of fabrics but a study of Acca's altar seemed an appropriate offering to make to a long-term friend and colleague whose earliest publications were focussed on Hexham.

∴

Introduction

Until relatively recently Acca, bishop of Hexham from AD 709, has attracted surprisingly little scholarly attention. This academic neglect is all the more puzzling when set against the catalogue of his contributions to Hexham's liturgy, relic collections, works of art, library, and buildings, his possible compilation of an influential *Martyrology*, his encouragement of the cult of St Oswald and of the cross, and his warm (if changing) relationship with the contrasting personalities of Bede and Wilfrid. In his early life he had shared in Wilfrid's perilous exiles and journeys to Frisia and Rome and, as his successor at Hexham, he had encouraged Stephen to produce his *Vita Wilfridi*; as Bede's diocesan and friend he supplied him with historical information, exchanged letters, and encouraged his production of theological commentaries, many of which were dedicated to him. His was an eventful life and an impressive episcopate.[1]

---

1   *The Life of Bishop Wilfrid by Eddius Stephanus*, ed. and trans. Bertram Colgrave (Cambridge, 1927), pp. 2, 46, 122; Bede, *Bede's Ecclesiastical History of the English People*, 3.13 (pp. 352–13), 4.13a (p. 376), 5.19 (p. 526), 5.20 (p. 530), 5.23 (p. 558), and p. 572, ed. and trans. Bertram Colgrave and Roger Mynors (Oxford, 1969); *Venerabilis Bedae, Opera Historica*, ed. Charles Plummer, 2 vols (Oxford, 1896), 1, pp. xv, xxxiii, xliv, xlix, cxlvii–cxlix, cliv; 2, pp. 330, 367; Dorothy Whitelock, "Bede and His Teachers and Friends," in *Famulus Christi*, ed. Gerald

© KONINKLIJKE BRILL NV, LEIDEN, 2021 | DOI:10.1163/9789004467514_014

Seemingly, however, his rule as bishop did not end well. One interpretation of a passage in Bede's preface to *De Templo* suggests that, at a date between 729 and 731, Acca was subject to some form of persecution – Bede sending the work to him knowing that the study of scriptures enabled the bishop "to daily gain relief from the present troubles of temporal affairs."[2] Whatever the implications of that remark, there is no doubt that in 731 he fled from his see, possibly as one casualty of the troubles which marked the early years of Ceolwulf's reign; certainly the king's difficulties and Acca's dismissal are linked together in an annal added to the *c.*737 Moore manuscript of the *Historia Ecclesiastica*:

Anno DCCXXXI *Ceoluulf rex captus et ad tonsus et remissus in regnum; Acca episcopus de sua sede fugatus*

731. King Ceolwulf was captured and tonsured and then restored to his kingdom; Bishop Acca was put to flight from his see.[3]

Bonner (London, 1976), pp. 19–39 at 26–27; Michael Lapidge, "Acca of Hexham and the Origin of the Old English Martyrology," *Analecta Bollandiana* 123 (2005), 29–78 at pp. 66–69 (but see Christine Rauer, *The Old English Martyrology* (Anglo-Saxon Texts 10) (Cambridge, 2013)); Michael Lapidge, *The Anglo-Saxon Library* (Oxford, 2006), pp. 42, 47–48, 233–34. The following papers track the subtleties of the evolving Bede/Acca relationship and fully reference earlier literature: Clare Stancliffe, "Disputed Episcopacy: Bede, Acca, and the Relationship between Stephen's Life of St Wilfrid and Early Prose Lives of St Cuthbert," *Anglo-Saxon England* 41 (2013), 7–39 and Clare Stancliffe, "Bede and Bishop Acca," in *Cities, Saints and Communities: Essays in Honour of Alan Thacker*, ed. Scott Gregorio and Paul Kershaw (Turnhout, 2020) pp. 171–194, together with Paul Hilliard, "Acca of Hexham through the Eyes of the Venerable Bede," *Early Medieval Europe* 26 (2018), 440–61.

2   "Praesentes rerum temporalium angores cotidie alleuare," *Bedae Venerabilis Opera, pars. II: Opera Exegetica*, ed. David Hurst (Corpus Christianorum, Series Latina 119A) (Turnhout, 1969), p. 144. Translation in: *Bede: On the Temple*, trans. Seán Connolly (Translated Texts for Historians 21) (Liverpool, 1995), pp. 2–3 where another interpretation is suggested.

3   Bede, *Bede's Ecclesiastical History*, pp. 572–73. Other translators prefer "fled from" for *fugatus* – see N.J. Higham, *(Re)reading Bede: the Ecclesiastical History in Context* (London, 2006), p. 64 and Joanna Story, "After Bede: Continuing the Ecclesiastical History," in *Early Medieval Studies in Memory of Patrick Wormald*, ed. Stephen Baxter, Catherine Karkov, *et al.* (Farnham, 2009), pp. 165–84 at 184 – but, as my colleague Jerry Paterson kindly observed, the form is more likely to be the past participle of *fugare* which would imply forced flight. For commentaries on this episode see: David Kirby, "Northumbria in the Time of Wilfrid," in *St Wilfrid at Hexham*, ed. D.P. Kirby (Newcastle upon Tyne, 1974), pp. 1–34 at 24–25; Whitelock, "Bede and his Teachers," p. 27; Lapidge, "Acca of Hexham," p. 68; Higham, *(Re)reading Bede*, pp. 62–65, 82–83, 192–93; Story, "After Bede," p. 172; Alan T. Thacker, "Wilfrid, his Cult and his Biographer," in *Wilfrid, Abbot, Bishop, Saint*, ed. N.J. Higham (Donington, 2013), pp. 1–16 at 16.

Where he sought refuge in this period is uncertain: Richard of Hexham (fl. 1141, d. 1163/1167) recorded a tradition of his spending a period at Whithorn while, among modern scholars, Woolf proposed an exile in Pictland, Fraser re-located him to Mercia, and Lapidge envisaged retirement at Hexham itself.[4] We have no evidence – as William of Malmesbury cautiously noted – as to whether he was ever reinstated to Hexham, though in 735 Archbishop Egbert consecrated Frithuberht as his successor to the bishopric.[5] Wherever he spent his final years he was clearly still widely recognised as sufficiently distinguished for his death in 740 to be recorded in northern chronicle sources.[6]

There is no direct contemporary, or even near-contemporary, evidence for Hexham as the location of his burial though, as we will see, twelfth-century writers asserted the truth of this tradition. There is, moreover, no trace of any early cult development at the site. Thus neither Acca nor Hexham figures in the c.1031 list of saints' resting places in Anglo-Saxon England (*De Locis Sanctis*),

---

4   Richard of Hexham, *de statu et episcopis Hagustaldensis ecclesie* in: *The Priory of Hexham*, ed. James Raine, 2 vols (Surtees Society 44, 46) (Durham, 1864, 1865), 1, p. 35. For other commentaries see Alex Woolf, "Onuist, Son of Uurguist, tyrannus carnifax or a David for the Picts," in *Aethelbald and Offa: Two Eighth-Century Kings of Mercia*, ed. David Hill and Margaret Worthington (British Archaeological Reports, British Series 383) (Oxford, 2005), pp. 35–42 at 37–38; Lapidge, "Acca of Hexham," pp. 68–69; James E. Fraser, *From Caledonia to Pictland: Scotland to 795* (Edinburgh, 2009), p. 309; Neil McGuigon, "Neither Scotland nor England: Middle Britain c. 850–1150," PhD thesis, University of St Andrews, 2015. Richard does not claim that Acca exercised episcopal powers at Whithorn (episcopal translation was in any case uncanonical though not unprecedented in the early Anglo-Saxon church: see Patrick Sims-Williams, *Religion and Literature in Western England, 600–800* (Cambridge, 1990), p. 338). Rather, his account refers to Acca preparing the foundations of an episcopal see at Whithorn which, since it was contiguous with the Hexham diocese, he may well have done – but not necessarily when in exile: see Peter Hill, *Whithorn and St Ninian: The Excavation of a Monastic Town* (Stroud, 1997), p. 18. William Skene, *Celtic Scotland: a History of Ancient Alban*, 3 vols (Edinburgh, 1876–1880), 2, pp. 272–74 argued, with some special pleading, for a St Andrews sojourn – a view supported more recently by Woolf, "Onuist," pp. 37–38, but rejected by Fraser, *From Caledonia*, p. 309. For a further suggestion see Éamonn Ó Carragáin, "The Company they Keep: Scholarly Discussion, 2005–2020 of the Original Settings for the Poems in the *Dream of the Rood* Tradition," Chapter 11 in this volume.

5   Bede, *Bede's Ecclesiastical History*, p. 572. For William of Malmesbury see *William of Malmesbury, Gesta Pontificum Anglorum*, ed. and trans. Michael Winterbottom, 2 vols (Oxford, 2007), 1, p. 389.

6   *Symeonis Monachi Opera Omnia*, ed. Thomas Arnold, 2 vols (Rolls Series 75) (London 1882–1885), 2, p. 33. The D, E, and F versions of the *Anglo-Saxon Chronicle* and John of Worcester record his death as in, respectively, 737 and 738: *The Anglo-Saxon Chronicle: a Collaborative Edition*, 7: MS E, ed. Susan Irvine (Cambridge, 2004), p. 36; *The Chronicle of John of Worcester*, ed. and trans. R.R. Darlington, P. McGurk, 3 vols (Oxford, 1995–1998), 2, p. 186.

parts of which were possibly assembled in the ninth century.[7] Curiously, the earliest record of the existence of *any* Accan cult sets it in Ripon, a location catalogued in a list of saints' resting places contained in the *Peterborough Chronicle* of Hugh Candidus, a work completed in or after 1155 but obviously drawing in part on pre-Conquest northern material.[8] While Hexham does figure in this list, it is only included as the resting place of King Ælfwald.[9]

All this uncertainty about the locations involved in Acca's final decade and the place of his burial thus provide a depressing prelude to the main purpose of this essay: assessing the evidence for the existence of an inscribed portable altar which one twelfth-century source claimed had been recovered, along with vestments, from the bishop's Hexham grave.

Recovering Accan Relics: The Earliest Records

Two early twelfth-century Durham texts give us our first glimpse of an Accan cult at Hexham, suggesting that it may already have been established by the eleventh century, if not long before. The first of these indications is provided by Symeon of Durham's *Libellus de Exordio*, a history of the Cuthbertine *Congregatio* and its successor Benedictine Durham community, which can be dated between 1104 and 1107/1115.[10] In it he gives a warm portrait of a sacristan in the pre-Benedictine body named Elfred who, at some date towards the middle of the eleventh century, gathered relics of early Northumbrian saints to Durham in acts designed to assert the legitimacy of the *Congregatio*'s position

---

7   D.W. Rollason, "Lists of Saints' Resting Places in Anglo-Saxon England," *Anglo-Saxon England* 7 (1978), 61–93; for doubts about the chronological distinctions within the consolidated list see Paul Everson and David Stocker, "Archaeology and Archiepiscopal Reform: Greater Churches in York Diocese in the 11th century," in *The Archaeology of the 11th Century: Continuities and Transformations*, ed. Dawn M. Hadley and Chris C. Dyer (London, 2017), pp. 177–202 at 197.

8   Rollason, "Saints' Resting Places," pp. 69–72; Lawrence Butler, "Two Twelfth-century Lists of Saints' Resting Places," *Analecta Bollandiana* 105 (1987), 87–103 at pp. 97, 98, and 102; *The Peterborough Chronicle of Hugh Candidus*, trans. Charles and William Thomas Mellows, 2nd ed. (Peterborough, 1997), pp. 25, 27; John Blair, *The Church in Anglo-Saxon Society* (Oxford, 2005), p. 502.

9   *Peterborough Chronicle*, p. 27; Butler, "Twelfth Century lists," pp. 94–99.

10   Text: *Symeon of Durham. Libellus de Exordio ... Dunhelmensis Ecclesie*, ed. and trans. David Rollason (Oxford, 2000); date: ibid., p. xlii; David Rollason, "Symeon of Durham's *Historia de Regibus Anglorum et Dacorum* as a Product of Twelfth-century Historical Workshops," in *The Long Twelfth-Century View of the Anglo-Saxon Past*, ed. Martin Brett and David A. Woodman (Farnham, 2015), pp. 95–112 at 98.

as the sole heir of the region's Christian past – and thus, vitally, to claim control of the churches and estates associated with those saints:

> *ossa sanctorum que in illis sepulta nouerat, de terra eleuauit, ac declaranda populis et ueneranda supra humum locata reliquit, ossa uidelicet ... Acce quoque et Alchmundi episcoporum Hagustaldensium ... De quorum omnium reliquiis aliquam secum partem in Dunhelmum asportauit, et cum patris Cuthberti corpore locauit.*[11]

He raised from the earth the bones of those saints whom he knew to be buried in these places and enshrined them above ground so that they might be better known to the people and venerated by them. The bones in question were ... the bishops of Hexham Acca and Alchmund ... He took a certain part of all these relics back to Durham with him, and enshrined them with the body of father Cuthbert.[12]

A second Durham document, *An account of the early provosts of Hexham*, composed at some date between 1083 and 1124/1127, gives a short summary of the same Elfredian intrusion at Hexham – while helpfully supplying the sacristan's patronymic:

> *Eluredus, Westou sune, secretaries Dunelmensis ecclesiæ, dono domini sui Edmundi episcopi, tenuit ecclesiam de Hagustaldaham ... Iste Eluredus partem de reliquiis episcoporum, qui apud Hagustal'h' antiquitus fuerant ibidemque sepulti, transtulit Dunelmo, et cum Sancto Cuthberto incorrupto collocavit.*

Elfred, the son of Westou, sacrist of the church of Durham, through the grant of his lord Bishop Edmund, held the church of Hexham ... This Elfred translated to Durham parts of the relics of the bishops, who had been in ancient times at Hexham and buried in the same place, and placed them with the incorrupt St Cuthbert.[13]

---

11 *Symeon, Libellus*, p. 162.
12 Rollason, trans., *Symeon, Libellus*, pp. 162–64.
13 Text: Richard of Hexham, Raine, *Priory*, 1, p. viii; translation: author. For date of composition see Ralph Walterspacher, *The Foundation of Hexham Priory, 1070–1170* (Papers in North Eastern History 11) (Middlesborough, 2002), p. 8.

Recovering Accan Relics: Twelfth-Century Hexham Sources

Later in date, though still within the twelfth century, are the accounts of the Elfred excavation preserved in three Hexham-derived sources. All were documents written against the background of the complex relationships between Benedictine Durham and Augustinian Hexham which played out in the course of the twelfth century and which have been sensitively analysed by Ralph Walterspacher and Naomi Luff in recent publications.[14]

The first of these texts is Richard of Hexham's *de Statu et episcopis Hagustaldensis ecclesie*.[15] This takes the story of Hexham from the Anglo-Saxon period through to 1113/1114; it was possibly composed before the 1154/1155 translation of Hexham's saintly relics into the new Augustinian church, and certainly pre-dates Richard's death in 1163/1167.[16] The focus of the work was on the legitimacy and transformational impact of the Archbishop of York's role in establishing the Augustinian priory at Hexham, together with an assertion of the strength of Hexham's relic collection when set against that of Durham. In chapter 15 Richard chronicled Acca's flight from Hexham, recording the tradition that, after a period in Candida Casa (Whithorn), he was subsequently buried at Hexham next to his sanctuary (*juxta secretarium suæ*).[17] While echoing Symeon's story of the eleventh-century discovery of the tomb he asserts, in contrast to Symeon's claims, that no relics were removed from Hexham by Elfred Westou; on the contrary, his corporeal remains were first set in a remote part of the church (*intra ecclesiam in remotioribus partibus*) but later given a place of prominence around the altar.[18] Richard further claims that it was a sign of Acca's saintly merits that the fabrics originally enclosing his remains (*sudarium lineum, et casula, et tunicæ sericæ*) were still visibly beautiful, pristine, and strong in his own day.[19]

The second Hexham text is Ailred of Rievaulx's *De sanctis ecclesiae Haugustaldensis*, which was written after Richard's death in 1163/1167, and was designed to be read at the annual commemoration of the 1154/1155 translation of relics of multiple saints into the Augustinian church; it may indeed be a re-writing of the sermon preached on that occasion since some chapters are

---

14 Walterspacher, *Foundation*; Alexandra Naomi Mary Luff, "The Place of Durham Cathedral Priory in the Post-Conquest Spiritual Life of the North East," PhD thesis, University of Durham, 2001, pp. 80–103, 133–44.

15 Raine, *Priory*, 1, pp. 1–106.

16 Luff, *Place of Priory*, p. 169; Walterspacher, *Foundation*, pp. 10, 33.

17 Raine, *Priory*, 1, pp. 34–35.

18 Raine, *Priory*, 1, p. 49.

19 Raine, *Priory*, 1, pp. 34, 36.

clearly additions to the original work, interrupting its narrative.[20] Like Richard he stressed Hexham's ecclesiastical autonomy but, in contrast to Richard's account, Ailred gave more attention to the role of the pre-Augustinian clerics, who were in fact members of his own family, in the preservation of relics and forging of links to York.[21] In pursuit of this agenda he naturally included the Accan translation by Elfred Westou, his great grandfather, and, like Richard, stressed that he did not remove any relics to Durham:

> *Sacras illas reliquias absportare noluit, uel non potuit; sedeas intra ecclesiam honeste recondens, uenerationi locorum, deuotioni presentium, profectui futurorum, diuina gratia disponente, consulit*[22]

He was unwilling, or unable, to take away these sacred relics [of Acca]. He concealed them decently inside the church, taking thought for veneration of places, the devotion of people of his time, and the improvement of those to come, as divine grace directed him.[23]

Like Richard, Ailred identifies a group of liturgical vestments which were still preserved at Hexham as having derived from Elfred Westou's excavation. They were "speaking signs" (*signa loquentia*) of Acca's sanctity which could still be seen and touched. These *signa* were:

---

20 Text: *Aelredus Rievalensis, Opera Omnia 6: Opera Historica et Hagiographica*, ed. Domenico Pezzini (Corpus Christianorum Continuatio Mediaevalis 3) (Turnhout, 2017), pp. 75–110; authorship: Anselm Hoste, *Bibliotheca Aelrediana* (Steenbrugge, 1962), pp. 127–28; re-writing explanation: Luff, *Place of Priory*, p. 133; recent studies: Marsha Dutton, "Saints Refusing to Leave: Aelred of Rievaulx's The Saints of Hexham as Inverted Translation: Tradition, Innovation, and Devotion in Twelfth-century Northern England," *The Medieval Translator* 12 (2012), 187–200 and Lauren L. Whitnah, "Aelred of Rievaulx and the Saints of Hexham," *Church History* 87 (2018), 1–30.

21 *Aelredus Rievalensis*, pp. 94–97. For Ailred's family connections see Luff, *Place of Priory*, fig. 2.3.

22 *Aelredus Rievalensis*, p. 94; similarly he asserts that Bishop Alchmund's corporeal remains could not be moved from Hexham: *Aelredus Rievalensis*, p. 99 and see also p. 103.

23 Translation from *Ailred of Rievaulx: the Lives of the Northern Saints*, trans. Jane Patricia Freeland and Marsha L. Dutton (Cistercian Fathers Series 71) (Kalamazoo, 2006), p. 88. In a subsequent passage Ailred does, however, admit that some parts of Acca's bones had indeed been removed: *Aelredus Rievalensis*, p. 99. The importance of the integrity of the relics and their unbroken association with Hexham is illuminatingly discussed in Dutton, "Saints Refusing." For post-Elfred translations see Pezzini, *Aelredus Rievalensis*, pp. 95–96, 99.

sanctissimas eius uestes, quibus sacre eius reliquie in terra trecentis annis fuerunt obuolute ... Habetis certe casulam eius sericam, similiter et dalmaticam, sudarium quoque lineum, in quibus uenustas antiqua seruatur, pristina fortitudo perdurat.[24]

sacred garments in which his holy relics were wrapped in the earth for three hundred years ... Surely you possess his silk chasuble and similarly his dalmatic, as well as a linen cloth in which the former beauty is preserved, and the original strength endures.[25]

The final twelfth-century Hexham-derived source gives us the fullest account of Westou's discoveries and, unlike all others, describes the finding of a portable altar along with the vestments identified in the other documents. It survives in a Durham manuscript, now Cambridge, Corpus Christi College 139, a complex work containing a number of chronicles which have been stitched together to provide a history from the late seventh century through to 1129.[26] The manuscript has been dated to 1164–1175 but may be as late as 1180.[27] Among

---

24   *Aelredus Rievalensis*, p. 88.

25   Translation from Freeland and Dutton, *Ailred of Rievaulx*, p. 80.

26   Text in *Symeonis Monachi*, 2, pp. 1–283. A new edition of the text, edited by M. Lapidge and D. Rollason, is forthcoming in which the title has been emended to *Historia de Regibus Anglorum et Dacorum*. Major studies of the manuscript, its components, provenance, and textual elements are Peter Hunter Blair, "Some Observations on the 'Historia Regum' Attributed to Symeon of Durham," in *Celt and Saxon: Studies in the Early British Border*, ed. Kenneth Jackson *et al.* (Cambridge, 1964), pp. 63–118; Hilary Seaton Offler, "Hexham and the Historia Regum," *Transactions of the Architectural and Archaeological Society of Durham and Northumberland* 2 (1970), 51–62; Derek Baker, "Scissors and Paste: Corpus Christi, Cambridge 139 again," *Studies in Church History* 11 (1975), 83–123; Michael Lapidge, "Byrhtferth of Ramsey and the Early Sections of the *Historia Regum* Attributed to Symeon of Durham," *Anglo-Saxon England* 10 (1982), 97–122 (reprinted in his *Anglo-Latin Literature 900–1066* (London, 1993), pp. 317–42); Cyril Hart, "Byhrtferth's Northumbrian Chronicle," *English Historical Review* 97 (1982), 558–82; Bernard Meehan, "Durham Twelfth-century Manuscripts in Cistercian Houses," in *Anglo-Norman Durham 1093–1193*, ed. David Rollason, Margaret Harvey, and Michael Prestwich (Woodbridge, 1994), pp. 439–49; Christopher Norton, "History, Wisdom and Illumination," in *Symeon of Durham: Historian of Durham and the North*, ed. David Rollason (Stamford, 1998), pp. 61–105; David Rollason, "Symeon's Contribution to Historical Writing in Northern England," in Rollason, *Symeon of Durham, Historian*, pp. 1–13 at 10; *Symeon, Libellus*, p. xlviii; *Historia de Sancto Cuthberto: a History of Saint Cuthbert and a Record of his Patrimony*, ed. Ted Johnson South (Anglo-Saxon Texts 3) (Cambridge, 2002), pp. 10–11; Rollason, "Symeon of Durham's *Historia de Regibus Anglorum et Dacorum*," pp. 95–112.

27   Luff, *Place of Priory*, p. 183; Walterspacher, *Foundation*, p. 25; Rollason, "Symeon of Durham's *Historia de Regibus*," p. 102 (for later date of 1180).

these texts is the only complete version of the *Historia Regum* (hereafter *Hist. Reg.*), which itself drew upon a wide range of source materials. In recent years a series of subtle analyses have demonstrated that the surviving text passed through a sequence of changes and amendments but, as it survives, was finally re-worked in Durham after passing through a Hexham recension.[28] Inevitably there has been disagreement as to the date when these 'Hexham interpolations' entered the chain of textual transmission though all historians agree that this took place no earlier than the twelfth century.[29] It should, of course, be noted that the date of entry to textual transmission does not furnish us with the origin date of its narratives.

Our concern here is with one of two long interpolations under the years 740 and 781 which have been inserted into a section consisting of a chronicle from 732–802, the contents of which are otherwise largely derived from Byrhtferth of Ramsey.[30] Both interpolations are distinctive in that under the year of a saint's death they give an account of a translation some 250/300 years later – and both are lengthy narratives set in the middle of short annals. The second of these, under the year 781, concerns the death of Bishop Alchmund, and the subsequent translation of his remains 250 years later by Elfred Westou. The earlier entry occurs under the year 740 where the *Hist. Reg.* records Acca's death and follows this with a long interpolated section describing how Acca was buried:

> *ad orientalem plagam extra parietem ecclesiæ Haugustaldensis ... Duæque cruces lapideæ mirabili celatura decoratæ positæ sunt, una ad caput, alia ad pedes ejus. ... De quo loco post annos plusquam ccc. depositionis suæ a quodam presbytero divina revelatione translatus est, ac in ecclesia intra feretrum condigno honore positus est ... Ob cujus sanctitatis meritum omnibus demonstrandum casula et tunica et sudarium, quæ cum sanctissimo ejus corpore in terra posita erant, non solum speciem, sed etiam fortitudinem pristinam usque in hodiernum diem servant. Inventa est etiam super pectus ejus tabula lignea in modum altaris facta ex duobus lignis clavis argenteis conjuncta, sculptaque est in illa scriptura hæc: "Almæ Trinitati, agiæ Sophiæ, Sanctæ Mariæ". ... Vestimenta vero ejus prædicta fratres ejusdem*

---

28   Walterspacher, *Foundation*, pp. 22–24; Luff, *Place of Priory*, p. 183.

29   Blair, "Some Observations," pp. 89–90; Offler, "Hexham and Historia," p. 53; Luff, *Place of Priory*, pp. 169, 183; Walterspacher, *Foundation*, p. 29; Rollason, "Symeon of Durham's *Historia de Regibus Anglorum et Dacorum*," pp. 101–04, fig. 6.1.

30   *Symeonis Monachi*, 2, pp. 32–38, 47–50. For Byrhtferth's role see Lapidge, "Byrhtferth of Ramsey."

Hagustaldensis ecclesiæ aliquotiens populo monstrare solent, a quo cum omni devotione deosculantur.[31]

on the outside of the wall, at the east end of the church at Hexham ... Two stone crosses, adorned with exquisite carving, were placed, the one at his head, the other at his feet. ... From this place, more than three hundred years after his burial, he was translated in consequence of a divine revelation made to a certain priest, and was placed in a shrine in the church ... As a testimony to all of the merit of his sanctity, the chasuble, tunic, and sudarium, which were placed in the tomb with his sacred body, preserve to this day not only their form but their original strength. There was found upon his breast a wooden tablet, in the form of an altar, made of two pieces of wood joined with silver nails, on which is the inscription: '*Almæ Trinitati; agiæ Sophiæ; Sanctæ Mariæ*'. ... The brethren of the church of Hexham are wont frequently to show the aforesaid vestments to the people by whom they are kissed with every mark of reverence.[32]

The text then goes on to list miracles associated with these relics.

There can be little doubt that the three Hexham-derived documents are describing the same translation event as was chronicled by Symeon and the *Early Provosts*, even though the *Hist. Reg.* does not record the name of the "certain priest" who organised the translation. It does however record his name for the associated Alchmund translation.[33]

Acca's Grave?

These accounts clearly raise questions about historical veracity. Three issues are immediately apparent: the plausibility of locating any such burial outside the east wall of the church as claimed by Richard and the *Hist. Reg.*; the likelihood of Acca's burial in the episcopal see from which he had earlier taken flight; and, finally, the possibility of Elfred identifying Acca's grave and remains some three centuries after their original interment.

There is no problem with the first issue. Burial outside the east wall of the main church, as in the *Hist. Reg.* account (or close to the *secretarium* as claimed

---

31   *Symeonis Monachi*, 2, p. 33.
32   Translation from *Symeon of Durham, A History of the Kings of England*, trans. Joseph Stevenson (1858; repr. Lampeter, 1987), p. 29.
33   *Symeonis Monachi*, 2, p. 48.

by Richard of Hexham) is archaeologically entirely plausible, for this does seem to have been a prestigious site both in Britain and in continental Europe: Eric Cambridge has shown that the small apsed structure lying to the east of Wilfrid's main monastic church at Hexham was possibly, by analogy with similar buildings at Whithorn, Repton, and Gloucester and in Gaul, the mausoleum of the martyred king Ælfwald (d. 788), and it was certainly surrounded by elaborate sarcophagi-enclosed burials which must pre-date the Augustinian church.[34] This was, then, a likely site for a high status burial of a bishop.

The difficulty of claiming that Acca had been buried in an episcopal foundation from which he had previously fled exposes our lack of information about the circumstances and the length of his exile. There are, however, two explanations which do not run counter to the meagre evidence we do possess.[35] We have seen that, in some way, his 731 flight was linked in near-contemporary records to Ceolwulf's deposition. Unfortunately we do not know with which of the warring secular parties Acca was aligned. If he was *opposed* to Ceolwulf then the bishop's withdrawal would have been a natural consequence of the king's return to power. But by 740 another member of Ceolwulf's family had succeeded to the throne and Acca may thus have returned to political and ecclesiastical favour, while never being restored to his original see. Alternatively, as a Ceolwulf *supporter*, he could have been temporarily exiled but then returned to Hexham to exercise his episcopal rights for a brief period before withdrawing to a contemplative life for his final years and being replaced by Frithuberht; the lengthy period between his 731 exile and Frithuberht's accession some four years later would thus be readily explained.[36] Whatever the circumstances, a burial at Hexham is thus not so improbable as at first appears.

Even assuming that Acca *was* buried at Hexham, what credence should we place on Elfred's claimed ability to identify his grave among the other high status burials in that area of the site? Was he for example – and to take the most cynical view – merely excavating *a* body from Hexham which could be claimed

---

34   Eric Cambridge and Alan Williams, "Hexham Abbey: a Review of Recent Work and its Implications," *Archaeologia Aeliana*, 5th ser., 23 (1995), 1–138 at pp. 79–80.

35   For material in this paragraph about Acca's factional alignments and his final years see Kirby, "Northumbria," pp. 24–25; Fraser, *From Caledonia*, p. 309; Higham, *(Re)reading Bede*, p. 64.

36   See Lapidge, "Acca of Hexham," pp. 68–69 and Higham, *(Re)reading Bede*, p. 64. The hiatus in the York episcopacy may also have contributed to a delay in consecration of a new Hexham bishop. For documented eighth-century episcopal resignations see Catherine Cubitt, "Wilfrid's 'usurping bishops': Episcopal Elections in Anglo-Saxon England, c. 600–c. 800," *Northern History* 25 (1989), 18–38 at pp. 28–29.

as Acca's, in order to boost Durham's relic collection of Northumbrian saints mentioned in the works of Bede?

As a first step towards answering such a basic question it is worth stressing that, as at Jarrow and Lindisfarne, the demise of Northumbrian monastic communities in the course of the ninth century did not result in a total loss of occupation or liturgical activity at these sites: the sculptural evidence for such continuity is clear at Hexham.[37] There is therefore no reason why historical traditions, including the location of famous burials, should not have been transmitted over the three centuries which separated Acca from Elfred Westou. Indeed, if we accept Neil McGuigan's recent suggestion that the Hexham see survived into the tenth century, then the possibility of episcopal graves being marked and honoured to a date nearer Elfred's intervention would be immeasurably strengthened.[38] Nor should we forget that Elfred, as well as being sacristan of Durham, was effectively 'prebendary' of Hexham.[39] His Durham duties would prevent him from exercising an active priesthood at Hexham – hence his appointment of two successive vicars in his place to look after spiritualities– but that position must have given him ready access to both the church and, through local informants, the history of Hexham. His excavation of Alchmund's remains was, indeed, informed by a local inhabitant called Dregmo.[40]

There is perhaps one further implication to be drawn from these three Hexham sources. Elfred's location problems would have been much eased if Acca's grave had remained marked as 'special' in some way in the years after his death. There is, admittedly, no written or archaeological evidence for the existence of an elaborate shrine centred on his grave before Westou's translation – at which eleventh-century stage Acca's bones (actual or assumed) were clearly regarded as those of a saint worthy of acquisition.[41] But this need not imply that there was no earlier local cult in existence, which could have been focussed on a below-ground interment: we know from parallel instances that formal

---

37   The evidence is summarised in Richard N. Bailey and Eric Cambridge, "Dating the Old English poem 'Durham,'" *Medium Ævum* 85 (2016), 1–14 at p. 7.

38   Neil McGuigon, "Neither Scotland nor England: Middle Britain c. 850–1150," PhD thesis, University of St Andrews, 2015, pp. 61–62, 79–80, 180–82.

39   Raine, *Priory*, 1, p. viii; Luff, *Place of Priory*, pp. 87–89, fig. 2.3.

40   *Symeonis Monachi*, 2, p. 47. Stevenson, *Symeon of Durham*, p. 38, suggested that "dregmo" was a description of the man's status. The *Hist. Reg.* does not record the name of the *quodam presbytero* who first translated Acca's remains, but he is identified as Elfred Westou in the Alchmund account: *Symeonis Monachi*, 2, p. 48.

41   *Symeon, Libellus*, p. 163.

translation of remains to an above-ground positioning was not a necessary concomitant of establishing sainthood.[42]

This brief review exposes the extent to which inference and special pleading are inevitably involved in any claim that Elfred Westou managed to recover the actual remains of Acca and associated relics. It is quite likely that he translated a high-status burial but – on the evidence available to us – not necessarily that of Acca himself.

The Portable Altar and Associated Relics

Even if we were to accept the veracity of Elfred Westou's translation of what could be identified as Acca's remains, we are then confronted by the problem of whether he also actually discovered the associated vestments and portable altar which are recorded in the Hexham-based accounts.[43] Are they, in essence, no more than a twelfth-century invention designed to match the vestments and portable altar discovered by the Durham monks on the opening of St Cuthbert's coffin in 1104?[44] Historians have frequently expressed their reservations on this issue; Hunter Blair, for example, commenting on the 'propagandist' nature of the *Hist. Reg.* interpolations, drew sceptical attention to these coincidences: "Acca's vestments were no less well preserved than Cuthbert's, and if there was a portable altar in the tomb of Cuthbert, so also was there one in Acca's."[45]

We begin with the fabrics. Richard, Ailred, and the *Hist. Reg.* all refer to the survival into the twelfth century of what were claimed to be Acca's

---

42   For variation in above-ground and subterranean enshrinement see John Blair, "A Saint for Every Minster? Local Cults in Anglo-Saxon England," in *Local Saints and Local Churches in the Early Medieval West*, ed. Alan Thacker and Richard Sharpe (Oxford, 2002), pp. 455–94 at 490–94; John Blair, *The Church in Anglo-Saxon Society* (Oxford, 2005), pp. 145–48. *Aelredus Rievalensis*, 89, 103 records liturgical celebrations of Acca's feast day in the pre-Augustinian period, but this is not, of course, evidence for any pre-Elfred feast.

43   Raine, *Priory*, 1, p. 36; *Aelredus Rievalensis*, p. 88; *Symeonis Monachi*, 2, p. 33. The near-contemporary evidence of St Cuthbert's burial attests to the tradition of burying a priest wearing sacerdotal vestments: *Two Lives of St Cuthbert*, ed. Bertram Colgrave (Cambridge, 1940), pp. 130–31.

44   *The Relics of St Cuthbert*, ed. C.F. Battiscombe (Oxford, 1956), pp. 375–525; *St Cuthbert, His Cult and his Community*, ed. Gerald Bonner, Clare Stancliffe, and David Rollason (Woodbridge, 1989), pp. 287–366; Eric Cambridge, "Reconsidering Cuthbert's Relics," in *The St Cuthbert Gospel: Studies on the Insular Manuscript of the Gospel of St John*, ed. Claire Breay and Bernard Meehan (London, 2015), pp. 115–27 at 116–17.

45   Blair, "Some Observations," p. 89.

ecclesiastical vestments. Richard catalogued them as consisting of *sudarium lineum, casula,* and *tunica sericæ* – a listing repeated in the *Hist. Reg.* – whilst Ailred offered the minor variation of *casulam ... sericam, dalmaticam, sudarium ... lineum.*[46] All three texts show that these vestments were accessible for veneration at Hexham in the mid-twelfth century, and miracles associated with them were recorded by Richard – and in the early thirteenth-century additions to the recension of Ailred's *De Sanctis* text which is now London, British Library, Additional 38816, fol. 16r.[47] Furthermore two Durham relic lists of the fourteenth century both catalogue Accan fabrics, including specifically *de sudario et de casulae jusdem.*[48] These presumably came to Durham in the course of the later twelfth century when Durham/Hexham relationships had reached a more amicable phase than earlier in that century.[49]

Unfortunately the undoubted twelfth-century existence of episcopal vestments in no way guarantees that they derived from an eleventh-century excavation of an eighth-century grave.

---

46   Raine, *Priory*, 1, p. 36; *Aelredus Rievalensis*, p. 88; *Symeonis Monachi*, 2, p. 33. For summary studies of these classes of vestment see Elizabeth Coatsworth and Gale R. Owen-Crocker, *Clothing the Past* (Leiden, 2018).

47   Raine, *Priory*, 1, p. 36; Cadwallader J. Bates, "Three Additional Miracles Attributed to Saint Acca of Hexham," *Archaeologia Aeliana*, ser. 2, 20 (1898), 289–94. As Walterspacher, *Foundation*, p. 22 notes, the wider impact of Hexham's vestment holdings can perhaps be seen in Reginald of Durham's *Libellus de Admirandis Beati Cuthberti*. Written in the 1160s, its description of the Cuthbert translation of 1104 devotes the whole of chapters 40 and 41 to the beauty of the vestments discovered: Battiscombe, *Relics*, pp. 109–12.

48   Raine, *Priory*, 1, p. ccccxxviii; *Durham Account Rolls*, ed. Joseph Fowler, 3 vols (Surtees Society 99, 100, 103) (Durham, 1899–1901), 2, p. 431. The non-appearance of Accan relics in the eleventh-century Old English poem *Durham* can be explained by its concentration on figures associated with St Cuthbert; for the date of this poem see Bailey and Cambridge, "Dating 'Durham'." Fourteenth-century Durham relic lists do include Accan items, respectively *sudario* and *casula* in the York manuscript (Raine, *Priory*, 1, p. ccccxxviii) and *casula, sindone,* and *sudario* in the de Segbruk list of 1383–1384 (*Durham Account Rolls*, 2, pp. 428, 431, 435). Both these later lists imply the presence also of other (unspecified) Accan relics. The earliest Durham relic list does not include Accan material: for text see Battiscombe, *Relics*, pp. 113–14 and for comments see Luff, *Place of Priory*, pp. 142, 181, 189 and Walterspacher, *Foundation*, p. 19.

49   Whether Peterborough's holding of an unspecified Accan relic, or relics, recorded by Hugh Candidus in 1115 represents a further onward transmission of material from Durham in the twelfth century, or was the result of much earlier gift or robbery from a putative Durham holding during the pre-Benedictine period is uncertain – as is the source of material held by Hyde Abbey; see Mellows, *Peterborough Chronicle*, p. 25. For Durham-Peterborough relationships in the mid-eleventh century see Bailey and Cambridge, "'Dating Durham'," pp. 7–9, 13 and, for Hyde Abbey holdings, see *Liber Vitae: Register and Martyrology of New Minster and Hyde Abbey, Winchester*, ed. Walter de Gray Birch (London, 1892), pp. 148, 149.

What, then, of the more interesting and challenging relic: the portable altar which is described in the *Hist. Reg.* as "a wooden tablet, in the form of an altar, made of two pieces of wood joined with silver nails: on which is this inscription: '*Almæ Trinitati; Agiæ Sophiæ; Sanctæ Mariæ*'."[50]

As we have seen, only the *Hist. Reg.* Hexham interpolator records its presence when (what were claimed to be) Acca's remains were translated by Elfred Westou in the mid-eleventh century; unlike the vestments it does not figure in the near contemporary accounts by Richard and Ailred.[51] This discrepancy in the records has inevitably raised suspicions that the object was a twelfth-century invention to match the portable altar discovered in 1104 at the translation of St Cuthbert in Durham.[52] There are, however, several possible arguments against such claims. First, if it were a response to Durham's possession of an altar associated with St Cuthbert, then it was a very modest one: silver nails holding two pieces of wood together can hardly be claimed to match the twelfth-century appearance of the Durham relic as it is described in *De Miraculis et Translationibus Sancti Cuthberti* (the so-called 'Anonymous Account') of 1124 or Reginald of Durham's account written in 1167: both refer to it as a *silver* altar (respectively *altare videlicet argenteum* and *altare argentium*).[53] Secondly, given that the Durham silver encasing represents enshrinement and further modifications of the eighth and early ninth century, it is at least arguable that the Hexham altar, with its wooden fabric and brief incised dedication, is closer to the original late seventh-/early eighth-century appearance of Cuthbert's altar than to the form of the Durham relic as it became known in the twelfth century.[54] What is more, the twelfth-century Durham accounts of the Cuthbertian altar make no mention of any dedication inscription – the threefold dedication of Hexham's altar cannot therefore be interpreted as any type of response to Durham's relic as it was recorded in the twelfth century.[55]

---

50   *Symeonis Monachi*, 2, p. 33.

51   Raine, *Priory*, 1, p. 36; *Aelredus Rievalensis*, p. 88.

52   C.A. Ralegh Radford, "The Portable Altar of St Cuthbert," in Battiscombe, *Relics*, pp. 326–35; Elizabeth Coatsworth, "The Pectoral Cross and Portable Altar from the Tomb of St Cuthbert," in *St Cuthbert, His Cult*, pp. 287–301 at 296–301.

53   *Symeonis Monachi*, 1, p. 255; *Reginald's Libellus de Admirandis Beati Cuthberti Virtutibus*, ed. James Raine (Surtees Society 1) (Durham 1835), p. 89. Translations in Battiscombe, *Relics*, pp. 103, 111.

54   For the dating of the various phases see Coatsworth, "Pectoral Cross," pp. 296–301; L[eslie] W[ebster], "Portable Altar," in *The Making of England*, ed. Leslie Webster and Janet Backhouse (London, 1991), pp. 134–35.

55   The earliest record of an inscription on the Cuthbert altar is contained in Raine's report on his 1827 excavations: James Raine, *St Cuthbert: with an Account of the State in which his Remains were Found ... in the year MDCCCXXVII* (Durham, 1828), pp. 199–202. Note

And, lastly and negatively, the figures and themes of the Hexham inscription in no way resemble those of dedications on known twelfth-century altars.[56] The fact that the *Hist. Reg.* describes the altar, whilst Richard and Ailred make no mention of the object – despite all three texts being near-contemporary in date and, presumably, drawing on similar local Hexham information – can also be readily explained: Richard and Ailred are concentrating on Hexham's (then) contemporary possession of miracle-working bones and *accessible, visible* vestments; the altar could well have rotted away by their date, and its former existence was not directly relevant to their agendas.[57]

All this granted, does the *Hist. Reg.* description suggest that such an object could have existed in Acca's period if not, as we have cautioned above, actually once the possession of the saint himself?

There is, first, no problem about an altar made of wood for, although successive church councils attempted to legislate for the use of stone, it is clear that many early examples were fashioned from timber.[58] Bede's account of the c. 695 martyrdom of the Hewalds in Germany in referring to their possession of a "consecrated board instead of an altar" (*tabulam altaris uice dedicatem*)

---

also that the *Hist. Reg.* claims not to know why the altar was placed with Acca and makes no cross-reference to Cuthbert's relics: *Symeonis Monachi*, 2, 33. See also Helen Foxhall Forbes, *Heaven and Earth in Anglo-Saxon England: Theology and Society in an Age of Faith* (Farnham, 2013), p. 326.

56   Rudolph Favreau, "Les Autels portatifs et leurs inscriptions," *Cahiers de civilization médiévale* 46 (2003), 327–52.

57   The agendas of Richard and Ailred are perceptively examined in Luff, *Place of Priory*, pp. 133–39, 168–77.

58   In general on portable altars see Joseph Braun, *Der christliche Altar in seiner geschichtlichen Entwicklung*, 2 vols (Munich, 1924), 1, pp. 419–523; Thomas Jerome Welsh, *The Use of the Portable Altar: A Historical Synopsis and a Commentary* (Washington, D.C., 1950); Lisa Bailey, "The Strange Case of the Portable Altar: Liturgy and the Limits of Episcopal Authority in Early Medieval Gaul," *Journal of the Australian Early Medieval Association* 8 (2012), 31–51. Catalogues of medieval portable altars can be found in Michael Budde, *Altare Portatile; Kompendium der Tragältare des Mittelalters 600–1600*, 3 vols (Münster, 1999) and Eric Palazzo, *L'Espace ritual et le sacré dans le christianisme: la liturgie de l'autel portative dans l'Antiquité et au Moyen Âge* (Culture et Société Médiévales 15) (Turnhout, 2008), esp. pp. 74–78, 135–48, 154–60. For insular medieval portable altars in stone see Charles Thomas, *The Early Christian Archaeology of North Britain* (London, 1971), pp. 194–98 and Blair, *Church in Anglo-Saxon Society*, p. 376. For an early sixth-century Gaulish synod's attempt to stipulate the use of stone for portable altars see Bailey, "Strange Case," p. 42 and for similar later initiatives see Favreau, "Les Autels," p. 328 and Palazzo, *L'Espace*, pp. 120–35. As late as the eleventh century in England, Wulfstan of Worcester was still attempting to enforce the use of stone for large-scale altars in his diocese: Blair, *Church in Anglo-Saxon Society*, pp. 496–97 with references.

shows that the Cuthbert and Hexham items were not alone in this respect.[59]
And though I can find no adequate parallel for the particular two-part form
of altar specified in the *Hist. Reg.*, a sandwiched arrangement would have permitted enclosure of some form of *brandea* between the two leaves – the presence of a relic within or below an altar was already accepted practice before
it became a formal requirement of full-scale altars after the second Council of
Nicaea in 787.

The intriguing element, of course, is the inscription:

ALMÆ TRINITATI: AGIÆ SOPHIÆ: SANCTÆ MARIÆ

All three of these invocations find their parallels within eighth-century texts.
Thus *almus* as a characteristic of the Trinity is evoked in the envoi to Aldhelm's
De Virginate and in Bede's *Historia Ecclesiastica*.[60] Similarly *Sanctæ Mariæ* is a
ubiquitous collocation in ecclesiastical and liturgical texts from, at least, the
time of Pope Sergius' establishment of Marian festivals in the period 687–701.[61]
En passant it might also be noted that Mary's very inclusion in the triple dedication chimes well with Bullough's deductions from a group of Alcuin antiphons
which, in his words, "points to a well-developed and largely unsuspected cult
of the Virgin, with an unmistakable doctrinal basis, in the northern English
church in which Alcuin spent his adolescence and early manhood," a cult
which is also reflected in the mid-eighth century Ruthwell cross.[62]

---

59   Bede, *Bede's Ecclesiastical History*, 5.10 (p. 482). For an example from early sixth-century
       Gaul see Bailey, "Strange Case," p. 32.

60   *Aldhelmi Malmesbiriensis Prosa de Virginitate*, ed. Scott Gwara, 2 vols (Corpus Chris-
       tianorum Series Latina 124, 124A) (Turnhout, 2001), 2, p. 761; Bede, *Bede's Ecclesiastical
       History*, 4.20 (p. 396). The collocation continues throughout the Anglo-Saxon period: see,
       i.a., the tenth- and eleventh-century charters, Peter Sawyer, *Anglo-Saxon Charters: an
       Annotated List and Bibliography* (London, 1968), nos. 836 and 947.

61   Donald Bullough, "Alcuin and the Kingdom of Heaven: Liturgy, Theology and the Carolin-
       gian Age," in *Carolingian Renewal: Sources and Heritage*, ed. Donald Bullough (Manches-
       ter, 1991), pp. 161–240 at 166. On the impact on Northumbria of Sergius' establishment
       of four Marian festivals see Mary Clayton, "Feasts of the Virgin Mary in the Liturgy of
       Anglo-Saxon Church," *Anglo-Saxon England* 13 (1984), 209–33 and Éamonn Ó'Carragáin,
       *Ritual and the Rood: Liturgical Images and the Old English Poems of the "Dream of the Rood"
       Tradition* (London, 2005), passim but especially pp. 97–99, 238, 246. On the dedication
       of the Wilfridian church in Hexham to *Sancta Maria* see Colgrave, *Life of Bishop Wilfrid*,
       pp. 123, 137. For the collocation in Anglo-Saxon litanies see *Anglo-Saxon Litanies of the
       Saints*, ed. Michael Lapidge (Henry Bradshaw Society 106) (London, 1991), pp. 93, 98,
       100, etc.

62   Bullough, "Alcuin and the Kingdom," p. 177; Ó'Carragáin, *Ritual and Rood*, passim.

It is, however, the central dedication to *Agiæ Sophiæ* which has naturally aroused more scholarly interest since it involves a Greek adjective for 'holy' and a Greek noun for the concept of Wisdom. But, like the other two dedications, this would also not be out of place in the eighth century. Explanation of the presence of both words, moreover, does not need to invoke discussions of Canterbury's late seventh-century Greek scholarship, with a potential transmission to Northumbria through John the Archcantor or through Acca's liturgical singer Maban.[63] Nor do we need to become involved in the problems of assessing knowledge of Greek at Jarrow in Bede's early eighth-century period.[64] Both words were well established in insular liturgical and exegetical literature by the late seventh century. Admittedly the use of *Sophia* for 'wisdom' is not found in Bede's numerous writings on this topic (many of which are dedicated to Acca), but in Bullough's words it is "commonplace in Aldhelm as well as in Alcuin's own writing."[65]

The adjective *Agios* was a similarly well-established lexical item. Its most obvious liturgical statement can be found in the Trisagion prayer (*O Agios …*) which was regularly used in the Gallican liturgy from the sixth century – a liturgy which contributed to the complex of usages employed in Anglo-Saxon England in the seventh and eighth centuries – and the presence of which can be inferred in England before the end of the eighth century through transliterated and translated copies preserved in two late Saxon manuscripts, London,

---

63   Bernhard Bischoff and Michael Lapidge, *Biblical Commentaries from the Canterbury School of Theodore and Hadrian* (Cambridge, 1994). For John the Archcantor and Maban see Bede, *Bede's Ecclesiastical History*, 4.18 (p. 388), 5.20 (p. 530).

64   On Bede's knowledge of Greek and Anglo-Saxon knowledge of Greek see Mary Catherine Bodden, "Evidence for Knowledge of Greek in Anglo-Saxon England," *Anglo-Saxon England* 17 (1988), 217–46. For possibility of loan of Greek material from Bede to Acca see Lapidge, "Acca of Hexham," p. 71.

65   Donald Bullough, "Alcuin before Frankfort," in *Das Frankfurter Konzil von 794 im Spannungsfeld von Kirche, Politik und Theologie*, ed. Rainer Berndt (Mainz, 1997), pp. 571–85 at 577. For Aldhelm see *Aldhelmi Opera*, ed. Rudolph Ehwald, 3 vols (Monumenta Germaniae Historica, Auctores Antiquissimi 15) (Berlin, 1913–1919), 2, pp. 489, 491. For Alcuin see Jean Deshusses, "Les Messes d' Alcuin," *Archiv für Liturgiewissenschaft* 14 (1972), 7–41 at p. 17; Mary Clayton, *The Cult of the Virgin Mary in Anglo-Saxon England* (Cambridge, 1990), pp. 59–60; Bullough, "Alcuin before Frankfort," p. 577, n. 28. Donald Bullough, *Alcuin, Achievement and Reputation* (Leiden, 2004), p. 322 notes that Alcuin distinguishes between *sophia* for Old Testament references to Wisdom and *sapientia* for New Testament expressions of the concept. On Bede's preoccupation with the concept of Wisdom see Arthur G. Holder, "The Feminine Christ in Bede's Biblical Commentaries," in *Bède le Vénérable entre Tradition et Postérité*, ed. Stéphane Lebecq, Michel Perrin and Olivier Szerwiniak (Villeneuve d'Ascq, 2005), pp. 109–18 and Faith Wallis, *Bede and Wisdom*, Jarrow Lecture (Jarrow, 2016).

British Library, Royal 2 A. xx and Cotton Galba A. xviii.[66] Less inferentially, the word is found in early insular liturgical contexts like the seventh-century *Antiphonary of Bangor* and the Latinised inscriptions, *O Agios Mattheus*, etc, accompanying the Lindisfarne Gospels' evangelist portraits.[67] Equally significant of the depth of penetration of the usage of this Greek adjective (and another indication of Northumbrian devotion to the Virgin) is found in the Greek plea neatly inserted in the interstices of the scalloped border of the titulus of an early eighth-century Gospels text now bound up in the Utrecht Psalter: "Holy (*agia*) Mary help the scribe".[68] Later in date we find the word employed in the formulae of charters, in lapidary texts – and in a magical incantation for fruitful fields.[69]

---

66 The fragmentary evidence for liturgical complexity and variety in seventh- and eighth-century Anglo-Saxon England is best summarised in Catherine Cubitt, *Anglo-Saxon Church Councils, 650–850* (London, 1995), pp. 125–52; Catherine Cubitt, "Unity and Diversity in the Early Anglo-Saxon Liturgy," *Studies in Church History* 32 (1996), 45–57; Richard Pfaff, *The Liturgy in Medieval England: a History* (Cambridge, 2009), pp. 30–52; Jesse D. Billett, *The Divine Office in Anglo-Saxon England 597–c. 1000* (Henry Bradshaw Society Subsidia 7) (London, 2014). For the use of the Trisagion in eighth-century England see Edmund Bishop, *Liturgica Historica: Papers on the Liturgy and Religious Life of the Western Church* (Oxford, 1918), pp. 141–46; Lapidge, *Anglo-Saxon Litanies*, pp. 13–16; Bischoff and Lapidge, *Biblical Commentaries*, p. 170. A recent summary of Merovingian liturgical influence in Northumbria can be found in David Ganz, "Merovingian Gospel Readings in Northumbria: the Legacy of Wilfrid?", in *Religious Franks: Religion and Power in the Frankish Kingdom: Studies in Honour of Mayke de Jong*, ed. Rob Meens, Dorine van Espelo, Bram van den Hoven van Genderen, Janneke Raaijmakers, Irene van Renswoude, and Carine van Rhijn (Manchester, 2016), pp. 317–30.

67 *The Antiphonary of Bangor: an Early Irish Manuscript in the Ambrosian Library at Milan*, ed. F.E. Warren, 2 vols (Henry Bradshaw Society 4, 10) (London 1893–1895), 1, pp. 12, 47, and 56 with extended discussion on p. 47; see also *The Winchester Troper: from Mss. of the 10th and 11th Centuries, with other Documents Illustrating the History of Tropes in England and France*, ed. Walter Howard Frere (Henry Bradshaw Society 8) (London, 1894), p. 48. *Lindisfarne Gospels* evangelist labels: *Evangelorium Quattuor Codex Lindisfarnensis*, ed. T.D. Kendrick, Julian Brown, and Rupert Bruce-Mitford, 2 vols (Olten and Lausanne, 1956–1960), 2, p. 49.

68 E.A. Lowe, "The Uncial Gospel Leaves Attached to the Utrecht Psalter," *Art Bulletin* 34 (1952), 237–38.

69 Charters: Ben Snook, *The Anglo-Saxon Chancery: the History, Language and Production of Anglo-Saxon Charters from Alfred to Edgar* (Cambridge, 2015), p. 150. Charm: Karen Jolly, "Tapping the Power of the Cross: Who and for Whom," in *The Place of the Cross in Anglo-Saxon England*, ed. Catherine Karkov, Sarah Keefer, and Karen Jolly (Woodbridge, 2006), pp. 58–79 at 68, 79. Lapidary text: Peter Kidson, "Lapidary Traditions in Anglo-Saxon England, II: Bede's *Explanatio Apocalypsis* and Related Works," *Anglo-Saxon England* 12 (1983), pp. 73–123 at p. 11. See also Advent Vespers hymn in Joseph Stevenson, *Latin Hymns of the Anglo-Saxon Church: with an Interlinear Anglo-Saxon Gloss* (Durham, 1851), p. 35.

The claimed dedication to *Agiæ Sophiæ* on Hexham's altar is thus perfectly appropriate as a statement from what we know of Northumbria's eighth- or early ninth-century monastic culture. And it is therefore no surprise to find the two words combined in two different Alcuin-associated contexts, a few decades after Acca's death. The first of these involves a church dedication. In his poem on York, Alcuin records the building of a church in the city by Archbishop Ælberht (767–778) which was dedicated to 'Alma Sophia,' a building of which the location and dedicatee has caused much scholarly controversy.[70] For our immediate purposes, however, what is significant is that the same church dedication is recorded among calendar entries in a continental manuscript (Berlin, Deutsche Staatsbibliothek, Phillips 1869) the contents of which, according to Bullough, received York modifications in *c.* 780.[71] Here the dedication is given as "*Agiæ Sophiæ*," precisely the combination recorded on the Hexham altar. The second collocation of the two words figures in the blessing of the *Missa De Sancta Sapientia* composed by Alcuin as one of a series of votive masses for days of the week when no festival occurs: *respice propitius super nos famulos tuos et praepara agiae sophiae dignam in cordibus nostris habitationem* ("look favourably upon your servants and prepare in our hearts a dwelling place worthy of your Holy Wisdom").[72]

Alcuin's devotion to *Sapientia/Sophia* is, of course, well-documented – he declared himself to be 'Sophia's slave' and his self-composed epitaph reads, "Alcuin was my name and Sophia always my love."[73] And earlier in eighth-century Northumbria there was obviously a strong interest in the concept, many of Bede's works centering on this theme.[74] All of this eighth-century evidence suggests that the claimed altar dedication would be perfectly consonant with

---

70   *Alcuin: the Bishops, Kings and Saints of York*, ed. and trans. Peter Godman (Oxford, 1982), p. 120. In this context the site and dedicatee of this church is irrelevant; see however Richard Morris, "Alcuin, York and the Alma Sophia," in *The Anglo-Saxon Church: Papers ... in Honour of Dr H.M. Taylor* (Council for British Archaeology Research Report 60), ed. Lawrence Butler and Richard Morris (London, 1986), pp. 80–89; Christopher Norton, "The Anglo-Saxon Cathedral at York and the Topography of the Anglian City," *Journal of the British Archaeological Association* 151 (1998), 1–42; Bullough, *Alcuin, Achievement*, pp. 155–56, 320–22. See also *Sources for York History to AD 1100* (Archaeology of York 1), ed. and trans. David Rollason, Derek Gore, and Gillian Fellows-Jensen (York, 1998), pp. 156–57.

71   Bullough, *Alcuin, Achievement*, pp. 324–25.

72   Deshusses, "Les Messes d' Alcuin," p. 18. Translation from Douglas Dales, *Alcuin: Theology and Thought* (Cambridge, 2013), p. 192.

73   "*Alchuine nomen erat sophiam mihi semper amanti*": *Poetae Latini Aevi Carolini*, 1, (Monumenta Germaniae Historica, Poetarum Latinorum Medii Aevi), ed. Ernst Dümmler (Berlin, 1881), p. 351.

74   Wallis, *Bede and Wisdom*; see also Holder, "Feminine Christ."

what we know of Northumbrian scholarship and intellectual preoccupations in Acca's period, even if we cannot prove that it came from his grave.

One further point should be made. There was clearly a depth of reference within, and a powerful inter-relationship between, the three dedications on the Hexham altar, springing from the concept of 'Sophia.' At the centre is the figure of Christ, whom Bede and other orthodox post-Augustinian commentators identified as foreshadowed in the Old Testament figure of Wisdom. Thus Alcuin's poem on York opens: *Christe deus, summi virtus sapientia patris* ("Christ divine, strength and wisdom of the Father") while one of the manuscripts containing Alcuin's votive mass for 'Sapientia' adds *quae Christus est* to the title, echoing Alcuin's own definition of Christ as the "wisdom of God."[75] Further, Wisdom was also seen as a collective attribute of the Trinity and, while the full statement of sapiential Mariology did not emerge until the twelfth century, readings for the Marian festivals were drawn from the Old Testament Wisdom books by the eighth century, and the association between Mary and Sapientia was clearly beginning to emerge at this date.[76] The central placing of an inscribed *Agiæ Sophiæ* on the altar, for the monastic ruminative mind, was thus profoundly significant, and it cannot be mere chance that Alcuin's votive masses similarly place the celebration of *Sancta Sapientia* on Wednesday – midway between Sunday's dedication to *Sancta Trinitate* and Saturday's to *Sancta Maria.*[77]

Conclusions

The record of Acca's claimed relics is clearly complex. But some facts are perhaps less uncertain than they once appeared. Acca might conceivably have been buried at Hexham. If he was, then Elfred Westou, through his Hexham contacts and family ties, *was* in a position to know of any local traditions about the site of his burial place. His excavations *did* yield bones, the continued

---

75   The biblical basis for the Christ/Wisdom equation is explicit in Luke 11:49 and 1 Corinthians 1:24; see also Colossians 2:3. For Bede's equation see Holder, "Feminine Christ" and Wallis, *Bede and Wisdom.* Alcuin poem: Godman, *Alcuin, Bishops, Kings*, p. 2; Mass textual variant: Deshusses, "Les Messes," p. 17.

76   For Alcuin's equation of Wisdom with the Trinity see *Alcuinus Eboracensis: De Fide Sanctae Trinitatiset de Incarnatione Christi*, ed. Eric Knibbs and E. Ann Matter (Corpus Christianorum Continuatio Mediaevalis 249) (Turnhout, 2012), pp. 57–58, 158. For the Mary/Wisdom equations see the discussion in Barbara Newman, *God and the Goddesses: Vision, Poetry and Belief in the Middle Ages* (Philadelphia, 2005), pp. 195–203.

77   Deshusses, "Les Messes."

veneration of which is attested through a series of translations at Hexham into the middle years of the twelfth century. Vestments *did* exist in the twelfth century which could be claimed to have originated from the grave excavated by Elfred. And, finally, the portable altar recorded in the *Hist. Reg.* cannot reasonably be seen, for the reasons set out above, as a twelfth-century Hexham invention to match Cuthbert's portable altar; it is, moreover, unlikely that a later forger would produce (or an inventive later chronicler describe) such a uniquely shaped object. We cannot be certain that it had emerged from a genuine Acca grave but its inscription fits well with eighth- or early ninth- century Northumbrian intellectual preoccupations.[78] If it is not to be associated with Acca himself, then it still remains a plausible product of his century.

Acknowledgements

I am grateful, as so often, to Eric Cambridge for his comments on earlier versions of this paper which have much improved its accuracy and clarity and also to Lisa Bailey, Clare Stancliffe, and Lauren Whitnah for facilitating access to their recent papers.

---

78 This is not, of course, to deny later preoccupations with the Wisdom concept; for a twelfth-century Durham example see Christopher Norton, "History, Wisdom and Illumination," pp. 61–105 at 90–96. As noted above, however, the lists compiled in Favreau, "Les Autels" show that the claimed Hexham inscription is not typical of figures and themes invoked on twelfth-century portable altars.

CHAPTER 13

The Hereford Gospels Reappraised

Michelle P. Brown and Peter Furniss

Elizabeth ('Betty') Coatsworth has ranged across media in her work, deploying a combined interdisciplinary art historical, archaeological and historical approach to bear upon metalwork, textiles, sculpture and manuscripts from the Insular cultural milieu. We owe her a debt of gratitude for this, and for her unfailing kindness and good humour. Her collaboration with Christopher Verey and Julian Brown on the Early English Manuscripts in Facsimile volume on the Durham Gospels is a good example of her approach. It therefore seemed fitting to offer this article on a related manuscript, approached in a similarly interdisciplinary way, with a focus on its materiality. The collaboration between a medieval manuscript scholar/cultural historian and a practitioner/reconstructor of techniques will, we hope, also appeal to her. It is offered with great affection.

∴

The Hereford Gospels – a Welsh Book Now in Hereford, or the Book of St Ethelbert the King's Shrine Still at Hereford, Its Place of Origin?

Michelle P. Brown

One of the greatest treasures of the famous chained library at Hereford Cathedral is an Insular Gospel book[1] which, by comparison with grander coun-

---

1   We should like to express our gratitude to Rosemary Firman, Hereford Cathedral Librarian, for facilitating our study of the manuscript and for sharing her expertise. We should also like to thank the other members of staff at the library for their unfailing kindness and professionalism. The two authors of this paper have different voices, one is an academic and the other a practising scribe and illuminator of high standing (Chair of Shropshire Scribes), himself from an academic background, who brings a different perspective to a material study of the manuscript. The article is therefore divided into two sections, but there is inevitably some overlap and each section contains areas of collaborative work between the two authors. This approach was also adopted in Michelle P. Brown and Patricia Lovett, *The British Library Historical Source-Book for Scribes* (London & Toronto, 1999).

terparts such as the Book of Durrow, the Echternach Gospels, the Lindisfarne Gospels and the Book of Kells,[2] has been considered modest and somewhat provincial in character. Yet this diminutive example of the genre has much still to teach us of the age in which it was produced.

Focused discussions of the manuscript by Lindsay, Lowe, McGurk, Alexander, Mynors and Thomson, Webb and Gameson have tended to favour a dating of c.800 and have accepted origins in Wales (although Gameson did allow the possibility of a western English origin).[3] This is largely owing to its comparatively simple appearance and materials, its Hereford provenance on the Welsh borders and perhaps to a romantic desire to furnish Wales with an illuminated manuscript that predates the Ricemarch Psalter (Dublin, Trinity College Library MS 50), which was presented between 1064 and 1082 by the scribe named Ithael to his brother Rhygyfarch (Old Welsh, Ricemarch), residing at the school at St David's where their father was bishop.

Lack of certainty concerning its actual place of origin has led to it being known, from its current location, as the Hereford Gospels (Fig. 13.1).[4] Following a recent detailed observation of the manuscript conducted along with Peter Furniss, Chairman of Shropshire Scribes, who has a particular interest in Insular scripts, it seems potentially useful to publish our observations on the manuscript, including his practitioner's view and my analysis and contextualization of it.

It is uncertain how early the manuscript was at Hereford. The chained library is largely a seventeenth-century construct, rather than a medieval one, and although the cathedral undoubtedly possessed a significant library during

2   Respectively Dublin, Trinity College Library, 57; Paris, Bibliothèque nationale de France, lat. 9389; London, British Library, Cotton Nero D. iv; Dublin, Trinity College Library, 58.

3   W.M. Lindsay, *Early Welsh Script* (Oxford, 1912), pp. 41–43; L.J. Hopkin-James, *The Celtic Gospels* (Oxford, 1934); E.A. Lowe, *Codices Latini Antiquiores*, 12 vols (Oxford, 1934–1971), 2.157; Patrick McGurk, *Latin Gospel Books: from AD 400 to AD 800* (Paris, 1961), no. 15; J.J.G. Alexander, *Insular Manuscripts 6th to the 9th Century* (A Survey of Manuscripts Illuminated in the British Isles), 1 (London, 1978), no. 38; Janet Backhouse, D.H. Turner, and Leslie Webster, eds, *The Golden Age of Anglo-Saxon Art, 966–1066* (London, 1984), p. 86; Nicholas Hart Webb, "Early Medieval Welsh Book Production," PhD thesis, University of London, 1985; R.A.B. Mynors, R.M. Thomson, and M. Gullick, *Catalogue of the Manuscripts of Hereford Cathedral Library* (Cambridge, 1993); R.G. Gameson, "The Hereford Gospels," in *Hereford Cathedral: A History*, ed. Gerald Aylmer and John Tiller (London, 2000), pp. 536–43; R.G. Gameson, "The Insular Gospel Book at Hereford Cathedral," *Scriptorium* 56–1 (2002), 48–79 (which contains a thorough description of the manuscript); M.P. Brown, *The Lindisfarne Gospels: Society, Spirituality and the Scribe* (London and Toronto, 2003), pp. 238, 380.

4   Cambridge, Pembroke College, 302, an Anglo-Saxon volume from the mid-11th-century, is also sometimes known as the Hereford Gospels, but the sobriquet is usually accorded to the earlier Insular manuscript that is the subject of this paper.

FIGURE 13.1   The Hereford Gospels, showing its chained binding, open at the St Mark
               Incipit page, fols 35v–36r.
               Courtesy of the Dean and Chapter, Hereford Cathedral

the high Middle Ages – a number of items from which remain there along with
medieval book chests and the famous thirteenth-century *Mappa Mundi* – by
the late sixteenth century it was reported as being poorly provisioned with
books.[5] The Hereford Gospels in now housed in a seventeenth-century chained
binding, but is likely to have been rebound for inclusion in the Hereford
post-Reformation chained library, so it may be surmised that it was at Hereford
by this time. During the Middle Ages such liturgical manuscripts tended to
reside in the sacristy or on the high altar, as working service-books and venerated icons, however, and the book may have had an earlier association with
the cathedral.

   At the head of the first vellum leaf of the medieval manuscript, at the top
of the Matthew *Incipit* page (Fig. 13.2), is the title in a sixteenth-century court
hand by the Hereford librarian – so the volume was evidently at the cathedral
by then. So, the manuscript was at Hereford from at least the sixteenth century,
but how much longer may it have been there? Local tradition of the Hereford
Gospels having been donated to the cathedral library by Bishop Athelstan

---

5   See Mynors, Thomson, and Gullick, *Catalogue*, on the library history.

(1013 × 1016–1056) during the early eleventh century, along with other of his books, appears unsubstantiated and probably stems from the inclusion in the book of documents relating to the Hereford area from his period in office. The blank lower half of the final leaf, at the end of John's Gospel (fol. 134r and v) and part of the concluding vellum flyleaf (fol. 135v) bear documents written in late Anglo-Saxon minuscule scripts. One is a shire moot record of King Cnut's reign (1016–35), in which a mother and her son disputed lands at Wellington and Cradley, which was enacted at Aylestone and, as the record notes, was subsequently recorded in a Gospel book at Hereford – probably this very entry in the Hereford Gospels.[6] This presumably conferred sacrality upon the oaths previously sworn orally in evidence. Another records a local land purchase by Leofwine, datable to 1043 × 1046. Someone has tried to cut out the latter document's text-block with a knife, the incisions having been repaired with paper patches. A third, on fol. 135v, was erased.[7] These documents all relate to the Hereford area and strongly suggest that the book was there when they were added during the second quarter of the eleventh century. Hereford Cathedral was evidently being regarded as the appropriate 'chancery' and repository for significant property transactions in the area by this period.

I have discussed elsewhere the use of other Insular Gospel books – the Lindisfarne Gospels, BL Royal MS 1.B.vii, the Chad Gospels, the Stockholm Codex Aureus, the Book of Kells and the Bodmin Gospels – as 'books of the high altar' in which certain legal transactions were recorded (in original blank areas and margins or on flyleaves or tipped in leaves).[8] These include property transactions, manumissions of slaves and redemption of book-hostages (an Armenian early Christian phenomenon) and there are indications that the performative enactment of such agreements, and the swearing of oaths upon the books into which the proceedings were entered, enhanced their legal status and conferred benefits upon the grantor's soul. Several of these books are associated with the shrines of early saints and were counted amongst their relics (doubling their efficacy in oath-swearing, as relic and sacred text). The

---

6   Gameson, "The Insular Gospel Book at Hereford Cathedral," pp. 71–72 and n. 111.

7   The Bodmin Gospels also contains erasures of documentary material added to it during the eleventh century, see M.P. Brown, *The Word and the Shaping of Cornwall before the Reformation: Stones, Scriptures and Playscripts* (London, 2021). Presumably such erasures were made because the transactions were now void.

8   Brown, *Lindisfarne Gospels*, pp. 118–23; Brown, "The Lichfield/Llandeilo Gospels Reinterpreted"; M.P. Brown, *The Book and the Transformation of Britain, c.550–1050: a Study in Written and Visual Literacy and Orality* (London and Chicago, 2011), pp. 94–95; Brown, *The Word and the Shaping of Cornwall*.

FIGURE 13.2   The Hereford Gospels, St Matthew *Incipit* page, fol. 1r.
                Photo: Peter Furniss, with kind permission of Hereford Cathedral

Hereford Gospels may have fulfilled a similar function in the Anglo-Saxon Hereford Cathedral. This also indicates that it functioned as a chancery and repository of legal documents and that it had a scriptorium.

The appending of documents to the end of Gospel books during Cnut's reign is paralleled in the York Gospels, a book that I have suggested was made as a gift from Cnut and Emma to "the Wolf" – the outspoken critic of their regime change, Archbishop Wulfstan of York.[9] Heslop has pointed to the use by the royal couple of book-gifts to court the support of secular and ecclesiastical aristocrats during the second and third decades of the eleventh century, along with grants of property and privileges.[10]

The practice of entering documents into Gospel books is, however, an earlier one. The role of Insular 'books of the high altar' as places of solemn enactment of legal processes has been previously discussed,[11] with copies of the resultant agreements and symbolic items being entered within them to ensure their sacrosanct, inviolable nature and the binding status of the oaths sworn thereupon by the major protagonists and witnesses – rather as we still swear upon copies of sacred texts in law courts today.

In the gutter at one point can be seen a piece of kermes-dyed bright pink sewing thread, which may be early, and possibly the remains of tacket stitching used to keep the quire in place prior to binding.[12] At the head of fol. 126v is a piece of white thread, possibly of silk, which may have formed part of the sewing attaching something to the page. This may bear some relationship to the heavy discoloration of this page and that facing it by brown reagent staining. During the nineteenth and early twentieth centuries, and perhaps even earlier, such reagents were used to render things that were otherwise illegible more visible. Sadly, this was a fleeting benefit which almost immediately resulted in the permanent defacement of the areas concerned. There are also signs here and on the adjacent openings of ink offsets and ferrous staining which may

---

9   M.P. Brown, "Review of Alexander *et al.*, *The York Gospels: A Facsimile with Introductory Essays,*" *The Book Collector* 38 (1989), 551–55.

10   T.A. Heslop, "The Production of De-luxe Manuscripts and the Patronage of King Cnut and Queen Emma," *Anglo-Saxon England* 19 (1990), 151–95 and T.A. Heslop, "Art and the Man: Archbishop Wulfstan and the York Gospels," in *Wulfstan, Archbishop of York*, ed. Matthew Townend (Turnhout, 2004), pp. 6–7, notes 14–15.

11   Brown, *Lindisfarne Gospels*, pp. 117–21; M.P. Brown, *The Book and the Transformation of Britain, c.550–1050: a Study in Written and Visual Literacy and Orality* (London and Chicago, 2011), pp. 94–96; M.P. Brown, "Concealed and Revealed: Insular Visualisations of the Word," in *Clothing Sacred Scripture*, ed. D. Ganz and B. Schellewald (Berlin and Boston, 2019), pp. 69–80.

12   J.P. Gumbert, "The Tacketed Quire: an Exercise in Comparative Codicology," *Scriptorium* 65.2 (2011), 299–320.

indicate that documents and relics or markers may have been inserted in this area. Michael Clanchy notes the practice of exchanging knife blades and the like as part of the legal performative process of conveying property and I have pointed to the forensic evidence for such items being formerly included in the Lindisfarne Gospels, prior to its clean-up (perhaps by Sir Robert Cotton) and the removal of extraneous materials.[13]

There are some stubs and the issue of lacunae is discussed by Peter Furniss, below. Three decorated Incipit pages remain – Matthew (see Fig. 13.2), Mark (see Fig. 13.1) and John (Fig. 13.3) but there are signs of two significant leaves bearing major decoration having been excised and of some leaves having been taken out and then reinserted during rebinding. The codicology therefore suggests that the decorative suite may originally have included evangelist miniatures and carpet pages. These excised leaves may have been removed from the Hereford Gospels owing to a connoisseur-based interest in them as 'art for art's sake,' as often happens with illuminated manuscripts, but in this case the removal of these important leaves may have been motivated also, or instead, by a concern with the validity of the contents of later documents added in their margins.

An analogy for this is the Chad Gospels (Fig. 13.4), which is in some respects the Hereford Gospels' closest relative. There the decorated suite of leaves introducing St Luke's Gospel has attracted greater emphasis, both in the original manufacturing campaign in which it is the only Gospel to have been accorded a Cross Carpet-Page as well as an evangelist miniature and decorated *Incipit* Page. The Luke miniature was selected to receive the marginal inscription recording the volume's redemption by the Welshman Gelhi, who swapped his best white horse for it during the mid-ninth century (a century after it had been made) and who gifted it to the altar of St Teilo at Llandeilo Fawr in Carmathenshire.[14] Gelhi took the opportunity to have his book-redemption/restitution to the Church of a sacred tome (an ultimately Armenian practice) recorded in the book, for the good of his soul, along with an assertion that

---

13　M.T. Clanchy, *From Memory to Written Record: England, 1066–1307* (Cambridge, 1979); Brown, *Lindisfarne Gospels*, pp. 117–21.

14　On the Welsh marginalia added to the Chad Gospels at Llandeilo Fawr, see D. Jenkins and M.E. Owen, "The Welsh Marginalia in the Lichfield Gospels," *Cambridge Medieval Celtic Studies* 5 (Summer 1983), 37–66, and 7 (Summer 1984), 91–120. On the Chad Gospels and their historical and stylistic contextualisation, see M.P. Brown, "The Lichfield Angel and the Manuscript Context: Lichfield as a Centre of Insular Art," *Journal of the British Archaeological Association* 160 (2007), 8–19; M.P. Brown, "The Lichfield/Llandeilo Gospels Reinterpreted," in *Authority and Subjugation in Writing of Medieval Wales*, ed. R. Kennedy and S. Meecham-Jones (New York and Basingstoke, 2008), pp. 57–70.

FIGURE 13.3   The Hereford Gospels, St John *Incipit* page, fol. 102r.
Photo: Peter Furniss, with kind permission of Hereford Cathedral

his family was the rightful owner of a contested gold mine. Other documents added on key decorated leaves of the Chad Gospels include the earliest extant medieval manumissions; for such Gospel books were places of public assembly and would be seen in use during the performative public liturgy and displayed on the high altars of leading ecclesiastical centres and shrines.[15] The emphasis upon St Luke's opening pages may be due to the exegetical equation of this evangelist, symbolized by the sacrificial bull, with the sacrifice on the Cross of the incarnate Divine.[16] The Chi-rho page, which I have suggested effectively forms an iconic representation of Christ as *Logos*, would also have been a particularly appropriate place to enter records of actions intended to honour the Saviour and seek redemption effected by the Divine's acceptance of human form (Matthew symbolising exegetically Christ's incarnation and nativity and Luke his Crucifixion).[17]

Like the Chad Gospels, Hereford opens with the decorated *Incipit* Page to Matthew's Gospel (see Fig. 13.2), and in both volumes this leaf shows signs of wear and dirt suggesting that at some point they functioned as the front covers. This implies that the original bindings had been removed, perhaps because they carried metalwork or ivory/bone elaborations and were, effectively, treasure bindings. If so, both volumes may have originally included prefatory matter. This could have included canon tables, but probably did not as neither book features the requisite marginal Eusebian section apparatus needed to make such tables of practical use.

The Chad Gospels also offer the closest textual analogy to the Hereford Gospels. Both are Mixed Latin/Vulgate texts of the 'Irish/Celtic family'. They share some sixty distinctive variant readings. This is sufficient to suggest a textual dependency of Hereford upon Chad, which may have been made as much as half a century earlier, or upon a shared textual exemplar.[18] I have pro-

---

15   *Ibid.* and n. 8, above.

16   M.P. Brown, *The Book of Cerne: Prayer, Patronage and Power in Ninth-Century England* (London and Toronto, 1996), pp. 75–79; M.P. Brown, "Embodying Exegesis: Depictions of the Evangelists in Insular Manuscripts," in *Le Isole Britanniche e Roma in Età Romanobarbarica*, ed. A.M. Luiselli Fadda and É. Ó Carragáin, Quadrini di Romano Barbarica 1 (Rome, 1998), pp. 109–27; Brown, *Lindisfarne Gospels*, pp. 346–69.

17   *Ibid.*

18   Gameson, "The Insular Gospel Book at Hereford Cathedral," states that there is only an 81% agreement between Hereford and Chad with regard to variant readings which depart from the Vulgate. He uses this to support his argument for Welsh origins for the Hereford Gospels. However, 81% is a high percentage of agreement in terms of Insular mixed texts and would support origins in a similar textual milieu (the Irish/Celtic Mixed Text Family) and, with 60 distinctive shared variant readings, there may even have been some mutual dependence upon the same ultimate textual exemplar or stemma. On the

posed that Chad was made either at Lindisfarne or at its daughter house of Lichfield, which was founded by St Chad of Holy Island in the mid-seventh century. Its artist was granted access to the major decorated openings of the Lindisfarne Gospels in order to design somewhat simplified versions of them for the Chad Gospels, whilst weaving in influences from other manuscripts too. Although the Lindisfarne Gospels, along with the Ceolfrith Bibles from Monkwearmouth-Jarrow, contain the purest version of Jerome's Vulgate Latin edition, made in Bethlehem in the late fourth century, this 'Italo-Northumbrian' textual family did not supplant the pre-existing mixed texts circulating in Britain and Ireland, or elsewhere in the latinate West. The Chad Gospels may therefore have taken as its textual model the mixed Celtic tradition used in the Columban and Cuthbertine *paruchiae* even after the scholarly and symbolic espousal of the Vulgate – with its potential for overcoming local variation in favour of international ecumenical harmony – was favoured in the Lindisfarne Gospels when it was made around 715–722 on Holy Island.[19]

The Chad Gospels, like many other Insular Gospel books, thus pays homage to another important book of the high altar from the same monastic federation (the Lindisfarne Gospels) by quoting some of its motifs – rather like Wren quoted Michelangelo's dome of St Peter's, Rome, at St Paul's in London, and it is reiterated in other monuments such as the Capitol in Washington DC;[20] but, as in those architectural instances, the visual rhetoric is adapted to present need and combined with other cultural allusions.

The Hereford Gospels may be a relatively simpler production, but it likewise quotes elements from other key manuscripts and regional traditions in its visual repertoire, indicating manufacture in a centre aware of a range of stylistic influences drawn from across the Insular milieu. Its Matthew '*Liber*' and John '*In Principio*' *Incipit*s (see Figs. 13.2–3) recall the monograms used in the corresponding pages of the Lindisfarne Gospels. The zoomorphic and rectilinear borders of the *Incipit* pages in Hereford are reminiscent of the Chad Gospels and the Irish-Northumbrian tradition of the Echternach Gospels. The arabesque Islamic-style motif filling the bow of "b" in Hereford's Liber *Incipit*

Mixed Text in Chad and related manuscripts, see Brown, *Lindisfarne Gospels*, pp. 173–75 and CD-ROM appendix of textual variant collations in the Lindisfarne Gospels and other Insular Gospel books.

19   Brown, *Lindisfarne Gospels*; M.P. Brown, "Reading the Lindisfarne Gospels: Text, Image, Context," in *From Holy Island to Durham: The Contexts and Meanings of the Lindisfarne Gospels*, ed. R.G. Gameson (London, 2013), pp. 84–95.

20   M.P. Brown, "The Visual Rhetoric of Insular Decorated *Incipit* Openings," in *Graphic Devices and the Early Decorated Book*, ed. M.P. Brown, I.H. Garipzanov, and B.C. Tilghman (Boydell Studies in Medieval Art and Architecture) (Woodbridge, 2017), pp. 127–42.

FIGURE 13.4   The Chad Gospels, St Mark *Incipit* page, p. 143.
Photo: Courtesy of the Dean and Chapter, Lichfield Cathedral

(see Fig. 13.2) resembles a more complex device – one of a number of near eastern influences – in the Book of Kells (probably made on Iona around 800). The black ribbon-like display lettering in the Hereford *Incipit* pages and the way in which it gives way to lines of text script at the foot of the pages, rather than being executed in display script throughout the whole page, recalls elements in the Barberini Gospels, which was probably made at Peterborough in eastern Mercia at the end of the eighth century.[21] The enhancement of the text script by slightly larger and more calligraphic forms in Hereford's Matthew and Mark *Incipit* Pages (see Figs. 13.1–2) suggests that the scribe may also be the artist, who is either following a recent Mercian (and Irish) trend of rapid diminuendo into the text script on display panels or is adapting designs from models with fewer words on the page and supplementing them with further words from the text (see Peter Furniss's discussion, below).

The closest parallels in manuscript art for the long-snouted beasts that form the terminals to major initials and frames in the Matthew and Mark *Incipit* Pages are to be found in the Chad Gospels, with their antecedents residing in Northumbrian works such as the Durham Gospels and the Durham Cassiodorus. The John *Incipit* eschews zoomorphic ornament in favour of purely geometric fret and key patterns and spiralwork of fine workmanship. The background to this lies in Hiberno-Northumbrian manuscripts and metalwork. A distinctive feature is the use of turgid pelta-like protuberances which adorn the sides of some of the major initials on these pages.

An interesting feature of the design of the *Incipit* Pages is that the crosses embedded in the Cross Carpet-Pages of the Book of Durrow, the Lindisfarne Gospels and the Chad Gospels have migrated from the carpets of ornament (which I have related to the use of the prayer-mat, or *oratorio*, in eighth-century England)[22] of Coptic origin to become part of the framing entablature of the decorated *incipit*s themselves. They form, in effect, 'cross-*incipit* pages' (see Figs. 13.1–3). The Mark *Incipit* page features a cross with lozenge-shaped terminals at its heart, set against a gleaming yellow infrastructure topped by a Latin cross. The yellow gleams like the gold of the *Crux gemmata* itself – the symbol of eternal life. The Book of Kells also eschews the use of gold in favour of a bright yellow, whereas the Lindisfarne Gospels features delicate touches of

---

21   Rome, Vatican City, Biblioteca Apostolica, Barberini Lat. 570. M.P. Brown, "The Barberini Gospels: Context and Intertextuality," in *Text, Image, Interpretation: Studies in Anglo-Saxon Literature and its Insular Context in Honour of Eamonn Ó Carragáin*, ed. A. Minnis and J. Roberts (Turnhout, 2007), pp. 89–116.

22   For the use of the prayer-mat (*oratorio*) in the period, and its influence upon carpet-pages, see Brown, *Lindisfarne Gospels*, p. 319.

both gold leaf and shell-gold.[23] In the John *Incipit* the cross terminals are circular. The formal variations of each of the crosses in the Cross Carpet-Pages of the Lindisfarne Gospels were intended, I have suggested, to signal the contribution of different churches (signified by the Latin cross, the Greek cross, the Celtic ring-headed cross and the Coptic/Ethiopic tau cross) to the Christian tradition. In Hereford this theologically grounded component has become more an aesthetic variation that permitted a reduction in the number of full decorated pages. This labour/resource-saving approach extends into the text, where the articulation of text breaks is handled solely by slightly enlarged penwork minor initials and *litterae notabiliores* in black ink, devoid of coloured infills, or (in the case of the Genealogy of Christ) by the introduction of further columns (Figs. 13.5–6.) The initials and *litterae notabiliores* are otherwise embedded in single columns of text and often follow punctuation by *distinctiones*, a system of systematic punctuation using rising numbers or positions (in respect to the writing line) of points to denote rising value of pause, known to the grammarians of late Antiquity and popularized by early Irish scribes.[24]

Script and the 'Mercian Schriftprovinz'

The text is pricked for 33 lines of continuous text, spaced at 5 mm between writing lines. Although the prick marks remain, executed with a tool that made round holes up to quire 8 and one that made slits thereafter, the hard-point ruling is only now visible on one leaf. The membrane is vellum of moderate quality, with some of it inclining to a mushroom hue and suede-like surface or to a stiff, fatty or celluloid character, with little hair/flesh-side distinction. This is consistent with usual Insular codicological manufacturing practices, rather than the occasional experiments with classical and continental preparation and assembly techniques, such as are sometimes found at Lindisfarne, Monkwearmouth-Jarrow and Canterbury.[25]

The script is fluid and accomplished, with text breaks denoted within the column by *distinctiones* marks, including triangles of points or a colon of points followed by a midpoint horizontal tongue. These are followed, where appropriate to sense and *sententia*, by enlarged 1.5- to 2-line initials in text ink by the single scribe. Writing a whole gospel book single-handedly, in the manner of the eastern desert fathers and Insular founding fathers such as St Columba, is

---

23   For observations on the artistic use of pigments in the Lindisfarne Gospels and related manuscripts and for the results of a non-destructive raman laser pigment analysis examination, see Brown, *Lindisfarne Gospels*, pp. 275–98 and appendix 1, pp. 430–51.

24   M.B. Parkes, *Pause and Effect: An Introduction to the History of Punctuation in the West* (Farnham, 1992).

25   Brown, *Lindisfarne Gospels*, pp. 200–05.

a spiritual practice favoured within the Columban and Cuthbertine monastic federations in which only the 'seniores', the most tried and tested and therefore usually high-ranking (bishop, abbot or anchorite) members of the community, might undertake on behalf of all, as I have discussed elsewhere.[26] This applied to the scribal work, which for transmitting Scripture was a priestly function akin to that of the Jewish sofer (Scribe), rather than that of the copyist of other texts. The artwork might be by another hand, more artistically gifted, but sometimes they might be one and the same, as in the Lindisfarne Gospels where one hand (probably that of Bishop Eadfrith, who died in 722) was responsible for every aspect of the work, in true eremitic fashion, other than the writing of the marginal numbering of the Eusebian sections needed to work with the canon tables – someone else was permitted to add these, perhaps after the maker's death at which some of the decoration was also left incomplete and never finished by another hand.[27] In the Hereford Gospels the end of each Gospel concludes with a scribal prayer-colophon, such as *"Finit amen d(e)o gratias" ago'* on fol. 35v at the end of Luke's Gospel.

An unusual feature of the script is that it is an Insular set minuscule, rather than an uncial or half-uncial hand of the sort usually employed for Scripture by Insular scribes. A slanted pen is used, producing angled heads to strokes, and minuscule letter-forms are often favoured, such as single-compartment a (rather than the formal 'oc' form of the letter 'a' featured in Insular Phase II half-uncial such as that found in the Lindisfarne Gospels, the Chad Gospels and the Book of Kells), flat-topped g, n and tall s. The overall appearance is elevated in formality, however, by the frequent lifts of the pen, even where ligatures might appear more natural, and by the use of uncial round d and capital R. Abbreviation bars are used and there is a liberal sprinkling of Tironian *notae* (shorthand symbols) of the sort often used by Insular scribes, including hooked h for *autem* and ÷ for *est*.

Within the Insular hierarchy of scripts, it is unusual to find set minuscule – albeit the highest grade of minuscule (or lower-case) script – except in the early formative and late phases of its development.[28] The Irish/Northumbrian scribes of the Echternach Gospels employed it in the late seventh century, as

---

26   Brown, *Lindisfarne Gospels*, pp. 213–71 and 395–409.

27   *Ibid.*

28   T. Julian Brown, "The Insular System of Scripts," in *A Palaeographer's View: the Selected Writings of Julian Brown*, ed. J. Bately, M.P. Brown, and J. Roberts (London, 1993); M.P. Brown, "Writing in the Insular World," in *The Cambridge History of the Book in Britain Volume 1: c.400–1100*, ed. R.G. Gameson (Cambridge, 2011), pp. 121–66.

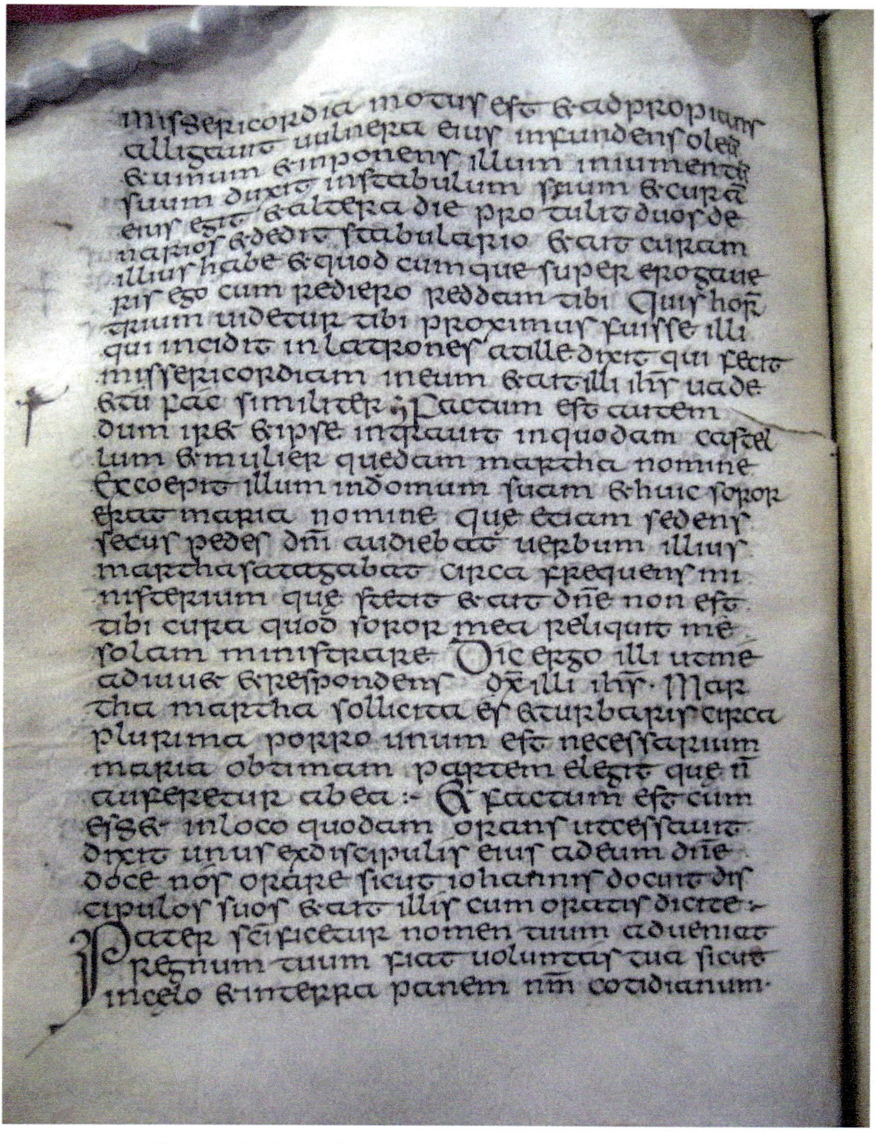

FIGURE 13.5   The Hereford Gospels, text script with penwork minor initial and enlarged
                 litterae notabiliores, fol. 78v.
                 Photo: Peter Furniss, with kind permission of Hereford Cathedral

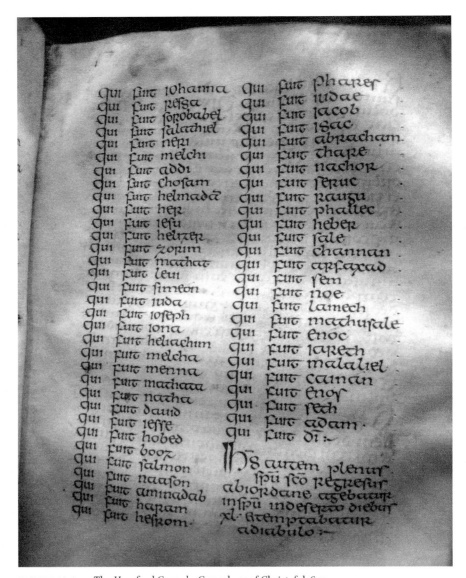

FIGURE 13.6   The Hereford Gospels, Genealogy of Christ, fol. 65r.
Photo: Peter Furniss, with kind permission of Hereford Cathedral

did those of the Royal Bible (British Library, Royal MS 1. E. vi) in Canterbury during the 830s–840s. The former case is probably due to the hierarchical canon of form and function not yet being fully established, or, due to time constraints. The latter case is likely to have been influenced by the promotion of caroline minuscule as the multi-purpose single script of choice throughout the Carolingian empire from the beginning of the ninth century onwards.

Yet Irish scribes were less constrained by a hierarchical developmental sequence of scripts and appropriate uses than their Anglo-Saxon counterparts. Scripts of Julian Brown's Phases I and II co-habit in areas of Irish influence, and I have suggested that, contrary to usual historical assumptions, the English Midland kingdom of Mercia was receptive to Irish influences in its book arts during the late eighth and ninth centuries, especially in the border areas of western Mercia.[29]

A similar use of set minuscule, an unwillingness to be subject to the regimen of uniform horizontal head and base-lines (of the sort so elegantly deployed in the Lindisfarne Gospels' reformed half-uncial script) and a desire to fracture the rounded aspect of half-uncials by breaking the bows of letters with pen-lifts, is found in some Mercian manuscripts of this period. Notable parallels include three of the prayerbooks of the Mercian 'Tiberius group': BL MSS Harley 7653, Harley 2965 and Royal 2. A. xx (see Fig. 13.7). I have suggested that all of these were written for, and probably by, women in western Mercia shortly before and after the year 800.[30] Similar script features are also found in Mercian charters of c.775–810.[31] In my analysis of what I have termed the 'Mercian Schriftprovinz,' encompassing those areas under the control of the Mercian 'hegemony,' or 'greater Mercia' (incorporating Kent, the eastern fenlands and Wessex) under kings Offa and Cenwulf, I have discussed contemporary Irish textual and palaeographical influences on western Mercia at this time.[32] The Stowe Missal and the St Gall Gospels are good examples of this sort of Irish set minuscule with *fractura* aspect,[33] similarly used for Scripture.

---

29   Brown, *Book of Cerne*, p. 118; M.P. Brown, "Mercian Manuscripts: the Implications of the Staffordshire Hoard, Other Recent Discoveries, and the 'New Materiality'," in *Writing in Context: Insular Manuscript Culture, 500–1200*, ed. Erik Kwakkel (Leiden, 2013), pp. 23–66.

30   M.P. Brown, "Mercian Manuscripts? The 'Tiberius' Group and its Historical Context," in *Mercia: An Anglo-Saxon Kingdom in Europe*, ed. M.P. Brown and C.A. Farr (Leicester, 2002), pp. 278–91; and Brown, "Writing in the Insular World."

31   M.P. Brown, *The Book of Cerne: Prayer, Patronage and Power in Ninth-Century England* (London and Toronto, 1996), pp. 164–72.

32   *Ibid.*, p. 118.

33   Respectively Dublin, Royal Irish Academy, D.II. 3 and S. Gallen 51.

I would suggest that the Hereford Gospels also originated in the milieu of Irish-influenced western Mercia/Welsh borders in the early ninth century.

Context and Historical Background

If then, the Hereford Gospels can be considered to exhibit cultural affinities with Hiberno-Saxon manuscripts of the earlier and contemporary Columban and Cuthbertine traditions, with contemporary Irish script and art styles and with Mercian manuscript culture of primarily western Mercian character, but also incorporating visual allusions to features found in works such as the Barberini Gospels from the farthest eastern fenland reaches of Mercia around 800, what might this lead us to conclude concerning its origins?

The Hereford Gospels' closest relative, in many ways, is the Chad Gospels which was probably made at or for the shrine of St Chad at Lichfield in the mid-eighth century (see Figs. 13.4–5). The only extant example of script likely, demonstrably, to be from Hereford itself at this period is a charter which remains in Hereford Cathedral Archives (HCA 4067; Fig. 13.8). This is a charter of Bishop Cuthwulf of Hereford, renting an estate on the River Frome to Ealdorman Ælfstan, dated 840–852. The Hereford scriptorium is the probable source of this document. It is written in an elegant Phase II pointed minuscule which finds its closest parallels in Mercian charters of the second quarter of the ninth century and in the Book of Cerne (Fig. 13.9), a prayerbook probably made at Lichfield for its bishop, Æthelwald (818–830).[34] The influence of Lichfield's scriptorium evidently continued to be exerted at Hereford, and it seems possible that its gospel book was in fact made at Hereford as part of the developmental phase of book production associated with western Mercia from c.780–820, after which Mercian practices were modernized in response to developments at the Canterbury Cathedral scriptorium which had begun under Archbishop Wulfred (805–832).[35] Although a Mercian noble, he was intent upon restoring Canterbury's privileges which had been rescinded by King Offa in favour of his new, and more amenable, if short-lived, archbishopric of Lichfield. Script reform, to produce more impressive appearing documents, was part of this agenda. The Hereford Gospels belongs to the preceding phase of script development and is probably of late eighth or, more likely, early ninth-century date. The palaeographical evidence confirms a stylistic

---

34   Brown, *Book of Cerne* and "Writing in the Insular World."

35   Brown, *Book of Cerne*, pp. 164–66, 182–83 and "The Lichfield Angel and the Manuscript Context: Lichfield as a Centre of Insular Art"; N.P. Brooks, *The Early History of the Church of Canterbury: Christ Church from 597 to 1066* (London, 1984).

FIGURE 13.7   The Royal Prayerbook (London, BL, Royal 2. A. xx), fol. 17r, detail.
Courtesy of the British Library Board

connection to Mercian manuscript culture of this period, but the question remains: could it have been made at Hereford?

It is intriguing, and may be telling, that the eastern Mercian artistic milieu of the Barberini Gospels, which I have suggested was made at Peterborough (Medeshamstede) around the year 800, should also be reflected in some aspects of the decoration of the Hereford Gospels. If the latter was indeed made at Hereford, the establishment there of a shrine dedicated to the cult of St Ethelbert the King during the early ninth century would fit well as a context for contact with eastern Mercia/East Anglia and may even provide a possible context for production of the Hereford Gospels itself.

The origins of Hereford Cathedral are uncertain. There had been missionary activity in the region by figures who feature in Wales (and further afield) – Sts David and Dyfrig[36] – and St Chad of Holy Island was active in Mercia from 669, moving his *cathedra* from Repton to Lichfield where a cathedral was built *c.*700. In 672, the year of Chad's death, Archbishop Theodore of Tarsus restructured the Mercian diocese, splitting it into five parts with that of the Magonsaete in SW Mercia (which was established *c.*676) corresponding to what became the Hereford diocese and the diocese of the Hwicce to Worcester. It may be that it took a while for Hereford itself, at a much-frequented ford of the River Wye, to rise to prominence within the existing landscape of church activity. Hereford cathedral is said to have been (re)founded by Putta (died 688), who settled there around 676 after he was driven from Rochester by Æthelred of Mercia. Close by the medieval cathedral site is that of a minster dedicated to St Guthlac (673–714), a princely Mercian warrior turned hermit-monk who trained at Repton and established a hermitage at Crowland in the Fens and whose associations extend from the western to the eastern extremities of Mercia.

The first reliably recorded bishop of Hereford, Wulfheard, appears in 803 and by around 830 the nobleman Milfrid is said to have constructed a stone cathedral and shrine on the site of a wooden one, at around the time that the ancient ford was being transformed into a fortified centre.

---

36   On this Welsh clerical presence, the role of the Minster at Leominster (14 miles from Hereford) which may have been associated with David and missionary activity from Lindisfarne in the area, see J. Hillaby, "The Early Church in Herefordshire: Columban and Roman" and K. Ray, "Archaeology and the Three Early Churches of Herefordshire," in *The Early Church in Herefordshire*, ed. A. Malpas *et al.*, (Leominster, 2001).

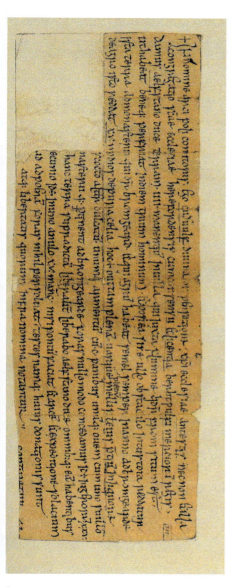

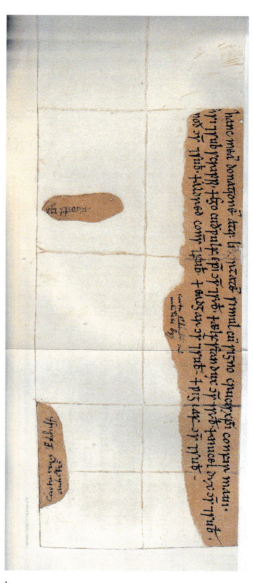

a   b

FIGURE 13.8   a (obverse) and b (reverse) Charter of Bishop Cuthwulf of Hereford, renting an estate on the River Frome to Ealdorman Ælfstan, Hereford, 840–852 (Hereford, HCA 4067). Courtesy of the Dean and Chapter, Hereford Cathedral

FIGURE 13.9   The Book of Cerne (CUL, Ll. I. 10), fol. 43r, detail.
              Courtesy of the Syndics of Cambridge University Library

Hereford Cathedral is dedicated to two saints, St Mary the Virgin and
St Ethelbert the King. The latter was King of East Anglia in the late eighth century. We know little about his reign, other than that he minted his own coin-
age, featuring images of Romulus and Remus which may indicate an ancestral
connection with the Wuffingas dynasty, of Sutton Hoo fame, and an aspira-
tion for diplomatic links with Rome. Such expressions of independence may
have led to him being beheaded by Offa, King of Mercia in the year 794. This
event is said to have taken place at the royal vill of Sutton Walls, four miles
from Hereford, during Ethelbert's visit to conclude his proposed marriage to
Offa's daughter, Ælfthyth/Alfreda (who is said subsequently to have become
a recluse at Crowland before heading to Rome on pilgrimage, thereby sig-
nalling either that she had not been complicit in his murder and/or that she
felt the need to expiate the sin of her father in this regard through her own
spiritual devotion).[37]

   Ethelbert's body is said to have been brought to Hereford cathedral by 'a
pious monk' and was buried there. Miracles occurred at the site during the
early ninth century and (by c. 830) Milfrid, a Mercian nobleman, was moved

---

37   East Anglian sources for the period are rare and we are reliant for details of King
      Ethelbert's life upon his surviving coins and fifteenth-century accounts by Richard of
      Cirencester and John of Brompton's *Chronicon*. The *Anglo-Saxon Chronicle* does state that
      he was beheaded in 794 at Offa's command.

by them to rebuild in stone the little wooden church which stood there, and to dedicate it to the sainted king. It was in this early ninth-century period that the shrine of St Chad of Holy Island, the founder-figure of Lichfield Cathedral, was being upgraded there (some 80 miles from Hereford) and the Lichfield Angel polychrome sculpture (Fig. 8.5) was being carved as part of a new tomb-shaped shrine. Its decoration echoes that of the mid-eighth-century St Chad Gospels, and I have suggested that this cross-media visual referencing was extended during the 820s to the illuminated prayerbook made at Lichfield for its bishop, Æthelwald.[38]

Might the Hereford Gospels, with its own complementary references to the Hiberno-Saxon saints of the past and to the western and eastern Mercian churches of the present, actually have been made at Hereford during the early ninth century, under the cultural stimulus of recent developments at Lichfield, for the shrine of King Ethelbert the King or for the bishop of Hereford? William of Malmesbury, writing in the early twelfth century, refers to royal and episcopal Saxon tombs and a cross adjacent to Hereford Cathedral.[39]

The manufacture of the Barberini Gospels at Peterborough Cathedral around 800 might also have been related in part to these political events, but rather than associating itself stylistically and culturally with the Hiberno-Saxon idiom (as the Hereford Gospels does), it wears instead a fashionable Southumbrian stylistic cloak of Italo-Byzantine artistic influences combined with contemporary Mercian Tiberius Group influences.[40] The visual rhetoric of the Hereford Gospels on the other hand, despite some signs of influence from such grand artistic trends, retains a provincial 'Celtic' feel consistent with its Welsh border location, and bears similarities in appearance to the earlier great Insular books of the high altar, notably the St Chad Gospels (probably then still at Lichfield), and to the grander of the Irish pocket gospel books, notably the MacDurnan Gospels, which I have suggested was made at Armagh in the early ninth century as a replacement for a book associated with the cult of St Patrick.[41]

38　Brown, *The Book of Cerne*; Brown, "Mercian Manuscripts? The 'Tiberius' Group'"; Brown, "The Lichfield Angel"; Brown, "Mercian Manuscripts: the Implications of the Staffordshire Hoard."

39　William of Malmesbury, *Gesta regum Anglorum*, book ii, ch. 134.5; William of Malmesbury *Gesta regum anglorum: the History of the English Kings*, ed. and trans R.A.B. Mynors, R.M. Thomson, and M. Winterbottom, 2 vols (Oxford, 1998–1999), 1, pp. 214–15.

40　Brown, "The Barberini Gospels."

41　London, Lambeth Palace Library 1370. M.P. Brown, "Ferdomnach and the Ninth to Twelfth-Century Books of Armagh: Exuberant Exhibitionist or Accomplished Antiquary?", in *Mapping New Territories in Art and Architectural History: Essays in Honour of Roger Stalley*, ed. Frances Narkiewicz, Niamh NicGhabhann, and Danielle O'Donovan (Turnhout, forthcoming 2021).

The scale of the Hereford Gospels places it, like the Book of Durrow, in an intermediate position between the full-size Insular Gospel books and the Irish pocket Gospel books.[42] It may have served as the portable Gospels of a leading prelate or have been intended to honour Irish ecclesiastical influence in Wales and the border area. The scale of its decoration and its probable use as a 'book of the high altar' in which important legal transactions were recorded to confer additional sacrality upon their status, situates it more in the realm of those Insular Gospel books which served a liturgical role in worship in leading centres, often associated with the cults of saintly figures.[43]

Returning to the Hereford historical context, the eighth century saw the rise of the kingdom of Mercia to a position of political supremacy in southern England. The dynasty of Kings Æthelbald and Offa was focused upon Tamworth and the Midlands but expanded its influence and overlordship by the late ninth century to form what might be considered 'Greater Mercia', incorporating Kent, East Anglia and Wessex. From the end of the century the seat of power in Mercia moved to western Mercia, focusing upon centres such as Winchcombe (50 miles from Hereford), where the abbey was the repository for the royal archives.[44]

The first of the rulers from this area, King Cenwulf of Mercia (ruled 796–821), was at pains to distance himself from much of Offa's policy and a rapprochement with East Anglia and Kent is marked during his reign. He restored to Canterbury many of the rights, lands and privileges which Offa had transferred to his more compliant short-lived archbishopric of Lichfield, but also ensured that it, and other ecclesiastical centres in his own western Mercian homeland, continued to enjoy the support of himself and the Mercian aristocracy.[45] It is possible that the Beonna who was elected Bishop of Hereford at the Synod of Clofesho in 824 and who remained in office until 830 was the same person of that name who was abbot of Medeshamstede in the late eighth and early ninth centuries and who disappears from view around 805.[46]

Milfrid's patronage of Hereford would fit into such a scenario, prior to the escalation of Viking incursions into England. His stone church would have contained the shrine, and both would have needed a copy of Scripture as a focal point. Given its historical and cultural associations and its relatively

---

42   *Ibid.* and Patrick McGurk, "The Irish Pocket Gospel Book," *Sacris Erudiri* 8 (1956), 249–70; Eleanor E. Jackson, "*To Hold Infinity in the Palm of Your Hand: the Insular Pocket Gospel Books Re-evaluated*," PhD thesis, University of York, 2017.

43   Brown, *Lindisfarne Gospels*, pp. 64–83 and "Writing in the Insular World."

44   Brown, "Mercian Manuscripts? The 'Tiberius' Group."

45   *Ibid.* and Brown, *Book of Cerne*, pp. 164–66.

46   Aylmer and Tiller, *Hereford Cathedral*, p. 12.

modest political and economic status as a Mercian border bishopric – one which was well aware of the need to preserve a visual rhetoric of association with its Celtic neighbours and antecedents – one would expect its book of the high altar to look something like the Hereford Gospels.

In the late ninth century the Hereford diocese passed from Mercian rule to that of the new West Saxon rulers of later Anglo-Saxon England and would have formed part of the kingdom's western boundary. William of Malmesbury later records Hereford at the place where King Athelstan (924–939) compelled the rulers of the Northern Britons to meet and pay him tribute.[47]

The documents entered in the final pages of the Hereford Gospels point to pragmatic literacy at Hereford in the second quarter of the eleventh century and Milfrid's stone cathedral stood until the reign of Edward the Confessor, when it was altered, but this new or refurbished church was sacked in 1055 by a combined force of Welsh and Irish led by the Welsh prince Gruffydd ap Llywelyn. Hereford Cathedral remained ruinous until rebuilt by Robert of Lorraine, who was consecrated as its bishop in 1079. Work was continued by Bishop Reynelm, who died in 1115, and it was completed under Bishop Robert de Betun (1131–1148).

The cult of St Ethelbert the King survived these changes and music for the *Office of St Ethelbert* survives in the thirteenth-century Hereford Breviary. It is conceivable that the Hereford Gospels may likewise owe its survival and its place of honour amongst the treasures of Hereford Cathedral to its origins there in the early ninth century as a shrine-book of St Ethelbert the King.

---

47   William of Malmesbury, *Gesta regum Anglorum*, book ii, ch. 134.5; Mynors *et al.*, vol. 1, pp. 214–15; see Aylmer and Tiller, *Hereford Cathedral*, p. 13.

Appendix: Observations on the Codicology and Palaeography of the Hereford Gospels, a Scribe's View

Peter Furniss

The manuscript is now bound in an early seventeenth-century leather binding with chain attachment, the overall size of approximately 23 cm × 17 cm, giving a Gospel Book of medium size. It has 135 folios which include the main text of the Gospels, three decorated *incipit* pages and two later Anglo-Saxon documentary additions which follow St John's Gospel (on fol. 134r–v, with a third, now erased, on fol. 135v) and were added at Hereford during the first half of the eleventh century.[48]

A paper pastedown and flyleaf at the front of the volume's seventeenth-century chained calfskin-covered binding bear the Hereford Cathedral shelf-mark P i 2 (the lower case 'i' represents 1). Also written on the pastedown are numbers in pencil in the top left-hand corner: 52 crossed out and replaced with 88. The flyleaf has the number 969 pencilled in at the bottom of its verso. At the head of the first vellum leaf of the medieval manuscript, at the top of the Matthew *Incipit* page (Fig. 13.2), is the title in a sixteenth-century Hereford librarian's court hand – so the volume was there by then. Written in two lines: the top line is crossed through and reads "*Testament(um) novu(m),*" the second line reads "*Quatuor Evangelia.*"[49]

Each page of the manuscript is written in single blocks of text approximately 170 mm × 115 mm in size, using a closely spaced script with distinct word separation. Pricking was done with an implement producing round holes up to quire 8 and slits thereafter. Ruling is mostly not visible, but where it does occur it is in hard-point.

The script is written in a competent hand and the whole manuscript appears to have been written by one scribe (see Figs. 13.5–6), with the exception of the later Anglo-Saxon documentary additions at the end of the manuscript. There is no decoration within the text except for enlarged initials and some diminuendo work, but the manuscript contains three decorated *incipit* pages, with the possibility that two others have been removed. This also points to an establishment that did not want to waste its limited resources on decoration or excessive use of vellum, although the monastery must have been reasonably well-founded with good contacts in the monastic world to have access to a good copy of the Gospels as an exemplar, or to possess some original copy of its own.

---

48   Gameson, "The Insular Gospel Book at Hereford Cathedral," pp. 71–72 and n. 111.

49   The 'v' has a tall lead-in stroke which makes it look like a 'b', and the last letter looks like a 'd' with a curling ascender; the second line is "*Quatuor Evangelia*" (the 'v' has a tall lead-in stroke which almost makes it look like a 'b').

That Hereford possessed earlier books is indicated by the palimpsested leaves that form part of the Hereford Gospels (see Fig. 13.10, below). Some fragments from an early eighth-century Insular copy of Matthew's Gospel book, with commentary,[50] written in an uncial script of Northumbrian character (see below), also survive as flyleaves and pastedown offsets on the boards of Hereford MS P.2.10, a mid-eleventh-century copy of Proverbs and Ecclesiastes. The uncial script was related by Lowe to that of the Ceolfrith Bibles, although it is smaller and differs in some details. However, Michelle Brown has proposed that Worcester and western Mercia also practised uncial script in the 8th century.[51] She suggests that Worcester Cathedral probably produced a fine uncial charter of King Æthelbald of Mercia, dated 736 (BL MS Cotton Augustus.II.3, known as the Ismere Diploma),[52] and Inkberrow under Abbess Cuthswith, c.700, also possessed an Early Christian uncial manuscript. Bodleian, Hatton 48, an Uncial *Rule of St Benedict* with an eleventh-century Worcester provenance, she proposed as an example of its work during the late eighth century, along with a manuscript of *Paterius* (Worcester, Cathedral Library, Add. MS 4) and possibly the Codex Bigotianus (Paris, B.N., lat. 281 and 298). She has also suggested that one of Ceolfrith's three Bibles was probably presented to Worcester by King Offa and was later attributed to Rome, presumably on the basis of its romanizing style.[53] Uncial script was therefore highly familiar in western Mercia and the borders (including Hereford) by the time the Hereford Gospels were being written and the flyleaves preserved in a volume that formed part of Worcester's Romanesque library may be another example of this.[54]

In poorer monasteries and churches, to save vellum and resources, extant copies of bibles would probably have been updated rather than new ones commissioned. This manuscript contains little alteration apart from small letters inserted as minor correction to the wording and spelling by the scribe, and there appears to be no major theological comment or updating, which probably implies that the manuscript was commissioned for a particular purpose by an establishment capable of a reasonable level of funding. The manuscript is of medium size, being smaller than some of the more well-known Insular Gospel Books, yet larger than the more readily portable

---

50   E.A. Lowe, *Codices Latini Antiquiores* (Oxford, 1934–1971), 2.158.

51   M.P. Brown on uncial in "Writing in the Insular World," in *A History of the Book in Britain Volume 1: From the Romans to the Normans*, ed. R.G. Gameson (Cambridge, 2011). Worcester was first suggested as a significant scriptorium by C.H. Turner, *Early Worcester Manuscripts: Fragments of Four Books and a Charter of the Eighth Century Belonging to Worcester Cathedral* (Oxford, 1916).

52   J.M. Backhouse and L. Webster, eds, *The Making of England: Anglo-Saxon Art and Culture, 600–900 AD*, BM/BL exhibition catalogue (London, 1991), no. 152.

53   Backhouse and Webster, *The Making of England*, no. 87. See also nn. 47 and 55, above.

54   For an overview of Insular uncial script, see Brown, "Writing in the Insular World."

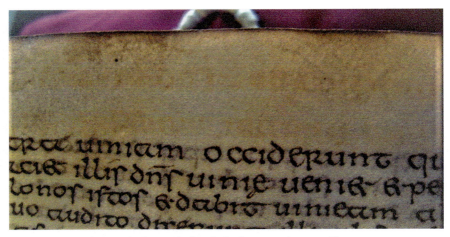

FIGURE 13.10   The Hereford Gospels, detail of palimpsested text on fol. 93v.
Photo: Peter Furniss, with kind permission of Hereford Cathedral

Pocket Gospel Books, which does appear to indicate that it was possibly made as a static book to be held in the monastery for scriptural readings or as an icon of veneration. It would have been a working book to use in services as the marginal crosses and enlarged capitals indicate various lections and readings. As it is more or less agreed that it was not produced at one of the mainstream important centres and was produced at a poorer monastery, it would probably be a symbol of great importance to them and have taken much of their resources to produce.

Rosemary Firman advised that the membrane had been investigated and found to be calfskin.[55] In subsequent discussions with Paul Wright – Parchment Maker at the firm William Cowley – he agrees, that in view of the vellum being fairly thick and stiff, it points to a maker that was not at the top of his profession and the creamy coloration of the material points to the hide from older beasts rather than young spring calves which give white skins. A consideration that the beasts had been allowed to grow to 18 months to almost full size to maximise the amount of meat for sale and the size of the hide to maximise the number of bifolia to be cut from one hide, points to a monastery that was being careful with its funds. He has suggested that approximately 12 bifolia of 14″ × 9.5″ (the size for this manuscript) could be cut from a hide, or possibly more if no account was taken of the holes in imperfect skins. He also indicated

55   The identification of the skin of both the main part and the palimpsest leaves as calf-skin was made in 2018 (from samples taken in Nov. 2017) by the "Books and Beasts" project at York University, led by Dr Sarah Fiddyment and Professor Matthew Collins of the BioARCH research facility in the Department of Archaeology. It has not been reported in print as far as we know.

that for spring births, September and October periods were good for harvesting calves after summer grazing and before the expense of winter feed in order to give good quality parchment. Harvesting the following year when calves were up to 18 months old and almost full grown would maximise both the meat production and the size of the hide.

Collation of the Manuscript and Lacunae (as at 8 February 2019)
Lacunae in the Decorative Scheme

There are some stubs but at each of their locations the verso and recto of the pages either side are continuous in text; nowhere does there appear to be any text missing. The most visible stub occurs after fol. 89 (McGurk classifies it as "leaf cut out").[56] The text from 89 to 90 is continuous and this means, as Rosemary Firman (the Cathedral Librarian) has suggested (pers. comm.), that it is a binding stub conjoint with fol. 100, which is an interesting singleton that has been erased prior to being rewritten to form part of the present volume (discussed below). Close inspection of the rest of the stubs indicates that they could at some stage have been glued to one of the adjacent leaves and were reinforcing strips used at the seventeenth-century rebinding to add support to weak sewing stations.

Three decorated Incipit pages remain, for Matthew (Fig. 13.2), Mark (Fig. 13.1) and John (Fig. 13.3). There are, however, signs of two significant leaves bearing major decoration having been excised and of some leaves having been taken out and then reinserted during rebinding as a separate gathering (quire 2), comprised of three single leaves. The modern pencil foliation has tried to indicate where these belong in the gospel text by foliating them accordingly in the order 8, 7, 5 so that the text would read continuously if those leaves were reinstated in that correct numerical order. One of the decorated leaf excisions would appear to have been an illuminated Chi-rho page with some 230 words on its verso, which would have come between what are now fol. 1v and fol. 2r: there is a stub between fol. 1v and fol. 2r which may indicate a Chi-rho page being removed after re-binding. The other excision occurs between fols 59v and 60r, where text and codicology conspire to indicate that a bifolium has been removed (stitching can be seen between fol. 59v and fol. 60r). Its right-hand leaf would have borne the decorated *Incipit* Page to Luke's Gospel and if its conjoint left-hand leaf was not blank it is likely to have carried a further page of major decoration, either an evangelist miniature, a four-evangelist symbols page or a carpet-page. By analogy with the Chad Gospels,[57] there may originally have been an evangelist miniature on the first recto of the bifolium, a cross-carpet page on its verso, Luke's decorated *Incipit* page on

---

56   P. McGurk, *Latin Gospel Books from AD 400 to AD 800* (Paris, 1961), p. 30.
57   Lichfield Cathedral, 1.

the facing recto and text on its verso. In Chad there is a cross-carpet page loosely modelled on that of St Matthew in the Lindisfarne Gospels and a Luke miniature which both echoes earlier stylized figures in the Echternach Gospels and predicts some of those in the Book of Kells.

Stubs Conjoint with Fols 8, 7 and 5

There were problems in the foliation of the first quire of the manuscript. McGurk leaves a question mark against his entry for the first quire of 8 folios.[58] Gameson refers to the first quire as "grievously mutilated" and "a modern reconstruction of irregular form" but gives no further indication.[59]

Three stubs appear after fol. 5, and fols 8, 7 and 5 appear to be bound separately and in reverse numerical order. Fol. 5v ends part way through Matthew 6:7 (*Nolite ergo adsimilare eis*) and fol. 6r which appears before this three-page section, continues from this starting point part way through Matthew 6:7 (*scit enim pater vester*). Fol. 7r continues from fol. 6v starting at Matthew 6:5 (*hipochrita eice primum*). Fol. 8r continues from fol. 7v starting part way through Matthew 8:4 (*monuis quod praecipit*).

There is complete continuity from fol. 5 through to fol. 8, although bound in the wrong order. Fol. 8v ends part way through Matthew 8:34 (*et ecce tota*) and fol. 9r continues from this point which implies that the three stubs after fol. 5 are conservation binding stubs conjoint with fols 8, 7 and 5.

On further inspection, Michelle Brown found that the first quire originally noted by McGurk as fol. 1 to fol. 8 was actually split into two parts and it was decided to re-examine the collation of the manuscript, leading to the following conclusion:

Manuscript Collation Undertaken on 19 December 2018

Blank flyleaf at front not numbered

1^6	fols 1 to 6	lacks 2 (possible decorated Chi-rho page)
2^4	fols 8, 7, 5,	lacks 4 – folio numbers in reverse order. Three stubs after fol. 5
3^{12}	fols 9 to 20	
4^{14}	fols 21 to 32	lacks 4 and 11. Stubs between fols 23–24 and 29–30
5^{10}	fols 33 to 42	
6^{12}	fols 43 to 54	

---

58   McGurk, *Latin Gospel Books*, p. 30.

59   Gameson, "The Insular Gospel Book at Hereford Cathedral," pp. 48–79.

7¹²	fols 55 to 64	lacks conjoint bifolium 6–7 (possible evangelist miniature and carpet page, followed by a decorated incipit page to Luke's Gospel and opening text page)
8¹⁴	fols 65 to 76	lacks 5 + 11 stubs
9¹⁴	fols 77 to 88	lacks 4 + 11 stubs
10¹⁴	fols 89 to 101	lacks 2 stub
11¹²	fols 102 to 113	fol. 112 is foliated twice
12¹⁴	fols 114 to 125	lacks 4 + 12 stubs
13¹⁰	fols 126 to 135	includes flyleaf fol. 135 with later inscriptions

Contents of Fols 1 to 8

Subsequent to this reappraisal of the manuscript's collation, Peter Furniss undertook a full analysis of the text on each folio of the first two gatherings. With the exception of the missing folio between fols 1v and 2r, all the Gospel text is continuous throughout these two gatherings, in the numerical sequence of the folios, despite the incorrect binding order of fols 6, 8, 7, and 5. In the next quire, fol. 9r also follows on with text continuity from fol. 8v. which confirms the initial assumption that the three stubs after fol. 5v are binding stubs conjoint with fols 8, 7, and 5. A full listing of the text sequence of this section is given below:

TABLE 13.1   Continuity of the text in the locations of stubs between leaves

fol. 1r	Matthew incipit + Matt 1:1	fol. 8r	Mid. Matt. 8:4 to mid. Matt 8:19
fol. 1v	Matt. 1:2 to Matt. 1:17	fol. 8v	Mid. Matt. 8:19 to mid. Matt 8:34
fol. 2r	Matt. 2:9 to middle of Matt. 2:21	fol. 7r	Matt. 7:4 to mid. Matt. 7:21
fol. 2v	Mid. Matt. 2:21 to mid. Matt. 3:12	fol. 7v	Mid. Matt. 7:21 to mid. Matt 8:4
fol. 3r	Mid. Matt. 3:12 to mid. Matt. 4:11	fol. 5r	Matt. 5:29 to Matt. 5:43
fol. 3v	Mid. Matt. 4:11 to Matt. 4:25	fol. 5v	Matt. 5:44 to mid. Matt. 6:8
fol. 4r	Matt 5:1 to mid. Matt. 5:17	fol. 9r	Mid. Matt. 8:34 to mid. Matt. 9:15
fol. 4v	Mid. Matt. 5:17 to Matt. 5:29		
fol. 6r	Mid. Matt. 6:8 to mid. Matt 6:24		
fol. 6v	Mid. Matt. 6:24 to 7:4		

Textual Lacunae between Fols 1v and 2r

Something is missing: fol. 1v ends at Matthew 1:17 and fol. 2r starts at Matthew 2:9. Matthew 1:17 is the end of the generations from Abraham and Matthew 1:18 heralds the birth of Christ. In most Gospel books the verse is opened with a Chi-rho symbol, usually in the form of a large, decorated piece of artwork. It does therefore appear that a Chi-rho symbol was incorporated in the Gospels but has been removed. Looking at the word count of the Passage between Matthew 1:17 and Matthew 2:9 there appear to be approximately 250 words in the Latin version of the gospel, both from a count in the St Chad Gospels and the modern Latin Vulgate.

From a sample group of pages from the Hereford Gospels, the word count per page (see list below) varies from around 210 to 240. Note that in the remaining three *incipit* pages the decorated symbol is also accompanied by smaller lettering to complete the opening verse. It is therefore possible that the missing folio would be a Chi-rho symbol with the completion of verse 18 in small letters on the recto side, and the section from Matthew 1:19 to Matthew 2:8 on the verso side.

Sample Page Word Count

Fol. 2v–221 words
Fol. 3r–230 words
Fol. 20r–242 word
Fol. 31v–229 words
Fol. 78v–206 words
Fol. 84r–215 words
Fol. 84v–207 words
Fol. 109v–213 words
Fol. 114r–206 words

Suspected Missing Text from the Remaining Part of the Manuscript

In his collation of the manuscript, McGurk identifies locations where stubs indicate the possibility of missing leaves. In the revised collation above, these stubs are also identified but in one instance the position of a stub differs from that given in the McGurk collation.

On the visit of 6 February, Peter Furniss took a more detailed inspection of the stubs and their positions and took photographs of the verso and recto of the leaves either side. In a subsequent study of the photographs, he found that, with the exception of the missing bifolia from the centre of fols 59v–60r, all the text was continuous in the areas of the stubs, indicating that no leaves had been taken from the gatherings. He now proposes that the stubs between the various leaves could be stiffening strips used to reinforce weak folds in some of the bifolia to aid stitching during the rebinding process, and there are indications that some of them may have been glued to the particular bifolia concerned.

The continuity of the text in the locations of these stubs is given in the table below:

TABLE 13.2   Continuity of text in locations of stubs

Location of stub	Text continuity
fol.23v–fol.24r	fol.23v ends, mid Matt. 20:30 – fol.24r starts, mid Matt. 20:30
fol.29v–fol.30r	fol.29v ends, mid Matt. 25:20 – fol.30r starts, mid Matt. 25:20
fol.30v–fol.31r (McGurk)	fol.30v ends, mid Matt. 26:5 – fol.31r starts, mid Matt. 26:5
fol.68v–fol.69r	fol.68v ends, Luke 6:8 – fol.69r starts, Luke 6:9
fol.73v–fol.74r	fol.73v ends, mid Luke 8:34 – fol.74r starts mid Luke 8:34
fol.79v–fol.80r	fol.79v ends, mid Luke 11:29 – fol.80r starts, mid Luke 11:29
fol.86v–fol.87r	fol.86v ends, mid Luke 15:25 – fol.87r starts, mid Luke 15:25
fol.89v–fol.90r	fol.89v ends, mid Luke 17:30 – fol.90r starts, mid Luke 17:30
fol.116v–fol.117r	fol.116v ends, mid John 9:21 – fol.117r starts, mid John 9:21
fol.123v–f,124r	fol.123v ends, mid John 13:31 – fol.124r starts, mid John 13:31

Lacunae between Fols 59v and 60r

Mark ends at line 15 on fol. 59v. Luke starts on fol. 60r part way through Luke 1:17 (*helie ut convertat corda partum in filios*). There are approximately 230 words missing from the beginning of Luke which appears to relate to a decorated *incipit* on the recto of the missing page together with smaller lettering to complete the opening verse, with the remainder of the missing text on the verso of the page. Stitching can be seen between fol. 59v and fol. 60r, indicating the centre of the quire but Michelle Brown was unable to identify any other missing folio in the gospels that would indicate a complete bifolium having been removed from the centre of the quire.

Michelle Brown proposed that this complete bifolium had been removed from the centre of this gathering and that it may have contained a carpet page in addition to the Luke incipit. She suggested that a search of the St Chad Gospels should be undertaken to identify any possible parallels with the start of Luke's gospel.

On further investigation of the St Chad Gospels it was found that the start of Luke's Gospel consisted of:

Pg. 219 – Four Evangelist symbols
Pg. 220 – Cross carpet page
Pg. 221 – Luke *incipit*
Pg. 222 – First text verses of Luke's Gospel

If a similar construction had been used in the Hereford Gospels this would account for the four sides of two missing bifolia.

Palimpsested Areas

Rosemary Firman advised that the bifolium comprising what are now fols 93–96 had been identified as palimpsested and pointed out that these folios were noticeably thicker and more rigid than the rest of the manuscript. She also thought that the singleton fol. 100 was palimpsested, as she had identified dry point ruling down the margin outside the text block similar to that on fol. 93, and it was a thicker sheet of vellum.[60] X-ray imaging techniques used at the bottom of fol. 93v clearly show two rows of writing under the text block written in *scriptura continua* in slightly larger letters than the Hereford text, although it is not possible to make out the letters. Peter Furniss's photographs of the top right-hand corner of fol. 93r shows a shadow of a former text line, and bottom of 93v shows two shadows of text lines; the top of fol. 93v also shows the shadows of a palimpsested line of text (Fig. 13.10).

Examination with a hand-held UV lamp did not render the texts legible, but it is possible from the faint images to tell that the script is a rounded Insular hand, probably a half-uncial, which is a little larger than the main text hand of the Gospels and that the word separation is not pronounced. It seems that these three leaves were reused from an earlier, probably eighth-century, manuscript written in the grade of script usual for penning sacred texts.

Notes on the Flyleaves of Hereford Cathedral Library, MS P. 2. 10

This mid-eleventh-century manuscript (P. 2. 10) containing Old Testament books of Proverbs and Ecclesiastes, has leaves from an earlier manuscript cut to size and reused as flyleaves. The flyleaves are from a commentary on Matthew, probably of Northumbrian origin, written in the eighth century in Uncial script. These leaves were formerly pasted down to the covers, and the glue, having wet the ink, has left an offset impression in a mirror image of the script. These leaves are now foliated as fol. i and fol. 61.

The back flyleaf, fol. 61 (Fig. 13.11a), is bound into the manuscript upside down and part of the mirror image is visible on the back cover (Fig. 13.11b) which has been rebound at the Bodleian Library, where the leaves were released from the covers and the back board recovered with two sections of vellum, leaving part of the mirror image

---

60   The palimpsest bifolium was first noticed by Richard Gameson and reported in his chapter "The Material Fabric of Early British Books," in *A History of the Book in Britain Volume 1: From the Romans to the Normans*, ed. Richard Gameson (Cambridge, 2011), p. 19. Further to this, Rosemary Firman reported to him that fol. 100 had similarities which might also point to it as a third leaf.

visible. The area of script relating to the image left on the back board is outlined in red on the photograph of fol. 61v (see Fig. 13.12a).

The leaves are written in uncial script in two columns of 32 lines each, and the script on the two leaves is contiguous, confirming E.A. Lowe's statement in CLA No. 158 that the leaves are from the inner bifolium of a quire cut in two.

The leaves contain sections of Matthew's Gospel together with exegetical commentaries, and are set out as follows:

Front Flyleaf
Recto of original manuscript – now bound in P.2.10 as fol. ir

LH column	Lines 1–5: Matthew 7:27
	Line 6: Blank between gospel section and commentary
	Lines 7–32: commentary on the gospel section
RH column	Lines 1–30: continuation of commentary
	Lines 31–32: blank at end of commentary

The last verses of Matthew 7:28–29 are not included. The commentary relates to Matthew 7:24–27, the words of Jesus about rock and sand foundations, indeed lines 17–19 contain the verse from 1 Corinthians 3:11, about Jesus being the foundation.

Verso of original manuscript – now bound in P.2.10 as fol. iv

LH column	Lines 1–15: Matthew 8:1–4
	Line 16: blank between gospel section and commentary
	Lines 17–32: commentary on the gospel section
RH column	Lines 1–32: continuation of the commentary

Rear Flyleaf
Recto of original manuscript – now inverted and bound in P.2.10 as fol. 61v

LH column	Lines 1–5: continuation of commentary on gospel section
	Lines 6–7: blank space between commentary and gospel section
	Lines 8–32: Matthew 8:5–12
RH column	Lines 1–6: Matthew 8:12–13
	Lines 7–8: blank space between gospel section and commentary
	Lines 9–32: commentary on gospel section

Verso of original manuscript – now inverted and bound in P.2.10 as fol. 61r

LH column	Lines 1–32: continuation of the commentary on the gospel section
RH column	Lines 1–28: completion of the commentary on the gospel section
	Lines 29–32: blank space at end of commentary on the gospel section

In CLA 2.158 (Fig. 13.12), Lowe attributes the leaves to production in England, probably in Northumberland, on the grounds of the abbreviations and initials. He further draws attention to the similarity of the uncial script of the flyleaves to that of British Library, Add. MS 37777 (Greenwell leaf; Fig. 13.13) which is considered to have been part of one of the two other Ceolfrith Bibles, written at Monkwearmouth-Jarrow, the Codex Amiatinus being the third.

When the script of our flyleaf is compared to that of the Greenwell leaf (see Fig. 13.13), it has similarities but it appears to have been written by a less expert scribe. Although our flyleaf is of smaller size, it still has the same characteristics of word spacing which is not quite perfect, and the letter shapes written with a flat pen angle are similar. The Greenwell leaf has forked terminals at the top exit strokes of 'c', 'e', 'f', 'g', 's', 't' and the lower stroke of 'l', with fine lower exit hairline. In our flyleaves however the terminals appear to be more wedge shaped where the fine lower exit hairline is not as distinct and merges into the main body of the serif, probably due to a scribe who is not as expert or that not enough care has been taken over the cutting and sharpening the quill. The 'a' in the Greenwell leaf is fairly uniform, with a delicate elongated bowl, whereas ours has a more rounded, clumsily executed bowl which can vary in shape. Another letter which demonstrates the difference in skill levels of the two scribes is the 'e' which in Greenwell has a definite separation of the top exit curve and the mid line, whereas in our flyleaves there is a variation, sometimes the curve is separate from the mid line and in other cases the top curve joins the mid line.

The Mynors and Thomson Catalogue for Hereford Cathedral Library also points out that our flyleaves are discussed by Glunz. Some anomalies occur in this discussion, Glunz uses an incorrect Hereford catalogue number, P.2.9, for the main manuscript and he also refers to the script of the flyleaves as half-uncial. He states that our flyleaves are part of a manuscript written in southern England, probably Canterbury, and appears to have reached that decision on the basis that they contain some Old Latin textual variations from the Vulgate, eg. 8: v3 omits 'iħs', 8: v5 includes 'iħs' and 'quidam', 8:v13 omits 'et' before sicut. He notes similarities with other manuscripts, containing Old Latin variants, known to have existed at Canterbury, such as the St Augustine Gospels (Cambridge, Corpus Christi College, 286) and Oxford, Bodleian Auct. D. 2. 14, and presumably he assumes these would have been used as models for our flyleaf manuscript. This appears to be quite a leap of assumption and does not preclude the fact that in the eighth century Old Latin variants associated with Irish influences or direct contact with Canterbury could still have appeared in Northumbria.

On balance it appears sensible to conclude the probability of a Northumbrian origin for our flyleaves, although, given Michelle Brown's suggestion of a West Mercian background of uncial script production, with an injection of Northumbrian influence from the Ceolfrith Bible given to Worcester by King Offa in the late eighth century, an origin in the Anglo-Welsh borderlands cannot be ruled out.

FIGURE 13.11A
Hereford Cathedral Library,
P. 2. 10, eighth-century uncial
flyleaves, fol. 61v.
Photo: Peter Furniss, with
kind permission of Hereford
Cathedral

FIGURE 13.11B
Back board pastedown.
Photo: Peter Furniss, with
kind permission of Hereford
Cathedral

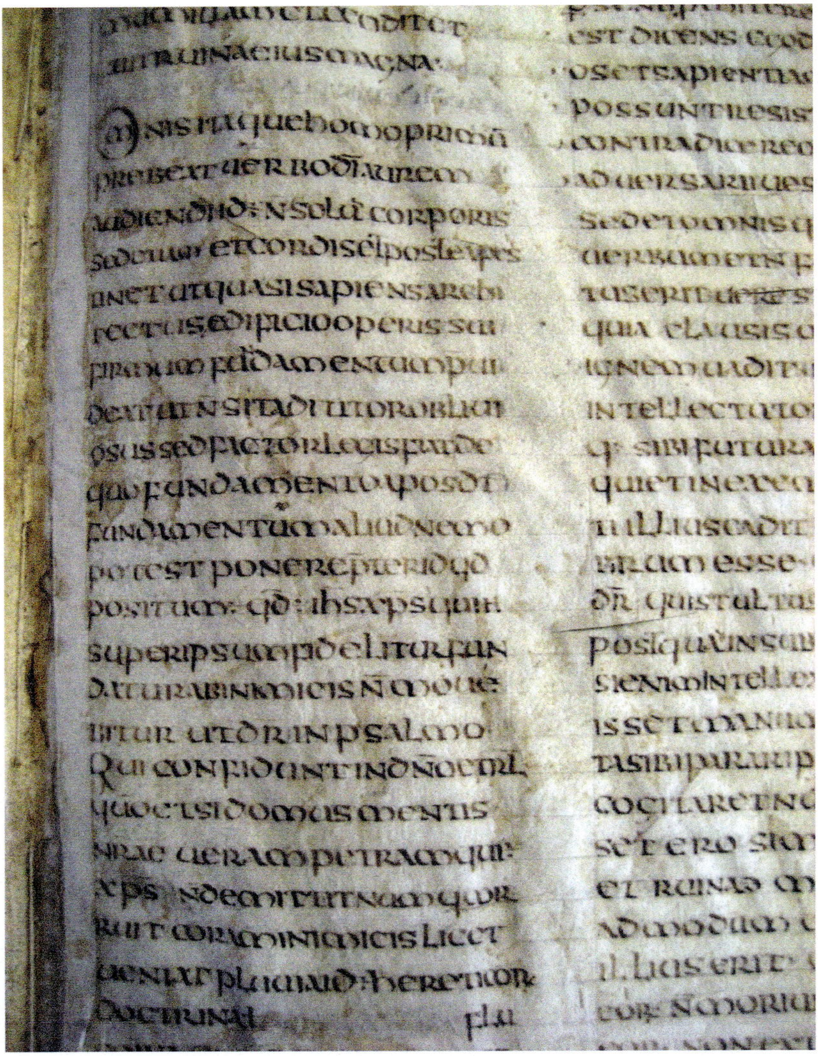

FIGURE 13.12 Hereford Cathedral Library, P. 2. 10, front flyleaf fol. ir (CLA 2.158). Photo: Peter Furniss, with kind permission of Hereford Cathedral

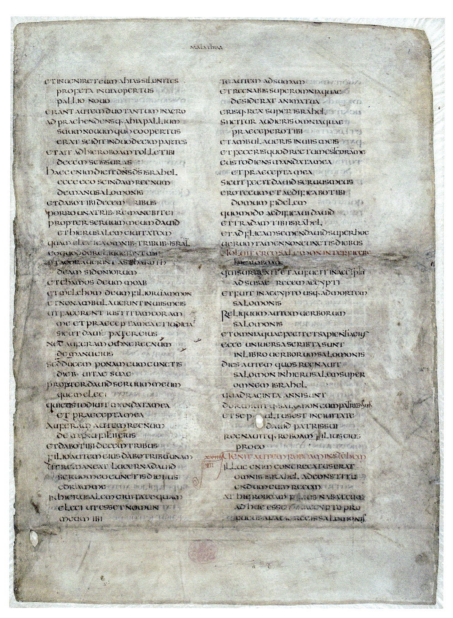

FIGURE 13.13   London, BL, Add. 37777, fol. 1 (Greenwell leaf) (CLA 2.177).
Photo: Creative Commons

Select Bibliography

Primary Sources

Bede, *Bede's Ecclesiastical History of the English People*, ed. and trans. Bertram Colgrave and R.A.B. Mynors (Oxford, 1969).

Cockayne, Oswald, ed. and trans., *Leechdoms, Wortcunning and Starcraft of Early England*. 3 vols (Rolls series 35) (London: 1864–66).

De Vriend, Hubert J., ed., *The Old English Herbarium and Medicina de quadrupedibus* (EETS, os 286), ed. (London, 1984).

Falileyev, Alexander, and Morfydd E. Owen, ed. and trans., *The Leiden Leechbook: A Study of the Earliest Neo-Brittonic Medical Compilation* (Innsbruck, 2005).

Raine, James, ed., *The Priory of Hexham*, 2 vols (Surtees Society 44, 46) (Durham, 1864, 1865).

Stoll, Ulrich, trans., *Das "Lorscher Arzneibuch": Ein medizinhistorisches Kompendium des 8. Jahrhunderts (Codex Bambergensis medicinalis 1): Text, Übersetzung und Fachglossar* (Stuttgart, 1992).

Symeon of Durham, *Symeonis Monachi Opera Omnia*, ed. Thomas Arnold, 2 vols (Rolls Series 75) (London, 1882–1885).

Symeon of Durham, *Libellus de Exordio … Dunhelmensis Ecclesie*, ed. and trans. David Rollason (Oxford, 2000).

Secondary Sources

Aird, W.M., "An Absent Friend: the Career of Bishop William of St Calais," in *Anglo-Norman Durham 1093–1193*, ed. David Rollason, Margaret Harvey, and Michael Prestwich (1994, repr. Woodbridge, 1998), pp. 283–971.

Alexander, J.J.G., *Insular Manuscripts 6th to the 9th Century* (A Survey of Manuscripts Illuminated in the British Isles) 1 (London, 1978).

Alton, Ernest H., Peter Meyer, and George O. Simms, ed., *The Book of Kells: evangeliorum quattuor codex Cenannensis*, 3 vols (Berne, 1950–51).

Ashby, Steve, *A Viking way of life: combs and communities in early Medieval Britain* (Stroud, 2014).

Ashby, Steve, "Technologies of Appearance: Hair Behaviour in Early Medieval Europe," *Archaeological Journal* 171.1 (2014), 151–84.

Ashby, Steve, and C.E. Batey, "Evidence of Exchange Networks: the Combs and Other Worked Skeletal Material," in *Being an Islander*, ed. James Barrett (Cambridge, 2012), pp. 229–43.

Bailey, Richard N., *England's Earliest Sculptors* (Toronto, 1996).

Bailey, Richard N., *Corpus of Anglo-Saxon Stone Sculpture Volume IX. Cheshire and Lancashire* (Oxford, 2010).

Bailey, Richard N., and Rosemary Cramp, *Corpus of Anglo-Saxon Stone Sculpture Volume II. Cumberland, Westmoreland and Lancashire North-of-the-Sands* (Oxford, 1988).

Battiscombe, C.F., *The Relics of St Cuthbert* (Oxford, 1956).

Bayer, Anja, and Caroline Vogt, "Neue textilkundliche Untersuchungen am sogenannten 'Hemd der Balthilde,'" *Zeitschrift für Archäologie des Mittelalters* 47 (2019), 31–52.

Bernstein, Meg, "A Bishop of Two Peoples: William of St Calais and the Hybridization of Architecture in Eleventh-century Durham," *Journal of the Society of Architectural Historians* 77.3 (2018), 267–84.

Birkett, Tom, *Reading the Runes in Old English and Old Norse Poetry* (London, 2017).

Bonner, Gerald, Clare Stancliffe, and David Rollason, ed., *St Cuthbert, His Cult and his Community* (Woodbridge, 1989).

Braun, Joseph, *Der christliche Altar in seiner geschichtlichen Entwicklung*, 2 vols (Munich, 1924).

Brown, Michelle P., *The Lindisfarne Gospels: Society, Spirituality and the Scribe* (London and Toronto, 2003).

Brown, Michelle P., "The Lichfield Angel and the Manuscript Context: Lichfield as a Centre of Insular Art," *Journal of the British Archaeological Association* 160 (2007), 8–19.

Brown, Michelle P., "The Lichfield / Llandeilo Gospels Reinterpreted," in *Authority and Subjugation in Writing of Medieval Wales*, ed. Ruth Kennedy and Simon Meecham-Jones (New York and Basingstoke, 2008), pp. 57–70.

Bryant, Richard, *Corpus of Anglo-Saxon Stone Sculpture Volume X. The Western Midlands* (Oxford, 2012).

Budde, Michael, *Altare Portatile; Kompendium der Tragältare des Mittelalters 600–1600*, 3 vols (Münster, 1999).

Budny, Mildred, and Dominic Tweddle, "The Early Medieval Textiles at Maaseik, Belgium," *The Antiquaries Journal* 65 (1985), 353–89.

Cambridge, Eric, and Alan Williams, "Hexham Abbey: a Review of Recent Work and its Implications," *Archaeologia Aeliana*, 5th ser., 23 (1995), 1–138.

Carruthers, Mary, *The Book of Memory: A Study of Memory in Medieval Culture* (Cambridge, [first edition 1990] second edition 2008).

Cavell, Megan, "Old English 'Wundenlocc' Hair in Context," *Medium Ævum* 82.1 (2013), 119–25.

Chazelle, Celia, *The Codex Amiatinus and its "Sister" Bibles: Scripture, Liturgy, and Art in the Milieu of the Venerable Bede* (Leiden, 2019).

Christie, Mrs A.G.I., *English Medieval Embroidery* (Oxford, 1938).

Coatsworth, Elizabeth, "Cloth-making and the Virgin Mary in Anglo-Saxon Literature and Art," in *Medieval Art: Recent Perspectives: A Memorial Tribute to C.R. Dodwell*, ed. Gale R. Owen-Crocker and Timothy Graham (Manchester and New York, 1998), pp. 8–25.

Coatsworth, Elizabeth, "Stitches in Time: Establishing a History of Anglo-Saxon Embroidery," *Medieval Clothing and Textiles* 1 (2005), 1–27 at p. 23.

Coatsworth, Elizabeth, "Cushioning Medieval Life: Domestic Textiles in Anglo-Saxon England," *Medieval Clothing and Textiles* (2007), 1–12.

Coatsworth, Elizabeth, "Text and Textile," in *Text, Image, Interpretation: Studies in Anglo-Saxon Literature and its Insular Context in Honour of Éamonn Ó'Carragáin*, ed. A. Minnis and J. Roberts (Turnhout, 2007), pp. 187–207.

Coatsworth, Elizabeth, *Corpus of Anglo-Saxon Stone Sculpture Volume VIII. Western Yorkshire* (Oxford, 2008).

Coatsworth, Elizabeth, and Gale R. Owen-Crocker, *Clothing the Past: Surviving Medieval Garments from Early Medieval to Early Modern Western Europe* (Leiden, 2018).

Coatsworth, Elizabeth, and Michael Pinder, *The Art of the Anglo-Saxon Goldsmith: Fine Metalwork in Anglo-Saxon England: its Practice and Practitioners* (Woodbridge, 2002).

Cramp, Rosemary, *Corpus of Anglo-Saxon Stone Sculpture Volume 1. County Durham and Northumberland* (Oxford, 1984).

Cramp, Rosemary, *Wearmouth and Jarrow Monastic Sites*, 2 vols (Swindon, 2005–06).

Cramp, Rosemary, *Corpus of Anglo-Saxon Stone Sculpture Volume VII. South-West England* (Oxford, 2006).

Daniels, Robin, *Anglo-Saxon Hartlepool and the Foundation of English Christianity: An Archaeology of the Anglo-Saxon Monastery* (Hartlepool, 2007).

Duffey, Judith E., "The Inventive Group of Illustrations in the Harley Psalter," PhD dissertation (University of California at Berkeley, 1997).

Favreau, Rudolph, "Les Autels portatifs et leurs inscriptions," *Cahiers de civilization médiévale* 46 (2003), 327–52.

Fell, Christine E., "Hild, Abbess of Streonæshalch," in *Hagiography and Medieval Literature, A Symposium*, ed. Hans Bekker-Nielsen, Peter Foote, Jørgen Højgaard Jørgensen and Tore Nyberg (Odense, 1981), pp. 76–99.

Fern, Chris, Tania Dickinson, and Leslie Webster, ed., *The Staffordshire Hoard: An Anglo-Saxon Treasure* (London, 2019).

Fowler, [Rev.] J.T., "An Account of Excavations Made on the Site of the Chapter-house of Durham Cathedral in 1874," *Archaeologia* 45.2 (1880), 385–404.

Fox, Peter, ed., *The Book of Kells, MS 58, Trinity College Library Dublin*, 2 vols, facsimile and commentary (Lucerne, 1990).

Gameson, R.G., "The Hereford Gospels," in *Hereford Cathedral: A History*, ed. Gerald Aylmer and John Tiller (London, 2000), pp. 536–43.

Gameson, R.G., "The insular Gospel book at Hereford Cathedral", *Scriptorium* 56.1 (2002), 48–79.

Granger-Taylor, Hero, "The Two Dalmatics of Saint Ambrose?" *Bulletin de Liaison du CIETA* 58 (1983), 127–73.

Granger-Taylor, Hero, and Frances Pritchard, "A Fine Quality Insular Embroidery from Llan-gors Crannog, near Brecon," in *Pattern and Purpose in Insular Art: Proceedings of the 4th International Conference on Insular Art*, ed. Mark Redknap, Nancy Edwards, Susan Youngs, Alan Lane, and Jeremy Knight (Oxford, 2002), pp. 91–99.

Griffiths, Fiona J., "'Like the Sister of Aaron': Medieval Religious Women as Makers and Donors of Liturgical Textiles," in *Female "vita religiosa" between Late Antiquity and the High Middle Ages: Structures, Developments and Spatial Contexts*, ed. Gert Melville and Anne Müller (Vita regularis, Abhandlungen 47) (Berlin, 2011), pp. 343–74.

Hawkes, Jane, "Reading Stone," in *Theorizing Anglo-Saxon Stone Sculpture*, ed. Catherine E. Karkov and Fred Orton (Morgantown, WV, 2003), pp. 5–30.

Hawkes, Jane, "East Meets West in Anglo-Saxon Sculpture," in *England, Ireland, and the Insular World: Textual and Material Connections in the Early Middle Ages*, ed. Mary Clayton, Alice Jorgensen, and Juliet Mullins (Tempe, AZ, 2017).

Hawkes, Jane, and Philip Sidebottom, *Corpus of Anglo-Saxon Stone Sculpture Volume XIII. Derbyshire and Staffordshire* (Oxford, 2018).

Henry, Françoise, *Irish Art During the Viking Invasions 800–1020 AD* (New York, 1967).

Henry, Françoise, *The Book of Kells* (London, 1974).

Hollis, Stephanie, *Anglo-Saxon Women and the Church: Sharing a Common Fate* (Woodbridge, 1992).

Hyer, Maren Clegg, "Recycle, Reduce, Reuse: Imagined and Re-imagined Textiles in Anglo-Saxon England," *Medieval Clothing and Textiles* 8 (2012), 49–62.

Hyer, Maren Clegg, "Precious Offerings: Dressing Devotional Statues in Medieval England," in *Refashioning Dress, Medieval to Early Modern*, ed. Gale R. Owen-Crocker and Maren Clegg Hyer (Medieval and Renaissance Clothing and Textiles 4) (Woodbridge, 2019), pp. 17–26.

Inman, Anne E., *Hild of Whitby and the Ministry of Women in the Anglo-Saxon World* (Lanham/Boulder/New York/London, 2019).

Jørgensen, Lise Bender, *North European Textiles until AD 1000* (Aarhus, 1992).

Keefer, Sarah Larratt, "'Either/And' as 'Style' in Anglo-Christian Poetry," in *Anglo-Saxon Styles*, ed. Catherine E. Karkov and George Brown (Albany, NY, 2003), pp. 179–200.

Lane, Alan, and Mark Redknap, *Llangorse Crannog: The Excavation of an Early Medieval Royal Site in the Kingdom of Brycheiniog* (Oxford, 2019).

Lang, James, *Corpus of Anglo-Saxon Stone Sculpture Volume VI. Northern Yorkshire* (Oxford, 2002).

Laporte, Jean-Pierre, *Le Trésor des Saints de Chelles* (Société Archéologique et Historique de Chelles) (Chelles, 1988).

Leatherbury, Sean V., *Inscribing Faith in Late Antiquity: between Reading and Seeing* (London, 2020).

Lester-Makin, Alexandra, *The Lost Art of the Anglo-Saxon World: The Sacred and Secular Power of Embroidery* (Oxford and Philadelphia, PA, 2019).

MacCarron, Máirín, *Bede and Time: Computus, Theology and History in the Early Medieval World* (London, 2020).

MacGabhann, Donncha, "The Making of the Book of Kells: Two Masters and Two Campaigns," PhD thesis (University of London, School of Advanced Study, 2016), available online: https://sas-space.sas.ac.uk/6920/.

MacGabhann, Donncha, "The *et*–ligature in the Book of Kells: Revealing the 'Calligraphic Imagination' of its Great Scribe," in *Islands in a Global Context: Proceedings of the Seventh International Conference on Insular Art*, ed. Conor Newman, Mags Mannion, and Fiona Gavin (Dublin, 2017), pp. 138–48.

MacGabhann, Donncha, "Turning the Tables: An Alternative Approach to Understanding the Canon Tables in the Book of Kells," in *Peopling Insular Art: Practice, Performance, Perception: Proceedings of the Eighth International Conference on Insular Art, Glasgow 2017*, ed. Cynthia Thickpenny, Katherine Forsyth, Jane Geddes, and Kate Mathis (Oxford and Philadelphia, 2020), pp. 13–22.

Macy, Gary, *The Hidden History of Women's Ordination: Female Clergy in the Medieval West* (Oxford, 2008).

McGurk, Patrick, *Latin Gospel Books: from AD 400 to AD 800* (Paris, 1961).

Miller, Maureen C., *Clothing the Clergy: Virtue and Power in Medieval Europe, c. 800–1200* (London, 2014).

Mittman, Asa Simon, and Patricia MacCormack, "Rebuilding the Fabulated Bodies of the Hoard-warriors," *postmedieval: a journal of medieval cultural studies* 7 (2016), 356–68.

Monk, Christopher, "Bedship and Sex-play: Sex and Sensuality in Early Medieval England," in *Sense and Feeling in Daily Living in the Early Medieval English World*, ed. Maren Clegg Hyer and Gale R. Owen-Crocker (Liverpool, 2020).

Murray, Griffin, *The Cross of Cong: a Masterpiece of Medieval Irish Art* (Dublin, 2014).

Muthesius, Anna, *Byzantine Silk Weaving AD 400 to AD 1200*, ed. Ewald Kislinger and Johannes Koder (Vienna, 1997).

Muthesius, Anna, "Silk in the Medieval World," in *The Cambridge History of Western Textiles 1*, ed. David Jenkins (Cambridge, 2003), pp. 325–54.

Myers, Cynthia, "Hairnet," in *Encyclopedia of Medieval Dress and Textiles of the British Isles c. 450–1450*, ed. Gale R. Owen-Crocker, Elizabeth Coatsworth, and Maria Hayward (Leiden and Boston, 2012), pp. 261–62.

Noel, William, *The Harley Psalter* (Cambridge, 1995).

Ó Carragáin, Éamonn, "A Liturgical Interpretation of the Bewcastle Cross," in *Medieval Literature and Antiquities: Studies in Honour of Basil Cottle*, ed. Myra Stokes and Tom Burton (Cambridge, 1987), pp. 15–42.

Ó Carragáin, Éamonn, *Ritual and the Rood: Liturgical Images and the Old English Poems of the Dream of the Rood Tradition* (London, 2005).

Ó Carragáin, Éamonn, "The Vercelli Book as a Context for *The Dream of the Rood*," in *Transformation in Anglo-Saxon Culture: Toller Lectures on Art, Archaeology and Text*, ed. Charles Insley and Gale R. Owen-Crocker (Oxford, 2017), pp. 105–28.

O'Mahony, Felicity, ed., *The Book of Kells: Proceedings of a Conference at Trinity College Dublin, 6–9 September 1992* (Aldershot, 1994).

O'Reilly, Jennifer, *Early Medieval Text and Image*, ed. Carol Farr, Elizabeth Mullins, Máirín MacCarron and Diarmuid Scully (Variorum Collected Studies), 3 vols (London, 2019).

Offler, Hilary Seaton, "Hexham and the Historia Regum," *Transactions of the Architectural and Archaeological Society of Durham and Northumberland* 2 (1970), 51–62.

Orton, Fred, and Ian Wood with Clare A. Lees, *Fragments of History: Rethinking the Ruthwell and Bewcastle Monuments* (Manchester, 2007).

Orton, Peter, *Writing in a Speaking World: the Pragmatics of Literacy in Anglo-Saxon Inscriptions and Old English Poetry* (Tempe, AZ, 2014).

Overbey, Karen Eileen, "Passing Time with the Staffordshire Hoard," *postmedieval: a journal of medieval cultural studies* 7 (2016), 378–87.

Owen-Crocker, Gale R., *Dress in Anglo-Saxon England: Revised and Enlarged Edition* (Woodbridge, 2004).

Owen-Crocker, Gale R., "Smelly Sheep, Shimmering Silk: The Sensual and Emotional Experience of Textiles," in *Sense and Feeling in Daily Living in the Early Medieval English World*, ed. Maren Clegg Hyer and Gale R. Owen-Crocker (Liverpool, 2020), pp. 197–218.

Peers, Charles, and C.A. Ralegh Radford, "The Saxon Monastery of Whitby," *Archaeologia* 89 (1943), 27–88.

Phelpstead, Carl, "Hair Today, Gone Tomorrow: Hair Loss, the Tonsure, and Masculinity in Medieval Iceland," *Scandinavian Studies* 85.1 (2013), 1–19.

Pitt, J., "Malmesbury Abbey and Late Saxon Parochial Development in Wiltshire," *Wiltshire Archaeological and Natural History Magazine* 96 (2003), 77–88.

Pugh, R.B., and Elizabeth Crittall, ed., *Victoria History of the Counties of England: Wiltshire, Vol. 7* (Oxford, 1953).

Pulliam, Heather, *Word and Image in the Book of Kells* (Dublin, 2006).

Raine, James, *A Brief Historical Account of the Episcopal Castle, or Palace of Auckland* (Durham, 1852).

Roberts, Jane, and Alan Thacker, *Guthlac: Crowland's Saint* (Donington, 2020).

Rollason, David, "Symeon of Durham's *Historia de RegibusAnglorum et Dacorum* as a Product of Twelfth-century Historical Workshops," in *The Long Twelfth-Century View of the Anglo-Saxon Past*, ed. Martin Brett and David A. Woodman (Farnham, 2015), pp. 95–112.

Schorta, Regula, "Catalogue des tissus et enveloppes de reliques textiles," in *L'abbaye de Saint-Maurice d'Agaune 515–2015, Vol. 2 – Le trésor*, ed. Pierre Alain Mariaux (Bern, 2015).

Sylvester, Louise M., Mark C. Chambers, and Gale R. Owen-Crocker, ed., *Medieval Dress and Textiles in Britain: a Multilingual Sourcebook* (Woodbridge, 2014).

Temple, Elżbieta, *Anglo-Saxon Manuscripts, 900–1066* (London, 1976).

Tilghman, Benjamin C., "On the Enigmatic Nature of Things in Anglo-Saxon Art," *Different Visions: a Journal of New Perspectives on Medieval Art* 4 (2014), 1–43, http://differentvisions.org/articles-pdf/four/tilghman-enigma-anglo-saxon-art.pdf.

Tweddle, Dominic, *Corpus of Anglo-Saxon Stone Sculpture Volume IV. South-East England* (Oxford, 1995).

Tweddle, Dominic, Martin Biddle, and Birthe Kjølby-Biddle, *Corpus of Anglo-Saxon Sculpture Volume IV. South-East England* (Oxford, 1995).

Verey, Christopher D., T. Julian Brown, and Elizabeth Coatsworth, ed., *The Durham Gospels, together with Fragments of a Gospel Book in Uncial: Durham, Cathedral Library, MS A. II. 17* (Early English Manuscripts in Facsimile 20) (Copenhagen, 1980).

Verhecken-Lammens, Chris, and Daniel De Jonghe, "Technical Report," in Monica Paredis-Vroon, Chris Verhecken-Lammens, and Daniël De Jonghe, "The Major Relics of Aachen Cathedral," *Bulletin du CIETA* 73 (1995–1996), 21–26.

Vierck, Hayo E.F., "La 'chemise de Sainte-Bathilde' à Chelles et l'influence byzantine sur l'art de cour Mérovingien au VIIᵉ siècle," in *Centenaire de l'Abbé Cochet 1975. Actes du Colloque international d'archéologie* (Rouen, 1978), 521–64.

Walton Rogers, Penelope, *Cloth and Clothing in Early Anglo-Saxon England, AD 450–700* (York, 2007).

Walton Rogers, Penelope, "Cloth, Clothing and Anglo-Saxon Women," in *A Stitch in Time: Essays in Honour of Lise Bender Jørgensen*, ed. Sophie Bergerbrant and Sølvi Helene Fossøy (Gothenburg, 2014), pp. 262–63.

Walton Rogers, Penelope, *The Anglian Artefacts from Whitby Abbey Excavations, 1993–2014* ASLab Report to Historic England, 9 April 2019, to appear in Tony Wilmott, in prep.

Waxenberger, G., *A Phonology of Old English Runic Inscriptions with a Concise Edition of the Old English Inscriptions and an Analysis of Graphemes* (Ergänzungsbände zum Reallexikon der Germanischen Altertumskunde) (Berlin, 2021).

Webb, Nicholas Hart, "Early Medieval Welsh Book Production," PhD thesis (University of London), 1985.

Webster, Leslie, and Janet Backhouse, ed., *The Making of England: Anglo-Saxon Art and Culture A.D. 600–900* (London, 1991).

Werckmeister, Otto Karl, "Three Problems of Tradition in Pre-Carolingian Figure-Style: From Visigothic to Insular Illumination," *Proceedings of the Royal Irish Academy* 63 (1962–4), 167–89.

Wilmott, Tony, "The Anglian Abbey of *Streonæshalch*-Whitby: New Perspectives on Topography and Layout," in *Anglo-Saxon Studies in Archaeology and History*, 20, *Early Medieval Monasticism in the North Sea Zone: Recent Research and New Perspectives*, ed. Gabor Thomas and Alexandra Knox (2017), pp. 81–94.

Withers, Benjamin C., and Jonathan Wilcox, ed., *Naked Before God: Uncovering the Body in Anglo-Saxon England* (Morgantown, 2003).

Electronic Resources

Frantzen, Allen, *Anglo-Saxon Penitentials: a Cultural Database*, http://www.anglo-saxon.net/penance/index.php?p=JUNIUS_88b&anchor=X04.02.01.

Harley Psalter, London British Library Harley 603, http://www.bl.uk/manuscripts/Viewer.aspx?ref=harley_ms_603_fs001r.

The Corpus of Anglo-Saxon Stone Sculpture, https://chacklepie.com/ascorpus/index.php.

Utrecht Psalter, Utrecht, Universiteitsbibliotheek, Utrecht Hs. 32; Website of Utrecht University Library Special Collections page on the Utrecht Psalter, https://www.uu.nl/en/utrecht-university-library-special-collections/the-treasury/manuscripts-from-the-treasury/the-utrecht-psalter; and https://psalter.library.uu.nl/.

Williams, Howard, "Tressed for Death in Early Anglo-Saxon England," *Internet Archaeology* 42 (2016), http://dx.doi.org/10.11141/ia.42.6.7.

Index of Bible References

Index of Manuscripts

General Index

Printed in the United States
by Baker & Taylor Publisher Services